THE OLD TESTAMENT IN MEDIEVAL ICELANDIC TEXTS

Studies in Old Norse Literature

Print ISSN 2514–0701
Online ISSN 2514–071X

Series Editors
Professor Sif Rikhardsdottir
Professor Carolyne Larrington

Studies in Old Norse Literature aims to provide a forum for monographs and collections engaging with the literature produced in medieval Scandinavia, one of the largest surviving bodies of medieval European literature. The series investigates poetry and prose alongside translated, religious and learned material; although the primary focus is on Old Norse-Icelandic literature, studies which make comparison with other medieval literatures or which take a broadly interdisciplinary approach by addressing the historical and archaeological contexts of literary texts are also welcomed. It offers opportunities to publish a wide range of books, whether cutting-edge, theoretically informed writing, provocative revisionist approaches to established conceptualisations, or strong, traditional studies of previously neglected aspects of the field. The series will enable researchers to communicate their findings both beyond and within the academic community of medievalists, highlighting the growing interest in Old Norse-Icelandic literary culture.

Proposals or queries should be sent in the first instance to the editors or to the publisher, at the email addresses given below.

Professor Sif Rikhardsdottir, sifr@hi.is

Professor Carolyne Larrington, carolyne.larrington@sjc.ox.ac.uk

Boydell & Brewer, editorial@boydell.co.uk

Previous volumes in the series are listed at the end of the volume.

The Old Testament in Medieval Icelandic Texts

Translation, Exegesis and Storytelling

Siân Elizabeth Grønlie

D. S. BREWER

© Siân Elizabeth Grønlie 2024

All Rights Reserved. Except as permitted under current legislation no part of this work may be photocopied, stored in a retrieval system, published, performed in public, adapted, broadcast, transmitted, recorded or reproduced in any form or by any means, without the prior permission of the copyright owner

The right of Siân Elizabeth Grønlie to be identified as the author of this work has been asserted in accordance with sections 77 and 78 of the Copyright, Designs and Patents Act 1988

First published 2024
D. S. Brewer, Cambridge

ISBN 978 1 84384 712 0

D. S. Brewer is an imprint of Boydell & Brewer Ltd
PO Box 9, Woodbridge, Suffolk IP12 3DF, UK
and of Boydell & Brewer Inc.
668 Mt Hope Avenue, Rochester, NY 14620–2731, USA
website: www.boydellandbrewer.com

A CIP catalogue record for this book is available from the British Library

The publisher has no responsibility for the continued existence or accuracy of URLs for external or third-party internet websites referred to in this book, and does not guarantee that any content on such websites is, or will remain, accurate or appropriate

This publication is printed on acid-free paper

For Andy

CONTENTS

Illustrations	viii
Abbreviations	ix
Introduction: Biblical Literature and *Stjórn*	1
1 Hebrew Sagas and Icelandic Sagas: Convergent Evolution	15
2 From Hebrew Bible to Old Testament: Traditions of Exegesis	42
3 Types and Shadows: The Old Testament in Homilies and Saints' Lives	70
4 World History and Biblical History: Exegesis and Encyclopaedic Writing	103
5 In the Beginning: Primeval History in Genesis 1–11	139
6 The God of Abraham, Isaac and Jacob: Family History in Genesis 12–50	171
7 Heroes, Heroines and Royal Biography: From Judges to 2 Kings	210
Epilogue: Biblical Literature and Saga Literature	245
Acknowledgements	259
Bibliography	261
Index	289

vii

ILLUSTRATIONS

1	The Fall of Man, AM 227 fol. 1v.	129
2	The Fall of the Angels, AM 227 fol. 1v.	147
3	Sarah or Hagar, AM 227 fol. 30r.	180
4	The Sacrifice of Isaac, AM 227 fol. 23v.	181
5	Abraham's Departure from Haran, AM 227 fol. 23v.	181

All illustrations reproduced by permission of the Árni Magnússon Institute for Icelandic Studies.

ABBREVIATIONS

CCCM   *Corpus Christianorum, Continuatio Mediaeualis* (Turnhout: Brepols, 1967–)

CCSL   *Corpus Christianorum, Series Latina* (Turnhout: Brepols, 1954–)

CSEL   *Corpus Scriptorum Ecclesiasticorum Latinorum* (Berlin: De Gruyter, 1866–)

DONP   *Ordbog over det norrøne prosasprog / A Dictionary of Old Norse Prose*, ed. Helle Degnbol, Bent Chr. Jacobsen, Eva Rode, Christopher Sanders, and Þorbjörg Helgadóttir (Copenhagen: Arnamagnæanske Kommission, 1989–); access to slips and draft entries at https://onp.ku.dk/onp/onp.php

NPNF   *A Select Library of the Nicene and Post-Nicene Fathers: Second Series*, ed. Philip Shaff and Henry Wace, 14 vols (Oxford: Parker, 1890–1900)

PL   *Patrologiae cursus completus sive bibliotheca universalis, integra, uniformis, commoda, oeconomica, omnium ss. Patrum, doctorum scriptorumque ecclesiasticorum qui ab aevo apostolico ad Innocentii III tempora floruerunt,... series Latina*, ed. J. P. Migne, 221 vols (Paris: Migne, 1844–64)

INTRODUCTION: BIBLICAL LITERATURE AND *STJÓRN*

It would be difficult to find a nation so markedly preoccupied from its earliest days with the question of its own origins.[1]

Feuds and rivalries form the basic structure of the work, and the motivation for the various episodes within it.[2]

The characterisation is complex, the motives mixed, the plot riddled with gaps and enigmas [...] Through a mimesis of real-life conditions of inference, we are surrounded by ambiguities.[3]

By consistently, though not slavishly, refusing to give the reader access to the inner lives of the characters [...] narrators force the reader to constantly negotiate and renegotiate the thoughts and feelings of characters and, thus, the motivation for their action.[4]

A conspicuously innovative narrative art, anticipating the modern novelist's craft.[5]

These quotations appear to give an insightful picture of the narrative art of the Icelandic family sagas.

---

[1]   Gerhard von Rad, 'The Beginnings of Historical Writing in Ancient Israel', in *The Problem of the Hexateuch and Other Essays* (Edinburgh and London: Oliver & Boyd, 1966), 168.

[2]   John van Seters, *The Biblical Saga of King David* (Winona Lake, IN: Eisenbrauns, 2009), 48.

[3]   Meir Sternberg, *The Poetics of Biblical Narrative: Ideological Literature and the Drama of Reading* (Bloomington, IN: Indiana University Press, 1985), 38, 47.

[4]   Tod Linafelt, 'Private Poetry and Public Eloquence in 2 Samuel 1:17–27: Hearing and Overhearing David's Lament for Jonathan and Saul', *Journal of Religion* 88.4 (2008), 506.

[5]   Robert Kawashima, *Biblical Narrative and the Death of the Rhapsode* (Bloomington, IN: Indiana University Press, 2004), 4.

The Old Testament in Medieval Icelandic Texts

Except they do not: all these comments are about the Hebrew Bible/Old Testament, written by scholars with little or no knowledge of Old Norse.[6] Yet one only has to omit the word 'biblical' to repurpose them as a convincing description of the sagas. While biblical scholars have long realised that the Icelandic sagas are a useful analogue for the stories in the Hebrew Bible, this interest has not really been reciprocated. In the many discussions about the origins of the sagas and their distinctive style, biblical narrative has always been eclipsed by hagiographical and homiletic writing.[7] In many ways, this is obvious and understandable: while the earliest manuscripts in Iceland and Norway contain homilies and saints' lives, there is no manuscript evidence of translations from the Old Testament before c. 1300. It is less obvious and understandable why later biblical translations have been neglected, but this apparent oversight is carried over into many handbooks and companions to Old Norse-Icelandic literature, only one of which to my knowledge contains a whole chapter on the Bible.[8] It is more usual for biblical translations to be relegated to a few pages or a brief reference in chapters on learned literature, as for example in McTurk's *Companion to Old Norse-Icelandic Literature and Culture* and, more recently, in *The Routledge Research Companion to the Medieval Icelandic Sagas*.[9] One only has to compare the sustained attention given to biblical translation in Old English to see the extent of this neglect: from Marsden's *The Text of the Old Testament in Anglo-Saxon England* and Remley's *Old English Biblical Verse* in the 1990s to Daniel Anlezark's *Water and Fire: The Myth of the Flood in Anglo-Saxon England* (2006), Zacher's *Rewriting the Old Testament in Anglo-Saxon Verse* (2013), McBrine's *Biblical Epics in Late Antiquity and Anglo-Saxon England* (2017), Fox and Sharma's

---

6   I use the terms Hebrew Bible and Old Testament more or less interchangeably in this book. Although 'Hebrew Bible' is preferable to 'Old Testament' with its implications of supercessionism, the Icelanders did not read the Bible in Hebrew and knew it as the Old Testament. For an overview, see John Barton, 'Old Testament or Hebrew Bible?', in *The Old Testament: Canon, Literature and Theology* (Aldershot: Routledge, 2007), 83–89.

7   See Jónas Kristjánsson, 'Learned Style or Saga Style', *Speculum Norroenum: Norse Studies in Memory of Gabriel Turville-Petre*, ed. Ursula Dronke et al. (Odense: Odense University Press, 1981), 260–92.

8   Ian Kirby, 'Biblical Literature', in *Old Icelandic Literature and Society*, ed. Margaret Clunies Ross (Cambridge: Cambridge University Press, 2000), 287–301.

9   See Svanhildur Óskarsdóttir, 'Prose of Christian Instruction', in *A Companion to Old Norse-Icelandic Literature and Culture* (Malden, MA: Blackwell Publishing, 2005), ed. Rory McTurk, 343–47; Annette Lassen, 'Indigenous and Latin Literature', in *The Routledge Research Companion to the Medieval Icelandic Sagas*, ed. Ármann Jakobsson and Sverrir Jakobsson (London: Routledge, 2017), 76, 81.

2

Introduction

collection on *Old English Literature and the Old Testament* (2017), and Schrunk Ericksen's *Reading Old English Biblical Poetry* (2020).[10]

This scholarly neglect is particularly striking given that the manuscripts containing translations from the Old Testament are among the most beautiful and imposing of the Icelandic Middle Ages. AM 227 fol., which dates to c. 1340–60 and was produced at either Þingeyrar or possibly Skálholt, is beautifully illuminated with historiated initials, including: Christ in majesty flanked by angels, the sacrifice of Isaac, the temptation of Christ, Isaac blessing Jacob, God speaking to Joshua, Samuel anointing David, and Solomon with his cupbearer.[11] Meanwhile, in the lower margins, and occasionally the side margin, narrative scenes unfold: the Fall of the Angels, the creation of the animals and the Fall of Man; Abraham setting out from Haran with his wife Sarah and his nephew Lot; the procession around Jericho before the walls tumble down; Samuel waking from sleep at God's call and thinking that Eli has called him.[12] Selma Jónsdóttir has shown that these illuminations are influenced by the Tickhill Psalter Group, which is associated with Augustinian communities within the archdiocese of York.[13] The manuscript

---

10 Richard Marsden, *The Text of the Old Testament in Anglo-Saxon England* (Cambridge: Cambridge University Press, 1995); Paul G. Remley, *Old English Biblical Verse: Studies in Genesis, Exodus and Daniel* (Cambridge: Cambridge University Press, 1996); Daniel Anzelark, *Water and Fire: The Myth of the Flood in Anglo-Saxon England* (Manchester: Manchester University Press, 2006); Samantha Zacher, *Rewriting the Old Testament in Anglo-Saxon Verse: Becoming the Chosen People* (London: Bloomsbury, 2013); Patrick McBrine, *Biblical Epics in Late Antiquity and Anglo-Saxon England* (Toronto: University of Toronto Press, 2017); *Old English Literature and the Old Testament*, ed. Michael Fox and Manish Sharma (Toronto: University of Toronto Press, 2017); Janet Schrunk Ericksen, *Reading Old English Biblical Poetry: The Book and the Poem in Junius 11* (Toronto: University of Toronto Press, 2020).

11 AM 227 fol., fols 1v, 23v, 33v, 38r, 71v, 88v, 155r. Another probably showed Samson and Delilah on fol. 83v, and there is a later illumination on fol. 96r, which may depict David and Jesse. For these identifications, see Selma Jónsdóttir, *Illumination in a Manuscript of Stjórn* (Reykjavík: Almenna Bókafélagið, 1971), 16–21; Guðbjörg Kristjánsdóttir 'Handritalýsingar í benediktínasklaustrinu á Þingeyrum', in *Íslensk klausturmenning á miðöldum*, ed. Haraldur Bernharðsson (Reykjavík: Miðaldastofa Háskóla Íslands, 2016), 241–50.

12 AM 227 fol., fols 1v, 23v, 71v, 88v. Selma Jónsdóttir (*Illumination*, 16) and Guðbjörg Kristjánsdóttir ('Handritalýsing', 245) identify the scene on fol. 23v as Abraham setting out to Moriah with one of his servants, but it seems more likely to depict what is happening on this page: Abraham leaving Haran with Sarah and Lot. Likewise, Selma Jónsdóttir (*Illumination*, 19) identifies the figures on fol. 88v as David and Saul, but they seem more likely to be Samuel and Eli in the story in 1 Sam. 3.

13 Selma Jónsdóttir, *Illumination*, 24, 35–43.

3

was copied by two scribes, one of whom (A) wrote up to fol. 59r and from fol. 90r to the end, while the other (B) wrote fols 59v–90r. Meanwhile, AM 226 fol., which is from Helgafell and dates to c. 1350–70, has been described by Stefan Drechsler as 'the most magnificent and complex illuminated manuscript from the Helgafell group'; the illuminations are by Magnús Þórðarson, who also made the illuminations in Flateyjarbók.[14] There are nine historiated initials relating to the biblical translations: God in majesty; Noah building the ark; Abraham and Lot; Isaac, Jacob and Rebecca; Joshua awoken by God; Elkanah or Saul; Samuel anointing David; David with his harp; and Solomon and the Queen of Sheba. These show the influence of northern French manuscripts of illuminated bibles, as well as East Anglian influence via Bergen.[15] Finally, AM 225 fol., which is a copy of AM 226 fol. made in Helgafell in c. 1390–1410, contains its own set of lively illustrations: Noah building the ark while his family squabble below, God answering Rebecca's prayer for a son, and Hannah praying for a child as Eli upbraids her from his chair.[16] In both AM 226 fol. and AM 225 fol., the biblical translations are followed by three further historical works – *Rómverja saga*, *Alexanders saga* and *Gyðinga saga* – forming a history of the world up to the birth of Christ. AM 225 fol. adds to this the *Vitae Patrum*, transitioning to the early history of monasticism in Egypt and Syria.

The biblical translations contained in these manuscripts are collectively known as *Stjórn*, a title that goes back at least as far as 1588, according to the Skálholt catalogue from 1674, which lists a 'Biblia skrifud er þeir kalla Stjörn' ('handwritten Bible which they call Stjörn').[17] *Stjórn* was edited by C. R. Unger in 1862 and by Reidar Astås in 2009.[18] However, the translations gathered under this title are neither by one author nor from one time period, and they only occur together in AM 226 fol. *Stjórn I* runs from the beginning of Genesis to Exodus 18 and probably dates to the beginning of the fourteenth century. It has a prologue that claims that it was commissioned by King Hákon Magnússon

---

14 Stefan Drechsler, *Illuminated Manuscript Production in Medieval Iceland: Literary and Artistic Activities of the Monastery at Helgafell in the Fourteenth Century* (Turnhout: Brepols, 2021), 90–92.

15 AM 226 fol., fols 1v, 12r, 22r, 34v, 70r, 79r, 81v, 88r, 96v; Drechsler, *Manuscript Production*, 236.

16 AM 225 fol., fols 9r, 23r, 48v. This last is my own identification. The image of Adam and Eve on 1r is later.

17 Jakob Benediktsson, 'Some Observations on *Stjórn* and the Manuscript AM 227 fol.', *Gripla* 15 (2004), 11.

18 *Stjorn: Gammelnorsk bibelhistorie fra verdens skabelse til det babyloniske fangenskab*, ed. Carl Rikard Unger (Christiania: Feilberg & Landmark, 1862); *Stjórn: Tekst etter håndskriftene*, ed. Reidar Astås, Norrøne Tekster 8 (Oslo: Riksarkivet, 2009).

Introduction

of Norway, who reigned from 1299 to 1319.[19] *Stjórn II* runs from Exodus 19 to the end of Deuteronomy, effectively filling in the rest of the Pentateuch. It is found only in AM 226 fol. (on fols 62–69) and these leaves were inserted after AM 225 fol. was copied, probably in the second half of the fifteenth century, although the translation may be earlier.[20] *Stjórn III* runs from Joshua to the Second Book of Kings, and its manuscript history is to some extent independent of *Stjórn I*: it is found separately in AM 228 fol., which dates to c. 1300 and is therefore the earliest manuscript of biblical translation; it was known as 'Minni Stiorn' ('the shorter Stjórn') when it was found at Hlíðarendi in 1671, while AM 226 fol. was apparently called 'Stœrri Stjórn' ('the Greater Stjórn').[21] Other manuscripts and fragments that contain only *Stjórn III* are: AM 229 II fol. (from c. 1350), AM 229 III fol. (from c. 1350–1400), NRA B I–II (c. 1350), NRA 60 C (c. 1300–50), AM 335 4to (c. 1390–1410); Thott 2099 I 4to (c. 1400–1500), Sth. Perg. 4to 36 I (from the later part of the fifteenth century) and AM 617 4to, which was written by Bishop Gísli Jónsson of Skálholt in c. 1560–70.[22] In addition to these, *Stjórn IV* is sometimes used as the title for the book of Joshua in AM 226 fol., which is translated not from the Vulgate, but from Peter Comestor's *Historia scholastica*.[23]

The date, provenance, and relationship between these different layers of biblical translation have been a matter of contention. In an article from 1886, Gustav Storm proposed five stages.[24] The first was a Norwegian translation of the historical books of the Old Testament dating to c. 1250. This is represented by *Stjórn III* in AM 228 fol. and was subsequently used by the authors of *Barlaams saga ok Josaphats* and *Konungs skuggsjá*. The second was the translation of Maccabees by the Icelander Brandr Jónsson – mentioned at the end of *Gyðinga saga* in AM 226 fol. – while he was in Norway in c. 1262–64 during the reign of Magnús Hákonarson. The third was the translation in c. 1310 of Genesis and Exodus by a Norwegian at the court of Hákon Magnússon, as suggested by the prologue to *Stjórn I*, and the fourth was the Icelandic translation of Joshua from Comestor's *Historia scholastica*. The final stage was an Icelandic summary of the rest of the Pentateuch, which Storm dated to the end of the fourteenth century, not long after the production of AM 226 fol.

Storm's belief that *Stjórn I* and *Stjórn III* were Norwegian, however, has been challenged on a number of counts. Einar Ólafur Sveinsson argued

---

[19] Kirsten Wolf, 'Brandr Jónsson and *Stjórn*', *Scandinavian Studies* 62.2 (1990), 165.

[20] Ian J. Kirby, *Bible Translation in Old Norse* (Genève: Librarie Droz, 1986), 52.

[21] Gustav Storm, 'De norsk-islandske bibeloversættelser fra 13de og 14de Aarhundrede og Biskop Brandr Jónsson', *Arkiv for nordisk filologi* 3 (1886), 244.

[22] Benediktsson, 'Some Observations', 27.

[23] Reidar Astås, 'Kilder for og særtrekk ved *Stjórn IV*', *Alvíssmál* 1 (1992), 55–64.

[24] Storm, 'De norsk-islandske bibeloversættelser', 256.

The Old Testament in Medieval Icelandic Texts

against Storm that the patterns of alliteration in *Stjórn III* were Icelandic and that most of the Norwegian vocabulary was in use in Iceland as well.[25] In her study of AM 227 fol., Selma Jónsdóttir suggested that the prologue to *Stjórn I* was spurious, better understood as a 'commonplace' designed to make the work as a whole look more 'impressive'.[26] She argued that *Stjórn* was an Icelandic work from c. 1340 and that it might be connected with the Benedictine monk Bergr Sokkason.[27] Meanwhile, both Hofmann and Bagge questioned the relationship between *Stjórn III* and *Konungs skuggsjá*. They argued independently that *Stjórn III* borrowed from *Konungs skuggsjá* rather than vice versa, dating it to c. 1260 or later.[28]

In the only full-length book on Bible translation in Old Norse, Kirby reassessed these relationships. He argued that the oldest layer of translation was represented by *Stjórn II*, on the basis that 'it is only to be expected that early translations of the Bible will be a close rendering of the original'.[29] He found some evidence that the exemplar dated to the first quarter of the thirteenth century and, therefore, that the translation was very early, possibly before the end of the twelfth century. *Stjórn III* he believed to be a 'reworking of an earlier translation', probably of the *Stjórn II*-type; he argued that it must originally have covered the Pentateuch as well, and that AM 228 fol. may have been the second of two volumes.[30] He suggested that this translation was made no earlier than the second half of the thirteenth century by an Icelander close to the king; following a suggestion of Hofmann's, he proposed Brandr Jónsson as a serious candidate.[31] Finally, he dated *Stjórn I* to the early part of the fourteenth century, arguing that the translator made use of an earlier translation of a *Stjórn III*-type alongside the Vulgate.[32] As a result, he argued for a theory of successive translations beginning as early as, or even before, the thirteenth century: first a 'straightforward translation' of

---

25   Einar Ólafur Sveinsson, 'Athugasemdir um *Stjórn*', in *Studia Centenalia. In honorem memoriae Benedikt S. Þórarinsson*, ed. B. S. Benedikz (Reykjavík: Typis Ísafoldianis, 1961), 31.

26   Selma Jónsdóttir, *Illumination*, 49–58.

27   Selma Jónsdóttir, *Illumination*, 71; cf. also Peter Hallberg, 'Some Observations on the Language of *Dunstanus saga*: With an Appendix on the Bible Translation *Stjórn*', *Saga-Book* 18 (1973), 346–53.

28   Dietrich Hofmann, 'Die Königsspiegel-Zitate in der Stiorn', *Skandinavistik* 3 (1973), 1–40; Sverre Bagge, 'Forholdet mellom *Kongespeilet* og *Stjórn*', *Arkiv for nordisk filologi* 89 (1974), 163–202. This has been contested by Odd Einar Haugen, 'Om tidsforholdet mellom *Stjórn* ok *Barlaams ok Josaphats saga*', *Maal og Minne* (1983), 18–28 and Kirby, *Bible Translation*, 169–81.

29   Kirby, *Bible Translation*, 60.

30   Kirby, *Bible Translation*, 64.

31   Kirby, *Bible Translation*, 66–69.

32   Kirby, *Bible Translation*, 54–56.

Introduction

the historical books of the Old Testament (of which *Stjórn II* gives us a small taste), then an 'elaborated translation' probably made by Brandr Jónsson in the mid-thirteenth century (which survives as *Stjórn III*), and finally an 'expanded version of the Bible Text' which probably never got past Exodus 18 and is now known as *Stjórn I*.[33]

Kirby's conclusions were largely adopted by Jakob Benediktsson in an article in *Gripla* in 2004. He too conjectured that *Stjórn II*, being 'a plain version' and 'without commentary', represented the earliest stage of translation, and that it must have covered the beginning of the Pentateuch and extended to the books of Kings.[34] He thought the style and phraseology of the translation pointed to the early thirteenth century. *Stjórn III* he described as 'a more "saga-like" narrative', probably contemporary with *Konungs skuggsjá* because of the close relationship between these two texts. He suggested that this translation too must have begun with the Pentateuch: 'There is nothing to be said in favour of the notion that such a work began with Joshua'.[35] He guessed that it might have been written by an Icelander in Norway, although he does not mention Brandr – perhaps because Kirsten Wolf had shown in 1990 that there were no good grounds for his authorship.[36] This leaves *Stjórn I* as the final stage in the process of ongoing translation, whether it is Norwegian or Icelandic.

More recently, however, this theory of successive waves of translation has been questioned. It has been pointed out that 'part-Bibles' were common in the Middle Ages, and that there is no particular reason to assume that *Stjórn II* and *Stjórn III* ever extended back to the beginning of Genesis or (in the case of *Stjórn II*) forward to Samuel and Kings. Svanhildur Óskarsdóttir argues that manuscripts like AM 228 fol. show the appeal of stories from Joshua, Samuel and Kings in their own right.[37] Samson, for example, is completely at home in AM 335 4to among romances and exempla showcasing 'young men ill-treated by cunning women'. Likewise, she suggests that, in AM 226 and 227 fol., Joshua follows naturally from Exodus 18, so *Stjórn II* may well be a separate undertaking, driven by the desire to produce a continuous biblical text.[38] Kleivane has come to similar conclusions about *Stjórn III*, suggesting that it should be viewed not as part of a longer biblical translation but as an

---

33 Kirby, *Bible Translation*, 72–73.
34 Jakob Benediktsson, 'Some Observations', 33–34.
35 Jakob Benediktsson, 'Some Observations', 35.
36 Wolf, 'Brandr Jónsson', 163–88.
37 Svanhildur Óskarsdóttir, 'Heroes or Holy People? The Context of Old Norse Bible Translations', in *Übersetzen in skandinavischen Mittelalter*, ed. Vera Johanterwage and Stefanie Würth (Vienna: Fassbaender, 2007), 117–18.
38 Svanhildur Óskarsdóttir, 'Heroes or Holy People?', 114.

The Old Testament in Medieval Icelandic Texts

independent 'mirror for kings'.[39] She revives Storm's suggestion that *stjórn* is a translation of Latin 'regnum' and refers to earthly government and kingship. Likewise, she points out that the concise nature of *Stjórn II* does not necessarily mean that it is early; on the contrary, it may reflect a later idea of the Bible as 'a more fixed text'.[40] *Stjórn I*, meanwhile, can be seen as complete in itself – a history 'ante legem' ('before the law').[41]

This leaves the issue of whether *Stjórn I* should be seen as Icelandic or Norwegian. Astås comes down firmly on the side of Norwegian, arguing that the work has its origins not just at the Norwegian court, but specifically in a Dominican context.[42] A number of things lead him to this conclusion: the importance of the Dominicans in Bergen to King Hákon Magnússon, the authenticity of the Prologue, the frequent appeals to 'reason', the use of Vincent of Beauvais and a general 'Dominican tendency' in the theology of the work. He suggests that it was composed towards the end of Hákon's reign and is the work of 'an able, well-read theologian' – perhaps someone like Bishop Jón Halldórsson of Skálholt.[43] The Dominican connection has also been stressed by Lars Wollin in an article comparing the translations in *Stjórn I* and *II* with the Swedish paraphrase of the Pentateuch. On the basis of similarities in the principles and strategies of translation, he suggests that these have a common Latin exemplar. This might have been, for example, a reworking of the Vulgate for preaching, composed in the milieu of the Dominican province of Dacia.[44]

It remains the case, however, that all surviving manuscripts of *Stjórn* are Icelandic, even if some were made for export to Norway. This poses a problem for those who want to argue that *Stjórn I* originated in Norway. Recently, Gunnar Harðarson has made a convincing case for associating *Stjórn I* with Skálholt. Although the consensus is that AM 227 fol. was produced at Þingeyrar, he points out that it belonged to the cathedral of Skálholt when Árni Magnússon acquired it in 1688, and that AM 229 I fol. (which contains fragments of *Stjórn* written in the same two scribal hands) was also in the diocese of Skálholt when it was acquired.[45] Hand A is also found in AM 657

---

39 Elise Kleivane, 'There is More to *Stjórn* than Biblical Translation', in *Speculum septentrionale. Konungs skuggsjá and the European Encyclopedia of the Middle Ages*, ed. Elise Kleivane and Karl G. Johansson (Oslo: Novus, 2018), 116, 120.

40 Kleivane, 'Biblical Translation', 144.

41 Kleivane, 'Biblical Translation', 140.

42 Reidar Astås, *An Old Norse Biblical Compilation: Studies in Stjórn* (New York: Peter Lang, 1991), 65, 78–81, 98, 110, 123, 125, 144, 148.

43 Astås, *Studies in Stjórn*, 150–51.

44 Lars Wollin, '*Stjórn* och Pentateukparafrasen: Ett sannordiskt dominikanprojekt i högmedeltiden', *Arkiv for nordisk filologi* 116 (2001), 245–51, 291–94.

45 Gunnar Harðarson, 'Music and Manuscripts in Skálholt and Þingeyrar', in *Dominican Resonances in Medieval Iceland: The Legacy of Bishop Jón*

Introduction

a–b 4to, a manuscript that contains a series of Dominican exempla and is therefore likely to originate in Skálholt.[46] *Stjórn* was certainly at Skálholt according to catalogues made in 1674, 1644 and 1588. In c. 1560–70, Bishop Gísli Jónsson copied a version of *Stjórn III*, adding later translations of Job and Sirach together with Luther's prefaces to these works.[47] From a careful study of post-Reformation book inventories, Gunnar shows that Skálholt owned all the main sources used in *Stjórn I*: Comestor's *Historia scholastica*, Vincent of Beauvais's *Speculum Historiale*, Durandus's *Rationale divinorum officiorum*, Leo's *Sermones*, Isidore's *Etymologiae*, and a work named *Flores Hugonis de Sancto Victore* (possibly referring to Richard's *Liber exceptionum*, which was often attributed to Hugh in the Middle Ages).[48] It also owned Gregory's Homilies on Ezekiel, which I have identified as a source of the Prologue (see p. 144). So, arguably, Skálholt is the only place in Iceland where *Stjórn I* could have been composed – and the only time, given its documented 'Dominican tendency', is during the episcopate of Bishop Jón Halldórsson (1322–39). Gunnar also notes that AM 226 fol. was being written in Helgafell around the time that Eysteinn Ásgrímsson had his headquarters there as *officialis* of Skálholt in 1349–50.[49] He identifies this Eysteinn with the 'brother Eysteinn' who was previously a canon in Þykkvibær and who composed the poem *Lilja*, which shows clear influence from *Stjórn I*. Drechsler has also noted the close relationship between Skálholt, Þykkvibær and Helgafell. He points out that scribes at Helgafell made copies of works associated with Brandr Jónsson and his nephew Rúnólfr Sigmundarson, who were both abbots of Þykkvibær: *Alexanders saga* and *Gyðinga saga* are included in AM 226 fol., *Jóns saga baptista II* is in AM 233 a fol., and *Augustinus saga* was in the library in Helgafell by c. 1377–78.[50]

Skálholt makes a lot of sense as the place of origin for *Stjórn I*, even if AM 227 fol. itself was copied or illustrated in Þingeyrar.[51] The use of Vincent of Beauvais, in particular, suggests an Icelandic provenance for *Stjórn I*: *Stjórn* is the only *Bible historiale* to use Vincent of Beauvais's *Speculum historiale* as a source, but this choice is understandable in an Icelandic context, given

---

    Halldórsson of Skálholt, ed. Gunnar Harðarson and Karl-Gunnar Johansson (Leiden: Brill, 2021), 277–78.

[46] Gunnar Harðarson, 'Music and Manuscripts', 279.

[47] Gunnar Harðarson, 'Music and Manuscripts', 279–8.

[48] Gunnar Harðarson, 'Music and Manuscripts', 283. For the inventories, see Kristján Eldjárn and Hörður Ágústsson, *Skálholt: Skrúði og áhöld* (Reykjavík: Hið íslenska bókmenntafélag, 1992), 292–312.

[49] Gunnar Harðarson, 'Music and Manuscripts', 285.

[50] Drechsler, *Manuscript Production*, 45, 236.

[51] Gunnar Harðarson ('Music and Manuscripts', 284) suggests that Arngrímr Brandsson may provide a point of contact between texts composed at Skálholt and manuscripts produced at Þingeyrar.

The Old Testament in Medieval Icelandic Texts

the extensive use of Vincent of Beauvais together with Comestor in compilations such as *Jóns saga baptista II*, *Mörtu saga ok Maríu*, *Pétrs saga postula I* and *Tveggja postula saga Jóns ok Jakobs*.[52] Moreover, the compiler's concern for piecing together the historical sequence of events before moving to higher levels of interpretation suggests a Victorine bent that fits well with the Augustinian communities at Þykkvibær and Helgafell, in the diocese of Skálholt, with their focus on teaching and book production: Helgafell was Victorine from 1458 and possibly from much earlier.[53] Drechsler has suggested that AM 226 fol. was produced in an educational context, to teach 'young readers' about world history up until the time of Christ.[54] One might question the limitation to 'young readers' here: the array of material in *Stjórn I* and its presentation on the page is clearly designed as an aid to biblical exegesis: it might be considered a vernacular equivalent to the *Glossa ordinaria*, providing a continuous gloss on the biblical text. Even if AM 227 fol. was at one stage intended for presentation to King Hákon Magnússon, in the event it too was used educationally within the cathedral school in Skálholt: the marginal notes, many of which are in Latin, draw out theologically significant points and make links to the liturgy.[55] Van Liere has suggested that one of the defining aspects of the Victorine reform was the practice of *lectio divina*, which the Victorines adapted into a school-room activity to be undertaken with written authorities to hand.[56] If so, then perhaps *Stjórn I* gives us a unique insight into how *lectio divina* was practised among the canons regular in the south of Iceland.

This book started life as a study of the translations collectively known as *Stjórn*, working on the assumption that these were Icelandic and so would in various ways show the influence of 'saga style phraseology', 'saga-style phrasing and elaboration', and perhaps even occasionally have 'the character of a family saga'.[57] However, it soon became clear to me that engagement with the historical books of the Hebrew Bible/Old Testament in medieval Iceland was much broader than I had realised. As elsewhere in Europe in the thirteenth and fourteenth centuries, the stories of the Hebrew Bible/Old Testament were breaking free from the allegorical mould and were becoming

---

52 It is also worth noting that all these compilations appear in manuscripts associated with Helgafell (AM 233 a fol., Codex Scardensis and AM 239 fol.) and Skálholt (AM 235 fol.).

53 See Chapter 2, pp. 52–60.

54 Drechsler, *Manuscript Production*, 115, 235.

55 See, for example, AM 227 fol., fols 4r, 5v, 13r, 31v, 36r, 38v, 61v, 66r, 66v.

56 Frans van Liere, '*Lectio divina*. Reading and Writing at St Victor in the Twelfth Century', paper given at The Order of St Victor, Scandinavia and Denmark, Odense Workshop, 2–3 June 2022.

57 Wolf, 'Brandr Jónsson', 178; Kirby, *Bible Translation*, 68; Astås, *Studies in Stjórn*, 92.

Introduction

popular as history and as narrative, fuelled by the enormous success of Peter Comestor's *Historia scholastica* and its reception in art and vernacular literature. But in Iceland, the stories of the Hebrew Bible/Old Testament were received not just as stories but also as sagas – stories that bore a remarkable likeness to Iceland's own saga literature even through the medium of Jerome's translation and the centuries of allegorical exposition. This, then, became the starting point of my book: how did the likeness between biblical 'sagas' and Icelandic sagas shape the reception of the historical books of the Old Testament in medieval Norway and Iceland?

In Chapter 1, I look at how scholars of the Hebrew Bible have used the Icelandic sagas as analogues, suggesting a range of similarities including a focus on family and genealogy, connections to place-names, and the shifting relationship between orality and literacy, and history and fiction. In particular, they comment on similarities between biblical and saga style, including narrative economy, indirection, ambiguity, and the impression of verisimilitude. More recent studies in both biblical and Old Norse scholarship have focused independently on the same techniques: 'self-effacement', 'a rhetoric of historicity', the presence of 'gaps' and 'blanks', and the rhetorical function of prosimetrum. As an illustration of how these similarities play out in practice, I look at two biblical stories – the sacrifice of Isaac and Jacob's wrestling with an angel – and compare them to passages from *Laxdœla saga*, *Hrafnkels saga*, *Grettis saga* and *Bárðar saga Snæfellsáss*. I discuss the possiblity that saga style was influenced by biblical style but, given the late date of the biblical translations, it seems more likely that the similarities between the two are the result of 'convergent evolution'. This is not to rule out the direct influence of well-known biblical stories on Old Norse-Icelandic literature. In fact, it could be argued that the closeness between these two traditions of narrative literature in fact makes borrowing easier.

In Chapter 2, I turn to the traditions of interpretation that shaped the reception of Old Testament literature in Iceland. I look at how allegorical readings developed in the works of Origen, Augustine and Gregory, as well as Jerome's preference for the 'Hebrew truth'. Particularly important for biblical narrative in Old Norse-Icelandic is the school of St Victor in Paris, and the centrality of history to the theology of Hugh and Richard. The idea of the Bible as a coherent historical narrative was carried over into vernacular literatures through Comestor's *Historia scholastica* and its reinvention in the *Bibles historiales* of the thirteenth, fourteenth and fifteenth centuries: Guiart's *Histoires escolastres*, the *Bible historiale completée*, the Middle English *Historye of the patriarchs*, the Saxon *Weltchronik*, the Middle Dutch *Rijmbijbel* and the German *Historienbiblen*. As biblical paraphrase strayed further from the Parisian schools, so it became ever more imaginative and creative.

Chapter 3 shifts the focus of attention from medieval Europe to Norway and Iceland and engages with the reception of Old Testament history in

The Old Testament in Medieval Icelandic Texts

homilies and saints' lives. In the homilies, passages from the Old Testament tend to be interpreted allegorically, as one might expect given that the purpose of homilies is to edify one's audience – although transforming Old Testament history into a neat pattern of moral exempla sometimes proves difficult for the homilist. In a few of Gregory's homilies, stories from the Old Testament are told twice, first as history and then as allegory, allowing them to be developed on both levels. In these cases, it is interesting to note that the homilist adopts different styles: the history is retold in idiomatic prose, while the allegory is much more complex and poetic. In later saints' lives, like *Maríu saga* and *Jóns saga baptista II*, this tendency to move between different styles is even more noticeable: the compiler of *Maríu saga* is comfortable both with complex poetic allegory and with entertaining rabbinic anecdote, while the prose of *Jóns saga baptista II* ranges from plain to high style depending on whether Grímr is telling a story, explicating a point, or exhorting his audience to beware the treachery of women. These compilations, although not focused on Old Testament history, give us an important insight into the stylistic and academic resources that were available to the compiler of *Stjórn I*.

Chapter 4 turns from homiletic and hagiographic literature to universal history and encyclopaedic writings. These were closely bound up with biblical exegesis in the Middle Ages: the purpose of an encyclopaedia like Isidore's was to provide its readers with all the information they needed to interpret the Scriptures. The main source for *Veraldar saga*, for example, may have been a version of Comestor's *Historia scholastica* followed by Richard of Victor's *Liber exceptionum*; this would make it more an aid to biblical exegesis than a work of secular historiography. Particularly interesting is the world history in AM 764 4to, which is quite different from *Veraldar saga* and shows little or no interest in allegorical readings. The translation of the book of Judith is very much in 'saga style', although the compiler is also capable of replicating quite closely stylistic effects in the Latin. The most imaginative engagement with biblical literature, however, comes in the Norwegian *Konungs skuggsjá* – a markedly Victorine work that brilliantly blends narrative and allegory to give whole new readings of well-known biblical stories. The story of Saul and David is a particular highlight, with the author intercalating narrative, commentary, dialogue and poetry to encourage a strongly ethical reading. While all these works are influenced by Victorine thinking, they develop biblical narrative in distinctively different way.

In Chapters 5 and 6, I turn to *Stjórn I*, which I divide into 'primeval' history (Genesis I–II) and 'ancestral' history (Genesis 12–50), separating the heavily commentated early chapters from the long stretches of narrative in the second part. Perhaps the most noticeable feature of the early chapters of *Stjórn I* is the sheer variety of material that it covers: from angelology to cosmology to world geography, and from liturgy to allegory. Rather than harmonising different biblical interpretations, the compiler is careful to

12

Introduction

cite and label each authority separately, even when this leads to conflicting views or works against the narrative flow. Precision and accuracy are a more important priority in this compilation than storytelling, and it is only in some of the shorter anecdotes, like Noah and his sons, that we start to see an interest in the human dimensions of the narrative and, consequently, a more informal and idiomatic style. In the second part of *Stjórn I*, however, this starts to shift as we move into stories that are clearly in some sense 'family history' and that revolve around familiar concerns like genealogy, inheritance and kinship. Although allegorical interpretations continue to be present, they are far more spaced out, and we start to see many more of the narrative techniques familiar from saga literature. A particularly compelling episode is the rape of Dinah, which the compiler retells brilliantly with an eye to stories of feud and violence in the sagas, focussing on family dynamics and the legal ramifications of the case. If, in the Hebrew Bible, this is a story about the evils of intermarriage and assimilation, in the Old Norse it has become a story in which a legitimate legal settlement violently collapses into blood-feud. Finally, the Joseph story with its romance structure relates to the sagas in a variety of ways: through the concept of *gæfa* ('luck'), through the vocabulary of dreams and, when it comes to the apocryphal story of Asenath, through the motif of the maiden-king romance and the trope of the Icelander abroad.

In Chapter 7, I turn at last to the translations in *Stjórn III*, with a particular focus on the 'saga' of Samson, the book of Ruth, and the story of Saul and David. It is here that we find the closest connections to saga literature, including direct loans from *Laxdœla saga*, *Egils saga Skalla-Grímssonar*, various kings' saga, and even from skaldic verse. The historical books of the Old Testament are richly reimagined in the language and style of the Icelandic sagas. Samson is completely at home in the saga world and should take his place alongside Egill and Grettir as the anti-social but verbally dexterous hero. We follow the life of David from the heroic exploits of his youth, through feud and intrigue, loss and love, to the old man who lies shivering in bed and cannot keep himself warm. Meanwhile, the book of Ruth, with its close focus on relationships between women, offers something new that the translator struggles to convey with the resources of the saga genre. In *Stjórn III*, for the first time, we can talk not just of a translator, but of a saga author: one whose work rivals *Heimskringla* and *Morkinskinna* in its rich texture and imaginative power.

Medieval Icelanders, I conclude, drew richly on the vernacular resources of the saga when translating and adapting stories from the Hebrew Bible/Old Testament – and this was facilitated in large part by the close likeness between biblical and saga narrative. In the Epilogue, though, I explore the possibility of an alternative scenario: that biblical narrative, in Latin or Old Norse, influenced the composition of some Icelandic sagas. I take three very different sagas as examples: Oddr's *Óláfs saga Tryggvasonar* (c. 1190), *Gísla saga* (c. 1225–50), and *Hrafnkels saga* (c. 1270). Although there is not space for a full investigation, I argue that loans from the Old Testament may be more common in the sagas than we have realised, obscured as they are by the close similarities between the two traditions.

Inevitably, and perhaps propitiously, this book-length study has shown how much more there is to say than there is room to say it. I have had, for example, to leave *Stjórn II* to one side, though it includes a masterful retelling of the story of Balaam and Balak in Numbers 22–24 and many of the anecdotes in 1 and 2 Kings would repay further study. While I have focussed on the process of translation and adaptation in *Stjórn I* and *III*, there is more work to be done on the question of who read and used these texts. I started from the observation that biblical stories and sagas are remarkably alike in the brilliance of their narrative art. It is my hope that this book will inspire further research on the biblical translations as literature and their close relationship to the Icelandic sagas.

❧ I ❧

Hebrew Sagas and Icelandic Sagas:
Convergent Evolution

Scholars of the Hebrew Bible have had considerably more to say about sagas than scholars of the sagas have had to say about the Hebrew Bible. There is a long tradition in biblical scholarship of comparing the stories in the Hebrew Bible to sagas, which stretches from Gunkel's landmark commentary on Genesis, published in 1901, to John Barton's *History of the Bible* from 2019.[1] The scholarly understanding of what a saga is changed significantly over this period, and this is reflected in biblical scholarship, which starts out by viewing 'sagas' as oral narratives, but moves towards a fuller appreciation of their literary and pre-novelistic features. Likewise, biblical scholars display differing levels of knowledge about the sagas, reflecting the availability of translated texts: Gunkel knows about them only through intermediaries, such as Klaeber's edition of *Beowulf*, while scholars like Sternberg and van Seters are familiar with *Njáls saga* – which they frequently cite – and Damrosch with *Snorra Edda*.[2] When comparing biblical stories and sagas, most scholars point to the shared focus on family and genealogy, the close connection to place-names, and the shifting relationship between orality and literacy. Some also note the similarity between biblical style and saga style, which will be the focus of this chapter: recent work in both areas has emphasised how biblical and saga narrative alike are characterised by

---

[1] Hermann Gunkel, *Genesis*, trans. Mark E. Biddle (Macon, GA.: Mercer University Press, 1997), vii–xi (in which German *Sage* is translated as 'legend'); this is a translation of the third edition from 1910; John Barton, *A History of the Bible: The Book and its Faiths* (London: Penguin, 2019), 40.

[2] Gunkel, *Genesis*, 352; Sternberg, *Poetics*, 377; David Damrosch, *The Narrative Covenant: Transformations of Genre in the Growth of Biblical Literature* (London: Harper & Row, 1987), 311–12; van Seters, *Biblical Saga*, 44–46.

The Old Testament in Medieval Icelandic Texts

'narrative economy', 'objectivity' and 'indirection'.[3] In this chapter, I will outline some of the important stages in the work of biblical scholars on the Icelandic sagas. I will then look at two biblical stories – the sacrifice of Isaac (Genesis 22) and Jacob's wrestling with an angel (Genesis 32) – and compare them with passages from the sagas of Icelanders. Although the medieval Icelanders received the Hebrew Bible primarily through the Latin Vulgate, I argue that they recognised in these biblical stories a storytelling tradition that was kindred to their own.

Oral Sagas

One of the earliest scholars to identify the stories in Genesis as 'sagas' was Gunkel, who understood it not as a literary genre *per se* but primarily as an alternative to 'history'.[4] Although German 'Sage' in this context is probably better translated as 'tale', I include it here because of Gunkel's influence on later scholarship. Gunkel came up with six criteria for identifying sagas or 'tales' in the Bible: an origin in oral rather than written tradition, a dependence on the imagination as well as on tradition, incredibility (the impossibly large number of animals on the ark), a tendency to anthropomorphism (God 'walking' in the Garden of Eden) and, most interestingly, a poetic 'tone'. By this he means not that these stories are poetry, but that they tend towards the mythic, with conflicts between tribes or peoples represented as conflict between individuals. He divides the stories in Genesis into two types: sagas about the origins of the world and sagas of the patriarchs. While he notes the 'brevity' and 'simplicity' with which these stories are told, he interprets this as a sign of 'primitiveness', commenting on how 'these simple artists had not learned how to reflect, but they were masters of observation'.[5] At the same time, he recognises how, in places, the 'primitive sagaman' attains to 'a mature, perfected, a very forcible art'.[6] It is not evident from Gunkel's references that he had read any Icelandic sagas; and when – in the third edition of his commentary from 1910 – he mentions *Grettis saga*, he is following a lead in Klaeber's edition of *Beowulf*, rather than having consulted the saga itself.[7]

---

3   See, for example, Sternberg, *Poetics*, 38 and Heather O'Donoghue, *Narrative in the Icelandic Family Saga: Meanings of Time in Old Norse Literature* (London: Bloomsbury, 2021), 1–10.

4   Hermann Gunkel, *The Legends of Genesis: The Biblical Saga and History*, trans. William Foxwell Albright (New York: Schocken, 1964), 1–12.

5   Gunkel, *Legends*, 62.

6   Gunkel, *Legends*, 78.

7   Gunkel, *Genesis*, 352; cf. *Klaeber's Beowulf and The Fight at Finnsburg*, ed. Robert D. Fulk and John D. Niles, 4th ed. (Toronto: University of Toronto Press, 2008), xl.

Hebrew Sagas and Icelandic Sagas

He compares Jacob's nocturnal wrestling with an angel to Beowulf's fight with Grendel and 'the Icelandic legends of Grettir and of Ormr Stórólfsson'; but Ormr's fight is not nocturnal, and has little in common with Jacob's (although it does follow the two-troll pattern in *Beowulf*). Grettir's fight with the revenant Glámr does in fact have some striking parallels with Genesis 32, but Gunkel's main interest was in the underlying folktale, rather than in the presenting stories. In his later work he moves away from the idea of 'saga' or 'tale' altogether to focus instead on how folkloristic motifs are incorporated into the Hebrew Bible.[8]

Gunkel's work was an influence on both von Rad and Coats, who refined Gunkel's understanding of the saga. In his commentary on Genesis from 1972, von Rad described Gunkel as 'the old master of saga interpretation', but he condemned Gunkel's opposition between history and saga as 'a crass misunderstanding'.[9] Far from being the opposite of history, saga is for him 'the form favoured by a people for depicting its early history'.[10] The difference is that, rather than being 'exact', 'rational', or 'logical', the sort of history that saga deals with is 'instinctive' and 'intuitive', even 'imponderable' and 'intimate'. So, for example, Jacob's wrestling with an angel is a way of representing Israel's relationship to its God. Like Gunkel, von Rad saw the art of these stories as 'primitive' but, also like Gunkel, he recognised that it could be very powerful: 'The Biblical traditions are characterised by a thorough-going economy of expression on the emotional side. What men thought or felt, what moved them, is subordinate to the objective events'.[11] There is much that is reminiscent of the Icelandic sagas here, but it does not spring from a close acquaintance with them. Von Rad's examples are all from myth or folktale: the 'Greek saga of Zeus, Poseidon, and Hermes' or 'all those sagas in which gods, spirits or demons attack a man'.[12] For him, as for Gunkel, saga was a useful way of describing narrative units: the story of Cain and Abel is a 'tribal saga', the tower of Babel is an 'aetiological saga', and the sacrifice of Isaac is 'a cult saga of a sanctuary'.[13] The greater the artistry, the less applicable the term 'saga': the story of Abraham does not qualify because of its 'theological reflection', while the Joseph story is more like a 'novella'.[14] Likewise, in *The Problem of the Hexateuch*, von Rad argues that the David story (the succession narrative in 1 and 2 Samuel) is 'too complex'

---

[8] Gunkel, *Legends*, 14.

[9] Gerhard von Rad, *Genesis: A Commentary* (Philadelphia: The Westminster Press,1972), 32, 280.

[10] von Rad, *Genesis*, 33.

[11] von Rad, *Genesis*, 34.

[12] von Rad, *Genesis*, 205, 321.

[13] von Rad, *Genesis*, 108, 150, 243.

[14] von Rad, *Genesis*, 185, 433.

to be a saga: 'These chapters contain genuine historical writing'.[15] Yet it is in discussing this story that von Rad sounds most like he is talking about a saga: he praises the 'masterly craftsmanship', the 'immense restraint' of the narrator, and the 'peculiarly secular mode of presentation': 'The narrator is at pains to conceal himself and his evaluations behind the material itself'.[16] For him, though, sagas are just precursors to this sophisticated historical narrative, which he views as one of the greatest achievements of Antiquity.

The idea of the 'saga' was taken further by Coats, both in his commentary on Genesis from 1983 and in his book on Moses from 1988. Following Gunkel, he distinguishes between 'primeval sagas' (the Creation and Fall, the Flood, the Tower of Babel) and 'family sagas' (Abraham, Isaac and Jacob), but he defines 'saga' much more convincingly than Gunkel as a 'long traditional prose narrative with an episodic structure, developed around stereotyped themes or topics'.[17] The family saga, likewise, is 'a narrative account of the events that comprise the past of the family unit': it centres on 'internal affairs' – travel, strife, separation, birth, marriage and death – but serves a wider purpose of 'legitimation for the group, by showing the[ir] genealogical, geographical, or historical origin'.[18] The term 'family saga' here does seem to be borrowed from scholarship on Old Icelandic literature, for Coats interjects 'See the Icelandic sagas' as an aside.[19] In his book on Moses, moreover, he carefully distinguishes between the English 'saga' and the German *Sage*: saga, he argues, is not a general category for narrative which is not – or is not yet – history, but a 'technical term' for 'a very particular genre of narrative literature'.[20] This is an important advance; however, Coats has little to say about what the characteristics of this genre might be. While he insists that the Moses narrative in Exodus is 'a heroic saga', he is less interested in the 'saga' than the 'heroic', for which he draws heavily on de Vries's *Heroic Song and Heroic Story*. Like Gunkel, he continues to see the saga as oral: 'Its intention is to capture the audience by the tensions in its storyline, thus, to entertain its audience with the skill of its storytelling. The consequence [...] is that the genre belongs primarily to the repertoire of the oral storyteller'.[21] Later in

---

15 von Rad, 'Beginnings', 192.

16 von Rad, 'Beginnings', 195.

17 George W. Coats, *Genesis with an Introduction to Narrative Literature* (Grand Rapids, MI: W. B. Eerdmans, 1983), 5–6.

18 Coats, *Genesis*, 7.

19 Coats, *Genesis*, 6.

20 George W. Coats, *Moses: Heroic Man, Man of God* (Sheffield: JSOT Press, 1988), 42, 219 (note).

21 Coats, *Moses*, 42.

Hebrew Sagas and Icelandic Sagas

the same book though – and in oddly contradictory terms – he describes the heroic saga as having a 'literary, folkloristic character'.[22]

Literary Sagas

For these scholars, sagas were a form of 'oral literature', whether defined in opposition to history, as a precursor to history, or as a traditional oral genre. This is to be expected for Gunkel, writing in 1901 but, by the 1970s, Icelandic scholars like Sigurður Nordal and Einar Ólafur Sveinsson – of the so-called 'book prose' school – had for some time been championing the sagas as literary works and distancing them from orality: Einar Ólafur Sveinsson's *Njáls saga: A Literary Masterpiece* was published in English in 1971.[23] This shift in perspective is reflected in the work of biblical scholars from the 1980s on, including Sternberg, Neff and Damrosch. Neff wrote a chapter entitled 'Saga' in a book edited by Coats in 1986 but, unlike Coats, he had read more extensively on the sagas and was aware of the debate over their origins. He cites Ker's *Epic and Romance*, Stefán Einarsson's *A History of Icelandic Literature* and Scholes and Kellogg's *The Nature of Narrative*, which defined the saga as a 'traditional prose narrative', but not necessarily an oral one.[24] On the basis of this secondary reading, Neff compares the stories in Genesis not with hypothetical oral sagas, but with real Icelandic ones. He lists that they share:[25]

> economy of detail, the absence of narrative digression, the importance of the principal characters, the conglomerate character of the interrelated narratives, the absence of plot, the description of character through action rather than word, the credibility of the story, the use of genealogy, and narrative composition of greater duration than a single story.

This combines the insights of earlier scholars on genealogy and character with new insights into narrative structure (the term 'conglomerate' is taken

---

[22] Coats, *Moses*, 156.

[23] See, for example, Sigurður Nordal, *Hrafnkels saga Freysgoða: A Study* (Cardiff: University of Wales Press, 1958); Einar Ólafur Sveinsson, *Njáls saga: A Literary Masterpiece* (Lincoln: University of Nebraska Press, 1971).

[24] Robert W. Neff, 'Saga', in *Saga, Legend, Tale, Novella, Fable: Narrative Forms in Old Testament Literature*, ed. George W. Coats (Sheffield; JSOT, 1985), 24–25; for his references, see William Paton Ker, *Epic and Romance: Essays on Medieval Literature* (New York: Dover, 1957); Stefán Einarsson, *A History of Icelandic Literature* (Baltimore, MD: John Hopkins, 1957); Robert Scholes and Robert Kellogg, *The Nature of Narrative* (New York: Oxford University Press, 1966).

[25] Neff, 'Saga', 31.

The Old Testament in Medieval Icelandic Texts

directly from Ker) and, above all, into biblical style: the aspects of style that Neff mentions had been identified before, but he was the first to connect them with the sagas.[26] He also corrects some of the misunderstandings about sagas that had persisted from Gunkel's work: Neff's emphasis on 'credibility' is the exact opposite of Gunkel's criterion of 'unbelievability'. Neff concludes that it is right to speak about 'sagas' in the Hebrew Bible, but that the term is better used for cycles of stories than for short, independent stories of origins: Genesis 12–25, he argues, should rightly be called the 'saga of Abraham'.[27]

An understanding of the literary qualities of the Icelandic sagas also underpins the work of Sternberg, one of the pioneers of a literary approach to the Hebrew Bible. Sternberg frequently uses examples from *Njáls saga* to contrast or compare with the literary techniques of biblical narrators – although not always accurately. When discussing, for example, how biblical portraits are a mode of narratorial foretelling ('proleptic portraiture'), he cites the portrait of Gunnarr in *Njáls saga*, singling out the detail that his nose was slightly upturned.[28] He argues that we are told this for 'solidity of specification' and contrasts it with the detail in 2 Samuel that David's son Absalom had beautiful thick hair. This he describes as 'realistic indirection': it takes on significance only at Absalom's death, when he hangs from a tree by his hair (see pp. 236–37). But Sternberg misses a much closer comparison here: Hallgerðr's beautiful long hair, which is described at the beginning of the saga, but takes on significance only at the moment of Gunnarr's death, when she refuses to lend him a strand of her hair to mend his broken bow.[29] When discussing retrospection, Sternberg notes that, in both biblical and saga narrative, information is sometimes temporarily withheld, reversing the sort of privilege that forecast gives: 'Only in retrospect does the reader of *Njals saga* discover Njal's foreknowledge of his trial by fire'.[30] This is an important point – and the function of 'gaps' has recently been discussed at length by O'Donoghue – but I am not sure that we do discover Njáll's foreknowledge in retrospect, as is suggested here.[31] Finally, Sternberg compares dreams in the Bible and in the sagas: 'Here, as always in the Icelandic saga, the dream is not an internal, but an external sign; not subjective and questionable [...] but objective and infallible'.[32] In fact, recent research on the sagas shows that

---

26 Ker, *Epic and Romance*, 198.

27 Neff, 'Saga', 32.

28 Sternberg, *Poetics*, 329; cf. *Brennu-Njáls saga*, ed. Einar Ólafur Sveinsson (Reykjavík: Hið íslenzka fornritafélag, 1954), 53.

29 *Brennu-Njáls saga*, 6, 189; compare the references to Absalom's hair in 2 Samuel 14.26 and 18.9–15.

30 Sternberg, *Poetics*, 377.

31 O'Donoghue, *Narrative*, 153–82.

32 Sternberg, *Poetics*, 395.

Hebrew Sagas and Icelandic Sagas

dreams can sometimes be 'subjective and questionable' (in *Gísla saga*, for example), but Sternberg's idea that dreams function as 'a foreshadowing of the narrator' is certainly true in *Njáls saga* and there is an even more notable parallel in Guðrún's dreams in *Laxdœla saga*.[33]

Damrosch's interest in the Icelandic sagas is different: for him, they provide an analogy for how a small and marginalised people like the Israelites came to produce such a great prose literature: 'In a small country, in a society younger and less prosperous than the great cultures of Egypt and Mesopotamia, literary composition reached a degree of power and beauty previously unknown in the Near East'.[34] His focus is on how the Pentateuch and the Deuteronomistic History came together, rather than on the individual stories that make them up. Drawing on von Rad's idea (p. 17) that sagas deal with the origins of a people, he describes how the Icelandic sagas, like the Deuteronomist, 'recall, collect, and adapt stories from the age of the settling and the founding of the nation'.[35] Like Sternberg, his main example is *Njáls saga*, but his interest is not in narrative technique so much as in the combination of different sources: he sees the author of *Njáls saga* as combining the stories of Gunnarr, Njáll, and the conversion of Iceland, just as the David story combines different layers of tradition about David and his kingship. It is this combination that produces their distinctive narrative styles: 'This is a form of composite artistry that produces characters and scenes of great ambiguity that resist any univocal reading'.[36] Damrosch's other example is Snorri Sturluson's *Edda* with its blend of myth, historiography and fiction, which he compares (less compellingly, perhaps) to the blend of verse and prose in Job. Still, *Snorra Edda* is useful for him because it is a prose account that draws on poetic sources, and Damrosch sees biblical historiography as arising out of the confluence of poetic epic and prose chronicle.[37] For Damrosch, the rise of historical prose writing in Israel is intimately connected to cultural identity: the sense of Hebrew culture as something 'distinctively new'. This sounds very like Schier's reflections on how the genre of the saga grew out of the Icelanders' sense of 'standing at the beginning, of having created something entirely new'.[38]

---

33 *Laxdœla saga*, ed. Einar Ólafur Sveinsson (Reykjavík: Hið íslenzka fornritafélag, 1934), 88–89. On the subjectivity of dreams, see Christopher Crocker, 'All I Do the Whole Night Through: On the Dreams of Gísli Súrsson', *Scandinavian Studies* 84.2 (2012), 143–62.

34 Damrosch, *Narrative Covenant*, 1.

35 Damrosch, *Narrative Covenant*, 310.

36 Damrosch, *Narrative Covenant*, 311–12.

37 Damrosch, *Narrative Covenant*, 3–4, 50.

38 Damrosch, *Narrative Covenant*, 43; compare Kurt Schier, 'Iceland and The Rise of Literature in "terra nova": Some Comparative Reflections', *Gripla* 1 (1975), 168–81.

The Old Testament in Medieval Icelandic Texts

Despite Neff's lead, neither Sternberg nor Damrosch describe biblical narratives as 'sagas'; rather, they draw on the Icelandic sagas as a comparative literature that deepens their understanding of biblical narrative. In fact, scholars like Gunn reject the term 'saga' as tending 'to court misunderstanding', even while he acknowledges a significant overlap in how sagas and biblical stories blend history, fiction and tradition.[39] Van Seters, on the other hand, has made a strong case for describing the David story as a 'saga'. Like Neff, his understanding of saga is distinctively Icelandic and very much of the book-prose school: 'I want to propose the term saga in the specific meaning of the Icelandic and Norse sagas as the most appropriate comparative literature for the David story'.[40] He specifies that he is not using the term as a faulty translation of German *Sage*, but rather as 'reflecting precisely the sort of written literature that one finds in the Icelandic sagas'. Drawing on the work of Magnús Magnússon and Theodore Andersson, as well as Scholes and Kellogg, van Seters defines a saga as a literary genre that includes some or all of the following features: it deals with the families of the 'founding age' of a people and extends over more than one generation; it is based on older written historical records, but many of its details are fictional; its anonymity is an aspect of style and is used alongside other literary techniques to create a veneer of 'realism'; it is intended as 'serious entertainment' (Magnús Magnússon's term); it uses type scenes and traditional motifs, but these are now literary conventions and not oral survivals; it expresses nostalgia for a glorious past, but can also parody it and subvert traditional narrative patterns.[41] In other words, it is precisely the qualities that, for von Rad, excluded the David story from the category of saga that make it, for van Seters, justifiably saga-like.

Saga Style

Despite the changing understanding of what a saga is, certain themes recur: a focus on family and origins; the blending of history, fiction and tradition; and the distinctiveness of 'saga style'. It is this last phrase that makes its way into Barton's 2019 *A History of the Bible*. Barton distinguishes three levels of

---

39 David M. Gunn, *Story of King David: Genre and Interpretation* (Sheffield: JSOT, 1978), 38.

40 Van Seters, *Biblical Saga*, 42.

41 Van Seters, *Biblical Saga*, 49–50; cf. *Njal's Saga*, trans. Magnús Magnússon and Hermann Pálsson (Harmondsworth: Penguin, 1960), 24. Van Seters' bibliography includes Theodore M. Andersson, *The Problem of Icelandic Saga Origins: A Historical Survey* (New Haven, CT: Yale University Press, 1964) and *The Growth of the Medieval Icelandic Saga (1180–1280)* (Ithaca, NY: Cornell University Press, 2006).

Hebrew Sagas and Icelandic Sagas

styles in Hebrew narrative, the first of which he describes as 'a plain laconic style, in which hardly anything is said about the emotions or the appearances of the characters, and we are left to make our own deductions about what is going on beneath the surface'.[42] He calls this 'saga style' on the basis of his own reading of the Icelandic sagas: 'The parallel with the clipped style of the Icelandic sagas seems to me to make it appropriate'. It contrasts with two other levels of style in the Hebrew Bible: 'deuteronomistic style', which is characterised by the accumulation of synonyms as well as overt moral judgements, and 'priestly style', which is marked by repetition, formulae and ritual.[43] Saga style seems to be the oldest of these three levels of style, dating perhaps as far back as the eighth century BCE, and its origins are obscure. In most books of the Bible, it occurs together with one or both other styles, and it is one of the methods by which different historical layers of material are identified. Barton comments that: 'We cannot say how the Israelites came to develop this sophisticated yet laconic style of narration in prose, and familiarity with the Bible can blunt our sense of how remarkable it is'.[44]

Barton's description of the style of the Icelandic sagas as 'clipped' echoes how it is typically described in Old Norse-Icelandic scholarship. Saga style is most often characterised by what is missing: complex subordination, rhetorical devices, figurative language and expressions of thought and feeling. At the same time, recent work has drawn attention to its sophistication. As far as I can tell, the similarity between biblical style and saga style was first recognised by Munro and Chadwick, as mentioned in the second volume of their *Growth of Literature*, published in 1936. On the story of David, they write:[45]

> The style is that of saga, though this fact in itself is rather inconclusive – for a literary style is often derived from saga. But it is worth noting that the narrative bears a rather close resemblance to the 'Sagas of Icelanders' and to some stories in the Icelandic 'Sagas of Kings' [...] These sagas show the same verisimilitude and liveliness together with fullness of detail, and in general, though they contain a large imaginative element, they may be regarded as historical authorities.

Other scholars mentioned above have also noted the common ground between biblical style and saga style in terms of 'realism' and 'economy': the

---

42 Barton, *History of the Bible*, 39–40.
43 Barton, *History of the Bible*, 41–45.
44 Barton, *History of the Bible*, 41.
45 Hector H. Munro and Nora K. Chadwick, *The Growth of Literature*, 3 vols (London: Cambridge University Press, 1932–40), II, 636. They also note that the sagas provide an analogy for how the David story weaves together older and more recent layers of material.

23

The Old Testament in Medieval Icelandic Texts

apparent absence of character, plot, and unnecessary descriptive detail.[46] But the full extent to which biblical style and saga style resemble each other has not really been explored, since scholars in both fields have written with little awareness of each other's work. In what follows, therefore, I want to examine the overlap between biblical style and saga style in four areas: economy, objectivity, the art of indirection, and the interplay between poetry and prose.

In an article from 1958, Bouman commented on the admirable way in which the Icelandic sagas 'economise': he described how 'their skill in handling the tools of language [is] like a precision-instrument'.[47] This narrative economy and precision is often pointed out by scholars, usually in a predictable number of adjectives: 'condensed and precise', 'succinct', 'spare and restrained', 'unadorned', 'subdued', 'blunt', 'brisk'.[48] This will all be very familiar to biblical scholars, who frequently use the term 'economy' when speaking of biblical style: from Gunkel's 'economy of substantial details', to von Rad's 'thorough-going economy of expression', to Alter's 'vigorous economy of means'.[49] Linafelt notes the 'limited vocabulary' of biblical narrative and the 'paucity of metaphorical description', while Alter describes it as 'bare of embellishment' and Gunkel speaks of the 'absence of inner life'.[50] Biblical style, like saga style, is also relentlessly paratactic: it is usually described in adjectives like 'laconic', 'terse', 'frugal', 'compact' and 'sparse', and typically characterised by 'restraint', 'tense understatement' and 'studied reticences'.[51] One might easily switch between these two lists of adjectives (from 'condensed' to 'compact', from 'spare' to 'sparse') without noticing that one has moved from Iceland to Israel.

---

46 See, for example, Gunkel, *Legends*, 62, 65, 68; von Rad, *Genesis*, 34.

47 A. C. Bouman, 'An Aspect of Style in Icelandic Sagas', *Neophilologus* 42.1 (1958), 50.

48 See, for example, Otto Springer, 'The Style of the Old Icelandic Family Saga', *Journal of English and Germanic Philology* 38.1 (1939), 115, 118, 121–22; Heather O'Donoghue, *Skaldic Verse and the Poetics of Saga Narrative* (Oxford: Oxford University Press, 2005), 6; Margaret Clunies Ross, *The Cambridge Introduction to the Old Norse-Icelandic Saga* (Cambridge: Cambridge University Press, 2010), 104; Sverre Bagge, 'The Old Norse Kings' Sagas and European Latin Historiography', *Journal of English and Germanic Philology* 115.1 (2016), 9–11.

49 Gunkel, *Legends*, 68; von Rad, *Genesis*, 34; Robert Alter, *The Art of Biblical Narrative* (London: Allen & Unwin, 1981), 24.

50 Gunkel, *Legends*, 58; Alter, *Art*, 23; Tod Linafelt, 'The Pentateuch', in *The Oxford Handbook of English Literature and Theology*, ed. Andrew Hass, David Jasper and Elizabeth Jay (Oxford: Oxford University Press, 2009), 214–15.

51 See, for example, Gunkel, *Legends*, 65; von Rad, 'Beginnings', 169, 195; Sternberg, *Poetics*, 158; Alter, *Art*, 22, 84, 127, 158; Jan P. Fokkelman, *Reading Biblical Narrative: A Practical Guide* (Leiden, Boston: Brill, 1999), 148–49, 175; Barton, *History of the Bible*, 40.

Hebrew Sagas and Icelandic Sagas

Likewise, objectivity and realism are important qualities of both biblical and saga style. Springer describes the saga author as a 'dispassionate observer', while Gunkel praises the biblical narrators as 'masters of observation'.[52] Scholars on the sagas have tried to tease out different strands of objectivity: lack of judgement or evaluation on the part of the narrator ('narrative objectivity'), external focalisation (in which the inner lives of characters are conveyed only by speech, action, or gesture), and striving for impartiality.[53] Exactly the same points have been made by biblical scholars. Gunkel and von Rad both speak about the subordination of character to action, while Alter notes the 'impassivity' of biblical narrative and the 'minimal authorial intrusions'.[54] Just as Lönnroth describes the Icelandic sagas as the 'opposite of anything homiletic, rhetorical or moralistic', so Sternberg dismisses moral didacticism as 'alien, if not antipathetic, to the spirit of Israelite storytelling'.[55] In a particularly close parallel, O'Donoghue writes about the 'self-effacement of the narrative voice' in the sagas, while Sternberg describes the biblical narrator as following a 'self-effacing policy' and pursuing a 'strategy' of 'self-effacement'.[56] Likewise, both consider the 'realism' of these texts to be the product of a particular mode of writing rather than evidence of their historical veracity: Sternberg speaks of a 'rhetoric of historicity', while O'Donoghue argues that the historical veneer of the sagas is due to the adoption of a non-fictional 'mode' of writing, even when the material is in fact fictional.[57]

Most recently, scholars in both fields have focussed on the presence of 'gaps' and 'blanks' in the narrative when the (omniscient) narrator deliberately withholds information. Sternberg includes in this the withholding of plot information, the refusal to elucidate structure and significance, and the absence of judgement on events. He pays particular attention to gaps as 'discontinuities' between the order of narration and the order in which events occur. The effect of this, he suggests, is to create a parallel between the 'process of reading' and the 'process of living': 'This generates a reading experience with clear implications for everyday life, where one normally is in the confidence neither of God nor of one's fellow men'.[58] Alter too

---

52 Springer, 'Style', 124; Gunkel, *Legends*, 62.

53 Lars Lönnroth, 'Rhetorical Persuasion in the Sagas', *Scandinavian Studies* 42.2 (1970), 158–59; Daniel Sävborg, 'Style', in *The Routledge Research Companion to the Medieval Icelandic Sagas*, ed. Ármann Jakobsson and Sverrir Jakobsson (London and New York: Routledge, 2017), 112–15.

54 Gunkel, *Legends*, 57; von Rad, *Genesis,* 34; Alter, *Art,* 109.

55 Lönnroth, 'Rhetorical Persuasion', 157; Sternberg, *Poetics,* 38.

56 O'Donoghue, *Narrative*, 113; Sternberg, *Poetics,* 77, 267.

57 O'Donoghue, *Narrative*, 2; Sternberg, *Poetics*, 157.

58 Sternberg, *Poetics*, 166.

The Old Testament in Medieval Icelandic Texts

comments how 'the suspension of judgement, weighing of possibilities, brooding on inner gaps' keeps us alert to how meaning is a 'process, requiring continual revision'.[59] O'Donoghue's most recent book on the sagas picks up on precisely these points: she argues that, while the saga authors are clearly positioned above the narrative, it is rare that they 'actively betray this all-knowing position'.[60] Rather, the readers must negotiate events themselves, as if at first hand – 'much as we do when we live in real human time ourselves, knowing little of others' motives and inner lives; and in ignorance of many salient facts and circumstances'. Miller says something very similar about reading *Hrafnkels saga*: 'Reading a person – like reading literature – is a probabilistic enterprise'.[61] Gaps and silences encourage 'extraordinarily close engagement' and purposefully foster ambiguity. Thus, both biblical and saga authors are masters in the 'art of indirection'.

One final area of style is the interplay between prose and verse. In *Skaldic Verse and the Poetics of Saga Narrative*, O'Donoghue argues that saga authors were able to exploit the marked contrast between the prose style of the sagas and the style of skaldic poetry: 'Nothing could be more different from the colloquial, spare, restrained style of family saga than the dazzlingly ornate, cryptic and sometimes even passionate quality of skaldic verse'.[62] In particular, she shows how verse is often used in the sagas for the 'expression of personal and deeply felt emotion', something which is not possible in the 'externally focalised' prose.[63] Verse thus allows for 'shifts of voice, perspective and authorial self-consciousness' when it is embedded in a prose narrative. Linafelt has recently made a similar argument for biblical prosimetrum, distinguishing between the different 'literary toolkits' of biblical prose and poetry: the use of prose for narrative and poetry for 'highly rhetorical genres'.[64] He argues that poetry gives access to resources that prose lacks, such as figurative language and the expression of interiority. He argues that: 'If biblical narrative trades in opaqueness of characterisation, biblical poetry fairly revels in the exposure of subjectivity'.[65] So, as in the Icelandic sagas, 'when biblical authors wanted to convey feeling or thought, they tended to resort to poetry'.

---

59   Alter, *Art*, 12.
60   O'Donoghue, *Narrative*, 5.
61   William Ian Miller, *Hrafnkel or the Ambiguities: Hard Cases, Hard Choices* (Oxford: Oxford University Press, 2017), 12.
62   O'Donoghue, *Skaldic Verse*, 6.
63   O'Donoghue, *Skaldic Verse*, 8.
64   Tod Linafelt, 'On Biblical Style', *St John's Review*, 54.1 (2013), 18. See also his 'Poetry and Biblical Narrative', in *The Oxford Handbook of Biblical Narrative*, ed. Danna Nolen Fewell (Oxford: Oxford University Press, 2016), 84–89.
65   Linafelt, 'Biblical Style', 39.

Hebrew Sagas and Icelandic Sagas

Two Biblical Stories

To illustrate some of the convergences between saga and biblical style, I would now like to look at a couple of stories which are foundational for our understanding of biblical narrative. The first is the sacrifice or binding of Isaac in Genesis 22:[66]

> And it happened after these things that God tested Abraham. And He said to him: 'Abraham!' and he said: 'Here I am.' And He said: 'Take, pray, your son, your only one, whom you love, Isaac, and go forth to the land of Moriah and offer him up as a burnt offering on one of the mountains which I shall say to you.' And Abraham rose early in the morning and saddled his donkey and took his two lads with him, and Isaac his son, and he split the wood for the offering and rose and went to the place that God had said to him. On the third day Abraham raised his eyes and saw the place from afar. And Abraham said to his lads: 'Sit you here with the donkey and let me and the lad walk ahead and let us worship and return to you.' And Abraham took the wood for the offering and put it on Isaac his son, and he took in his hand the fire and the cleaver and the two of them went together. And Isaac said to Abraham his father, 'Father!' and he said: 'Here I am, my son.' And he said: 'Here is the fire and the wood but where is the sheep for the offering?' And Abraham said: 'God will see to the sheep for the offering, my son.' And the two of them went together. And they came to the place which God had said to him, and Abraham built there an altar and laid out the wood and bound Isaac his son and placed him on the altar on top of the wood. And Abraham reached out his hand and took the cleaver to slaughter his son. And the LORD's messenger called to him from the heavens and said, 'Abraham, Abraham!' and he said, 'Here I am.' And he said: 'Do not reach out your hand against the lad and do nothing to him for now I know that you fear God and you have not held back your son, your only one, from me.'

This is the passage that Auerbach famously described as 'fraught with background' in *Mimesis*, in his comparison between the style of Homer and 'an equally ancient and equally epic style' – that of biblical narrative.[67] Auerbach's analysis is focussed on what is missing from the passage: he points out, for example, that we know neither where God is, nor where Abraham is, and that the repeated expression 'here I am' or 'behold me' (הִנֵּנִי) indicates a moral rather than a physical position. The syntax is overwhelmingly

---

[66] The translation is taken from Robert Alter, *Genesis: Translation and Commentary* (New York and London: Norton, 1996), 103–06. For the passage in Hebrew, see *Biblia Hebraica Stuttgartensia* (Stuttgart: Deutsche Bibelgesellschaft, 1997), 31.

[67] Erich Auerbach, *Mimesis: The Representation of Reality in Western Literature*, trans. Willard R. Trask (Princeton, NJ: Princeton University Press, 2013), 38–42.

The Old Testament in Medieval Icelandic Texts

paratactic and there are no epithets or adjectives. Auerbach powerfully describes Abraham's journey as 'a silent progress through the indeterminate and the contingent, a holding of the breath, a process which has no present, which is inserted, like a blank duration, between what has passed and what lies ahead, and which yet is measured: three days!'[68] Likewise, the only thing we are told about Abraham's feelings towards Isaac is in the relative clause 'whom you love', and this is not in the narrative itself but in the direct speech of God to Abraham. Neither Abraham's speech nor his dialogue with Isaac externalises their thoughts or emotions: 'Everything remains unexpressed'. Rather, Abraham's emotions can only be guessed through his history and actions: 'His soul is torn between desperate rebellion and hopeful expectation; his silent obedience is multi-layered, has background'. Auerbach roots this extraordinary style not only in the historical imperative and divine authority of the biblical texts, but also in their concept of the sublime: 'In the Old Testament stories, the sublime, tragic and problematic take shape precisely in the domestic and commonplace'.[69]

One might add to this that parataxis and repetition become powerful rhetorical devices in such an 'economic' or pared-back style. While Abraham's thoughts are entirely blanked, the series of concrete verbs hints at his concealed emotion: 'And Abraham rose early in the morning and saddled his donkey and took his two lads with him, and Isaac his son'.[70] The placing of 'Isaac' last in the series and the repetition of 'his son' (which is technically redundant information) suggest indirectly his reluctance to do what he has been told, despite his unquestioning obedience. Likewise, the long run of verbs at the end is almost unbearable in its forward drive, stalling only at the moment when Abraham reaches out his hand in intention: 'and Abraham built there an altar and laid out the wood and bound Isaac his son and placed him on the altar on top of the wood. And Abraham reached out his hand and took the cleaver to slaughter his son'. This is the moment that is so dramatically captured in medieval iconography, with Abraham often depicted in the act of turning from Isaac to the angel, his knife raised ready to strike.[71] The heart of his dilemma is captured by the repetition of 'Here I am': how can he be fully present to both God and his son in the face of the divine command?

---

68   Auerbach, *Mimesis*, 40.
69   Auerbach, *Mimesis*, 50.
70   On blanks and ellipses, see Jean-Louis Ska, 'Genesis 22 or the Testing of Abraham', in *The Exegesis of the Pentateuch: Exegetical Studies and Basic Questions* (Tübingen: Mohr Siebeck, 2009), 97–98.
71   See, for example, the Genesis initial in the twelfth-century Winchester Bible (fol. 5r), where Abraham twists his head backwards towards the angel with the knife still raised in his hand.

Hebrew Sagas and Icelandic Sagas

Only on the third occurrence is the dilemma resolved, when the angel interrupts Abraham to announce that God has changed his command.

The dialogue in the passage is particularly effective, especially between Abraham and Isaac. The gaps in knowledge create a subtle play of limited perspectives: we know that God is testing Abraham, but not why; Abraham knows that he must sacrifice Isaac, but not that God is testing him; Isaac knows that he is going to a sacrifice, but not that the sacrifice will be him.[72] When Abraham tells his servants 'let us worship and return to you', is he lying to them or does he still hope that that they might both return? When Isaac asks about the 'sheep for the offering', does he suspect the part that he will soon be called to play? When Abraham replies, 'God will see to the sheep for the offering, my son', does he identify the 'sheep' with his son (are they grammatically in apposition?) or does he anticipate that a real 'sheep' will be provided? We can only speculate as to what Abraham and Isaac are thinking, and the same is true of their emotions. Their love for one another is hinted at only by the repeated phrase 'the two of them went together' and the painful repetition in the dialogue of 'father', 'my son', 'my son'. The power of the passage lies precisely in the way in which we must negotiate our own ignorance, must 'read between the lines' and constantly revise our sense of what is happening and what it might mean. While scholars like Sternberg interpret these gaps as a way of defining human knowledge as limited in contrast with the omniscience of God, others, like Kawashima, see this new and innovative style as more of a literary phenomenon, one that anticipates 'the modern novelist's craft'.[73]

Gaps and blanks in the Icelandic sagas encourage very similar ways of reading, as the following conversation from *Laxdœla saga* shows. Sävborg has noted that, although *Laxdœla saga* is very much influenced by continental romance, and revolves around love relationships, the expression of emotion is very much in line with saga convention and must be inferred from verbal cues.[74] The scene that follows takes place after Kjartan has returned to Iceland and has found out that Guðrún – the woman whom he loves – has married his foster-brother Bolli. He marries Hrefna instead, and gives to her a headdress which was given to him by Princess Ingibjǫrg in Norway as a gift for his future wife:[75]

Viku skyldi haustboð vera at Ólafs. Annan dag eftir rœddi Guðrún í hljóði til Hrefnu, at hon skyldi sýna henni motrinn; hon kvað svá vera skyldu.

---

[72] Ska, 'Genesis 22', 99–100.

[73] Sternberg, *Poetics*, 46–47; Kawashima, *Biblical Narrative*, 4–8.

[74] Daniel Sävborg, 'Kärleken i *Laxdœla saga* – höviskt och sagatypiskt', *Alvíssmál* 11 (2004), 100. On emotion, see further Sif Rikharðsdóttir, *Emotion in Old Norse Literature: Translation, Voices, Contexts* (Cambridge: Brewer, 2017).

[75] *Laxdœla saga*, 140.

The Old Testament in Medieval Icelandic Texts

Um daginn eptir ganga þær í útibúr þat, er gripirnir váru í. Lauk Hrefna upp kistu ok tók þar upp guðvefjarpoka, en ór pokanum tók hon motrinn ok sýndi Guðrúnu. Hon rakði motrinn ok leit á um hríð og rœddi hvárki um lost né lof; síðan hirði Hrefna motrinn, ok gengu þær til sætis síns. Eptir þat fór þar fram gleði og skemmtan.

There was to be an autumn feast at Óláfr's for a week. The following day Guðrún said in private to Hrefna that she should show her the headdress. Hrefna said it should be so. Later in the day, they go up to the storehouse which the valuables were in. Hrefna opened up the chest and took out a velvet bag, and out of the bag she took the headdress and showed it to Guðrún. She unwound the headdress and looked at it for a while and said nothing in praise or blame. Then Hrefna put away the headdress and they went back to their seats. After that, the fun and entertainment continued.

Like the Old Testament passage, the syntax is paratactic, and there are no adjectives; series of clauses are joined by 'ok' and 'en'. The structure (as in Genesis 22) is symmetrical: the passage begins and ends with reference to the feast, which both Kjartan's new wife Hrefna and his previous love Guðrún are attending. So, this private moment is bookended by references to the public setting in which it is placed, the 'gleði' ('fun') of which is painfully juxtaposed to the raw emotions in this scene. At the same time, although it is a private scene, it is described entirely from the outside. We are told what the two women do and what they say, but crucially not what either of them feel. The significance of their actions depends entirely on their history: both Guðrún's prior history with Kjartan, and the prior history of the headdress itself, which was given to Kjartan by a woman who – it is implied but never stated directly – may have hoped to marry him herself.[76] We can only speculate as to what these two women think and feel: why does Hrefna show Guðrún the headdress when she knows that Kjartan does not wish her to? Does she intend to evoke jealousy in Guðrún or does she naively interpret Guðrún's interest as a conciliatory move? Likewise, one might ask why Guðrún wishes to see it and whether she asks or commands Hrefna to show it to her. Is she feigning indifference, hoping that the headdress is less impressive than rumoured, or consciously feeding her jealousy and resentment? That she feels something is clear from the time that elapses while she looks at it, but the nature of her feelings can only be guessed. The alliterating 'lost né lof' ('praise or blame') draws attention to her silence even as it refuses to tell us what it means. This silence is just one of a series of meaningful silences in the saga, of which the most telling is the deliberate silence of the slave-girl

[76] *Laxdœla* saga, 131.

Hebrew Sagas and Icelandic Sagas

Melkorka, who is sold into slavery, brought to live with her owner's wife, and gives birth to his child, all without speaking a word to her oppressors.[77]

The second scene that I want to look at is that of Jacob wrestling with an angel in Genesis 32. In this scene too, one can observe parataxis, repetition and external focalisation, but my focus will be on ambiguity and the subversion of folkloric themes:[78]

> And he rose on that night and took his two wives and his two slave-girls and his eleven boys and he crossed over the Jabbok ford. And he took them and brought them over the stream, and he brought across all that he had. And Jacob was left alone, and a man wrestled with him until the break of dawn. And he saw that he had not won out against him and he touched his hip-socket of his hip and Jacob's hip-socket was wrenched as he wrestled with him. And he said, 'Let me go, for dawn is breaking.' And he said, 'I will not let you go unless you bless me.' And he said to him, 'What is your name?' And he said, 'Jacob.' And he said, 'Not Jacob shall your name hence be said but Israel, for you have striven with God and men, and won out.' And Jacob asked and said, 'Tell your name, pray.' And he said, 'Why should you ask my name?' And there he blessed him. And Jacob called the name of the place Peniel, meaning, 'I have seen God face to face and I came out alive.' And the sun rose upon him as he passed Penuel and he was limping on his hip.

The best-known and most compelling analysis of this scene is that of Barthes, who argues that its power and strangeness derive from the overturning of folkloric expectations.[79] The influence of folktale on this story is well established, both in relation to the night-time setting and the crossing of the river. The Three Billy Goats Gruff is the most obvious analogue, although it would be easy to come up with specifically Icelandic equivalents of trolls that cannot abide the light.[80] What Barthes showed, however, was that this story – far from being a genuine cultic or aetiological folktale – deliberately subverts folkloric expectations. We start out with a Subject (Jacob), a Sender who initiates the Quest (God), and an Opponent who tries to prevent it (the 'man').[81] As a result, we expect Jacob to defeat the Opponent, with the aid of a Helper. But these expectations are overturned when we discover, in

---

[77] *Laxdœla saga*, 23–28.

[78] Alter, *Genesis*, 180–83; *Biblia Hebraica*, 53.

[79] Roland Barthes, 'The Struggle with the Angel: Textual Analysis of Genesis 32:23–33', in *Structural Analysis and Biblical Exegesis: Interpretational Essays*, trans. Alfred M. Johnson (Pittsburgh, PA: Pickwick, 1974), 21–33.

[80] See John Lindow, *Trolls: An Unnatural History* (London: Reaktion Books, 2014), 40–41, 65–66.

[81] Barthes, 'Struggle with the Angel', 30–31.

The Old Testament in Medieval Icelandic Texts

Jacob's own retrospective assessment, that the Sender and the Opponent are the same: 'I have seen God face to face'. Barton compares this to a modern detective novel in which the detective turns out to be the murderer, or to discovering, upon a first reading of *Sir Gawain and the Green Knight*, that the Green Knight is Bertilak.[82] The ensuing disorientation plays a significant part in the 'uncanny' feel that this story has for most of us.

Barthes also notes, however, the significant 'ambiguity' that the style of the story produces. The first few sentences seem to conjure two different scenarios: one in which Jacob crosses the river with his family and belongings, and one in which he sends them on ahead and remains behind alone. This, Barthes suggests, produces two potential stories: an 'etymological saga' in which the trial is the literal crossing of the river, and a psychological story, which is about Jacob's spiritual rebirth.[83] Then there is the 'man' (אִישׁ) who comes out of nowhere with no explanation of why or how he is suddenly there. The question of identity is blurred further by the repetitive use of third-person verb forms – Barthes calls this style 'embrouillé' or 'intertwined' – so that one can only find out who is saying what by working backwards from the moment that Jacob speaks his name.[84] In the dark night of their struggle, the identity of both wrestlers is put in doubt. Likewise, the outcome of the wrestling is ambiguous: the 'man' appears to win when he wrenches Jacob's hip, yet it is Jacob who seems to be in a position to make demands ('I will not let go until you bless me'). How exactly Jacob 'wins out' over this unidentified figure who can disable him at a touch, is not explained: Barthes speaks of the 'illogical and inverse character of the victory', in which the weaker defeats the stronger and is permanently branded by his victory. Then there is the curious echo between Jacob (יַעֲקֹב), Jabbok (יַבֹּק) and the Hebrew verb 'to wrestle' (אבק), which might suggest that, in some sense, this story is taking place inside Jacob, that it is centrally bound up with his identity, as embodied in his change of name.[85] The setting by a river at the break of day – the sun rising as Jacob finally crosses – creates a doubly liminal space, a boundary to be crossed, a strong sense of a rite of passage.

I would like to argue that many of the features that make this passage so uncanny and subversive are shared by similar scenes in the Icelandic sagas. At the beginning of *Hrafnkels saga*, for example, Hrafnkell's father Hallfreðr

---

82 John Barton, *Reading the Old Testament: Method in Biblical Study* (London: Darton, Longman & Todd, 1984), 116–18.

83 Barthes, 'Struggle with the Angel', 23–26.

84 Barthes, 'Struggle with the Angel', 26.

85 Steven Molan, 'The Identity of Jacob's Opponent: Wrestling with Ambiguity in Genesis 32: 22–32', *Shofar* 11.2 (1993), 17–21.

32

Hebrew Sagas and Icelandic Sagas

is visited at night by an unidentified figure who directs him away from Geitdalr to the place where he will successfully settle:[86]

> En um várit fœrði Hallfreðr bú sitt norðr yfir heiði ok gerði bú þar, sem heitir í Geitdal. Ok eina nótt dreymði hann, at maðr kom at honum ok mælti: 'Þar liggr þú, Hallfreðr, ok heldr óvarliga. Fœr þú á brott bú þitt ok vestr yfir Lagarfljót. Þar er heill þín ǫll'. Eptir þat vaknar hann ok fœrir hann bú sitt út yfir Rangá í Tungu, þar sem síðan heitir á Hallfreðarstǫðum, ok bjó þar til elli. En honum varð þar eptir gǫltr ok hafr. Ok inn sama dag, sem Hallfreðr var í brott, hljóp skriða á húsin, ok týndusk þar þessir gripir, ok heitir þat síðan í Geitdal.

> And in the spring Hallfreðr moved his household north over the heath and built a farm at a place called Geitdalr. And one night he dreamed that a man came to him and said: 'There you lie, Hallfreðr, and rather unwarily. Move your household away and west over Lagarfljót. There is all your good fortune'. After that he wakes up and moves his household out over Rangá in Tunga, to a place that is since called Hallfreðarstaðir. And he left behind a boar and a goat. And the same day Hallfreðr left, a landslide fell onto the house, and these animals died, and it has since been called Geitdalr.

Like the story of Jacob, this anecdote clearly has an 'etymological' element to it, providing an explanation for the place-names Hallfreðarstaðir and Geitdalr. It takes place at night – in this case in the context of a dream – and the 'maðr' ('man') who appears is unidentified. It has been suggested that he may be the god Freyr or a nature spirit (*landvættr*), but the saga author leaves his identity obscure.[87] It is not clear either why he chooses to redirect Hallfreðr and what his connection is to the landslide that destroys the old farm, whether he causes or simply foreknows it. Only the cryptic reference to 'heill' ('luck', 'warning', 'omen') suggests that he may be benevolently inclined. The result of the encounter is, as for Jacob, the crossing of a body of water – in this case, Lagarfljót or Rangá.[88]

Another 'wrestling' match that bears affinity to that of Jacob is Grettir's fight with the revenant Glámr. Although the identity of Glámr is known before the fight, the description of his night-time arrival is purposefully

---

[86] *Hrafnkels saga*, in *Austfirðingasǫgur*, ed. Jón Jóhannesson (Reykjavík: Hið íslenzka fornritafélag, 1950), 97–98.

[87] Preben Meulengracht Sørensen, 'Freyr in den Isländersagas', in *Germanische Religionsgeschichte: Quellen und Quellenprobleme*, ed. Heinrich Beck et al. (Berlin: De Gruyter, 1992), 720–35.

[88] Hermann Pálsson has connected it to a different biblical story: the crossing of the Jordan in Joshua. See his '*Hrafnkels saga og Stjórn*', in *Sjötíu ritgerðir helgaðar Jakobi Benediktssyni, 20 júlí 1977*, ed. Einar G. Pétursson and Jónas Kristjánsson, 2 vols (Reykjavík: Stofnun Árna Magnússonar á Íslandi, 1977), I, 335–43.

The Old Testament in Medieval Icelandic Texts

ambiguous in a similar way to the biblical narrative, although in this case the saga author uses the passive voice to recreate Grettir's own limited vision: 'Var þá farit upp á húsin ok riðit skálanum ok barit hælunum, svá at brakaði í hverju tré. Því gekk lengi. Þá var farit ofan af húsunum' ('[Something] then climbed onto the houses and sat astride the hall and beat [it] with its heels, so that it creaked in every beam. That went on for a long time. Then [it] climbed down from the houses').[89] Glámr is not mentioned until he opens the door, and Grettir sees his monstrous head appear. As for Jacob, the outcome of the wrestling match is ambiguous and, at the crucial moment, Grettir is overcome by faintness ('mœði') just as Jacob is overcome by the disabling touch of his adversary. This is what allows, in both cases, for the supernatural opponent to deliver a verdict, which is in some sense narratorial as much as it is supernatural: in Jacob's case a blessing and promise for the future, in Grettir's case the inverse: a curse, a curtailing of the future that would have been his.[90] The wrestling match and its pronouncement mark the turning point in both of their lives. This sense of liminality or boundary crossing is heightened by the unusual details of the natural setting: for Jacob, the breaking of day; for Grettir, the light of the full moon, as the clouds passing over it suddenly disperse. Both heroes are left permanently changed by their encounter with the Other: while Jacob limps away into the sunrise, Grettir is left with a crippling fear of the dark, which will haunt him for the rest of his life.

Moreover, the way in which Jacob's wrestling match subverts the conventions of folktale has been amply documented in the Icelandic sagas. Sävborg and Bek-Pedersen have written about 'how easily the saga genre incorporates both literary and folktale elements side-by-side', while Aðalheiður Guðmundsdóttir comments on how sagas can manipulate the relationship between structure and meaning in the folktale: they can make use of folktale material but are not obliged to follow the same rules.[91] In particular, Ingjaldr's fishing trip in *Bárðar saga* can be thought of as parallel to Genesis 32. Ingjaldr is out fishing when he has his paranormal encounter, and here the darkness is replaced by mist and fog drifting over 'svá sterkt ok myrkt, at eigi sá stafna í milli' ('so strong and dark that one couldn't see between

---

89   *Grettis saga Ásmundarsonar*, ed. Guðni Jónsson (Reykjavík: Hið íslenzka fornritafélag, 1936), 119.

90   William Sayers, 'The Alien and Alienated as Unquiet Dead in the Sagas of the Icelanders', in *Monster Theory: Reading Culture*, ed. Jeffrey J. Cohen (Minneapolis: University of Minneapolis Press, 1996), 253.

91   Daniel Sävborg and Karen Bek-Pedersen, 'Introduction', in *Folklore in Old Norse – Old Norse in Folklore*, ed. Daniel Sävborg and Karen Bek-Pedersen (Tartu: University of Tartu Press, 2014), 11; see also Aðalheiður Guðmundsdóttir, 'The Other World in the *Fornaldarsögur* and in Folklore' in the same volume, 33–36.

Hebrew Sagas and Icelandic Sagas

the prow and stern').[92] Ingjaldr glimpses first 'mann á báti' ('a person on a boat'), who later calls himself Grímr and is said to be 'red-bearded', which suggests rather than tells us that it is Þórr. Ingjaldr suggests that they row back to land, but Grímr refuses to let him: 'ok máttu bíða, þar til er ek hefi hlaðit bátinn' ('and you must stay there until I have loaded the boat'). How he can compel Ingjaldr to stay is entirely mysterious, but one suggestion is that Ingjaldr – believing himself to be in a folktale – thinks that he will get a supernatural boon from this stranger, just as Jacob does from his adversary.[93] In fact, it turns out that he is not in a folktale, but in a miracle story and, as he reaches the point of death, still unable to leave, he thinks to call upon Bárðr, who comes to rescue him. The same story type can be found in many Norwegian folktales, but the difference here is that the saga author is not only aware of the conventions he is following, but also able to subvert them, and he expects his audience to recognise this. The effect, as in Jacob's wrestling match, is to disorientate the reader, and so force us to confront things from an unfamiliar point of view.

Convergence or Dependence?

The close similarity between biblical and saga narrative – partly in terms of their content, but above all in terms of style – raises the question of whether there is a direct dependence between the two traditions or whether the resemblance is purely coincidental. Since biblical style, according to Barton, developed as early as the eighth century BCE, any relationship of dependence would clearly run from the Bible to the sagas.[94] But, of course, the Icelanders did not read the Bible in Hebrew: they read it in the Vulgate, Jerome's fourth-century Latin translation. Although there may well have been some knowledge of Hebrew in medieval Iceland, it was not extensive: Richard Cole has documented Hebrew in runic inscriptions in Norway, and suggests that most come from the Christian use of Hebrew in the liturgy, although there are details that suggest some Old Norse speakers may have known more 'esoteric' terms, perhaps because they were trained at the abbey of St Victor in Paris.[95] The author of The *First Grammatical Treatise* (c. 1125–75) thinks that the letter 'z' is made up of Hebrew ד (daleth) and צ

---

[92] *Bárðar saga Snæfellsáss*, in *Harðar saga, Bárðar saga*, ed. Þórhallur Vilmundarson and Bjarni Vilhjálmsson (Reykjavík: Hið íslenzka fornritafélag, 1991), 126.

[93] See Camilla Asplund Ingemark, 'The Trolls in *Bárðar saga* – Playing with the Conventions of Oral Texts', in *Folklore in Old Norse*, ed. Sävborg and Bek-Pedersen, 132–33.

[94] Barton, *History of the Bible*, 47.

[95] Richard Cole, 'Hebrew in Runic Inscriptions and Elsewhere', *Viking and Medieval Scandinavia* 11 (2015), 33–78.

35

The Old Testament in Medieval Icelandic Texts

(tsade), which suggests that he knew what these two letters sounded like. The author of *The Third Grammatical Treatise* (c. 1250) compares dotted runes to the variable vocalic values of א (aleph) and ע (ayin). Although he wrongly thinks that these two letters are vowels, he does at least know something about Masoretic pointing.[96] Both Cole and O'Donoghue have explored the possible circulation of Hebrew traditions in Iceland, probably also via St Victor in Paris, where there was significant interaction between Jewish and Christian scholars.[97] However, there is no evidence that this knowledge was wide-spread or competent enough for Icelandic prose style to be influenced by Hebrew.

The next question is how far 'saga style' in the Hebrew Bible comes through into the Latin Vulgate. Jerome is often quoted in translation studies as having exempted the Bible from the usual 'sense for sense' method of translation: 'except in the case of the holy scriptures, where even the order of the words is a mystery'.[98] Kamesar has suggested, though, that we should not take him at his word; he may here be referring not to his own preferences, but to the strategy adopted in earlier Greek and Old Latin translations.[99] In other writings, Jerome makes it clear that his own aim in translating the Bible is 'to attain elegance in Latin and achieve stylistic fidelity'. Either way, it appears that, even if Jerome's theory was to translate 'word for word', this does not align with his practice, which varies between books of the Bible and over time, but certainly involves much 'sense for sense'.[100] While certain aspects of Jerome's translation do follow the Hebrew closely (e.g. undeclined proper names, Hebraic temporal expressions, the infinite absolute), Kraus notes his 'strong proclivity towards elegant Latin style'.[101] Jerome avoids at least some

---

96 Cole, 'Hebrew in Runic Inscriptions', 41.

97 Richard Cole, 'The French Connection, or Þórr versus the Golem', in *Medieval Encounters: Jewish, Christian and Muslim Culture in Confluence and Dialogue* 20.3 (2014), 238–60; Heather O'Donoghue, 'What has Lamech to do with Baldr: The Lethal Shot of a Blind Man in Old Norse Myth and Jewish Exegetical Traditions', *Medium Ævum* 72.1 (2003), 82–107.

98 Jerome, Ep. 57.5, CSEL 54 ('abseque Scripturis sanctis, ubi et uerborum ordo mysterium est'), trans. in *The Letters of St Jerome*, in *NPNF*, VI, 294.

99 Adam Kamesar, 'Jerome', in *The New Cambridge History of the Bible*, ed. James Carleton Paget and Joachim Schaper, 4 vols (Cambridge: Cambridge University Press, 2012–15), I, 669.

100 Benjamin Kedar, 'The Latin Translations', in *Mikra: Text, Translation, Reading and Interpretation of the Hebrew Bible in Ancient Judaism and Early Christianity*, ed. M. J. Mulder and Henry Sysling (Assen: Van Gorcum, 1988), 323–29; H. F. D. Sparks, 'Jerome as Biblical Scholar', in *The Cambridge History of the Bible, Volume 1: From the Beginnings to Jerome*, ed. P. R Ackroyd and C. F. Evans (Cambridge: Cambridge University Press, 1970), 525.

101 Matthew A. Kraus, *Jewish, Christian and Classical Exegetical Traditions in*

Hebrew Sagas and Icelandic Sagas

of the characteristics of the Hebrew that have been noted above, including parataxis and meaningful repetition, which he replaces with asyndeton, subordination and variation, and Latin idioms and expressions. For example, while Hebrew typically begins new clauses with the conjunction ו (waw), Jerome uses 'an abundance of clause connectors and participles', preferring to specify the relationship between clauses rather than leave it open.[102]

If one looks at the sacrifice of Isaac in Genesis 22, for example, the divergences from Hebrew style are easily detected.[103] The run of verbs joined by ו (waw) has been replaced by a variety of connectives ('et', 'que', 'autem', 'igitur', 'cum'). Compare, for example, the beginning of verse 3 in the Latin Vulgate with the translation of the Hebrew above (p. 27): 'Igitur Abraham de nocte consurgens stravit asinum suum ducens secum duos iuvenes et Isaac filium suum' ('So Abraham, getting up at night, saddled his donkey, taking with him the two youths, and Isaac his son'). Instead of a series of short clauses joined by 'and', we have one main clause using two present participles. Likewise, in place of the effective paratactic sequence of verbs in verse 9, we find: 'Veneruntque ad locum quem ostenderat ei Deus in quo aedificavit altare et desuper ligna conposuit cumque conligasset Isaac filium suum posuit eum in altari' ('And they came to the place that God had shown him, in which he built an altar, and arranged the wood on it. And once he had bound Isaac his son, he laid him on the altar'). The repetition of 'and he said' (וַיֹּאמֶר) in the Hebrew has been replaced by a variety of verbs: 'dixit', 'ait', 'respondit', 'inquit'. Where the Hebrew uses one word for 'his young men' or 'his lads' (נְעָרָיו), the Vulgate has 'pueros' ('boys') and 'iuvenes' ('youths'). For the Hebrew thrice-repeated verb אמר ('to say') in the phrase 'that God had said to him', the Vulgate uses three different verbs: 'monstravero', 'praeceperat' and 'ostenderat'. Where the Hebrew repeats 'the two of them' (שְׁנֵיהֶם) before and after the dialogue between Abraham and Isaac, Jerome goes for 'duo … simul' and 'pariter'. Instead of the repeated Hebrew idiom 'Here I am' or 'Behold' (הִנֵּנִי or הִנֵּה), he uses three different expressions: 'adsum' ('I am here'), 'quid vis' ('what do you want?'), and 'ecce' ('behold'). The 'restrained' or 'laconic' aspects of biblical style are not as evident in his translation.

Despite his preference for 'stylistic variation', though, Jerome did understand the peculiarity of Hebrew style, and replicated some aspects of it. In Graeco-Roman culture, many educated people felt that the Bible was lacking in literary qualities, and Jerome engaged with this both by justifying the

---

Jerome's Translation of the Book of Exodus: Translation Technique and the Vulgate (Leiden: Brill, 2017), 52.

[102] Kraus, *Exegetical Traditions*, 94.

[103] *Biblia Sacra iuxta Vulgatam Versionem*, ed. Roger Gryson et al., 4th ed. (Stuttgart: Deutsche Bibelgesellschaft, 1994), 29–30. The translations of this passage are my own.

The Old Testament in Medieval Icelandic Texts

simplicity of biblical style and by advocating for its beauty.[104] In a letter to Paulinus of Nola, for example, he urges him: 'Let not the simplicity of the scripture or the poorness of its vocabulary offend you', suggesting that this should either be blamed on the translators (presumably of the Old Latin Bible) or understood as a 'deliberate purpose' to make allowances for the unlearned: 'For in this way it is better fitted for the instruction of an unlettered congregation as the educated person can take one meaning and the uneducated another from one and the same sentence'.[105] Writing to Pammachius about his own translation of the Old Testament into Latin, he cautions: 'You must not in my small writings look for any such eloquence as that which for Christ's sake you disregard in Cicero. A version made for the use of the Church, even though it may possess a literary charm, ought to disguise and avoid it'.[106] In his prefaces to Isaiah, Jeremiah and Ezekiel, he attempts to characterise the style of each prophet, aligning them with the classical categories of 'elevated', 'smooth' and 'simple' style. Kamesar describes his study of the style of the Prophets as 'the most creative application of Graeco-Latin scholarship to the biblical corpus'.[107] For Jerome, style was an important part of translation, and he actively tried to preserve something of the Bible's original flavour ('sapor').

If we turn back to Genesis 22, then, we can see that some aspects of Hebrew style are still present. For example, Jerome preserves the symmetry between the beginning and the end of the passage, although with a slight variation: 'dixit ad eum Abraham ille respondit adsum' ('he said to him, "Abraham". He replied, "Here I am"'); 'dicens Abraham Abraham qui respondit adsum' ('saying "Abraham, Abraham", who replied: "Here I am"'). In the dialogue between Abraham and Isaac, we still find the repetition of 'pater mi' ('my father'), 'fili' ('son'), 'fili mi' ('my son'). Towards the end of the passage, some of the parataxis is retained, although the conjunction itself is varied: 'cumque conligasset Isaac filium suum posuit eum in altari super struem lignorum extenditque manum et arripuit gladium ut immolaret filium' ('and once he had bound Isaac his son, he placed him on the altar on the pile of wood, and extended his hand, and took the knife to sacrifice his son'). The word-order, when meaningful, may be kept as well, such as the postponement of 'Isaac' in God's command to Abraham and 'his son' in Abraham's obedient response: 'tolle filium tuum unigenitum quem diligis Isaac' ('take your son, the only-begotten, whom you love, Isaac'); 'ducens secum duos iuvenes et Isaac filium suum' ('taking with him two youths and Isaac his son'). Aspects

---

104 Kamesar, 'Jerome', 665–66.
105 Jerome, Ep. 53.10; trans. *NPNF*, VI, 102.
106 Jerome, Ep. 49.4, trans. *NPNF*, VI, 79–80.
107 Kamesar, 'Jerome', 666–67.

Hebrew Sagas and Icelandic Sagas

of style that are not reliant on syntax also remain in the Vulgate: the lack of adjectives and the absence of description, characterisation or commentary.

It seems possible, then, that some aspects of biblical style could have been transmitted through the Vulgate, and reinforced through the ideal of the 'plain style' as part of the teaching of rhetoric in cathedral and monastery schools.[108] Some of the earliest texts to be translated into Old Norse-Icelandic in the twelfth century – the lives of saints and apostles – were written primarily in this style (sometimes called 'popular style' in scholarship on the sagas), and it is generally agreed that they provided one model for the first saga authors.[109] The biblical translations, however, date from significantly later – the mid-thirteenth century – which makes it difficult to argue that they could have had any influence on vernacular style. On the contrary, it seems more likely – or at least it is easier to prove – that aspects of saga style have influenced the biblical translations.

The overall likeness between biblical and saga narrative, therefore, is difficult to explain through a theory of direct dependence. It seems more likely to be rooted in shared circumstances, circumstances that led in both cases to the refinement of a particular style of prose to a high level of artistry. Elsewhere I have suggested a biological model for this in 'convergent evolution': the way in which, in response to environmental pressures, two species – which are otherwise independent – may evolve similar features that are not present in any common ancestor.[110] One well-known example is filter feeding in whales and sharks; another is echolocation, which evolved independently in bats and dolphins and shrews. In the same way, what we seem to be dealing with here are two convergent forms of storytelling, which have come to resemble each other not because they share a common ancestor, but because of the sort of environment in which they arose.

Exactly which environmental factors were prevalent, though, is difficult to tell, since scholars from within each tradition disagree on how 'saga style'

---

[108] For some important discussions of rhetoric and style in Old Norse-Icelandic, see Sverrir Tómasson, *Formálar íslenskra sagnaritara á miðöldum* (Reykjavík: Stofnun Árna Magnússonar, 1998), 33–44; Ian McDougall, 'Studies in the Prose Style of the Old Icelandic and Old Norwegian Homily Books', PhD thesis, University of London, 2013; Lucy Collings, 'Codex Scardensis: Studies in Icelandic Hagiography', PhD thesis, Cornell University, 1979, 149–53; Philip Roughton, 'Stylistics and Sources of the *Postola sögur* in AM 645 4to and AM 652/630 4to', *Gripla* 16 (2005), 10–15; Þórir Óskarsson, 'Rhetoric and Style', in *A Companion to Old Norse-Icelandic Literature and Culture*, ed. Rory McTurk (Malden: Blackwell, 2005), 355–64.

[109] Gabriel Turville-Petre, *Origins of Icelandic Literature* (Oxford: Clarendon Press, 1967), 142; Jónas Kristjánsson, 'Learned Style or Saga Style?', 260–92.

[110] Siân Grønlie, '"Cast out this bondwoman": Hagar and Ishmael in Old Norse-Icelandic Literature', *Arkiv for nordisk filologi* 134 (2019), 28.

arose. The unique characteristics of Hebrew storytelling have been explained either as a theological phenomenon – relating to the rise of monotheism and/ or a new concept of divinity working through history – or as purely literary, the coming together of epic poetry with the prose chronicle, or a response to the decline of the epic arts.[111] The genesis of Icelandic 'saga style' is similarly debated, with differing emphases on its oral origins, its relationship to the circumstances of settlement, and its dependence on the earliest translations from Latin.[112] While they are hard to pin down, it is clear that, in both cases, cultural circumstances have led to the rise of an extraordinarily rich prose out of oral traditions of storytelling. For scholars of both literatures, an element of mystery remains: how such small and apparently insignificant peoples, living on the edge of great civilisations (Egypt and Mesopotamia; Western Latin Christendom), came to produce such masterful narrative prose.

It is important to note that the model of convergent evolution does not rule out direct borrowing from the Old Testament in Old Norse-Icelandic literature. Clearly some saga authors would have read parts of the Bible either in Latin or in translation and/or known stories from the Old Testament through sermons, encyclopaedic literature, or word of mouth. Likewise, some of the Old Norse-Icelandic translations of the Old Testament are clearly influenced by the Icelandic sagas. But what I want to argue is that the kinds of borrowings we find in both directions are possible precisely because there is an already existing likeness between saga narrative and Old Testament historical stories. In other words, while saints' lives may have taught the saga authors how to do things that they did not already know how to do – how to represent subjectivity or use allegory, for example – in the Old Testament, the Icelanders found a storytelling tradition that was very much kindred to their own.

Conclusion

In this chapter, I set out to show that there is a close relationship between the stories in the Hebrew Bible and Icelandic saga narrative. This relationship consists not only in a shared interest in family and origins, genealogy and place-names, but above all in the shared use of a prose style – called 'saga style' – characterised by economy, objectivity and indirection. While biblical

---

[111] See, for example, von Rad, 'Beginnings', 202–04; Damrosch, *Narrative Covenant*, 41–50; Kawashima, *Biblical Narrative*, 190–92.

[112] Turville-Petre, *Origins*, 142; Jónas Kristjánsson, 'Learned Style or Saga Style', 291. There is a brief discussion and further bibliography in Jónas Wellendorf, 'Ecclesiastical Literature and Hagiography', in *The Routledge Research Companion to the Medieval Icelandic Sagas*, ed. Ármann Jakobsson and Sverrir Jakobsson (London: Routledge, 2017), 51–52.

Hebrew Sagas and Icelandic Sagas

scholars were already beginning to discuss these similarities at the turn of the twentieth century, it has taken longer for scholars of Old Norse-Icelandic literature to catch up – no doubt for the understandable reason that few scholars of the sagas are conversant with biblical Hebrew. I have argued here that the similarities between these two traditions may be best understood as driven by the environments in which they arose, rather than by a relationship of literary dependence. However, when biblical narrative did arrive in Iceland in the years after the conversion to Christianity in 999–1000, one might expect the Icelanders to show a particular interest in stories so closely related to their own storytelling tradition. The issue is complicated, of course, by the successive translations of the Hebrew Bible into Greek and then Latin: the Icelanders first encountered the Hebrew Bible as the Old Testament in the Latin translation of St Jerome. However, some aspects of biblical style do survive these layers of translation, not least because Jerome himself – like St Augustine and other Fathers of the Church – both recognised and defended the distinctiveness of biblical style. The aim of this book is to explore how the curious affinity between biblical stories and Icelandic sagas shaped the reception of Old Testament narrative in Old Norse-Icelandic. I start, in the next chapter, by looking at some of the interpretative traditions through which the Old Testament was read in medieval Norway and Iceland.

⤏ 2 ⤎

From Hebrew Bible to Old Testament:
Traditions of Exegesis

The Hebrew Bible came to the Icelanders not only through successive translations, but also through successive layers of exegesis that transformed it into
the Old Testament: Christian Scripture that speaks of Christ and the Church.
In fact, translation and exegesis are closely linked, to the extent that the latter
might be thought of as a development of the former: exegesis as a translation of the reality that lies behind the words.[1] All early Christian exegesis
is dependent on translation: the Scripture of the early Church was not the
Hebrew Bible, but the Greek Septuagint (LXX), a translation supposedly
made independently by 72 scholars, who all miraculously produced the
same text.[2] Some of the earliest biblical exegetes were actively involved in
translation and textual criticism: one of Origen's great achievements was the
compilation of the *Hexapla*, a multiple-column parallel Bible in which the
LXX was set out alongside the Hebrew, a transliteration into Greek, and three
other Greek translations.[3] Likewise, Jerome was initially asked to translate
the LXX into Latin, but turned instead to the Hebrew Bible – a choice that
attracted criticism at the time, most notably from Augustine.[4] His translation,
which became the Vulgate, was not fully accepted by the Church until the

---

1   Frances Young, *Biblical Exegesis and the Formation of Christian Culture*
     (Cambridge: Cambridge University Press, 1997), 119; Reinhart Ceulemans, 'The
     Septuagint and Other Translations', in *The Oxford Handbook of Early Christian
     Biblical Interpretation*, ed. Paul M. Blowers and Peter W. Martens (Oxford:
     Oxford University Press, 2019), 33.
2   Kristin De Troyer, 'The Septuagint', in *The New Cambridge History of the
     Bible*, I, 272–73. Ronald Heine, *Origen: Scholarship in the Service of the Church*
     (Oxford: Oxford University Press, 2010), 65–66.
3   Heine, *Scholarship*, 74; Gilles Dorival, 'Origen', in *The New Cambridge History
     of the Bible*, I, 608.
4   Kamesar, 'Jerome', 662.

42

From Hebrew Bible to Old Testament

sixth century, by which time it had accrued some of the sanctity that originally applied to the LXX. Augustine, who knew very little Hebrew, used Old Latin translations probably made in North Africa, although in his *De doctrina christiana* he did recommend learning Hebrew and Greek, as well as Latin, before taking on the task of biblical exegesis.[5] By the twelfth century, it was rare to read the Bible without some form of commentary, whether prefaces, glossaries, lists of Hebrew names, or the huge interpretative framework of the *Glossa Ordinaria*, which incorporated both interlinear and marginal annotations.[6] In this chapter, I look at some of the ways in which the Old Testament was read in the Middle Ages, from Origen and Augustine, to Hugh of St Victor and Peter Comestor, to the vernacular translations known as *Bibles historiales*. I focus, in particular, on the development of allegorical readings, and the rediscovery in the twelfth century of the Bible as historical narrative.

Types and Figures

The earliest allegorical readings of the Old Testament are within the New Testament itself. Paul, for example, writing about Sarah and Hagar in Genesis 21, comments: 'Which things are said by an allegory [ἀλληγορούμενα]: for these [women] are the two testaments'.[7] In 1 Corinthians 10, he reads the events of the Exodus as an allegory of baptism, describing them as 'types' (τύποι). But figurative readings of the classics had a long pre-Christian history: in Alexandria, where the LXX was translated, there was a continuous history of textual criticism and commentary-writing on Homer, the format of which Origen adopted in his writings on the Christian Scriptures.[8] Hellenistic Jews like Philo, who was writing in the first century BCE, used allegory as a literary tool to develop readings of the Hebrew Bible that construed Greek culture in specifically Jewish terms: the belief that Plato was inspired by Moses – popularised by Aristobulus – was one expression of this desire to assert the priority of Jewish culture over Greek.[9] So Philo, just like Paul, reads the story of Sarah and Hagar as an allegory: 'It is not women who are

---

5   Augustine of Hippo, *De doctrina christiana*, II.16; *On Christian Teaching*, trans. R. P. H. Green (Oxford: Oxford University Press, 2008), 42.

6   Laura Light, 'Non-Biblical Texts in Thirteenth-Century Bibles', in *Medieval Manuscripts, their Makers and Users: A Special Issue of Viator in Honor of Richard and Mary Rouse* (Turnhout: Brepols, 2011), 169–83. On the *Glossa ordinaria*, see Lesley Smith, *The Glossa ordinaria: The Making of a Medieval Bible Commentary* (Leiden: Brill, 2009).

7   Gal. 4.24. All translations of the Vulgate are from the Douay-Rheims translation of the Bible, unless otherwise stated.

8   Heine, *Scholarship*, 22–24.

9   Heine, *Scholarship*, 19; Young, *Biblical Exegesis*, 68.

The Old Testament in Medieval Icelandic Texts

spoken of here; it is minds'.[10] The existence of rival texts and interpretations of the Bible posed a problem for the early Church and drove the need for a unitive reading – a feature of Greek literary tradition – that would emphasise the organic unity of the whole. Young describes this in terms of a 'culture war' or 'take-over bid' in which the Bible came to replace the classics in the formation of a Christian culture.[11]

Origen, who was probably born in Alexandria in c. 185 CE, was the most prolific and influential of these early Christian interpreters, although much of his work survives only in Latin translations made by Rufinus of Aquileia and Jerome. For Origen, the Old and the New Testaments are in perfect harmony, and the task of exegesis is to discover Christ's presence in the Scripture so that he can complete his work of redemption in the human soul.[12] Just as Christ is both human and divine, so the Bible has both a literal and a spiritual sense:

> Just as he is cloaked by the flesh, so also he is clothed with the garment of these words, so that the words are that which is seen, just as the flesh is seen, but hidden within (the words) the spiritual sense is perceived, just as the flesh is seen and the divinity perceived.[13]

The true coherence or unity of Scripture is to be found in the spiritual sense, which is always useful or edifying, advancing the soul towards perfection. So, discussing Isaac's wells in Genesis 26, Origen writes: 'Do you think these are tales and that the Holy Spirit tells stories in Scriptures? This is instruction for souls and spiritual teaching which instructs and teaches you to come daily to the wells of the Scriptures'.[14] While Origen has been criticised – both in his own time and more recently – for neglecting the historical sense of Scripture, it is rather that his understanding of history is different: history, for him, is 'the figurative representation of the spiritual reality' made known directly in the incarnation.[15] Rather than destroying the historical sense, Origen saw

---

10 Philo, 'On Mating with the Preliminary Studies', in *Philo*, trans. F. H. Colson and G. H. Whitaker, vol. 4 (Cambridge, MA: Harvard University Press, 1932), 550–51.

11 Young, *Biblical Exegesis*, 51–54, 286, 292.

12 David Dawson, *Christian Figural Reading and the Fashioning of Identity* (Berkeley: University of California Press, 2002), 71; Karen Jo Torjesen, *Hermeneutical Procedure and Theological Method in Origen's Exegesis* (Berlin and Boston: De Gruyter, 2011), 148.

13 Quoted in Torjesen, *Origen's Exegesis*, 110.

14 Origen, *Homilies on Genesis and Exodus*, trans. Ronald Heine (Washington, DC: Catholic University of America Press, 1982), 160. The Latin text of the Homilies can be found in *Origenes Werke: Band 6, Homilien zum Hexateuch in Rufins Übersetzung, Teil 1: Die Homilien zu Genesis, Exodus und Leviticus*, ed. W. Baehrens (Leipzig: J. C. Hinrichs'sche Buchhandlung, 1920). The above quotation is on p. 95.

15 Torjesen, *Origen's Exegesis*, 140; Henri de Lubac, *History and Spirit: The*

the spiritual sense as preserving or even redeeming it: the contradictions, lack of logic, and moral 'scandals' of the Old Testament are justified by their spiritual interpretation. As de Lubac has shown, he 'transposes the history of Israel's wars, its captivities, its deliverances, its victories to apply them to the Christian life'.[16] The historical event is reproduced in the individual as a drama of the soul; it is not a one-off happening, but continually relevant and available to the reader.

Origen's homily on the sacrifice of Isaac (Genesis 22) is a good example of his hermeneutic method; it was translated into Latin by Rufinus and part of it was incorporated into Vincent of Beauvais's *Speculum historiale*, whence it made its way into *Stjórn*. Origen was aware of the allegorical equation of Isaac with Christ – which goes back to at least the end of the second century CE – but he alludes to this only in passing; rather he is interested in Abraham's inner conflict, which is precisely what is left unexpressed in the biblical text.[17] Following a prompt from the Epistle to the Hebrews, he construes it as a test of Abraham's faith in the resurrection: 'Abraham knew himself to prefigure the image of future truth [...] He knew that Christ would be born of his seed, who was to be offered as a truer victim for the whole world'.[18] In other words, Abraham already knows that the events of his life are symbolic of Christian doctrine. Origen reinterprets details of time and place as interior movements: Abraham is ordered to go 'into the high land' so that 'exalted by faith, he might abandon earthly things and ascend to things above'; it is 'early morning' because 'the beginning of light shone in his heart'.[19] The three days of the journey – as well as containing a theological 'mystery' – create a space in which 'the parent's heart is tormented with recurring anxieties'. This internal focus allows Origen to locate his audience imaginatively within the text, to recreate historical event as an inner drama, the 'total warfare of the flesh [...] against the faith of the soul'.[20] When Abraham raises his hand to strike, Origen even addresses fathers in his congregation, appealing to any who have experienced the death of a child through illness to show 'that faith in God is stronger than the affections of the flesh'.[21] The 'scandal' of God's command to kill one's child is reconceptualised or redeemed as the need to

---

    Understanding of Scripture according to Origen, trans. Anne Englund Nash (San Francisco, CA: Ignatius Press, 2007), 105, 122.

[16] De Lubac, *History and Spirit*, 206.

[17] Paba Nidhani De Andrado, '"A Model of Christ": Melito's Re-Vision of Jewish Akedah Exegeses', *Studies in Christian-Jewish Relations* 12.1 (2017), 1–18.

[18] Origen, *Homilies*, 137.

[19] Origen, *Homilies*, 139.

[20] Origen, *Homilies*, 138.

[21] Origen, *Homilies*, 142.

The Old Testament in Medieval Icelandic Texts

relinquish earthly joys, so that God may return them to us multiplied. For Origen, the shape of history is replicated in the movements of the soul.

Jerome (d. 420 CE) inherited the Greek exegetical tradition represented by Origen, and, for him too, the spiritual sense was paramount and the locus of Christian salvation. His attitude towards the Hebrew text of the Bible, however, marked a significant departure from tradition. The LXX had been the authorised Bible of the Christian Church for over 300 years, so Jerome's decision to translate from the Hebrew rather than the Greek was not a choice between the 'original' and a 'copy', but between 'two independent textual traditions, each with its own history'.[22] Although Jerome was in practice deeply indebted to Origen's textual work in the *Hexapla*, he was keen to annex the truth of the Hebrew Scriptures as his own: in the famous 'helmeted prologue' to his translation of the books of Samuel and Kings, he comments that 'I am not in the least conscious that I have deviated in any way from the Hebrew original' ('hebraica veritate').[23] This 'Hebrew truth', for Jerome, includes not just the Hebrew text of the Bible, but also a whole body of rabbinical interpretations, as well as Jewish material gained indirectly from Origen and his successors. Jerome's exegetical works, such as the *Quaestiones Hebraicae in Genesim*, were written to defend and make sense specifically of the Hebrew text of the Bible:[24]

> Our purpose therefore will be either to refute the errors of those who suspect that the Hebrew books are unreliable, or to restore by means of their authority the errors that can be seen to abound in the Greek and Latin codices, and in addition to explain by recourse to their native tongue the etymologies of things, names, and places, which are unintelligible in our language.

Williams describes it as a work of 'great originality', showing extensive assimilation of Jewish exegetical traditions. In Jerome's great commentaries on the Prophets, he comes to associate the text 'iuxta Hebraeos' ('according to the Hebrews') with the literal or historical level of interpretation and the LXX with the allegorical level. This leaves him with the awkward dilemma

---

22 Megan Hale Williams, *The Monk and the Book: Jerome and the Making of Christian Scholarship* (Chicago: University of Chicago Press, 2006), 7; see also Adam Kamesar, *Jerome, Greek Scholarship and the Hebrew Bible: A Study of the Quaestiones Hebraicae in Genesim* (Oxford: Clarendon Press, 1993), 176–87.

23 Jerome's Prologue is in *Biblia sacra*, ed. Gryson, 364–66; it is translated in *NPNF*, II, 490.

24 Jerome, *Hebraicae quaestiones in libro Geneseos*, CCSL 72, 1–2; trans. in Williams, *The Monk and the Book*, 83–84.

From Hebrew Bible to Old Testament

that the most authoritative text of the Scripture (the Hebrew) is associated with the least satisfactory level of interpretation (the literal or historical).[25]

Jerome's 'Hebrew truth' re-emerges strongly with the Victorines in the twelfth century but was viewed with doubt and suspicion by his contemporary St Augustine (354–430 CE). Augustine inherited from Ambrose the figurative tradition of Philo and Origen and fully embraced the potential of allegorical readings to transform the biblical text, which he knew from the Old Latin translations. In his *Confessions*, he vividly dramatises for us the difficulties posed by the Old Latin Bible for an educated reader trained in oratory and rhetoric. He describes how he was initially revulsed by biblical style: 'It seemed to me unworthy in comparison with the dignity of Cicero. My inflated conceit shunned the Bible's restraint, and my gaze never penetrated to its inwardness'.[26] This all changed when Augustine heard Ambrose preach for the first time:[27]

> I was delighted to hear Ambrose, in his sermons to the people saying, as if he were most carefully enunciating a principle of exegesis: 'The letter kills, the spirit gives life' (2 Cor. 3:6). Those texts which, taken literally, seemed to contain perverse teaching he would expound spiritually, removing the mystical veil.

Allegorical readings thus offered a way of resolving things which appeared 'perverse' or incongruous, such as the anthropomorphism of God, which Augustine came to understood through the doctrine of condescension: God's accommodation of himself to the paucity to human language. More importantly for Augustine, it offered a way of dealing with the apparent unliterariness of biblical style: 'lowly to the beginner but, on further reading, of mountainous difficulty'.[28] Augustine explains this as an accommodation to the abilities of the reader, condescending to the weak and challenging the more able: 'It was open to everyone to read, while keeping the dignity of its secret meaning for a profounder interpretation. The Bible offered itself to all in very accessible words and the most humble style of diction, while also exercising the concentration of those who are not light of heart'.[29] Just as Augustine's conversion was enabled by a shift from literal to figurative reading, so figurative reading itself can be understood as a form of conversion, a redemptive 'turning' of loss into the 'gain' of Christian salvation: 'Allegorical exegesis repeats in miniature the crisis through which loss and death became gain and eternal

---

25 Williams, *The Monk and the Book*, 117.
26 Augustine of Hippo, *Confessionum librum XIII*, iii.5; *Confessions*, trans. Henry Chadwick (Oxford: Oxford University Press, 1991), 40.
27 Augustine, *Confessionum*, vi.4, trans. Chadwick, 94.
28 Augustine, *Confessionum*, iii.5, trans. Chadwick, 40.
29 Augustine, *Confessionum*, vi.5, trans. Chadwick, 96.

life'.[30] So it is entirely appropriate that Augustine's *Confessions* ends with an allegorical interpretation of Genesis 1, as the story of creation is recast as the conversion of the individual soul.

Augustine sets out the methods of biblical interpretation more discursively in *De doctrina christiana*, a work focussed not just on how to read, but – as the title suggests – on how to teach. As teacher, he was concerned to set out basic principles that would enable biblical exegetes to develop interpretations of their own. In book II, he develops his theory of signs, distinguishing between literal signs ('signa propria') that refer to 'those things for which they were invented' and figurative signs ('signa translata') that point beyond this: the word 'ox', for example, may signify a literal ox or, figuratively, a preacher of the gospel. Augustine suggests various ways in which the obscurity of proper 'signs' may be dealt with before moving onto the understanding of figurative signs. He warns about the dangers of not going beyond the literal, quoting (as in the *Confessions*) from 2 Corinthians 3.6:[31]

> For when something meant figuratively is interpreted as if it were meant literally, it is understood in a carnal way. No 'death of the soul' is more aptly given that name than the situation in which the intelligence, which is what raises the soul above the level of animals, is subjected to the flesh by following the letter.

The literal meaning, even when acceptable, is not always edifying, and this is particularly the case for the Old Testament, on which Augustine spends some time. He instructs his readers that 'all, or nearly all, of the deeds contained in the books of the Old Testament are to be interpreted not only literally, but also figuratively'. Moreover, he warns that, when reading about unethical acts such as Solomon's womanising, 'one should take up the figurative meaning into one's understanding but not take over the deed itself into one's own behaviour'.[32] He recommends that all Scripture is to be prayed and meditated on 'till an interpretation be found that tends to establish the reign of love'. All interpretation is grounded in the 'Catholic faith' of the Church, and all words in the incarnate Word.

Particularly interesting are Augustine's musings on difficult or obscure passages of the Bible. Westra has commented on how Augustine was able to make 'an aesthetic virtue out of a hermeneutic vice', so that obscurity in the Bible became for him, through allegory, a creative catalyst for 'its fecundity, its richness of meanings, and its beauty'.[33] The poetic and aesthetic quality

---

30 Lynn M. Poland, 'Augustine, Allegory and Conversion', *Literature and Theology* 2.1 (1988), 39.

31 Augustine, *De doctrina christiana*, iii.5; trans. Green, 72.

32 Augustine, *De doctrina christiana*, iii.18–22, trans. Green, 84.

33 H. J. Westra, 'Augustine and Poetic Exegesis', in *Poetry and Exegesis in*

of exegesis for Augustine is very much evident when he writes about the interpretation of Song of Songs 4.2:[34]

> And yet somehow it gives me more pleasure to contemplate holy men when I see them as the teeth of the church, tearing men away from their errors and transferring them into its body, breaking down their rawness by biting and chewing. And it is with the greatest of pleasure, too, that I visualise the shorn ewes, their worldly burdens set aside like fleeces, ascending from the pool (baptism) and all giving birth to twins (the two commandments of love).

Allegorical reading trains the mind, stimulates the intellect, and encourages us to value more deeply that which has taken more effort to uncover. It can be thought of as replicating the incarnation, and so inculcating humility in its readers, as they stoop below or 'under' the literal sense in imitation of God's own self-abasement.[35] Moreover, Augustine allows amply for multiple readings of one and the same passage, even if it cannot be shown that this was the writer's intention: 'Could God have built into the divine eloquence a more generous or bountiful gift than the possibility of understanding the same words in several ways, all of them deriving confirmation from other no less divinely inspired passages?'[36] The correct interpretation is determined not by the text alone, but by the love that the reader brings to it, opening it up to an infinite play of significances.

Augustine's strongest defence of the Old Testament in both its historical integrity and its spiritual figuration comes in book xii of his *Contra Faustum*. Here he argues that all of the Old Testament, even the smallest details, point to Christ: 'For everything that is contained in those books is said either about him or on account of him'.[37] He takes his readers on a rapid tour of Old Testament stories that point to Christ and the Church – including the creation of Eve out of Adam and Noah and the ark – commenting that 'those ideas are more pleasant to contemplate, to the extent that they are dug out of more

---

Premodern Latin Christianity: The Encounter between Classical and Christian Strategies of Interpretation, ed. Willemien Otten and Karla Pollmann (Leiden and Boston: Brill, 2007), 21.

[34] Augustine, *De doctrina christiana*, ii.6, trans. Green, 33 ('Your teeth are like a flock of shorn ewes that have come up from the washing, all of which bear twins').

[35] Mark D. Jordan, 'Words and Word: Incarnation and Signification in Augustine's *De Doctrina Christiana*', *Augustinian Studies* 11 (1980), 186–87.

[36] Augustine, *De doctrina christiana*, iii.27, trans. Green, 87.

[37] Augustine of Hippo, *Contra Faustum manichaeum*, xii.7; *Answer to Faustus, a Manichean*, trans. Roland Teske (Hyde Park, NY: New City Press, 2007), 129.

The Old Testament in Medieval Icelandic Texts

recondite passages'.[38] In Jacob's wrestling with the angel, for example, he sees the mystery of Christ's passion:[39]

> Who else wrestled with Jacob in the angel when, on the one hand, the weaker and the defeated blessed the winner as the stronger and, on the other hand, lamed the socket of his thigh but him who allowed the people of Israel to prevail against himself and blessed those who believed in him? But the socket of Jacob's thigh was lame in the multitude of the fleshly people.

Moreover, he sees the figurative level of understanding as giving meaning to what would otherwise be meaningless:

> If one of us who is ignorant of Hebrew letter, that is, of the Hebrew alphabet, saw those letters written on a wall in some place of honor, who would be so foolish as to think that the wall was simply painted in this way? Would he not rather understand it to be writing so that, even if he could not read it, he would still have no doubt that those strokes signified something?[40]

In this hermeneutic, the Jews play a double role, for on the one hand they are the 'keepers' or 'book-bearers' of the law, but on the other they are enslaved by their 'carnality', which causes them to limp, subjected to the letter of the law because they refuse to perceive the spiritual.[41] In fact, Augustine asserts that, even on the literal level, Jews must seek the assistance of Christians to understand what the Scriptures mean: 'For, unless they grant that they signify something, they do not defend books of such divine authority from the ignominious charge of being silly myths'.[42]

As one might expect, Augustine was well known in Iceland, not least in the Augustinian foundations: Viðey owned copies of *De doctrina christiana* and *Tractatus in Evangelium Iohannis* by 1397; Augustine's homilies are referenced in inventories from churches at Grenjaðarstaðr (1391), Múli (1318) and Vellir (1318) as well as at Möðruvellir (1461) and Skálholt; AM Acc. 7 Ms. 104 contains fragments of *De civitate Dei*.[43] Much more

---

38 Augustine, *Contra Faustum*, xii.14, trans. Teske, 134.

39 Augustine, *Contra Faustum*, xii.26, trans. Teske, 142.

40 Augustine, *Contra Faustum*, xii.37, trans. Teske, 149.

41 Augustine, *Contra Faustum*, xii.23, trans. Teske, 140. On Augustine's 'witness doctrine' and the 'hermeneutical' Jew, see Paula Fredricksen, *Augustine and the Jews: A Christian Defence of Jews and Judaism* (New York and London: Doubleday, 2008), 319–23; and Jeremy Cohen, *Living Letters of the Law: Ideas of the Jews in Medieval Christianity* (Berkeley: University of California Press, 1999), 24–54.

42 Augustine, *Contra Faustum*, xii.39, trans. Teske, 150.

43 *Diplomatarium Islandicum*, ed. Jón Sigurðsson, 16 vols (Copenhagen: Hið

From Hebrew Bible to Old Testament

widely read in Iceland, though, was Gregory the Great (d. 604), whose *Expositio in Canticum Canticorum, Homiliae in Hiezechihelem, Homiliae XL in Evangelia* and *Moralia in Job* are all attested there.[44] Gregory was an important intermediary between the Church Fathers and the Middle Ages: he drew on Origen and Augustine, but infused their work with a distinctively monastic spirituality.[45] His *Moralia* serves as a handbook of allegorical interpretation in which, like Origen, he espouses a threefold model of interpretation: 'First, we lay the historical foundations; next, by pursuing the typical sense, we erect a fabric of the mind to be a stronghold of faith; and moreover, as the last step, by the grace of moral instruction, we as it were clothe the edifice with an overcast of colouring'.[46] This sounds much tidier than his exegesis actually is: he describes it elsewhere as a meandering river, which sometimes overflows and must at other times be diverted, or as a kind of buffet lunch at which a range of different dishes will be served.[47] Gregory's overriding concerns, though, are pastoral and contemplative; he describes Scripture as a 'mirror' in which we see 'our inward face' and by which we are transformed as we read:[48]

> It changes the heart of him that reads it from earthly desires to the embracing of things above; that by its obscurer statements it exercises the strong, and by its humble strain speaks gently to the little ones; that it is neither so shut up, that it should come to be dreaded, nor so open to view as to become contemptible; that by use it removes weariness, and is the more delighted in the more it is meditated on; that the mind of him, who reads it, by words of a low pitch it assists, and by meanings of a lofty flight uplifts; that in some sort it grows with the persons reading.

íslenzka bókmentafélag, 1857–1972), II, 435, 455; IV, 20, 110–11; V, 288; Eldjárn and Hörður Ágústsson, *Skálholt*, 309; Merete Geert Andresen, *Katalog over AM Accessoria. De latinske fragmenter*, ed. Jonna Louis-Jensen (Copenhagen: C. A. Reitzels forlag, 2008), 93.

[44] See *Diplomatarium Islandicum*, ed. Jón Sigurðsson, II, 435, 455, 781; III, 102; IV, 20, 110, 162; V, 193, 288. Fragments of Gregory's *Moralia in Job* survive in AM Acc. 7 Ms. 100, 1r–12v and in AM Acc. 7 Ms. 101, 1r–2v. On Gregory's XL Homilies on the Gospels, see further Chapter 3, pp. 70–72.

[45] Scott DeGregorio, 'Gregory's Exegesis: Old and New Ways of Approaching the Scriptural Text', in *A Companion to Gregory the Great*, ed. Bronwen Neil and Matthew Dal Santo (Boston: Brill, 2013), 269.

[46] Gregory the Great, *Moralia on Job*, Ep. iii; *Morals on the Book of Job*, 3 vols (Oxford: John Henry Parker, 1844–50), I, 7.

[47] On these images, see Grover A. Zinn, 'Exegesis and Spirituality in the Writings of Gregory the Great', in *Gregory the Great: A Symposium*, ed. John C. Cavadini (Notre Dame, IN: University of Notre Dame Press, 2001), 171–72.

[48] Gregory, *Moralia in Job*, xx.i; translated in *Morals*, II, 446.

This lovely idea of Scripture 'growing with the reader' is also reflected in the more comic image of it as a river in which 'lambs wade and elephants swim'.[49]

Gregory's close focus on the inner life can be seen clearly in his exegesis of Genesis 32, which contrasts with Augustine's reading. While both read the angel as a figure for the divine, Augustine is interested in salvation history, and what Jacob tells us about the Church and its relationship to the Jews. For Gregory, on the other hand, it is an allegory of the contemplative life, focussing on the individual soul: 'Therefore the Angel stands for God, and Jacob who fights with the Angel, symbolises the soul of each perfect man who is placed in contemplation'.[50] In this effort to see God as God is in himself, the soul sometimes conquers and is sometimes conquered: 'As if engaged in a struggle [the soul] now conquers, as it were, because by understanding and perceiving it grazes the hem of the uncircumscribed light, but now succumbs because even in touching it falls once more'. Jacob's wrestling mirrors what is sometimes called the contemplative game of 'hide-and-seek', and the withering of his hip is the withering away of earthly desires and passions as the soul is filled through contemplative prayer with the desire for God: 'When Almighty God is already recognised through yearning and the understanding He withers every carnal desire in us'. For Augustine, it is a story about salvation history that highlights the ambivalent role of the Jews; for Gregory, it is a psychological allegory of the contemplative life that reflects on our struggle to hold onto a vision of God which is, by necessity, always fleeting and partial in this life.

The School of St Victor

The Church Fathers continued to be important throughout the Middle Ages: Dahan describes medieval exegesis as an 'unbroken tradition', in which interpretation is both 'cumulative' and 'infinite' ('infinie'), poised between tradition and innovation.[51] At the same time, the rise of the schools in northern France and the emergence of theology as an academic discipline led to changes in how Scripture was read and to a renewed emphasis on the literal or historical level of interpretation. The school of the Abbey of St Victor in Paris, founded in 1108, played an important role in this, working to reconcile the monastic tradition of *lectio divina* – in which the purpose of reading is the restoration of the divine image in the reader – with the

---

49 Gregory, *Moralia in Job*, Ep. iii; translated in *Morals*, I, 9.
50 Gregory the Great, *Homilies on Ezekiel*, ii.2.12; *Homilies on the Book of the Prophet Ezekiel*, trans. Theodosia Tomkinson, 2nd ed. (Etna, CA: Centre for Traditionalist Orthodox Studies, 2008), 288.
51 Gilbert Dahan, 'Les pères dans l'exégèse mediévale de la Bible', *Revue des Sciences Philosophiques et Théologiques* 91.1 (2007), 109–27.

From Hebrew Bible to Old Testament

academic rigour of the schools and their emphasis on reason and logic.[52] As Zinn puts it, St Victor 'remained open to the currents of intellectual life stirring in the Parisian schools, while maintaining a steadfast fidelity to the ancient tradition of monastic spirituality'.[53] St Victor trained many students and novices, and there is evidence that it was attended by a number of high-ranking Scandinavians, including Archbishops Eskil (1137–77) and Absalom (1178–1201) of Lund, Bishop Theodoricus (Þórir) of Hamar (1189/90–96), and Archbishops Henricus or Eiríkr Ívarsson (1188–1204/05) and Theodoricus (1206–14) of Nidaros.[54] Another student may have been St Þorlákr, who was bishop of Skálholt in 1178–93, and who is said to have studied abroad in Paris and Lincoln.[55] He was not formally affiliated with St Victor, since his name is not recorded in any lists, but he may well have been among the poorer students who flocked to the abbey in the 1160s. While the heyday of St Victor was the twelfth century, when Hugh (d. 1141), Andrew (d. 1175) and Richard (d. 1178) were all working and writing there, the Victorines remained active long beyond this in preaching and pastoral care in the university. Victorine writings continued to be read throughout France and northern Europe right through to the fifteenth century.[56]

Hugh was abbot of St Victor by 1133, and much of his writing consists of study guides for students to prepare them for the work of biblical

---

[52] Gillian R. Evans, *The Language and Logic of the Bible: The Earlier Middle Ages* (Cambridge: Cambridge University Press, 1984), 28; Christopher Ocker, *Biblical Poetics Before Humanism and Reformation* (Cambridge: Cambridge University Press, 2002), 3.

[53] Grover A. Zinn, '*Historia fundamenta est*: The Role of History in the Contemplative Life according to Hugh of St Victor', in *Contemporary Reflections on the Medieval Christian Tradition. Essays in Honor of Ray C. Petry*, ed. George H. Shriver (Durham, NC: Duke University Press, 1974), 137.

[54] On Scandinavian students in Paris, see Fourier Bonnard, *Historie de l'abbaye royale et de l'ordre de chanoines réguliers de Saint-Victor de Paris*, 2 vols (Paris: A. Savaète, 1905–07), I, 166, 214, 239, 273; Birger Munk-Olsen, 'Trois étudiants danois á Paris au XIIe siècle', in *Mélanges d'histoire, de littérature et de mythologie Hugur offerts à Régis Boyer pour son 65e anniversaire*, ed. Claude Lecouteux (Paris: Presses de l'Université de Paris-Sorbonne, 1997), 87–96; Gunnar Harðarson, *Littérature et spiritualité en Scandinave médiévale: La traduction norroise du De arrha animae de Hugues de Saint-Victor* (Paris: Brepols, 1995), 27–35. Scandinavian students are also listed in *Necrologium abbatiae Sancti Victoris Parisiensis*, ed. Ursula Vones-Liebenstein, Monika Seifert and Rainer Berndt (Aschendorff: Monasterii Westfalorum, 2012).

[55] *Biskupa sögur II*, ed. Ásdís Egilsdóttir (Reykjavík: Hið íslenzka fornritafélag, 1998), 52.

[56] See Torsten K. Edstam, 'The Reception of the Victorines', in *A Companion to the Abbey of St Victor in Paris*, ed. Hugh Feiss and Juliet Mousseau (Leiden: Brill, 2017), 547–50.

interpretation. In many ways, his thinking was deeply traditional: Origen, Gregory and especially Augustine were read at mealtimes in the Victorine refectory, and Hugh was known in his own time as *secundus Augustinus* ('a second Augustine'), completing Augustine's project in *De doctrina christiana* of integrating the arts into a specifically Christian programme of study.[57] The purpose of reading for the Victorines, as Harkins and others have shown, was still ascetic and contemplative: to bring about the reordering of the human person and the restoration of the image of God.[58] The difference is that, for Hugh, history plays a foundational role in this process; it cannot simply be eclipsed as the mystic moves from the letter to its mystical meaning. In his *Didascalicon*, written in c. 1120, Hugh adapts Gregory's metaphor of a building with three levels, but insists on the importance of the first: 'The foundation and principle of sacred learning, however, is history, from which, like honey from the honeycomb, the truth of allegory is extracted'.[59] He defines history in two ways: 'the recounting of actual deeds' and 'the first meaning of any narrative which uses words according to their proper nature'.[60] Students are to begin their study by memorising historical events: Hugh cites as most useful for this Genesis, Exodus, Joshua, Judges, Kings and Chronicles in the Old Testament, and the Gospels and Acts in the New Testament. In other words, the Bible should be read, as far as possible, in chronological sequence. It is striking that the Old Testament books listed here are almost exactly those represented in the Old Norse translations in *Stjórn*. Although Hugh labels particular books as historical, he also asserts that the whole of Scripture is sacred, distinct from other literature, precisely because it is historical, both in the sense of being about 'deeds done in time' ('rebus in tempore gestis') and in the sense that it is free from falsehood.[61]

Likewise, in *De scripturis* – sometimes described as his *accessus* to the study of the Bible – Hugh adapts Augustinian sign theory to emphasise the importance of 'things' ('res') as a language in their own right.[62] While

---

[57] Grover A. Zinn, 'The Influence of Augustine's *De doctrina christiana* upon the writings of Hugh of St Victor', in *Reading and Wisdom: The De Doctrina Christiana of Augustine in the Middle Ages*, ed. Edward D. English (Notre Dame, IN: University of Notre Dame Press, 1995), 48–60.

[58] Zinn, '*Historia*', 136; Franklin T. Harkins, *Reading and the Work of Restoration: History and Scripture in the Theology of Hugh of St Victor* (Toronto: Pontifical Institute of Medieval Studies, 2009), 185–87.

[59] Hugh of St Victor, *Didascalicon*, vi.3; *The Didascalicon of Hugh of St Victor: A Medieval Guide to the Arts,* trans. Jerome Taylor (New York: Columbia University Press, 1991), 138.

[60] Hugh, *Didascalicon*, vi.3; trans. Taylor, 137.

[61] Hugh, *Didascalicon*, iv.1; trans. Taylor, 102; Harkins, *Reading*, 148–49.

[62] See Grover A. Zinn, 'Hugh of St Victor's *De scripturis et scripturibus* as an *accessus* treatise for the study of the Bible', *Traditio* 52 (1997), 111–34.

From Hebrew Bible to Old Testament

Augustine argues that words as signs ('signa') can be either proper or figurative, Hugh goes into more detail about this process: words ('voces') signify things ('res$_1$'), but these things ('res$_1$') can signify other things ('res$_2$').[63] So, while Augustine explains that the word 'lion' can refer either to the animal or to Christ, Hugh specifies that it is not the word 'lion' that signifies Christ (res$_2$), but the actual animal (res$_1$) to whom the word refers. In order to understand what the sign refers to, one therefore needs to know about the animal's nature: 'To ignore the letter is to ignore what the letter signifies and what is signified by it'.[64] More than this, the significance of 'things', which God has inscribed into creation, is superior to the language of words. While the relationship between words and their referents is purely arbitrary, decided by convention, the meaning of 'things' is a God-given language: 'In Sacred Scripture, the meaning of things is much more excellent than the meaning of words [...] The first is the voice of human beings, but the second is the voice of God speaking to human beings'.[65]

To illustrate the importance of paying attention to the letter, Hugh uses the parable of the man born blind from John 9.1–12. Just as Jesus uses mud to give sight to the blind man, so the Scriptures use the visible material of the world to signify that which is invisible: 'You think that the entire word of God has mud on its surface, and therefore you boldly trample it with your feet, and you despise what the letter narrates as having been done physically ("corporaliter") and visibly ("visibiliter"). But listen! The mud that you tread with your feet is used to illumine the eyes of the blind man'.[66] He warns his students not to look down on 'humility' in the Bible, because 'through humility you are illuminated towards divinity'. For Hugh, the Holy Spirit has painted 'similitudes' or 'likenesses' onto the letter of the Scripture as a means of signifying that which lies beyond the powers of earthly language. If we ignore the outward shape of the letter, we will not understand its inner meaning.

For Hugh, then, history is 'the foundation of all instruction' and it begins with the memorisation of times, places, people and events, as in his *Chronicon*, a study guide that summarises world history. Hugh describes it as 'the foundation of the foundation, that is the first foundation'.[67] But Hugh

---

[63] On the Victorine understanding of 'things' and 'signs', see further Ocker, *Biblical Poetics*, 32–36.

[64] Hugh of St Victor, *De scripturis et scripturibus*, v; translated in 'On Sacred Scripture and its Authors', trans. Frans van Liere, in *Interpretation of Scripture: Theory: A Selection of Works by Hugh, Andrew Godfrey and Richard of St Victor*, ed. Franklin T. Harkins and Frans van Liere (Turnhout: Brepols, 2012), 216.

[65] Hugh, *De scripturis*, xiv; trans. van Liere, 225.

[66] Hugh, *De scripturis*, v; trans. van Liere, 218.

[67] On Hugh's *Chronicon*, also known as *De tribus maximis*, see R. W Southern,

The Old Testament in Medieval Icelandic Texts

uses history as the structural principle for his theological and mystical works as well. *De sacramentis* – the first theological *summa* of the Middle Ages – is organised on 'historical-biblical' principles.[68] Hugh divides sacred history into two parts: *opus conditionis* (the work of creation: the first six days) and *opus restaurationis* (the work of restoration: the first six ages). The former is classified as the subject of profane literature and history, while the latter is the subject of the sacred Scriptures: 'the Incarnation of the Word with all its sacraments, both those that have gone before from the beginning of time, and those which come after, even to the end of the world'.[69] Unlike Augustine, who believed that creation was simultaneous, Hugh himself thought that God brought creation to completion 'through intervals of time'. History itself is sacramental, and he sees God as revealing himself through time and in every historical period as Creator and Redeemer: 'Let us not doubt that from the beginning through the succession of the times faith has grown in the faithful themselves by certain increases'.[70] Finally, in his treatises on Noah's ark, Hugh lays out a visual plan for the memorisation of salvation history. Whereas it was usual to interpret the flood as baptism, and the ark as the Church, Zinn has shown that Hugh characterises the waves as the 'flux of time, the ebb and flow of events', and the keel of the ark as 'the sweep of salvation history, from Creation to Consummation'.[71]

Hugh's own exegetical work follows the plan that he laid out: it begins with commentaries of the historical books of the Old Testament, including the Pentateuch and the four books of Kings. His *Adnotationes in Pentateuchem* – written early in his career – focus explicitly on 'the truth of the events and the form of the words', which Hugh sees as interdependent.[72] After a brief

---

'Aspects of the European Tradition of Historical Writing: 2. Hugh of St Victor and the Idea of Historical Development', *Transactions of the Royal Historical Society* 5th ser. 21 (1971), 159–79. The prologue is edited in William M. Green, 'Hugo of St Victor: *De tribus maximis circumstantiis gestorum*', *Speculum* 18 (1943), 483–93 (see p. 491 for the quotation above). Further sections can be found in Lars Bøje Mortensen, 'Hugh of St Victor on Secular History', *Cahiers de l'institut du Moyen-Age grec et latin* 62 (1992), 3–30.

68 Harkins, *Reading*, 208.

69 Hugh of St Victor, *De sacramentis christiane fidei* i.2; *Hugh of St Victor on the Sacraments of the Christian Faith*, trans. Roy J. Deferrari (Eugene, OR: Wipf & Stock, 2007), 3.

70 Hugh, *De sacramentis*, i.10, trans. Deferrari, 177.

71 Zinn, 'Historia', 152.

72 Hugh, *Adnotationes in Pentateuchem*, translated in 'Notes on Genesis', trans. Jan van Zwieten, in *Interpretation of Scripture: Practice. A Selection of Works of Hugh, Andrew, and Richard of St Victor, Peter Comestor, Robert of Melun, Maurice of Sully and Leonius of Paris*, ed. Frans van Liere and Franklin T. Harkins (Turnhout: Brepols, 2015), 61.

accessus, which discusses the title in Hebrew and Greek, the author (Moses, who is described as a 'historian'), and authorial intention, the notes cover issues such as person, time and place, context, sentence construction, the order of narrative (which is not always the order of events), and aspects of the Hebrew text.[73] Hugh is clearly familiar with aspects of biblical style (which he describes in the *Didascalicon* as 'concise'), and points out recapitulation, ellipsis, proverbs, figures of speech, hyperbole, omission and repetition.[74] In establishing the order and coherence of the narrative, he also pays close attention to motive and psychological realism, often explaining what people think or mean. So, for example, he tells us that Abraham is 'playing on Lot's emotions' (Genesis 13.9), that Jacob is 'flattering Esau to save his own life' (Genesis 33.10) and that in Joseph's brothers 'envy was kindled and stirred up' (Genesis 37).[75] When discussing the sacrifice of Isaac (Genesis 22), Hugh weighs up the apparent contradiction between identifying Moriah as the site of the crucifixion and the fact that it took Abraham as long as three days to get there. He chooses a naturalistic interpretation: the journey took Abraham longer than it needed because he travelled 'as a man who was very worried, now about the death of his son, now about the Lord's command, and who did not pay much attention to his journey'.[76]

Hugh's emphasis on historical exegesis has been compared to the focus on *peshat* (literal or contextual meaning) that characterises Jewish exegesis of the Northern French school.[77] Hugh was certainly acquainted with Jewish interpretation of the Scriptures through personal contacts and possibly from his own reading.[78] Although it seems unlikely that he knew much Hebrew, he does occasionally cite Hebrew characters or provide Latin transliterations, and he defends the Hebrew text of the Bible over the LXX.[79] While some

---

[73] Hugh, *Adnotationes*, trans. van Zwieten, 58–59, 61–62.

[74] Hugh, *Adnotationes*, trans. van Zwieten, 58–59; on Hugh's attention to biblical style, see Gilbert Dahan, 'La méthode critique dans l'étude de la Bible (XII–XIIIe siècles)', in *La méthode critique au Moyen Âge*, ed. Mireille Chazan and Gilbert Dahan (Turnhout: Brepols, 2006), 118–19.

[75] Hugh, *Adnotationes*, 13.9, 33.10, 37.3, trans. van Zwieten, 90, 101, 102.

[76] Hugh, *Adnotationes*, 22.5, trans. van Zwieten, 95.

[77] Michael A. Signer, '*Peshat, Sensus Litteralis* and Sequential Narrative: Jewish Exegesis and the School of St Victor in the Twelfth Century', in *The Frank Talmage Memorial*, vol. I, ed. Barry Walfish (Haifa: Haifa University Press, 1993), 203–16; Robert A. Harris, 'Jewish biblical exegesis', in *The New Cambridge History of the Bible*, II, 596–611. An older but still important study is Herman Hailperin, *Rashi and the Christian Scholars* (Pittsburgh: University of Pittsburgh Press, 1963).

[78] Rebecca Moore, *Jews and Christians in the Life and Thought of Hugh of St Victor* (Atlanta, GA: Scholars Press, 1998), 79–80.

[79] Moore, *Jews and Christians*, 81–85.

The Old Testament in Medieval Icelandic Texts

of Hugh's references to Hebrew come from Bede, Augustine and Jerome, he also corrects Jerome's translation in places and engages with ideas that have parallels in the writings of Rashi (1040–1105), Rashbam (1080–1200), Abraham Ibn Ezra (1093–1167), Joseph Bekhor Shor (1130–1200) and Joseph Kara (1050–1155).[80] This is seen most clearly in his commentaries on the Old Testament. His *Adnotationes* contain 60 Hebrew glossary notes, as well as drawing on Jewish exegesis and tradition, for example in the case of Lamech's blindness, hunting skills, and infallible bow.[81] Most striking, though, is his reworking of Jewish midrash in Psalm 84 (85), which became the Christian allegory of the Four Daughters of God and makes an appearance in the Norwegian *Konungs skuggsjá* (pp. 125–27). Hugh's resistance to giving this allegory a Christological interpretation contrasts with the version of Bernard of Clairvaux, for whom it is an allegory about the atonement.

Hugh's willingness to consult with Jewish scholars on the literal or historical meaning of the Old Testament was taken further by Andrew, who was at St Victor in c. 1138–49 (when he became abbot of Wigmore) and again during the 1150s.[82] Andrew's work, too, shows familiarity with the exegesis of Rashi and his successors, although they are never mentioned by name. Berndt has calculated that, of the 248 references Andrew makes to 'Hebrei' in his *Heptateuch*, only 85 come from a Latin tradition (including 36 that are first recorded in Hugh's work), and 140 are loans from Jewish sources with over half coming from the commentaries of Rashi, Rashbam and Joseph Kara, the Midrash Rabbah and the Talmud.[83] Others probably came from oral teaching in and around the Parisian schools. For Andrew, Hebrew was the 'first of all languages', and Berndt theorises that he must either have been able to translate Hebrew himself or (more likely) have used a Latin translation of the Hebrew Bible made by Jewish scholars in Paris; he often privileges rabbinic interpretations over Christian, especially in his commentaries on the historical books.[84] While Andrew is clearly following a path laid out by Hugh, his decision to restrict himself to literal commentary is strikingly original and got him into some trouble with his contemporaries, most notoriously over the translation and interpretation of Isaiah 7.14 'virgo concipiet'

---

80 Hugh, *Adnotationes*, trans. van Zwieten, 56.

81 Hugh, *Adnotationes*, trans. van Zwieten, 113 (n. 85).

82 Rainer Berndt, 'The School of St Victor in Paris', in *Hebrew Bible/Old Testament: The History of its Interpretation, Volume 1 From the Beginnings to the Middle Ages (until 1300). Part 2 The Middle Ages*, ed. Magne Sæbø (Göttingen: Vandenhoeck & Ruprecht, 1996), 479.

83 Rainer Berndt, *André de Saint-Victor (d. 1175): Exégète et Théologien* (Paris: Brepols, 1991), 223.

84 Berndt, *André de Saint-Victor*, 158, 163, 201–03, 261–62.

From Hebrew Bible to Old Testament

('a virgin shall conceive').[85] This was a standard point of contention between Jewish and Christian scholars, and Andrew's refusal to enter into the polemics of it (what van Liere calls his 'methodical doubt') was roundly condemned by Richard of St Victor in his work *On Emmanuel*.[86] As a whole, Andrew's exegesis moves away from traditional Christological 'rereadings' of the Old Testament; his aim is 'to interpret in translating' ('interpréter en traduisant') by paying close attention to the Hebrew text.[87]

Richard took Hugh's teaching in a different direction from Andrew's textual work, reasserting the importance of reading the Bible within the structure of salvation history. He entered the Abbey of St Victor in the 1140s, a few years after the death of Hugh, and was prior in 1162–73.[88] His *Liber exceptionum* ('Book of Notes') – written in the 1150s – was popular as a 'condensed version' of the programme of reading articulated in Hugh's theoretical works. Coulter describes it as a 'crash course' on the liberal arts, biblical exegesis and the theology of creation and restoration.[89] It is divided into two parts that correspond to Hugh's division between *opus conditionis* and *opus restaurationis*. The first part covers 'the origins of the arts, the setting of the earth's lands, and the course of history from the beginning to our own times' and is heavily dependent on the *Didascalicon*. The second part provides a summary of allegorical-tropological interpretations 'arranged according to the sequence of the underlying history'.[90] Books 1–9 stretch from the Creation to the Maccabees, book 10 comprises sermons, while books 11–14 cover the New Testament. It offers the reader a series of 'hermeneutical keys' by which the surface of the historical narrative can be decoded. Here is the summary of Genesis 22, for example: 'Abraham, therefore, God the Father; Isaac, Christ; the mountain, divine charity; the two youths, unbelieving Jews

---

85 Frans van Liere, 'Andrew of St Victor and his Franciscan Critics', in *The Multiple Meanings of Scripture: The Role of Exegesis in Early-Christian and Medieval Culture*, ed. Ineke van't Spijker (Boston: Brill, 2009), 291–309.

86 Frans van Liere, 'Introduction to Richard of St Victor, *On Emmanuel*', in *Interpretation of Scripture: Practice*, ed. van Liere and Harkins, 349–452 (at p. 354).

87 Berndt, *André de Saint-Victor*, 263.

88 Dale M. Coulter, *Per visibilia ad invisibilia: Theological Method in Richard of St Victor (d. 1173)* (Turnhout: Brepols, 2006), 19–20.

89 Dale M. Coulter, 'Introduction to Richard of St Victor, *The Book of Notes* (selections)', in *The Interpretation of Scripture: Theory*, ed. Harkins and van Liere, 289–95; Coulter, *Per visibilia*, 38–39.

90 Richard of St Victor, *Liber exceptionum: texte critique avec introd., notes et tables*, ed. Jean Châtillon (Paris: J. Vrin, 1958), 7. The first part is translated in Richard of St Victor, 'The Book of Notes (selections)', trans. Hugh Feiss, in *The Interpretation of Scripture: Theory*, ed. Harkins and van Liere, 297–326 (at p. 297).

The Old Testament in Medieval Icelandic Texts

and Gentiles; the donkey, the folly of their unbelief; the altar, wood, bush, the standard of the cross; Isaac, divinity; the ram, humanity; the fire, the anguish of the passion'.[91] This part of the *Liber* was often transmitted separately in manuscripts as 'Allegories on the Old and New Testaments', sometimes accompanying Comestor's *Historia scholastica*. Although Richard retains Hugh's sense of history as having 'first place', this does not mean that he is interested in it, and his exegetical works focus on the Old Testament Prophets and Wisdom Literature, rather than the Pentateuch.[92] For Richard, reading the Bible allegorically was an essential stage in the contemplative ascent: it produces 'perseverance in prayer, fervour in devotion and clarity in heavenly contemplation'.[93] In his *Benjamin Minor*, an allegorical treatise on contemplation, he characterises Scripture as the bedchamber of Rachel, where 'divine wisdom is hidden under the veil of attractive allegories'.[94] She is there to be accessed 'as often as spiritual understanding is sought out in sacred reading'.

Comestor and the *Bible historiale*

The turn towards historical exegesis in the twelfth century is common to both Jewish and Christian exegesis, facilitating scholarly collaboration between Jews and Christians, although not necessarily reducing anti-Semitism.[95] Signer has noted how, in both the school of St Victor and the school of Rashi, we see a trend towards innovation, as biblical interpretation becomes 'loosened' from tradition.[96] One of the results of this is a move away from the 'non-sequential' readings of the Church Fathers towards an understanding of the Bible as a coherent historical narrative that needs to be read in sequence. Perhaps the fullest expression of this new understanding of the Bible as history and narrative is Peter Comestor's *Historia scholastica*, written as an introduction or study-guide to the historical exposition of the Bible. Peter

[91] *Liber exceptionum* ii.2.
[92] Berndt, 'St Victor', 476; see also Ineke van't Spijker, 'The Literal and the Spiritual: Richard of St Victor and the Multiple Meanings of Scripture', in *The Multiple Meanings of Scripture*, ed. van't Spijker, 232.
[93] *Liber exceptionum* ii. prologus; trans. Feiss, 318–19.
[94] Richard of St Victor, *Benjamin Minor* iv, translated in *The Twelve Patriarchs, The Mystical Ark, Book III of the Trinity*, trans. Grover A. Zinn (New York: Paulist Press, 1979), 56.
[95] A. Sapir Abulafia, 'The Bible in Jewish-Christian Dialogue', in *The New Cambridge History of the Bible*, II, 616–37; Cohen, *Living Letters*, 115–16.
[96] Michael Signer, 'Restoring the Narrative', in *With Reverence for the Word: Medieval Scriptural Exegesis in Judaism, Christianity and Islam*, ed. Jane Dammen McAuliffe, Barry D. Walfish and Joseph W. Goering (New York: Oxford University Press, 2003), 71–78.

From Hebrew Bible to Old Testament

– whose nickname *comestor* ('eater') may refer to his voracious appetite for books – was dean of the cathedral school in Troyes from c. 1164 and became chancellor of Notre-Dame in 1164–67.[97] He wrote the *Historia* in 1168–73, possibly at the Abbey of St Victor, to which he seems to have retired after 1169, and where he was buried next to Hugh at the high altar. The influence of the *Historia* is difficult to over-state: it was used in the Parisian schools from 1173 on, and Stephen Langton lectured on it twice between 1180 and 1200. It was approved by the Pope at the Lateran Council of 1215 as a standard part of the curriculum and, in 1228, the General Chapter of the Dominican Order stipulated that is was one of three books essential for theological study.[98] There are 800 extant manuscripts of it dating from between the twelfth and the fifteenth centuries, with copies found in Augustinian, Benedictine and Cistercian monasteries, as well as in cathedral schools.[99] As a result of the difficulties this poses for editing, the only part for which there is currently a critical edition is the book of Genesis, on which I will focus in this section.

The influence of the Victorines on Comestor's *Historia* is evident from its preface, where Comestor describes the Scriptures as a 'cenaculum' or dining hall, drawing on Gregory's metaphor of a house, as used by Hugh in the *Didascalicon*:[100]

Cenaculi huius tres sunt partes, fundamentum, paries, tectum. Historia fundamentum est [...] Allegoria, paries superinnitens, que per factum aliud factum figurat. Tropologia, doma culminis superpositum, que per factum quid a nobis sit faciendum insinuat. Prima planior, secunda acutior, tertia suauior.

There are three parts of this dining hall: the foundation, the walls, the roof. History is the foundation [...] Allegory, the wall resting on it, which through one deed signifies another. Tropology, the roof placed on top, which through what is done suggests what should be done by us. The first is plainer, the second keener, the third sweeter.

---

[97] Saralyn R. Daly, 'Peter Comestor: Master of Histories', *Speculum* 32.1 (1957), 65–68.

[98] Daly, 'Comestor', 71; Mark J. Clark, *The Making of the Historia scholastica, 1150–1200* (Toronto: Pontifical Institute of Mediaeval Studies, 2015), 5–15. The other two were the Glossed Bible and Peter Lombard's *Sentences*.

[99] Clark, *Making*, 14.

[100] *Petri Comestori Scolastica historia. Liber Genesis*, ed. Agneta Sylwan, CCCM 191 (Turnhout: Brepols, 2005), 4–5, with 'dogma' corrected to 'doma' as in the edition of the prefaces in Clark, *Making*, 262. On this analogy, see Lucie Dolezalova, 'The Dining Room of God: Petrus Comestor's "Historia scholastica" and Retelling the Bible as Feasting', in *Retelling the Bible: Literary, Historical and Social Contexts*, ed. Lucie Dolezalova and Tamas Visi (Frankfurt am Main: Peter Lang, 2011), 229–44.

The Old Testament in Medieval Icelandic Texts

Comestor undertakes to speak first of 'the foundation, indeed the beginning of the foundation' (echoing Hugh of St Victor's words on p. 55). Likewise, in the Prologue, he borrows another metaphor of Gregory's to speak of how 'I have composed an historical rivulet ['riuulum historicum'] up to the ascension of our Lord, leaving the sea of mysteries ['pelagus mysteriorum'] to the more skilled'.[101] Like Andrew, Comestor restricts his exegesis (though not entirely consistently) to the literal or historical sense. He describes being spurred on in this task by the need to recover a sense of historical sequence (spread 'widely, but too briefly' in the glosses) and to follow the 'truth of history' ('veritas historiae').[102] So the sweep of the *Historia* corresponds closely to Hugh's list of biblical books that are essential to the historical sense: The Pentateuch; Joshua to IV Kings (including Ruth); Tobias, Judith, Daniel and Esther; Maccabees; and a harmony of the Gospels. A second contributor later added the Acts of the Apostles to complete the historical sequence. Smalley has described the success of the *Historia* as 'the greatest triumph for the Victorine tradition'.[103]

The content of the *Historia* is in itself fairly traditional, and recent research has shown how deeply indebted it is to the *Glossa Ordinaria* and to the exegesis of Jerome. However, the form that it took was completely new. Comestor's innovation was to integrate text and gloss into a single unit, blurring the boundaries between them. As Clark has said, he unites 'Scripture, gloss and extra-Scriptural sources in a cogent narrative'.[104] This fusion is achieved by a combination of 'precision and flexibility': as well as citing named authorities, Comestor carefully incorporates commentary into the biblical text, paraphrasing the Vulgate using phrases from the *Glossa Ordinaria* and from the *Vetus Latina* to produce a 'finely honed' texture in which the gap between text and gloss is broken down. He includes not only biblical history, but also 'incidentia', events in pagan history which are chronologically related to those in the Bible, giving the *Historia* an encyclo-paedic feel and bringing it closer to 'universal history'. Above all, Comestor emerges as a master storyteller, filling in the gaps in Scripture, explaining psychological motivations, and giving depth to the biblical characters. In order to do this, he draws extensively on Jewish sources, most explicitly Josephus, whom he cites 72 times, but also through the works of Jerome, Hugh and Andrew, and perhaps also independently: the fact that Comestor

---

101 Comestor, *Liber Genesis*, 3.

102 David Luscombe, 'Peter Comestor and Biblical Chronology', *Irish Theological Quarterly* 80.2 (2015), 137–38.

103 Beryl Smalley, *The Study of the Bible in the Middle Ages* (Notre Dame, IN: Notre Dame University Press, 1964), 214.

104 Clark, *Making*, 151.

From Hebrew Bible to Old Testament

was dean of the cathedral school in Troyes, where the school of Rashi was based, is often cited in this respect.[105]

Comestor's treatment of Genesis 22 (the sacrifice of Isaac) is exemplary of his working method. True to purpose, there is no reference to allegory, despite the well-established significance of this scene. Instead, Comestor reconstructs the narrative using Jewish traditions, taken from the *Glossa Ordinaria*, from Josephus, and from oral tradition. From the Gloss, he cites a Hebrew tradition about how Solomon's temple was built on the site of Abraham's sacrifice, the name of the bush in which the ram was caught and how it got there (it was transported by an angel), a proverb connected with the place-name, and the sounding of trumpets to commemorate Isaac's release (most of which is also in Jerome).[106] From Josephus, he takes Isaac's age (he is 25) and he supplies a long addition which explains why Isaac in particular is obedient to God's command:[107]

> But Josephus reports the words of the father saying to the boy that, just as by God's will, he had entered the world miraculously, so too by God's will it was necessary for him to exit miraculously, since the Lord also judged him worthy to end his life not by illness, nor by war, nor by any human passion, but with prayers and sacrifices to call his spirit to him, and that he might raise him for the fulfilment of his promises. And so Isaac freely went to the altar and death.

This is followed by – and substantiates – a shorter comment from Alcuin via the Gloss, praising Abraham's 'undoubting mind' and his constancy and

---

[105] On Comestor's Jewish sources, see Ari Geiger, '*Historia Judaica*: Petrus Comestor and His Jewish Sources', in *Pierre le mangeur ou Pierre de Troyes, maître du XIIe siècle*, ed. Gilbert Dahan (Turnhout: Brepols, 2013), 125–45 and Louis Feldman, 'The Jewish Sources of Peter Comestor's Commentary on Genesis', *in Begegnungen zwischen Christentum und Judentum in Antike und Mittelalter: Festschrift für Heinz Schreckenberg*, ed. Dietrich-Alex Koch et al. (Göttingen: Vandenhoek & Ruprecht, 1993), 93–122. Older accounts of Comestor's Jewish sources tend not to take into account how many of these come via Latin Christian authors like Jerome; see, for example, Esra Shereshevky, 'Hebrew Traditions in Peter Comestor's *Historia scholastica*: I. Genesis', *Jewish Quarterly Review* 59.4 (1969), 268–89.

[106] The gloss on Genesis 22 has been edited in Devorah Schoenfeld, *Isaac on Jewish and Christian Altars: Polemic and Exegesis in Rashi and the Glossa ordinaria* (New York: Fordham University Press, 2013), 124–63; for the commentary above, see especially pp. 140–41, 148–50.

[107] Comestor, *Liber Genesis*, 110; cf. Flavius Josephus (Latin translation), *Antiquities*, I.xiii.3, ed. R. M. Pollard et al. (2013–2019) at https://www.latinjosephus.org/.

The Old Testament in Medieval Icelandic Texts

faith.[108] It is striking that the longest addition to this scene is from Josephus and that it serves to bolster the psychological credibility of Isaac's consent. Finally, the dating of this event to the first day of September is attributed to 'Hebrei' ('the Hebrews'). This is paralleled in the Genesis Rabbah, and perhaps comes from oral teaching either in Troyes or in Paris.[109]

Karp has argued that Josephus's *Antiquities* contributes to both the style and content of Comestor's work, providing him not only with 'historical material', but more importantly with 'historical perspective'.[110] Although it has been shown that, in Genesis at least, Jerome provides far more haggadic material (90 details as opposed to 40), it is Josephus who is more frequently named.[111] Karp argues that loans from Josephus serve specific purposes: they provide Comestor with a 'wealth' of historical material, they offer 'causal and psychological insights', and they transform biblical events into 'historic epic'. She suggests that they are sometimes used to replace allegorical interpretation, for example in the account of the creation of Eve out of Adam, where Comestor substitutes for the expected allegory of Christ and the Church a Jewish tradition that God previously made a wife for Adam out of mud.[112] Comestor also draws on Josephus to illuminate Cain's state of mind once he realises that he is outcast ('Cain, therefore, either fearing that wild beasts would devour him if he were to leave the company of men, or fearing on account of his sin that they would kill him') and to describe Adam's emotional reaction to the loss of both his sons ('the desire for children violently tormented him').[113] Clark describes how Comestor uses a range of different sources to 'spice up' the narrative, before returning to the *brevitas* of Genesis. He points in particular to Comestor's use of apocryphal narratives, even when he does not endorse these, such as the story that the Chaldeans threw Abraham and Haran into the fire because they refused to worship it.[114] Clark sees Comestor as situating his work somewhere between the literal exposition of Andrew and the historical narrative of Josephus.[115] In the process, he reinvents the Bible as narrative, and this was to have a profound and long-lasting effect.

The *Historia* was written as a scholastic text, but it did not take long for its influence to spread beyond the Parisian schools. Eventually translated into

---

108 Schoenfeld, *Isaac*, 143.
109 Comestor, *Liber Genesis*, III (n. 48/49).
110 Sandra Karp, 'Peter Comestor's *Historia scholastica*: A Study in the Development of Literal Scriptural Exegesis', PhD thesis, Tulane University, 1978, 183–97.
111 Feldman, 'The Jewish Sources', 94–102.
112 Karp, 'Peter Comestor', 210; Feldman, 'Jewish sources', 117.
113 Comestor, *Liber Genesis*, 51, 56; cf. Josephus, *Antiquities*, I.ii.1, I.ii.3.
114 Comestor, *Liber Genesis,* 80; Clark, *Making*, 133–43; Feldman, 'Jewish sources', 106.
115 Clark, *Making*, 36–43, 126.

From Hebrew Bible to Old Testament

every major west European vernacular, it became 'the single most important medium through which a popular Bible took shape'.[116] Lobrichon has outlined four stages in the history of its expanding influence: the addition of an *accessus ad auctorem* (c. 1180–90); the addition of Acts and the *Compendium Historiae*, together with Langton's commentary (c. 1190–95) and later that of Hugh of St Cher (1230s); Leoninus's *Historiae veteris testamenti* and Peter Riga's *Aurora*, a versified version of the *Historia*, which was popular in ecclesiastical circles (c. 1200); and finally the repackaging of the *Historia scholastica* for lay aristocratic audiences (c. 1220–50).[117] This shift towards a lay audience can already be seen in the use of Comestor in works produced in or for royal courts, such as Vincent of Beauvais's *Speculum historiale* (1248–64), the *Sachsenspiegel* (1225) and Rudolf von Ems's *Weltchronik* (1250–55). From 1225 on, the *Historia* was also translated into images in the *Bible moralisée*, a 'picture book of the Bible', each page of which hosted four extracts of text followed by four moralising and allegorising commentaries, each accompanied by an image within a medallion.[118]

The first translator of the *Historia scholastica* into French was Guiart Desmoulins (1251–1322), whose translation – which came to be known as the *Bible historiale* – played a significant role in shaping a vernacular Bible. Guiart was canon and later dean at St Peter's at Aire-sur-Lys, and he says in his preface that he wrote his *Histoires escolastres* in 1291–95.[119] There was already a long history of biblical translation and adaptation in France, including *Li Quatre Livre des Reis* from the late twelfth century, an anonymous abridged Old Testament (known as 'La Bible abrégée'), and 'La Bible du XIIIe siècle' (or 'The Old French Bible'), available from c. 1220–50.[120] Guiart produced his own translation of the biblical books in the *Historia scholastica*, and then added some of those Comestor omitted: I Maccabees, a 'short' Job, a selection of Proverbs, and a summary of the

---

[116] James Morey, 'Peter Comestor, Biblical Paraphrase and the Medieval Popular Bible', *Speculum* 68.1 (1993), 6.

[117] Guy Lobrichon, 'Le mangeur au festin. L'*Historia scholastica* aux mains de ses lecteurs : Glose, Bible en images, Bibles historiales (fin XIIIe–XIVe siècle)', in *Pierre le mangeur*, ed. Dahan, 291–95.

[118] John Lowden, 'The *Bible moralisée* in the Fifteenth Century', *Journal of the Warburg and Courtauld Institutes* 68 (2005), 73–136.

[119] Rosemarie Potz McGerr, 'Guyart desmoulins, the Vernacular Master of Histories, and his *Bible historiale*', *Viator* 14 (1983), 212, 228.

[120] Margriet Hooguliet, 'The Medieval Vernacular Bible in France as a Flexible Text: Selective and Discontinuous Reading Practices', in *Form and Function in the Late Medieval Bible*, ed. Eyal Poleg and Laura Light (Leiden: Brill, 2013), 283–386; Clive R. Sneddon, 'The Old French Bible', in *A Companion to Medieval Translation*, ed. Jeannette M. A. Beer (Leeds: Arc Humanities Press, 2019), 23–36.

The Old Testament in Medieval Icelandic Texts

Babylonian captivity drawing on Jeremiah, Ezekiel, Daniel, Judith and Esther.[121] In the second version, from 1297, he added a preface, tables of contents and the second book of Maccabees, as well as a translation of Acts and some short apocryphal texts. He also introduced a distinction between the script used for the text of the Bible and the script used for Comestor's glosses.[122] The *Bible historiale* continued to evolve and grow, soon passing beyond Guiart's control: a third version – known as the *Bible historiale complétée* – was produced in 1317, which divided it into two volumes. The first covers Comestor's Old Testament Books (Genesis–Esther), while the second is a complete translation from Proverbs to Revelation from the 'Bible du XIIIe siècle'.[123] This composite text has been described by Sneddon as 'the publishing success of mediaeval French Bibles': it survives in 70 complete manuscripts and 20 early editions.[124] As Sneddon has noted, this history of continuing expansion of the *Bible historiale* shows an 'intense concern for the text' and the 'public demand' for a complete Bible.

McGerr has described the *Bible historiale* as a 'combination of scholastic text-book and vernacular story book': often lavishly illustrated, but with an academic layout (based on the *Glossa ordinaria*), it met the needs of a non-scholastic audience who were interested in scholastic learning.[125] As biblical paraphrase became more and more distanced from its original context in the schools and universities, with their scholarly apparatus of tables and charts, so it encouraged a greater freedom of imagination and creativity in the adaptation of the biblical text for a contemporary audience: 'Cette ré-formulation directionelle incite au bricolage et tout particulièrement, au mélange des genres, afin de captiver, de séduire, de nourrir, de convaincre et transporter' ('This reformulation in a particular direction lends itself to bricolage and particularly to the mixing of genres, in order to captivate, seduce, nourish, convince, and transport').[126] The art of paraphrase – according to Lobrichon – is to 'juggle' different languages and literary genres in a way that leads to the 'proliferation' of stories, even of romance. This is narrative exegesis, in which one story is explained by another: Lobrichon calls it 'cette exégèse affranchie, vagabonde,

---

121 Guy Lobrichon, 'The Story of a Success: The *Bible historiale* in France (1295–1500)', in *Form and Function in the Late Medieval Bible*, ed. Poleg and Light, 314.

122 Lobrichon, 'Success', 318.

123 Lobrichon, 'Success', 320.

124 Sneddon, 'Old French Bible', 29–30.

125 Potz McGerr, 'Guyart desmoulins', 218.

126 Guy Lobrichon, 'Un nouveau genre pour un public novice: la paraphrase biblique dans l'espace roman du XIIᶜ siècle', in *The Church and Vernacular Literature in Medieval France*, ed. Dorothea Kullmann (Toronto: Pontifical Institute of Mediaeval Studies, 2009), 97.

From Hebrew Bible to Old Testament

poétique, lumineuse, qui parle directement à l'imagination et au cœur, sans jamais céder á l'émotion des mystiques' ('this liberated, vagabond, poetic, luminous exegesis, which speaks directly to the imagination and to the heart, without ever ceding to the emotion of the mystics').[127]

In England, surprisingly perhaps, there was no full translation of Comestor's work, although glosses from the *Historia scholastica* were added to the Old English Hexateuch – a prose translation from c. 1000 – in the late twelfth century (c. 1180).[128] The first post-Conquest work to draw on Comestor was *Genesis and Exodus* (c. 1250), which in fact covers the whole Pentateuch, although only the narrative parts.[129] Comestor was a source of *Cursor mundi*, an ambitious 'verse history of the world' written towards the end of the thirteenth century.[130] It was the major source for the *Middle English Metrical Paraphrase*, which survives in two manuscripts from the early to mid-fifteenth century: Livingston describes it as 'the most sustained translation – though one that is so loose as to seem at times a paraphrase of Comestor's paraphrase'.[131] All these poets are writing for lay people and understand the Bible primarily as narrative or 'stories': Lee comments that the poet of *Genesis and Exodus* is a 'storyteller' rather than a 'moralist', and the intelligibility of the narrative ranks more highly for him than either doctrine or revelation.[132] Likewise, Livingston describes the *Middle English Metrical Paraphrase* as a 'work of edification', which uses 'stories as exempla': it is 'filled with debates of action rather than debates of scholarship and exegesis'.[133] The only prose translation of Comestor's *Historia* from England was the fifteenth-century *Historye of the Patriarks*, which survives in one manuscript and covers only Genesis. It appears to draw on both the Latin text and the French *Bible historiale,* following the latter in including the text of Genesis alongside Comestor.[134]

---

[127] Lobrichon, 'Le mangeur', 306.

[128] Frans van Liere, *An Introduction to the Medieval Bible* (Cambridge: Cambridge University Press, 2014), 189. See also Richard Marsden, 'The Bible in English in the Middle Ages', in *The Practice of the Bible in the Middle Ages: Production, Reception and Performance in Western Christianity*, ed. Susan Boyton and Diane Reilly (New York: Columbia University Press, 2011), 272–95 (at p. 285).

[129] Brian S. Lee, 'Transforming the Vulgate: Comestor and the Middle English *Genesis and Exodus*', *Mediaevistik* 31 (2018), 136.

[130] *The Southern Version of Cursor mundi*, vol. 1, ed. Sarah M. Horral (Ottawa: University of Ottawa Press, 1978), 29–30

[131] Michael Livingston, 'Introduction', in *The Middle English Metrical Paraphrase of the Old Testament*, ed. Michael Livingston (Kalamazoo, MI: TEAMS, 2011), 20.

[132] Lee, 'Transforming the Vulgate', 137, 147.

[133] Livingston, 'Introduction', 5, 41.

[134] *The Historye of the Patriarks*, ed. Mayumi Taguchi (Heidelberg: Winter, 2010), xi.

The Old Testament in Medieval Icelandic Texts

In Dutch and German, too, Comestor was important in the transmission of biblical knowledge to lay people. Sherwood-Smith has examined four different works that show his influence: the thirteenth-century Schwarzwälder sermon cycle, the *Weltchronik* of Rudolf von Ems, the Middle Dutch *Rijmbijbel* or *Scolastica* of Jacob van Maerlant (c. 1271) and the *Historiebijbel van 1360.*[135] Of these, the *Rijmbijbel* is a verse adaptation of the *Historia*, covering the whole of its original span from Genesis up to the Ascension, while the *Historiebijbel* imitates the French *Bible historiale complétée* by translating the Vulgate with additions from a free translation of Comestor. Thirty manuscripts survive from c. 1425–75, of which 13 are illustrated. While each of the four works uses Comestor in a different way, there are communalities. In particular, the narrative texts borrow from Comestor for information on historical background, for the explanation of difficult passages, and for additional material either from Jewish sources or pagan history (Comestor's 'incidentia'). Finally, in Germany, over 100 manuscripts of *Historienbiblen* survive from the fourteenth and fifteenth centuries. They come from all over the German-speaking area and are concentrated in the years 1440–80. They draw on the Vulgate, the *Historia scholastica* and the *Weltchronik*. They were used by the laity, and perhaps women in particular, but were eventually displaced by Luther's sixteenth-century Bible translation.[136]

In Iceland, Comestor was well known and widely used in the lives of biblical saints to add 'fullness and detail' to the narrative: he is mentioned in *Mörtu saga ok Maríu*, *Pétrs saga I*, *Páls saga II*, *Stephanus saga*, and *Jóns saga baptista II*.[137] This last *vita*, which will be discussed in Chapter 3, quotes copiously from the *Historia scholastica* to provide historical and geographical detail, explanations of difficult passages, apocryphal stories, and as a source for the names of authorities like Josephus or Chrysostom. Comestor was also an essential read for some of the first Icelanders to write 'world history', including the author of *Veraldar saga*, which will be discussed in Chapter 4. Several partial translations of the *Historia scholastica* into Old Norse-Icelandic have survived: a single leaf from c. 1300 with a translation of 1 Samuel 22.10–28 (in AM 1054 4to IV), a version of the Book of Joshua in AM 226 fol. (one of the two main manuscripts of *Stjórn*); and

---

135 Maria Sherwood-Smith, 'Die "historia scholastica" als Quelle biblischer Stoffe im Mittelalter', in *Die Vermittlung geistlicher Inhalte im deutschen Mittelalter*, ed. Timothy R. Jackson, Nigel F. Palmer and Almut Sauerbaum (Tübingen: Niemeyer, 1996), 155–56.

136 Patricia McAllister, 'The Middle Low German *Historienbibel* Helmstedt 611.1: A Critical Edition of Genesis and Exodus', PhD thesis, Indiana University, 1988, 1–10.

137 Kirsten Wolf, 'Peter Comestor's *Historia scholastica* in Old Norse Translation', *Amsterdamer Beiträge zur älteren Germanistik* 33 (1991), 151.

From Hebrew Bible to Old Testament

parts II (chapters 21–32) and III (chapters 33–38) of *Gyðinga saga*, a translation of Maccabees made by Brandr Jónsson, who became abbot of the Augustininan monastery in Þykkvibær in 1247. Finally, Comestor is a major source for the Old Norse-Icelandic translations of the Old Testament collectively known as *Stjórn*, which will be discussed in Chapters 5–7. In fact, the two main manuscripts of *Stjórn* – AM 226 fol. and AM 227 fol. – may best be understood as imitations of the Old French *Bibles historiales*. Like the Old Testament volume of the *Bible historiale complétée*, AM 227 fol. covers material ranging from Genesis to the four books of Kings, while AM 226 fol. adds historical texts which update it to the birth of Christ. Like the *Bible historiales*, both manuscripts might fittingly be described in McGerr's words as a 'combination of scholastic text-book and vernacular story book'. They appeal to the needs of an audience who wanted to know more about scholastic learning, but who also appreciated the art of storytelling and the imaginative potential of biblical paraphrase.

Conclusion

This chapter has explored the development of biblical exegesis from Origen in the second century to the Victorines in the twelfth century, and the subsequent mediation of biblical stories to a lay audience through the *Bibles historiales*. While allegorical, poetic, and meditative readings of the Bible continued throughout the Middle Ages, there was a clear shift in the twelfth century to prioritising the literal level of exegesis and thinking about the Bible in terms of historical sequence and narrative coherence. Although Augustine and Gregory were known and read in Iceland throughout the medieval period, it is evident that the Victorines also had a significant influence on how Icelanders read the Bible, not only through clerics like St Þorlákr who studied in Paris, but also through translations of Peter Comestor's *Historia scholastica*. This opened the way not only to reading the Old Testament as history, but also encouraged the accumulation of many other kinds of extra-biblical material, including Jewish traditions and stories. In addition, it seems more than likely that the Icelanders would have been aware of and keen to imitate the kinds of biblical translations being made in medieval France. Before moving on to these later biblical translations, however, I want to spend some time exploring how knowledge of the Old Testament was mediated in earlier texts, including homilies, saints' lives, and world histories. In the next chapter, then, I look at how the Old Testament was translated and interpreted in the Old Icelandic Homily Book and in a selection of the lives of biblical saints.

❧ 3 ❧

Types and Shadows:
The Old Testament in Homilies and Saints' Lives

There was no complete translation of the Old Testament into Icelandic before Guðbrandur Þorláksson's *Biblia*, which was printed in Hólar and published in 1584.[1] However, a range of Old Testament material was available in the vernacular from the second half of the twelfth century on. The Old Norse-Icelandic homilies frequently cite verses from the Old Testament, especially those based on Gregory the Great's XL Homilies on the Gospels, which contained nearly 300 quotations from the Old Testament.[2] Although many of the citations found in homilies consist of single verses taken out of context from the Psalms or Prophets, there is also some Old Testament history, including the sacrifice of Isaac and two retellings of chapters 1–2 of Job. Fragments from two allegorical commentaries on the Psalms survive in AM 655 XXIII 4to (c. 1225–49) and AM 696 XXIV 4to (c. 1200–24), covering parts of Psalms 50, 31 and 37.[3] Old Testament exegesis also plays an important

---

[1]   On the pre-existing translations used by Guðbrandur Þorláksson for this Bible, see *Makkabear*, ed. Karl Óskar Ólafsson and Svanhildur Óskarsdóttir (Reykjavík: Stofnun Árna Magnússonar í íslenskum fræðum, 2020), xix–xx; Chr. Westergård-Nielsen, *To bibelske visdomsbøger og deres islandske overlevering* (Copenhagen: Munksgaard, 1957), xiv–xv, 68–74; Páll Eggert Ólason, *Menn og menntir siðskip-taaldarinnar á Íslandi*, 4 vols (Reykjavík: Bókaverslun Ársæls Árnarsonar, 1919–26), II, 530–69, IV, 373–83; and Einar G. Pétursson, 'Guðbrandur Þorláksson og bókaútgáfa hans', in *Hulin pláss. Ritgerðasafn* (Reykjavík: Stofnun Árna Magnússonar í íslenskum fræðum, 2011), 93–109.

[2]   Stephen Kessler, 'Gregory the Great: A Figure of Tradition and Transition', in *Hebrew Bible/Old Testament*, ed. Sæbø, 137.

[3]   AM 655 XXIII 4to is edited in Konráð Gíslason, *Um frumparta íslenzkrar túngu í fornöld* (Copenhagen: Trier, 1846), lxxxii–lxxxiii and James W. Marchand, 'An Old Norse Fragment of a Psalm Commentary', *Maal og Minne* (1976), 24–29. AM 696 XXIII 4to has not yet been edited, but there is a brief discussion in Hans

Types and Shadows

part in the lives of biblical saints like the Blessed Virgin Mary and St John the Baptist, in whose lives the 'types and shadows' of Old Testament history can be seen to be fulfilled. The later and more scholarly lives, in particular, are rich in biblical quotation: Kirby has counted over 100 biblical quotations or allusions in *Pétrs saga I*, *Jóns saga baptista II* and *Tveggja postula saga Jóns ok Jakobs*, although the majority are from the New Testament.[4] The later lives draw copiously on Comestor's *Historia scholastica* and Vincent of Beauvais's *Speculum historiale*, grounding the biblical narrative in historiographical detail and paying close attention to chronology as well as to secular history.[5] The Norwegian *Konungs skuggsjá* ('The King's Mirror') from c. 1240–63 provides a range of entertaining and instructive narratives from Genesis and from the four books of Kings (1 and 2 Samuel and 1 and 2 Kings). Finally, universal histories like *Veraldar saga* (c. 1155–90) integrate Old Testament history into a wider history of the world from the Creation to the sixth age. In this chapter, my focus is on Old Testament exegesis as it appears in homilies and saints' lives. I argue that, although we might expect allegorical interpretations to dominate, this is not always the case. Alongside traditional Gregorian exegesis – often executed with great skill and imagination – we also find some short historical narratives that show aspects of 'saga style'.

Old Norse-Icelandic Homilies

There are 33 or so manuscripts of homilies from medieval Norway and Iceland, not all of which have as yet been published.[6] They date from the mid-twelfth to the mid-sixteenth century: the oldest is AM 237 a fol. (from c. 1140–1160), a fragment of two leaves containing part of a homily for the dedication of a church, and a translation of Gregory's 34th Homily on the Gospels.[7] The two main collections are the Icelandic Homily Book (Stock. Perg. 4to 15) from c. 1200, which may have been made at the episcopal see in Skálholt, and the Norwegian Homily Book (AM 619 4to), which was copied

---

Bekker-Nielsen and Ole Widding, 'Fra ordbogens værksted', *Opuscula* I (1960), 341–42. The psalms themselves are in Latin, and the commentary is in Old Norse.

4 Ian J. Kirby, *Biblical Quotation in Old Norse-Icelandic Religious Literature*, 2 vols (Reykjavík: Stofnun Árna Magnússonar, 1976–80), I, 23, 31, 37.

5 Wolf, 'Peter Comestor', 151.

6 Thomas N. Hall, 'Old Norse-Icelandic Sermons', in *The Sermon*, ed. Beverly Mayne Kienzle (Turnhout: Brepols, 2000), 664.

7 Hall, 'Sermons', 681. It is edited in *Leifar fornra kristinna fræða íslenzkra: Codex Arna-Magnæanus 677 4to auk annara enna elztu brota af íslenzkum guðfræðisritum*, ed. Þorvaldur Bjarnarson (Denmark: Hagerup, 1878), 162–67.

The Old Testament in Medieval Icelandic Texts

in or around Bergen in c. 1200.[8] These have 11 pieces in common, which are listed in a recent collection of essays on the Norwegian Homily Book, and may derive from a shared twelfth-century exemplar.[9] Hall describes the Norwegian Homily Book as 'the most conservative representative of a Continental homiliary', containing seven topical pieces and 31 sermons that follow the liturgical year.[10] However, a more recent assessment describes it as 'a diverse and untypical sermon collection', even if much of the material is traditional.[11] The Icelandic Homily Book is less obviously well-ordered, and Hall has suggested that it contains two originally independent series of sermons to which various non-sermonic pieces have been added.[12] In addition to these, AM 677 4to from c. 1200–25 contains translations of ten of Gregory's Homilies, as well as parts of his *Dialogues*. There are witnesses to a further nine of his Homilies in other manuscripts, and it seems likely that there was a full translation by the mid-twelfth century, which was widely disseminated.[13] Hall – like Conti – describes the Old Norse-Icelandic Homilies as 'conservative' and 'backward-looking', based on sources like Gregory and Bede, but there is a preponderance of material of English provenance and twelfth-century authors are also represented, such as Abbot Absalon of Springiersbach (who was a canon of St Victor) and Ralph d'Escures, Archbishop of Canterbury in 1116–22.[14] For many homilies, the

8   *The Icelandic Homily Book: Perg. 15 4to in the Royal Library Stockholm*, ed. Andrea de Leeuw van Weenen (Reykjavík: Stofnun Árna Magnússonar á Íslandi, 1993), 1; Odd Einar Haugen and Åslaug Ommundsen, 'Nye blikk på homilieboka', in *Vår eldste bok: Skrift, miljø og biletbruk i den norske homiliebok*, ed. Odd Einar Haugen and Åslaug Ommundsen (Oslo: Novus, 2000), 12.

9   Haugen and Ommundsen, 'Nye blikk', 19.

10   Hall, 'Sermon', 669–70.

11   Kirsten M. Berg, 'Homilieboka – for hvem og til hva?', in *Vår eldste bok*, ed. Haugen and Ommundsen, 39–40; English translation on p. 260.

12   Hall, 'Sermons', 670.

13   Hall, 'Sermons', 675.

14   Hall, 'Sermons', 669; Aidan Conti, 'Gamalt og nytt i homiliebokens prekeunivers', in *Vår eldste bok*, ed. Haugen and Ommundsen, 168. On the English connection and twelfth-century sources, see Olaf Tveito, 'Wulfstan av York og norrøne homilier', in *Vår eldste bok*, ed. Haugen and Ommundsen, 187–215; Christopher Abram, 'Anglo-Saxon Influence in the Old Norwegian Homily Book', *Mediaeval Scandinavia* 14 (2004), 1–35 and 'Anglo-Saxon Homilies in their Scandinavian Context', in *The Old English Homily: Precedent, Practice and Appropriation*, ed. Aaron J. Kleist (Turnhout: Brepols, 2007), 425–44; Stephen Pelle, 'A New Source for Part of an Old Icelandic Christmas Homily', *Saga-Book* 36 (2012), 102–16; 'Twelfth-Century Sources for Old Norse Homilies: New Evidence from AM 655 XXVII 4to', *Gripla* 24 (2013), 45–75; 'An Old Norse Homily and Two Homiletic Fragments from AM 624 4to', *Gripla* 27 (2016), 263–89.

Types and Shadows

sources are difficult to pin down, and the question remains open as to how many should be considered original works rather than 'just' translations.

None of the Old Norse-Icelandic Homilies are on Old Testament topics, but they frequently engage with Old Testament material and show a ready familiarity with the allegorical method of interpretation. This is clear from the sermon on the wedding at Cana in the Old Icelandic Homily Book. It begins with a translation of John 2.1–11, followed by a discussion of marriage and virginity based on 'orðin sjálf' ('the words themselves'), in other words *ad litteram* ('according to the letter').[15] The homilist then turns to the allegorical sense: 'Nú hǫfum vér rœtt nǫkkut of ina ýtra skilning guðsp-jallsins, en þó eru enn eptir in innri ok in œðri tákn þess óliðuð' ('Now we have said something about the outer meaning of the gospel, but the inner and nobler significance is as yet untouched'). He goes on to read Christ as the bridegroom, the Church as his bride, the six jars of water as the six ages of the world, while the water 'merkir helgar ritningar' ('signifies holy Scriptures'). The miracle by which water is changed into wine thus becomes an allegory of biblical interpretation:[16]

> *Dominus* gerði vín ór vatni, þá er hann bauð at skilja þat andliga er í inum fornum lǫgum var boðit at halda líkamliga. Ór vatni gerði hann vín heldr en ór ǫngu, *quia* hann kom eigi at brjóta in fornu lǫg heldr at bœta, þat er at snúa því ǫllu til andligrar skilningar, er líkamliga var boðit í lǫgum.

> *The Lord* made water out of wine, when he commanded to interpret spirit-ually what was commanded in the old law to keep carnally. He made wine out of water rather than out of nothing, *because* he came not to break the old law, rather to fulfil it, that is to turn into a spiritual sense all that was commanded carnally in the law.

The homilist then links the effects of wine to what the disciples say on the road to Emmaus about how their hearts are burning within them (Luke 24.32): 'Makliga kallask andlig skilning heilagra ritninga vín, því at svá sem vín tekr mœði af manni ok gleðr hjarta hans, svá gerir ok andlig skilning manni létt erfiði fyrir guðs ást, ok gleðr huginn himneskri huggun' ('It is fitting that the spiritual sense of the holy Scriptures is called wine, because just as wine

---

[15] *Homilíubók: Isländska homilier efter en handskrift från tolfte århundradet: Isländska skinnboken 15 qu. å Kungl. Biblioteket i Stockholm*, ed. Theodor Wisén (Lund: Gleerup, 1872), 188–89.

[16] *Homilíubók*, 190. The Homily Book follows here the lines of Augustine of Hippo's interpretation in *In Iohannis evangelium tractatus*, ix.3; *Tractates on the Gospel of John 1–10* (Washington, DC: Catholic University of America Press, 1988–95), 196–95. All translations from texts in diplomatic editions have been silently normalised for ease of reading.

The Old Testament in Medieval Icelandic Texts

relieves a man of exhaustion and gladdens his heart, so the spiritual sense makes a man's toil seem light on account of the love of God and rejoices the heart with heavenly comfort'). The spiritual interpretation of the Old Testament follows Augustine's 'rule of love' and directs us away from carnal things towards the spiritual joys of Heaven.

The metaphor of weight in this last quotation is also central to the interpretation of Moses' prayer (from Exodus 17.12) in the Norse translation of Gregory's 33rd Homily:[17]

> Of þessi lǫg er svá ritat: Hendr Moysi váru þungar, þá var steinn lagðr undir hann, en þeir Aaron ok Ur héldu upp hǫndum hans. Moyses sitr á steini, því at lǫg hvílask í kristni. En þessi lǫg hafa þungar hendr, því at þau bjóða harða refsing synda en veita eigi miskunn. Aaron þýðisk styrktar fjall. En Ur þýðisk eldr. Fjall styrktar merkir lausnara várn, svá sem spámaðr mælti: 'Á inum efstum dǫgum mun [...] fan fjall dróttins hæra ǫllum fjǫllum'. En heilagr andi merkisk fyrir eld svá sem dróttinn mælti: 'Ek kom at senda eld á jǫrð'. Aaron ok Ur héldu upp hǫndom Moysi, því at dróttinn vár IHC sýndi oss fyrir andliga skilning léttbær vera þau lǫg er vér máttum eigi bera í líkamligri skilningu. Léttar gerði hann hendr Moysi, því at hann sneri til miskunnar þungum boðorðum laga.

> Of this law it is written: Moses' hands were heavy, then a stone was placed under him, and Aaron and Moses held up his hands. Moses sits on a stone because the law rests on Christianity, and this law has heavy hands, because it offers hard punishment for sins and shows no mercy. Aaron means mountain of strength, and Ur means fire. Mountain of strength signifies our Redeemer, just as the prophet said: 'In the last days will [...] on the mountain of the Lord higher than all mountains'. And the Holy Spirit is signified by fire, as our Lord said: 'I came to bring fire on earth'. Aaron and Ur held up Moses' hands, because our Lord IHC showed us that the laws we could not bear in the carnal sense are easy to bear according to the spiritual sense. He makes Moses' hands light because he turns to mercy the heavy commandments of the law.

This showcases several tools of the allegorical interpreter: etymology (which usually comes, as here, straight from Jerome's *Liber interpretationis Hebraicorum nominum*), the explanation of one Bible passage by another, no

---

17 *Leifar*, 83–84. For the Latin, see Grégoire le Grand, *Homélies sur l'évangile*, 2 vols, ed. Raymond Étaix, Charles Morel and Bruno Judic (Paris: Cerf, 2005–08), II, 314–16 and, for an English translation, Gregory the Great, *Forty Gospel Homilies*, trans. Dom David Hurst (Kalamazoo, MI: Cistercian Publications, 1990), 276–77. The fragmentary Old Testament quotation is Isaiah 2.2 ('And in the last days the mountain of the Lord shall be prepared on the top of all mountains').

Types and Shadows

matter how far apart they may be (here Isaiah 2.2 and Luke 12.49), and the curious way in which the allegorical interpretation is expressed as if it makes sense of the literal meaning in a process of retrospective justification.[18] This can be seen in the repetition throughout the passage of the conjunction 'því at' ('because'): Moses sat on a stone not because he was tired, but because the law rests on Christ; Aaron and Ur hold up his hands not because he needs support, but in order to show that the spiritual interpretation of the law makes it easier to bear. In all this, the translator follows Gregory closely, and the few small changes he makes show a clear understanding of how the allegory works: while Gregory describes the spiritual understanding of the law as 'tolerabilia nobis' ('bearable for us'), the translator makes more explicit the significance of heaviness at the start of the passage by choosing the adjective 'léttbærr' ('light to carry' or 'easy to bear'). Likewise, where the Latin speaks of the 'pondus' or 'weight' of the old commandments at the end, the translator uses instead the adjective 'þungr' ('heavy'), which links more directly back to the initial 'þungar' ('heavy') hands of Moses.

The vocabulary used in these two passages recurs throughout the Icelandic homilies: 'merkja' ('to signify'), 'tákn' ('sign'), 'kallask' ('to be called') and 'þýðask' ('to translate/interpret') are frequently used to signal allegorical readings. Likewise, the paired adjectives or adverbs 'líkamligr'/'andligr' ('carnal'/ 'spiritual') and 'líkamliga'/'andliga' ('carnally'/ 'spiritually') are used to distinguish between literal readings of the Old Testament and its allegorical interpretation.[19] In the homily for Ember Days in the Old Icelandic Homily Book, the homilist explains how the laws of the Old Testament are helpful to us only if we understand them spiritually: 'En ǫll boðorð, þau er í inum fornum lǫgum váru boðin líkamliga, veita oss mikla hjálp ef vér skiljum þau andliga' ('And all the commandments, which were commanded carnally in the old law, are a great help to us, if we interpret them spiritually').[20] Likewise, in the sermon for All Saints, the homilist exhorts that the historical deeds performed by the patriarchs be re-enacted spiritually by the congregation: 'Helgum aldarfeðrum vígjum vér musteri, ef vér skiljum ok fyllum andliga verk þau, er þeir gerðu líkamliga' ('We consecrate the church to the patriarchs, when we understand and fulfil spiritually the works that they performed carnally').[21] Perhaps the longest sustained passage of this kind is in the sermon 'Dróttinsdaga mál' ('Sermon on Sundays'), in which the congregation is encouraged to let the historical events which God performed 'sýniliga' ('visibly') be fulfilled 'andliga' ('spiritually') within their hearts:[22]

---

[18] See Chapter 2, pp. 44–45.
[19] *Homilíubók*, 16, 35, 46, 83, 152, 190; *Leifar*, 19, 25–26, 35–36, 48–49, 76, 85.
[20] *Homilíubók*, 35.
[21] *Homilíubók*, 42.
[22] *Homilíubók*, 26–27.

The Old Testament in Medieval Icelandic Texts

Guð skapar þá himin í hjǫrtum várum, er vér rennum hug várum með elsku til himinríkis dýrðar. Jǫrð skapaðisk þá i brjóstum várum, er vér minnumsk með lítillæti at vér erum jǫrð, ok skulum enn í jǫrð fara. Þá skiljum vér ljós frá myrkrum, er vér látum skína trúljós í hjǫrtum várum at útibyrgðum villumyrkrum. Á endrhreinsaða jǫrð stígum vér af ǫrk þeiri, er guð stýrði í miklu hafi ok flóði, þá er líkamir várir ok andir hreinsask frá syndum í skírnarbrunni fyrir almenniliga trú. Ór Egiptalands ánauð leysumsk vér at sǫkktum óvinum várum í it rauða haf, þá er vér ráðumsk frá syndum í iðranartárum, svá at þeir sǫkkvi í helvítisdjúp, en vér hjálpimsk fyrir iðran vára. Þá komum vér til fyrirheitsjarðar af eyðimǫrk eptir .xl. vetra. er vér erum leiddir frá syndum heims til paradísarfagnaða fyrir varðveizlu .x. lagaorða, þeira er fylldusk í boðorðum .iiij. guðspjalla, svá sem fjórum sinnum tíu fylla .xl.

God creates heaven in our hearts, when we turn our mind with love to the glory of heaven. Earth is created in our breasts, when we remember with humility that we are earth and shall return to earth again. We separate light from darkness, when we let the light of faith shine in our hearts, having shut out the darkness of error. We step onto newly cleansed earth from the ark, which God guided through the stormy sea and flood, when our bodies and souls are cleansed from sin in the well of baptism in the catholic faith. We are saved from the slavery of Egypt while our enemies are drowned in the Red Sea when we turn from sin with tears of repentance, so that they sink into the depths of hell, but we are saved through our repentance. We come to the promised land after forty years in the wilderness, when we are led from sin home to the joy of Paradise by keeping the ten commandments, which are fulfilled in the commands of the four gospels, just as four times ten is forty.

The historical sweep of the Old Testament – Creation, the Flood, the Exodus, the Promised Land – becomes an allegory of Christian salvation. Through wordplay and metaphorical compounds, the action is moved within: the light and darkness of the first day become 'trúljós' ('the light of faith') and 'villumyrkr' ('the darkness of error'), and the waters of the flood become 'skírnarbrunnr' ('the well of baptism') and 'iðranartár' ('tears of repentance'). The Old Testament is fulfilled in the New and only there reveals its true meaning. The homilist here links his two clauses not with 'because', but with 'when': the events of the Old Testament take on their true meaning 'when' we act them out in our moral lives.

Although many of the Old Testament quotations are taken entirely out of context in the Icelandic Homilies, they can be developed in exciting and imaginative ways. This is particularly the case in the sermon entitled

Types and Shadows

'Resurrectio Domini' ('Resurrection of the Lord'), in which the homilist draws on Gregory's 25th Homily to give an exposition of Job 40.20:[23]

> Sjá gleypandi hvalr merkir gráðgan andskota, þann er svelgja vill allt mannkyn í dauða. Agn er lagt á ǫngul, en hvass broddr leynisk. Þenna orm tók almáttigr guð á ǫngli, þá er hann sendi son sinn til dauða, sýniligan at líkam en ósýniligan at guðdómi. *Diabolus* sá agn líkams hans, þat er hann beit ok vildi fyrirfara. En guðdómsbroddr stangaði hann svá sem ǫngull. Á ǫngli varð hann tekinn, því at hann beiddisk at grípa líkams agn þat, er hann sá, en hvass guðdómsbroddr, sá er leyndr var, særði hann. Á ǫngli varð hann tekinn, því at hann fekk skaða af því, er hann beit, ok glataði hann þeim, er hann hafði áðr veldi yfir.

> That gaping whale signifies the greedy enemy, who wishes to swallow all mankind in death. A bait is placed on the hook, and the sharp point is hidden. Almighty God caught that serpent on a hook when he sent his son to death, visible in body but invisible in divinity. The devil saw the bait of his body, which he bit and wished to destroy. But the point of divinity stabbed him like a hook. On a hook he was caught, because he tried to snap up the bait of the body, which he saw, but the sharp point of divinity, which was hidden, wounded him. On a hook he was caught, because he was damaged by what he bit, and he lost what he previously had power over.

It is a famous metaphor, but the Icelandic translator captures it particularly well, setting the visible against the invisible, and that which is seen against that which is hidden. The style is vivid, with its figurative compounds ('guðdómsbroddr', 'líkams agn'), the startling participle 'gleypandi', and dramatic verbs linked by alliteration and rhyme ('svelgja', 'bíta', 'stanga', 'grípa'). It is tempting to deduce that the translator was drawn to this passage because of the myth of the *miðgarðsormr*, but the word 'ormr' here does correspond to 'serpent' in the Latin and the image of 'gleypandi hvalr' is a creative adaptation of Latin 'cetus ille deuorator' ('that gluttonous sea-monster'), from 'devorare' ('to swallow, devour').[24]

In the translated homilies of Gregory in AM 677 4to, there are longer stretches of Old Testament narrative, mostly, but not always, followed by allegorical interpretations. In the translation of his 36th Homily, we are told

---

23 Job 40.20 'an extrahere poteris Leviathan hamo' ('Canst thou draw out the leviathan with a hook?'); *Homilíubók*, 75. The first part of this allegory can be found in *Leifar*, 19. For the Latin, see Gregory, *Homélies*, II, 122–24 and *Gospel Homilies*, 195–96.

24 On the relevance of typology and 'figura' to the iconography of Þórr fishing for the Miðgarðsormr ('middle-earth-serpent'), see Lilla Kopár, *Gods and Settlers: The Iconography of Norse Mythology in Anglo-Scandinavian Sculpture* (Turnhout: Brepols, 2012), 173–75.

The Old Testament in Medieval Icelandic Texts

the story of the Amalekites from 1 Samuel 30.11–16 as an example of how God privileges the weak and the despised:[25]

> Svá er sagt í einni fornri sǫgu er þjóðir þær herjuðu er Amelechite heita. Þá lá eptir sveinn þeirra sjúkr á gǫtu hungraðr ok þyrstr ok hurfu þeir frá. En David fann hann þegar ok gaf honum át ok drykk ok styrktisk hann þegar ok gerðisk hann síðan hertogi Davids konungs. Þá kom hann at þar er Amalechite sátu at drykkju ok hefndi hann þá þess sterkliga er þeir fyrirlétu hann sjúkan.

> It is said in an old story that a people called the Amalekites were raiding. Then one of their servants was left behind sick on the road, hungry and thirsty, and they turned away from him. But David found him at once and gave him food and drink and he grew strong at once and later became one of King David's commanders. Then he came to where the Amalekites were sitting over their drink and he avenged fiercely the fact that they had left him behind sick.

The way this has been translated is very striking: the introductory formula 'Svá er sagt' ('It is said') and the mention of a 'forn saga' ('old story') makes it sound more like an episode in an actual saga than a moral exemplum. It certainly would not feel out of a place in a saga: the detail about the Amalekites sitting unsuspectingly over their drink (the Latin has 'feasting' or 'conuiuantes') as the avenger approaches sounds like a type scene from a heroic poem, as in the 'hall-attack' topos discussed by Battles.[26] The Latin has 'prostrauit' ('overthrew') rather than 'hefndi'; the point is that the weak overcome the strong, not that a slight is avenged. The syntax too is very obviously paratactic, where the Latin uses participles, ablative absolutes, and complex subordination. In short, the scene has been reshaped into a saga in miniature, the kind of story an Icelandic audience might recognise and appreciate.

The allegory that follows uses Jerome's etymology of 'Amalekites' as 'sleikjandi lýðr' ('a lapping people') to take us through a spiritual interpretation phrase by phrase:[27]

> Hvat er sleikjandi lýðr nema hugir jarðligra manna, þeir er þessa heims sælu hyggja vera allan sœtleik ok fǫgnuð. Þá herjar sjá sleikjandi lýðr,

---

[25] *Leifar*, 52. For the Latin, see Gregory, *Homélies*, II, 406–08 and *Gospel Homilies*, 318–19.

[26] Paul Battles, 'Dying for a Drink: "Sleeping after the Feast" Scenes in *Beowulf*, *Andreas*, and the Old English Poetic Tradition', *Modern Philology* 112.3 (2015), 435–57 (at p. 437). An example from Old Norse is Jörmunrekkr's wild feasting as Hamðir and Sǫrli approach his hall; see *Eddukvæði*, ed. Jónas Kristjánsson and Vésteinn Ólason, 2 vols (Reykjavík: Hið íslenzka fornritafélag, 2014), II, 411.

[27] *Leifar*, 52.

Types and Shadows

er elskendr jarðligra hluta vilja gera sér at ávexti annarra skaða. En þeir fyrirlétu sjúkan svein á gǫtu, því at hverr syndugr verðr lítilsvirðr af þessa heimsmǫnnum, ef hann þrýtr at veraldar auðœfum. En David veitti honum át ok drykkju, því at dróttinn velr opt þá er heimrinn rækir ok leiðir til sinnar mildi er liggja svá sem sjúkir á gǫtu ok megu eigi fylgja heimsunnǫndum ok gerir hann þá hertoga sína, þat eru kennimenn. En sá fann Amalechitas at drykkju ok hjó þá með sverði Davids, því at kennimenn vega með krafti orða Guðs drambláta heimsunnendr. Sveinn sá er fyrirlátinn var á gǫtu drap Amalekitas, því at þeir stíga oft yfir veraldliga hugi í kenningum er fyrr mættu eigi fylgja veraldarmǫnnum í heims farsælum.

What is a lapping people but the minds of earthly men, who think the bliss of this world is all sweetness and joy. That lapping people raid when the lovers of earthly things wish to benefit themselves at the expense of others. And they forsake the servant sick on the road because every sinner is despised by worldly men, if he runs out of worldly wealth. And David gave him food and drink because the Lord often chooses those whom the world rejects and leads to his mercy those who lie as if sick on the road and cannot follow the lovers of this world, and he makes them his commanders, that is clerics. And he found the Amalekites drinking and struck them with David's sword, because clerics strike with the power of God's words the proud lovers of this world. The servant who was left on the road killed the Amalekites because those who earlier could not follow worldly people in the joys of the world often triumph over worldly minds in their preaching.

The Old Testament passage is treated here like a code that can be deciphered, with the allegorical level of reading making sense of the literal level: as was noted above, the conjunction 'því at' ('because') is repeated throughout, as if it were the spiritual sense that came first. The syntax is not complicated, but it is not paratactic either: there is subordination with 'when' and 'because' as well as relative clauses. Moreover, the passage is heavy in compounds and noun phrases, which slow the pace in a way that focuses the mind and dissipates the narrative flow: the minds of earthly men, the lovers of earthly things, the men of this world, the pride of the lovers of this world, the men of this world, worldly minds. The lexical variation here may well be deliberate on the translator's part: the Latin uses only 'mentes saecularium' and 'saecularibus'. In other words, the allegorical explanation has been translated quite differently from the plain narrative that came first.

Another interesting example where narrative seems to take over is the story of Samson (Judges 16), which is retold in Gregory's 21st Homily as a type of the Resurrection, and which survives in translation in the late manuscript AM 624 4to (c. 1490–1510). This also contains, perhaps not coincidentally, a rather good summary of Augustinian sign theory in the translation of Ralph

The Old Testament in Medieval Icelandic Texts

d'Escures's Assumption Homily. Again, the way in which the story is told shows a clear interest in its narrative dynamics:[28]

> Þetta verk hans merkir Samson inn sterki, þá er hann kom í borg þá er Gaza heitir. En er borgarmenn sá hann kominn, þá byrgðu þeir ǫll borgarhlið, ok settu varðhaldsmenn ok þóttusk hafa gripinn Samson inn sterka; en hann braut borgarhlið á miðri nótt ok sté upp á fjall. Samson merkir lausnara várn í verki; en Gaza merkir helvíti, en þeirrar borgarlýðr merkir Gyðinga, þá er sáu IHm dauðan, ok líkam hans í grǫf lagðan, þá settu þeir varðhaldsmenn um grǫfina ok hugðusk byrgðan hafa lífs hǫfðingja sem Samson í Gaza. En Samson braut borgarhlið ok sté til fjalls, því at lausnari várr braut helvítis byrgi, ok sté upp til himins.

> This deed of his is signified by Samson the strong, when he came to the town called Gaza. And when the city-dwellers saw him come, they shut all the gates to the city, and set guards and thought that they had captured Samson the strong, but he broke the city gates in the middle of the night and went up the mountain. Samson signifies our Redeemer in deed, and Gaza signifies Hell, and the city-dwellers signify the Jews who, when they saw Jesus dead and his body laid in the grave, set guards around the grave, and thought they had shut in the chieftain of life, like Samson in Gaza. But Samson broke the city gates and went up the mountain, because our Redeemer broke the ramparts of hell and went up to Heaven.

There are several differences from the Latin worth noting here, in addition to the paratactic syntax: the repetition of Samson's nickname 'the strong', where the Latin has just once the adjective 'fortissimum' ('strongest'); the use of 'braut' for Latin 'abstulit' ('removed'), which heightens the drama of the literal actions (the verb 'destruxit' is used only once in the Latin of Christ breaking the gates of Hell). The repetition of 'braut' ('broke') also allows for the alliteration and wordplay on 'borg' ('city'), 'byrgja' ('to shut'), and 'byrgi' ('rampart'), none of which is in the Latin. Finally, the choice of the compound 'lífs hǫfðingi' ('chieftain of life') for 'auctor vitae' ('author of life') extends the military action into the allegorical level of interpretation. The force of the heroic narrative spills over into the allegory, helped by the heroism both of Samson's great feat and of Christ's harrowing of Hell.

Gregory comments in his 40th Homily that 'andlig skilning eflir trú, en siðbót saga' ('spiritual interpretation increases faith, and history [increases] morals') and the Old Testament is also used in the Icelandic homilies as a

---

[28] *Leifar,* 153. For the Latin, see Gregory, *Homélies,* II, 38 and *Gospel Homilies,* 162–63. The homily for Assumption is edited in Pelle, 'An Old Norse Homily', 268–71.

Types and Shadows

source of moral exempla.[29] More often than not, this involves the simplification of quite complex and ambiguous narratives to make them fit a particular Christian moral. We see this in the Homily for Christmas Day, which draws from Gregory's 38th Homily on the Gospels:[30]

> Tvá sonu átti inn fyrsti maðr Adam, ok var annarr þeirra góðr, en annarr vándr: Abel var góðr, en Cain vándr. Þrír váru synir Nóa í ǫrkinni með honum; váru .ij. góðir, en einn var vándr: Sem ok Iafeth váru góðir, en Kam var illr. Tvá sonu átti Abraham, ok var annarr góðr en annarr illr: Isaac var góðr, en Ismael illr. Átti Isaac ok tvá sonu; var annarr góðr en annarr vándr: er Iacob góðr ok inn helgasti maðr, en Esau vándr. Tólf sonu átti Iacob, ok var einn sá, er ǫllum gaf þeim líf, en þeir hǫfðu hann seldan mansali fyrir ǫfundar sakar ok illsku. Joseph gaf þeim ǫllum líf ok fekk þeim atvinnu of hallærit, þar er þeir myndu svelta elligar ok farask.

> The first man, Adam, had two sons, and one of them was good, and the other bad: Abel was good, and Cain bad. Three of Noah's sons were in the ark with him. Two were good, and one was bad: Shem and Japheth were good, and Ham was bad. Abraham had two sons, and one was good and the other bad: Isaac was good, but Ishmael bad. Isaac also had two sons; one was good, and the other bad: Jacob is good and the holiest man, but Esau bad. Jacob had twelve sons, and one of them gave life to them all, though they had previously sold him into slavery out of envy and malice. Joseph gave them all life and got them food during the famine, when they would otherwise have starved and died.

This looks like a surprising and unwarranted erasure of moral ambiguity: how is Ishmael bad? Is Esau really much worse than Jacob? What about Benjamin, who was not involved in selling Joseph into slavery, or Reuben, who tried to save his life? On the other hand, how exactly is Jacob, who tricks his brother out of his birth-right and deceives his father into giving him Esau's blessing, 'the holiest man'? The passage makes more sense in Gregory's Latin, where there is a small, but significant difference: Gregory divides each pair of brothers not into 'good' and 'bad', but into 'chosen' and 'rejected', according to the Old Testament theology of election.[31] He concludes the paragraph with the comment that: 'In the Church, then, there can be no bad without good, nor good without bad'. The Norse homilist translates this: 'Eigi megu góðir menn án of vera vánda mennina' ('There can be no good men without bad

---

29 *Leifar*, 37.
30 *Homilíubók*, 165–66. For the Latin, see Gregory, *Homélies*, II, 466 and *Gospel Homilies*, 345.
31 On the Old Testament theology of election, see Joel S. Kaminsky, *Yet I Loved Jacob: Reclaiming the Biblical Concept of Election* (Nashville, TN: Abingdon Press, 2007).

The Old Testament in Medieval Icelandic Texts

men').[32] It looks as if he has extended Gregory's judgement on the Church of his day back into Old Testament history, in which moral distinctions are considerably more difficult to make. It may be significant that, while Gregory never specifies which son is elected and which rejected, the Icelandic homilist carefully names them all. Perhaps it was not self-evident to him that his audience could distinguish which son was which.

The other extended Old Testament passage in the Icelandic Homily Book is found in the list of patriarchs in the second sermon for All Saints. This begins by running through the names of the most important patriarchs: Adam, Abel (described as 'inn helgasti maðr' or 'the holiest man'), and Enoch, who is also called 'heilagr maðr' ('a holy man'). After a long digression on Enoch, Elijah and the Anti-Christ, the homilist comes back to the patriarchs to tell the story of Abraham's near-sacrifice of Isaac:[33]

> Kenndi inn helgi Abraham ok þeir langfeðr, Isaac oc Iacob, mǫnnum góð dœmi í atferð sinni. Skyldum vér vera jafntrúfastir sem þeir, ok svá hlýðnir guðs boðorðum sem Abraham, at þá er guð reyndi til, hvé hlýðinn Abraham myndi honum vera ok mælti, at hann skyldi taka Ysaac son sinn, þann er hann unni sem sjálfum sér, ok hǫggva ok fœra hann svá guði í fórn. En þér meguð ætla, hvárt nǫkkut myndi honum jafnmikit þykkja sem þat, ok vildi hann þó þat virða meira, *er guð mælti* en sinn vilja, tók sveininn, ok brá sverði oc vildi hǫggva hann, *sem guð hafði mælt*. En guð sendi til engil sinn at stǫðva hǫggit, ok mælti við Abraham: 'Nú sé ek, at þú vill því hlýða, er bauð ek þér, ok þessu á móti skal koma, at í þínu kyni skulu allar þjóðir blezask, ok þitt kyn skal betr at þrifum verða en ekki kyn hafi fyrr orðit, ok inir gǫfgustu konungar munu frá þér koma. Nú svá sem þú vildir eigi þyrma einkasyni þínum, heldr vildir þú hǫggva hann fyrir guðs sakar, *þegar er hann mælti þat*, svá mun guð ok gera at móti við þik, at hann mun eigi vægja einkasyni sínum, ok mun hann senda hann af himni hingat í heim til lausnar ǫllu mannkyni, því er frá þér kømr'. [my italics]

The holy Abraham and his male descendants, Isaac and Jacob, set people a good example through their conduct. We should be as faithful as them and as obedient to God's commands as Abraham, when God tested how obedient to him Abraham would be, and said that he must take Isaac his son, whom he loved as himself, and kill him and thus offer him to God as a sacrifice. And you can imagine whether anything would have affected him as much as that, and yet he wished to honour *what God said* more than his own desire, took the boy, and drew a sword, and intended to kill him, *as God had said.* And God sent his angel to stop the blow and said to Abraham: 'Now I see that you will obey what I command and, in return,

---

32 *Homilíubók*, 166.
33 *Homilíubók*, 157.

82

Types and Shadows

through your kin all nations will be blessed, and your kin will flourish more than any kin has done before, and the most noble kings will descend from you. Now just as you did not spare your only son, but intended to kill him for God's sake *when he said so*, so God will do this for you in return, that he will not spare his only begotten son, and he will send him from Heaven into this world to redeem all mankind, who are descended from you'.

The sacrifice of Isaac is used as an exemplum of obedience, but the strain this puts on the translator is evident from the way he rewrites the biblical account. Firstly, he paraphrases the words of God, in order to make it quite explicit that Abraham is commanded to kill ('hǫggva') Isaac and that Abraham loves Isaac 'sem sjálfum sér' ('as himself'). Into Abraham's unfathomable silence in the Bible, he then projects his own sense of dilemma, asking his audience to imagine 'hvárt nǫkkut myndi honum jafnmikit þykkja sem þat' ('whether anything would have affected him as much as that'). In this respect, he is not so far from Origen, although his imagining of Abraham's internal dilemma is curiously understated, and Abraham's desire to honour 'er guð mælti' ('what God had said') wins out from the start. The homilist omits the three-day journey and the dialogue between Isaac and Abraham, so full of unexpressed emotion, and skips straight to the key moment, when Abraham draws his sword to kill his son, adding again (in case we had forgotten the first couple of times) 'sem guð hafði mælt' ('as God had said'). He makes the same crucial addition to God's final speech, when he commends Abraham for being willing to kill his son 'þegar er hann mælti þat' ('when he said so'). There is clearly some anxiety here that an audience should not understand the willingness to kill one's son as a virtue in its own right. Perhaps because of the cracks this story exposes, the homilist concludes with an allusion to Romans, focussing on a retrospective justification of Abraham's actions: the typological parallel with God's sacrifice of his only son.[34] This both fulfils the prophecy that all nations will be blessed in Abraham's kin, and hints at what Isaac's near sacrifice prefigures.

The other Old Testament character who receives attention in the homilies is Job, whose story is told twice in the Icelandic Homily Book: in an untitled sermon for the dedication of a church, and in the second sermon for All Saints.[35] These both follow the Ambrosian tradition of reading Job as a moral exemplum or 'dœmisaga', rather than as a type of the suffering Christ.[36]

---

34 Rom. 8.32: 'Qui etiam Filio suo non pepercit sed pro nobis omnibus tradidit illum' ('He that spared not even his own Son, but delivered him up for us all').

35 *Homilíubók*, 95–98, 153–54.

36 On homiletic treatments of Job, see Lawrence L. Besserman, *The Legend of Job in the Middle Ages* (Cambridge, MA: Harvard University, 2014), especially chap. 3 on the Middle Ages, 66–113; Alberto Ferreiro, 'Job in the Sermons of Caesarius of Arles', *Recherches du théologie ancienne et médiévale* 54 (1987), 13–26;

The Old Testament in Medieval Icelandic Texts

I will focus on the first of these two sermons, as the second is largely an abbreviated version of the first. In both, Job (like Abel, Jacob and Enoch) is described as 'heilagr' ('holy') and so assimilated into the body of the saints. The story needs to be heavily rewritten, though, in order to make it function as a moral exemplum. The complex poetry is excluded, and the homilist focuses purely on the prose sequence in chapters 1–2 with a brief summary of the end. For him, the important point is that the devil needs God's permission to tempt Job, and that God tests him for our benefit:[37]

> Eigi mælti guð af því svá, at eigi vissi hann áðr hversu Iob myndi við verða, þótt þess væri freistat, heldr af hinu, at hann vill, at þeir er þetta heyra, skyli vita, at hann vill reyna alla sína vini, vita hvárt þeir geri góðgerninga sína meir fyrir trú sakar ok ástar við guð ok snuggi eigi til annars af honum at móti en til eilífrar sælu, eða geri þeir meir til þess, at guð veiti þeim veraldliga giftu, bæði fjárhluti ok metorð ok heilsu hér innan heims.

> God did not say this because he did not already know how Job would react, if this were put to the test, but rather because he intends those who hear this to know that he will test all his friends, find out whether they are doing their good deeds more out of faith and love for God and don't look for anything from him in return other than eternal bliss, or whether they do it more so that God will give them worldly luck, both in property and honour and health in this world.

There are two issues here: one is theological, to do with divine omniscience, while the other is moral, to do with one's attitude towards wealth and property and one's motivation for good works. The homilist omits – perhaps unsurprisingly – God's disturbing admission that he has tested Job 'without cause'.[38] The other important point – which is also theological – is to do with Job's apparent blamelessness, and here the homilist eschews the Pelagian view that Job was in fact without sin.[39] He omits the two references to Job's sinlessness in the Latin, and instead has Job say of God: 'Sér hann, at ek þarf þess fyrir syndir mínar [...] Til þess em ek makligri miklu at þola hart' ('He sees that I need this on account of my sins [...] I am much more deserving of hard suffering').[40] It is a significant difference from the biblical book of Job,

---

    Kenneth B. Steinhauser, 'Job in Patristic Commentaries and Theological Works', in *The Cambridge Companion to Job in the Middle Ages*, ed. Franklin T. Harkins (Leiden: Brill, 2017), 66–69.

37 *Homilíubók*, 95.

38 See Job 2.3 'tu autem commovisti me adversus eum ut adfligerem illum frustra' ('thou hast moved me against him, that I should afflict him without cause').

39 On Augustine and Jerome's anti-Pelagian interpretations of Job, see Steinhauser, 'Job', 60–66.

40 *Homilíubók*, 98. Contrast Job 1.22 'in omnibus his non peccavit Iob' ('in all these

Types and Shadows

but it is a pragmatic moral for an Icelandic audience, for whom Job becomes a model of how to cope in times of adversity. This is stated explicitly in the second sermon on Job, when the homilist explains that he has digressed because: 'þat er styrking mikil þeim mǫnnom er fyrir vanheilsu verða eða mannamissi eða fjárskaða' ('this is a great support to those people who are subject to ill-health or bereavement or loss of property').[41]

Although the narrative is very much subordinate to its moral meaning in both sermons, there is some narrative art in how Job's ordeal is retold. Most noticeable is the account of his serial misfortunes, which is dramatically rendered in Old Norse with characteristic unmarked shifts from indirect to direct speech, which are not present in the Latin or the Hebrew, where only direct speech is used:[42]

En þá er þau váru at boðinu bǫrn Iobs, þá kom maðr of dag til fundar við Iob ok sagði, at hermenn hǫfðu tekit ǫxn hans alla ok drepit þá menn, er varðveitt hǫfðu áðr – 'en ek komumk einn undan at segja þér'.

And while Job's children were at the feast, a man came during the day to meet Job and said that raiders had taken all his oxen and killed the men who had looked after them – 'and I alone escaped to tell you'.

Þá kom inn fjórði til fundar við Iob ok sagði, at þar er synir hans ok dœtr sátu at boði, þá kom hregg ok felldi ofan hús á þau – 'ok fórusk þau þá ǫll bǫrn þín. Ek einn komumk á braut þeirra manna, er þar váru, at segja þér þessi tíðindi'.

Then the fourth [man] came to meet Job, and said that while his sons and daughters were sitting at the feast, a storm came and pulled down the house on them – 'and all your children then died. I alone escaped of those present there to tell you this news'.

In the Hebrew, each of the four messengers is described in exactly the same way, and each account of disaster ends with exactly the same words: 'And I alone escaped to tell you'.[43] The Old Icelandic, following the Latin, chooses to vary the wording more, but the parallelism has still been carefully reproduced. Finally, in some of the speeches, Hebrew idioms that are translated literally in the Vulgate have been replaced with Icelandic ones. Whereas, in the Latin, Satan taunts God with the exclamation 'pellem pro pelle' ('skin

---

     things Job sinned not') and 2.10 'in omnibus his non peccavit Iob labiis suis' ('in all these things Job did not sin with his lips').

41 *Homilíubók*, 154.

42 *Homilíubók*, 97.

43 Job 1.15–19; *Biblia Hebraica*, 1228: רַק־אֲנִי לְבַדִּי לְהַגִּיד לָךְ

for skin'), the homilist chooses a more homely saying: 'Sá þykkir eldrinn heitastr, er á sjálfum liggr' ('That fire seems hottest which lies on oneself').[44] When Job is afflicted with sores, the Latin describes him as afflicted 'a planta pedis usque ad verticem eius' ('from the sole of the foot even to the top of his head'), but the homilist replaces this with 'allt ór hvirfli ofan ok niðr á tær' ('from the ring of his head and down to his toes').[45] Although the primary purpose of the story is moral, the Icelandic homilist draws on the resources of vernacular storytelling to get the tone and drama of it exactly right.

What we see in the Old Norse-Icelandic homilies is that, while the allegorical method of interpretation is dominant, as one might expect in the context of preaching, there is nevertheless a real interest in the narrative dimension of the Old Testament. In some of Gregory's homilies, which were translated in the twelfth century, the historical narrative is rendered in a style evocative of the Icelandic sagas, with formulaic expressions such as 'Svá er sagt' and other stylistic traits that are not present in the Latin; these passages are stylistically quite distinct from the allegorical interpretations that follow them, which are typically rendered with figurative language and heavy noun-phrases. Likewise, while the Icelandic Homily Book prefers the allegorical or tropological mode when translating the Old Testament, some narrative passages also show careful literary shaping, including switches from indirect to direct discourse, and the use of familiar idioms and proverbs. Even in these early works, then, I would argue not only that some Icelanders perceived a likeness between Old Testament narratives and their own storytelling traditions, but also that they were willing to enhance this likeness by using stylistic resources of their own.

Saints' Lives and the Bible

Saints' lives, as one might expect, do not engage at length with Old Testament narrative, although the lives of biblical saints – the Blessed Virgin Mary, John the Baptist, the Apostles, Mary and Martha – do engage closely with the New Testament, and so contain relevant discussions of biblical exegesis and allegorical modes of reading. In so far as the Old Testament was believed to prefigure the New Testament, they also – like the homilies – cite verses from the Psalms and Prophets, and mention people, places and events from the Old Testament as well.[46] The later saints' lives, in particular, are

---

44 Job 2.4. This proverb also occurs in *Grettis saga*, 192.

45 Job 2.7. For other examples of this idiom, including one in *Heiðarvíga saga*; see *DONP*, s.v. 'hvirfill, 2' at https://onp.ku.dk/onp/onp.php?o38659 (accessed 15 December 2021).

46 A typical example is the way Adam is mentioned in *Andreas saga postola I* in *Postola sögur: Legendariske fortællinger om apostlernes liv, deres camp for

Types and Shadows

sophisticated and learned compilations, which draw on a wide range of historical material, including Comestor's *Historia scholastica* and Vincent of Beauvais's *Speculum historiale*, as well as patristic writers like Augustine, Jerome, Gregory and Bede.[47] As such, they are important forerunners for the kind of scholarly engagement that lies behind the compilation in *Stjórn I*.

In *Maríu saga*, for example, the compiler gives a short account of how to read Old Testament prophecies, but rather discourages readers from doing this without a firm basis in the Church Fathers. The discussion takes its starting point from Song of Songs: 'Quae est ista quae progreditur quasi aurora consurgens pulchra ut luna electa ut sol terribilis ut acies ordinate'.[48] This is understood to prefigure the Assumption of Mary, as in the saga's source at this point: the pseudo-Hieronymian letter *Cogitis me*, which is now known to be a forgery by Pascharius Radbertus, a monk at the Benedictine Abbey of Corbie (c. 785–c. 860).[49] After quoting the Latin and then translating it, the compiler explains how the obscurity of Old Testament prophecy requires illumination by 'holy men', who can interpret it in two different ways: either by using name-etymology ('þýðing nafna þeira') or by exploring the nature of 'things' ('náttúra þeira hluta') and searching for the 'líking' ('likeness') between 'res' and 'signum'. This leads on to a brief discussion of the properties of 'things':[50]

> Ok fyrir því at inn sami hlutr hefir fleiri náttúrur en eina, þá er hans nafn stundum sett fyrir góða merking eptir góðri náttúru, sem it óarga dýr, er merkir dróttin várn guð foður, fyrir þá náttúru er þat lífgar sonu sína á þriðja degi; þetta it sama dýr merkir ok fjándann eptir náttúru grimmleiks síns. En fyrir sakir myrkleiks spásagna þá gætir sá varligar síns vits ok

---

    kristendommens udbredelse, samt deres martyrdöd, ed. Carl R. Unger (Oslo: Bentzen, 1874), 338, where he stands in a complex set of relations to Christ: made of pure earth, as Christ was born of a pure virgin, bringing death where Christ brought life, and whose sin in taking from the 'tree of desire' is redeemed by Christ on the tree of the cross.

[47] In her *Legends of the Saints in Old Norse-Icelandic Prose* (Toronto: University of Toronto Press, 2013), Kirsten Wolf lists Peter Comestor and Vincent of Beauvais among the sources of *Pétrs saga I* (p. 314), *Jóns saga baptista II* (p. 164), and *Mörtu saga ok Maríu Magðalenu* (p. 223).

[48] Song of Songs 6.9: 'Who is she that cometh forth as the morning rising, fair as the moon, bright as the sun, terrible as any army set in array?' This verse was used as an antiphon for the Assumption and is cantus ID 004425 in the Cantus Index: Online Catalogue for Mass and Office Chants at https://cantusindex.org/id/004425.

[49] See Hannah W. Matis, *The Song of Songs in the Early Middle Ages* (Leiden: Brill, 2019), 176–213.

[50] *Maríu saga: Legender om jomfru Maria og hendes jertegn*, ed. Carl R. Unger (Oslo: Brögger & Christie, 1871), 58.

The Old Testament in Medieval Icelandic Texts

snildar, er tekr skýringar heilagra feðra til frásagnar, hvat þeir hlutir merkja, er spámenn hafa fyrir spát, heldr en hinn er tekr af sjálfum sér, ok á þá at hafa svǫr fyrir við guð ok menn.

And because the same thing has more than one property, its name is sometimes used to signify a good thing in accordance with a good property, like the lion, which signifies our Lord, God the Father, because of the property that it resurrects its sons on the third day; this same animal also signifies the devil in accordance with the property of ferocity. And, because of the obscurity of prophecies, he guards his wisdom and eloquence more carefully who uses the interpretations of the holy fathers to explain what the things the prophets have prophesied signify, rather than the one who works it out himself, and will then have to answer for it before God and man.

This is a good summary of Augustinian sign theory, but with one important difference: while Augustine encouraged a multiplicity of interpretations – even incorrect ones – as long as they obeyed the 'rule of love', this compiler sees potential multiplicity as a problem rather than a virtue and encourages his readers to stick with authorised interpretations. Likewise, when discussing earlier how John the Baptist declared himself unworthy to untie the Lord's sandal, he refers his readers to a warning of St Jerome: 'þat skal hverr kennandi varask at sveigja eigi ritningar eptir sínum vilja, heldr sinn vilja til ritninga' ('every teacher must beware not to bend the Scriptures to his will, but rather his will to the Scriptures').[51]

This does not prevent him, though, from devoting three pages in the printed edition to the exegesis of this one verse from Song of Songs, exploring in what ways Mary might be thought of as 'dagsbrún' ('dawn'), 'tungl' ('moon'), 'sól' ('sun') and 'fylking hermanna' ('formation of warriors'). He explains that Mary is like the dawn up to the moment of incarnation, when the 'sun of righteousness' began to shine in her breast. She is like the moon because she bore the likeness of God, as the moon is illuminated by the sun and brighter than all the stars. Thus, the Old Testament verse is used to reflect on the theological nature of Mary. When he comes to the sun, however, the exegesis tips over into lyricism, as he describes the effect of Mary's prayers on the sinner's hardened heart:[52]

Hon flóar ok heitir af sínu árnarðarorði við guð kólnuð hjǫrtu af ástleysi við guð ok jǫkli harðari, frosin af langri heipt eða rangri ágirni ok margfǫldum illvilja, svá at hverr sá, er sinna synda iðrask ok krýpr til hennar, þá gefsk sú miskunn ok gefizk hefir til dœma, at hugrinn blotnar, ok bráðnar harðýð-gisjökullinn, ok sprettr iðrunarvatnit upp í hjartanu ok fellr fram um augun.

---

51 *Maríu saga*, 20. Cf. Jerome, Ep. 48.17, translated in *NPNF* VI, 76–77.
52 *Maríu saga*, 60.

Types and Shadows

She floods and warms – by means of her words of intercession with God – hearts chilled by lack of love towards God and harder than a glacier, frozen by long resentment or wrong desire and all kinds of ill-will, so that to everyone who repents of their sins and kneels to her, to them mercy is given – and has been given as an example – so that the heart softens, and the hardened ice melts, and the water of repentance springs up in the heart and flows out from the eyes.

Here exegesis comes very close to poetry, although the passage remains prose: through complex metaphor, the compiler not only creates an inner landscape that feels distinctively Icelandic, but also captures the inner movement of the emotion of repentance: from the fixity of sin – 'harder than a glacier' – to the fluidity of mercy, unfolding between the alliterating verbs *flóa* ('to flood') and *fella* ('to flow'). As Mary – the sun – warms the freezing heart, it softens, melts, and up from the frozen depths springs a fresh stream of water – tears streaming from the eyes. The lyricism of the language, the interplay of alliteration and rhyme, and the use of the present tense all invite the readers to share in this emotional experience, to allow the same spring of tears to well up within themselves.

The longest sustained passage of allegory in *Maríu saga* is the allegory of the 15 steps to the temple, each of which is associated with a particular psalm, a particular virtue, and a particular stage of human history. This must be at least in part inspired by Jerome's exegesis of the gradual psalms, where he links each psalm with a particular step of the temple as part of an ascent towards God.[53] However, the author of *Maríu saga* ties this in with the Augustinian allegory of the six ages of the world, creating a visual scheme for human history that is reminiscent of Hugh of St Victor's *De Archa Noe*.[54] The first five steps symbolise the first five ages of the world, and from each age one or two biblical characters are chosen to represent the virtue of that age: Enoch, the abandonment of the world; Noah, hope and Abraham, joy; Moses, the joys of heaven; David and Manasseh, trust and protection. A single incident is then chosen to illustrate each virtue: Enoch's ascent into Heaven, Noah's Flood, the promise made to Abraham, David's defeat of

---

[53] See Hans Bekker-Nielsen and Ole Widding, 'The Fifteen Steps of the Temple: A Problem in the *Maríu saga*', *Opuscula* 2.1 (1961), 80–91, who appealed for help in finding the source for this passage. The most likely source seems to me to be Jerome's *Tractatus sive homiliae in psalmos*; for an English translation, see *Homilies of Saint Jerome Volume 1 (1–59 On the Psalms)*, trans. Sister Marie Liguori Ewald (Washington, DC: Catholic University of America Press, 1964), 300–15 (Hom. 41 on Ps. 119) and 341–52 (Hom. 46 on Ps. 133).

[54] On Hugh's use of visual aids, see Patrice Sicard, *Diagrammes médiévaux et exégèse visuelle, Le libellus de formation arche de Hughes de Saint-Victor* (Turnhout: Brepols, 1993).

The Old Testament in Medieval Icelandic Texts

Goliath. But, in the case of King Manasseh, the compiler tells a longer story, perhaps because Manasseh is useful as a type of the apparently hopeless sinner, who is nevertheless redeemed:[55]

Á þeim inum sama palli stóð Manases konungr dótturson Ysayas spámanns, er drepa lét Ysayam ok síðan blótaði skurðgoðum. Ok þá er hann var hertekinn af Babilonis mǫnnum, eptir sǫgn gyðinga, ok dœmðr til dauða með þeim hætti, at gerr var uxi ór eiri ok settr Manases þar í ofan, ok lokit aptr uxanum, en síðan gǫrt bál undir ok slegit eldi í. Manases tók at blóta ok at heita á skurðgoð sín, ok þá er þat týði ekki ok uxinn hitnaði, þá snerisk hann til iðranar ok hét á himna guð, ok sýndi guð honum trúlyndi ok traust síns fyrirheits, at á hverigri tíð er syndugr maðr iðrask glœpa sinna ok snýsk til guðs, þá mun guð honum miskunn veita. Þá kom engill guðs ok tók Manasen á brott ór uxanum luktum, ok setti hann niðr á Gyðingaland, ok tók hann síðan ríki sitt ok brásk eigi guði.

On the same step stood King Manasseh, the son of the prophet Isaiah's daughter, who had Isaiah killed and then sacrificed to idols. And when he was taken captive by the Babylonians, according to the account of the Jews, he was condemned to death in this way: an ox was made of brass and Manasseh [was] put inside it, and the ox sealed up again, and then a fire [was] made under it and set alight. Manasseh began to sacrifice and call on his idols, and when that didn't work and the ox grew hotter, then he turned to repentance, and called on the God of Heaven, and God showed him faithfulness and protection according to his promise, that at any time that a sinful man repents of his sins and turns to God, then God will show him mercy. Then God's angel came and took Manasseh out of the sealed ox and set him down in the land of the Jews, and he returned to his kingdom and did not turn from God.

The story of Manasseh is told in 2 Kings 20 and 2 Chronicles 33; but although 2 Chronicles mentions his captivity, change of heart, and restoration to the throne, the account of Isaiah's martyrdom and of the brazen ox are rabbinic in origin, as is suggested by the formula 'according to the account of the Jews'.[56] The martyrdom of Isaiah is told in Comestor's *Historia scholastica*, where we also learn that 'secundum Hebraeos' ('according to the Hebrews'),

---

55 *Maríu saga*, 10.

56 On the sources of this fascinating tradition, see Gideon Bohak, 'Classica et Rabbinica I: The Bull of Phalaris and the Tophet', *Journal for the Study of Judaism in the Persian, Hellenistic and Roman Period* 31.1–4 (2000), 203–16; Matthias Henze, 'King Manasseh of Judah in Early Judaism and Christianity', in *On Prophets, Warriors and Kings: Former Prophets through the Eyes of their Interpreters*, ed. George J. Brooke and Ariel Feldman (Berlin and Boston: De Gruyter, 2016), 181–228.

Types and Shadows

Isaiah was Manasseh's maternal grandfather.[57] The story of the brazen ox is paralleled in various rabbinic sources, but since it is not in Josephus (whom the compiler refers to as 'sagnameistari') nor in the *Historia scholastica*, it is not clear to me where the author of *Maríu saga* found it; possibly in Pseudo-Jerome's *Quaestiones Hebraicae in Libros Regum et Paralipomenon*, although this does not mention an ox:[58]

> Dum enim in Babylonem ductus fuisset, et in vase aeneo perforato missus, admoto igni, invocavit omnia nomina idolorum, quae colebat: et cum non fuisset ab eis exauditus neque liberatus, recordatum fuisse, quod a patre crebro audierat: *Cum invocaveris me in tribulatione, et conversus fueris, exaudiam te,* ut in Deuteronomio scribitur: exauditumque esse a Domino, et liberatum et reductum in regnum suum.

> For when he had been taken to Babylon and placed in a perforated bronze container, once a fire had been applied to it, he invoked all the names of the idols he worshipped, and when he had been neither heard nor rescued by them, it is said that he remembered what he had often heard from his father: *When you call on me in tribulation and are converted, I will hear you,* as it is written in Deuteronomy, and [it is said that] he was heard by the Lord, and freed, and returned to his kingdom.

Wherever it comes from, it is striking that this vivid and dramatic story from Jewish extra-biblical tradition has found its way into an Icelandic life of the Virgin Mary.

The compiler of *Maríu saga* is comfortable with a range of different approaches to the Old Testament, including Marian allegory (as one might expect), but also a historical approach that includes haggadic (narrative) material. He not only has a range of sources at his disposal, but also a range of different styles.[59] Both the allegorical exegesis of the Song of Songs and the account of Manasseh's repentance are in a sense about the same thing: the extravagance of God's mercy and his forgiveness of even the most hardened sinner. Yet one works by creating a poetic image of an interior landscape; the other is a lively anecdote in narrative form. One recreates the inner change that prompts repentance; the other describes Manasseh's experience from the outside. One works by metaphor and aural effects; the other by temporal

---

57 Comestor, *Historia Libri IV Regum*, PL 198, 1414.

58 Pseudo-Jerome, *Quaestiones Hebraicae in Libros Regum et Paralipomenon*, in PL 23, 1399D–1400A. The same story is found in AM 764 4to, where it presumably comes from *Maríu saga*, and in *Stjórn III*, 1201–02.

59 On these different styles, see also Laura Tomassini, 'Attempts at Biblical Exegesis in Old Norse: Some Examples from *Maríu saga*', *Opuscula* 10 (1996), 129–35.

The Old Testament in Medieval Icelandic Texts

sequence. In handling the first, the author uses the resources of vernacular poetry; in the second he draws on the resources of vernacular prose.

Maríu saga is sometimes paired in manuscripts with *Jóns saga baptista*, another biblical saint with strong Old Testament connections, as both the last Old Testament prophet and a forerunner or type of Christ.[60] Whereas *Maríu saga* caters for a more mixed audience, Grímr Hólmsteinsson's *Jóns saga baptista II* is extraordinarily learned, and probably written primarily for the cloister and the cathedral school.[61] It was commissioned by Rúnólfr Sigmundarson, nephew of Brandr Jónsson and abbot of the Augustinian monastery of Þykkvibær not far from Skálholt, Iceland's southern episcopal see.[62] Marner has dated it very specifically to 1282–88 in the midst of the dispute over the ownership of the Icelandic *staðar*. She has identified more than 37 sources, some of which are cited in the text: the preface lists Gregory, Augustine, Ambrose and Jerome; and Josephus, Comestor and the *Speculum historiale* are all cited in the text.[63] Even more than *Maríu saga*, it is primarily a compilation, and the compiler's own work is mainly limited to the selection and presentation of his source material. As Battista has commented, in later works like this: 'the *auctoritas* of the Latin text is being transferred to its vernacular counterpart'.[64]

Like *Maríu saga*, Grímr's *Jóns saga baptista* includes a number of passages that instruct the reader in biblical interpretation. In his exegesis of the *Benedictus*, for example, he teaches that: 'ǫll ritning ins forna lǫgmáls allt til várra tíma sagði spár af Kristi, ok allir helgir feðr bera bæði með verkum sínum ok orðum vitni guðligri tilskipan' ('All the Scripture of the Old Testament up to our own time was a prophecy of Christ, and all the holy fathers in both their deeds and words bear witness to divine providence').[65] Not only words, but also deeds, signify something other than themselves. The Mosaic law is described as 'skuggi eða figúra ókominna hluta' ('a shadow or figure of future things'), which is fulfilled in Jesus Christ.[66] Grímr also

---

60 Daniel C. Najork, *Reading the Old Norse-Icelandic 'Maríu saga' in its Manuscript Contexts* (Kalamazoo, MI: Medieval Institute Publications, 2012), 76–79; Astrid Marner, 'glosur lesnar af undirdiupi omeliarum hins mikla Gregorij, Augustini, Ambrosij ok Jeronimi ok annarra kennifedra: Väterzitate und Politik in der Jóns saga baptista des Grímr Hólmsteinsson', PhD thesis, University of Bonn, 2013, 77.

61 Christelle Fairise, 'Relating Mary's Life in Medieval Iceland: Similarities and Differences with the Continental Lives of the Virgin', *Arkiv for nordisk filologi* 129 (2014), 195; Marner, 'glosur', 413.

62 *Jóns saga baptista II*, in *Postola sögur*, 849–50; Marner, 'glosur', 58.

63 For a full list of sources, see Marner, 'glosur', 90–254.

64 Simonetta Battista, 'The "Compilator" and Contemporary Literary Culture in Old Norse Hagiography', *Viking and Medieval Scandinavia* 1 (2005), 11.

65 *Jóns saga baptista II*, 864.

66 *Jóns saga baptista II*, 887.

Types and Shadows

frequently uses the term 'glósur' ('glosses'), which only became common from c. 1275.[67] He employs the same image of the honeycomb used by Hugh of St Victor in his *Didascalicon* when talking about 'words' ('voces') and 'signs' ('signa'):[68]

> Má kalla í hans sǫgu svá mǫrg orðin sem stórmerkin, þau er sem inn feitasti seimr eru, því sœtari sem þau eru smæra mulit. Hafa þau svá margfalldan skilning, ef fróðir menn líta á þau, at æ ok æ finnsk í þeim hulit annat ágæti, þá er annat er uppgrafit.

> One might say there are as many great signs as there are words in his saga, which are like the richest honeycomb, the sweeter the smaller they are chewed up. They have multiple meanings, if wise men examine them, so that there is always some further excellence hidden in them, whenever one thing is discovered.

Unlike the compiler of *Maríu saga*, who is nervous about multiplicity, Grímr encourages his readers to keep on excavating the hidden treasures buried in his text.

For Grímr, biblical history is held together by a system of abstract correspondences that breaks down time and history and creates a single unity or truth. This can be seen most clearly in his discussion of why Jesus identifies John the Baptist as Elijah:[69]

> Því kallaði hann Jóhannem Eliam, at hann var á þá leið skipaðr til þess at vera fyrirrennari lausnarans í inni fyrri hans tilkvámu, sem Elias mun vera fyrirrennari dómandans í inni síðarri hans hingatkvámu. Báðir váru þeir skírlífir ok báðir neyttu þeir sparliga fœzlu, báðir váru þeir í eyðimǫrk, báðir váru þeir ófagrliga búnir, báðir þoldu þeir reiði konungs ok dróttningar, annarr Achab ok Jezabel, en annarr Herodes oc Herodiaden. Helias stemdi Jordan, meðan hann gekk yfir hana, en Jóhannes skírði dróttin í þeiri sǫmu á. Elias var numinn af jǫrðu, til þess at eigi yrði hann fanginn af sínum óvinum, en sæll Jóhannes var fyrir orð sjálfs sannleiksins kórónaðr með píslarvættis kórónu, til þess at hann vægi deyjandi sígr á ǫllum sínum óvinum.

> He called John Elijah, because he was appointed to be the forerunner of the Redeemer in his first coming, just as Elijah will be the forerunner of

---

67 Marner, 'glosur', 244.

68 *Jóns saga baptista II*, 928; cf. Hugh, *Didascalicon*, v.3 and vi.3, trans. Taylor, 121, 138.

69 *Jóns saga baptista II*, 910. This is from Bede, *Homilies on the Gospels*, trans. Lawrence T. Martin and David Hurst (Kalamazoo, MI: Cistercian Publications, 1991), II, ii.23; see Marner, 'glosur', 153–54.

the Judge in his second coming. Both of them were chaste, and both of them ate sparingly, both were in the wilderness, both of them were dressed plainly, both suffered the anger of a king and queen, one Ahab and Jezebel, the other Herod and Herodias. Elijah stemmed the Jordan, while he walked through it, and John baptised the Lord in the same river. Elijah was taken from earth, so that he would not be caught by his enemies, and the blessed John was crowned by the word of truth himself with a martyr's crown so that by dying he would gain victory over all his enemies.

It is not so much that the events of Elijah's life prefigure those of John the Baptist, but rather that both lives signify a single truth: spiritually, they are one person. The same mechanism lies behind Grímr's diatribe on woman and the 'ancient evil' she represents:[70]

> Hon gerði himneska menn jarðliga ok drekkti allt mannkyn í helvíti, ok tók lífit frá ǫllum heiminum fyrir epli ins óleyfða trés. Þetta grand leiðir mennina til eilífs aldrtila. Hana flýði Elias spámaðr, sá er með sinni tungu lukti ok lauk upp himininn, ok hann fór fyrir henni hrjáðr ok rekinn, ok þann manninn, sem hon finnr hreinan, gerir hon saurgan. Hon leiddi ok í girndarbruna ok þrøngving David psalmistam, ok drap nú Jóhannem baptistam.

> She made heavenly men earthly and drowned all mankind in hell, and took life from all the world through the apple of the forbidden tree. This harm leads men to eternal loss of life. The prophet Elijah fled from her, who with his tongue closed and opened heaven, and he departed before her harassed and driven away, and the man whom she finds pure, she makes dirty. She also led into the fire of lust and affliction David the Psalmist, and now killed John the Baptist.

The conflation of Eve, Jezebel, Bathsheba and Herodis into a single woman – the source of all evil in the world – is rhetorically very powerful (and Grímr claims to draw on the great rhetor Augustine here).[71] The effect – just for a moment – is to collapse historical time and difference so that one can see the eternal truths – the 'now' that lies behind it all.

Although Grímr can effectively use rhetoric to appeal to his audience's emotions, much of his exegesis is technical in character rather than lyrical or poetic.[72] Marner suggests that Grímr uses a particular style for commentary,

---

70 *Jóns saga baptista II*, 914.

71 In fact, this appears to be from a sermon by Peter Chrysologus; see David McDougall, 'Pseudo-Augustinian Passages in *Jóns saga baptista II* and *The Fourth Grammatical Treatise*', *Traditio* 44 (1988), 477.

72 On Grímr's effective use of rhetoric and different levels of style, see further Marner, 'glosur', 341–52; McDougall, 'Pseudo-Augustinian Passages', 463–83.

Types and Shadows

which she calls 'middle style' ('mittleres Stilregister') and which aims primarily at accuracy and precision.[73] His interpretation of Isaiah 40.4–5 provides a good example of this. First he translates the verses into Old Norse: 'Hverr dalr mun fyllask en fjǫll ok hálsar munu lægjask, rangir hlutir munu réttask, en snarpir sléttask, ok allt hold mun sjá hjálpráð guðs' ('Every valley will be filled, and mountains and ridges will be made low, wrong things will be righted, and rough things smoothed over, and all flesh will see the salvation of God').[74] He then poses the case that someone should ask why John the Baptist said these words and what they mean, before turning to the glosses of the Church Fathers for an answer. These explain that the valleys signify the heathens, who were initially 'low' in God's sight, before their humility and faith raised them to honour and filled them with divine mercy. Judah, on the other hand, which previously stood on the 'heights of virtue', is because of its arrogance and lack of faith brought low. Wrongs will be righted in that the hearts of evil men, which are corrupted by all kinds of evil, will be ruled by righteousness, while 'rough' thoughts that hamper the efforts of preachers will be turned to patience and 'smooth' the way for true teaching. We move from allegorical to tropological interpretation here, and the explanation ends with anagogy:

> En þó at eigi mætti í þessarri verǫld hverr maðr guðs son sjá, munu allir góðir menn ok illir sjá hann í enda þessarrar veraldar; góðir menn til óætlanligrar aukningar eilífra dýrða ok fagnaða, en illir menn til eilífrar fyrirdœmingar ok ørskemdar ok bótlausrar bǫlvanar, þá er þeir fyrirdœmask til endalauss ófagnaðar.

> And though not every man was able to see God's son in this world, all good men and evil will see him at the end of this world – good men to the unimaginable increase of eternal glories and joys, and evil men to eternal condemnation and shame and irremediable cursedness, when they are condemned to endless sorrow.

There is a bit of a rhetorical flourish here as Grímr brings his exegesis to the end, and it gives a good sense of his characteristic style: the parallelism between 'good' and 'evil' men, the matching word-pairs ('dýrðir ok fagnaðir', 'fyrirdœming ok ørskemd'), the alliterative collocations ('óætlanligrar aukningar', 'bótlausan bǫlvanar', 'endalauss ófagnaðar'), as well as the preference for complex syntax and polysyllabic words.

Grímr's main concern, though, is the accuracy of his interpretation: he comments at one point that John's words are 'óleysiligt lǫgmal almáttigs guðs […] ef þau eru rétt skilit' ('the indissoluble law of Almighty God […]

---

[73] Marner, 'glosur', 349–51.
[74] *Jóns saga baptista II*, 869–70; cf. Is. 40.4–5, as quoted in Lk. 3.5.

The Old Testament in Medieval Icelandic Texts

if they are correctly interpreted').[75] Part of this accuracy – as in the school of St Victor – has to do with getting the historical level of the narrative right. For this, Grímr draws copiously on Comestor, as well as on the Fathers of the Church.[76] He uses the *Historia scholastica* to explain Jewish festivals (like the 'dies propitionis', which he translates as 'líknardagr' or 'day of reconciliation' and compares to the ember days), to identify objects like the 'pugillaris' ('lítit vaxspjald eða bleikjuspjald at lykja má hnefa': 'a little wax tablet or blackboard which can be held in the hand'), and to clarify genealogical details.[77] He also draws on Comestor to explain things that appear puzzling or contradictory: how John's baptism relates to Jesus's baptism, why John denies that he is a prophet when Jesus says he is, why he eats locusts when this is supposedly forbidden by the law; whether the dove at Jesus's baptism was real.[78] He describes in some detail, from Comestor, the difference between the Pharisees and the Sadducees, transliterating the Hebrew word 'torath' (תּוֹרָה) and Greek 'philaxe' ('φυλακτήριον').[79] Occasionally, he adds an explanatory story. When interpreting John's words in Luke 3.8 ('I say unto you, that God is able of these stones to raise up children to Abraham'), he explains that:[80]

> Commestor segir, at hann mun sýnt þeim hafa þá .xii. steina, sem .xii. hǫfðingjar Israels ættar báru af þurrum Jordanar veg á þurt land, at sá grjótvarði væri verǫndum mǫnnum oc viðkomǫndum til sanns vitnisburðar um þá jartegn, er þeir gengu þurrum fótum yfir fyrrnefnda á. Einn af þessum steinum segisk sæll Jeronimus sét hafa svá þungan, sem þá máttu tveir mann létta, ok eigi fyrir því at steinarnir hefði vaxit, heldr fyrir því at mannfólkit hafði þorrit.

> Comestor says, that he must have showed them the twelve stones that the twelve leaders of the tribes of Israel carried from the dry bed of the Jordan onto dry land, so that the stone memorial would be for present and future generations a true witness of the miracle that they walked through the aforementioned river with dry feet. The blessed Jerome says that he saw one of those stones, which was as heavy as two men could lift, and not because the stone had grown heavier, but rather because humankind had grown weaker.

---

75 *Jóns saga baptista II*, 876.

76 Ole-Jörgen Johannessen, 'Litt om kildene', in *Opuscula septentrionalia: Festskrift til Ole Widding*, ed. Bent Christian Jacobsen et al. (Copenhagen: C. A. Reitzel, 1977), 102–08.

77 See for example *Jóns saga baptista II*, 852, 862, 868.

78 *Jóns saga baptista II*, 869, 873, 888, 892–93.

79 *Jóns saga baptista II*, 873–74.

80 *Jóns saga baptista II*, 875–76; Comestor, *Historia Evangelica*, c. 30, PL 198, 1552C.

Types and Shadows

These 12 stones are mentioned in Joshua 4 and, together with Jerome's personal comment, serve to authenticate the biblical account. Jerome's testimony that he had himself seen the stones and witnessed their weight adds just a hint of saga in the close connection between landscape and story, recalling the many stones said to have been lifted by Grettir the Strong in Iceland.[81] But, whereas Comestor restricts himself to the literal level of meaning, this is just the first stage for Grímr: he goes on to cite from 'the masters' a range of allegorical readings, including Bede's comments on the 'stony' hearts and 'stone' gods of the heathens, a strong warning against heresy, and even a mention of the theological controversy around Abelard. Other additions from Comestor are more explicitly allegorical. When explaining why John calls Jesus 'the lamb' of God, Grímr comments:[82]

> Commestor segir, at enn mun sá skilningr finnask í þessum orðum Jóhannis, at hann hafi fyrir þá sǫk kallat Jesum lamb guðs, at lambit veitir af sér þrjá hluti, ull til klæða, mjólk til drykkjar, hold til vistar. Svá veitir ok várr dróttinn sínum mǫnnum í himinríki ódauðleiks stólu, þá er réttlátir menn skína sem sól í ríki fǫður þeira; hann veitir ok mjólk einfaldrar kenningar þeim sem næringar þurfu í hans almenniligri trú; hann veitir ok af heilǫgu altari vist síns eiginligs líkama fólkinu til syndalausnar.

> Comestor says, that there is yet another interpretation to be found in these words of John, that he called Jesus lamb of God because a lamb gives of itself three things: wool for clothes, milk to drink, flesh to eat. So our Lord gives his people in heaven the stoles of incorruptibility, when the righteous shine like the sun in their father's kingdom; he also gives the milk of simple teaching to those who need nourishment in his catholic faith; he also gives from the holy altar the food of his own body for the forgiveness of people's sins.

This is, in fact, from the *Glossa ordinaria*, although Grímr may have got it through a gloss in the *Historia scholastica*.[83] The garments of incorruptibility might be thought of as anagogical; the milk of teaching as tropological, and

---

[81] Jerome mentions these stones in Ep. 108.12 (trans. in *NPNF*, VI, 490) and again in his *Liber de situ et nominibus locorum Hebraicorum* (PL 23, 900A), but neither source mentions that he had seen them himself or that he knew how much they weighed. For Grettir's stones, see *Grettis saga*, 48 and for other stones named after him, see Emily Lethbridge's interactive saga map at http://sagamap.hi.is/is/# (accessed 16 December 2021).

[82] *Jóns saga baptista II*, 895.

[83] Marner, 'glosur', 243. See *Glossa ordinaria cum Biblia latina* (Jn 1. 19*)*, ed. Martin Morard et alii, in *Glossae Scripturae Sacrae electronicae*, IRHT-CNRS, 2023, at https://gloss-e.irht.cnrs.fr/php/livres-liste.php?id=glo (accessed 24 July 2023).

The Old Testament in Medieval Icelandic Texts

the sacrament of the altar as allegory. Although Grímr does once refer to Comestor as 'magister in historiis' ('Master of Histories'), he is in the end less interested in telling a story well than in assembling authoritative glosses to ensure that his readers interpret the Bible correctly.[84] The historical detail provides the foundation for this vast exegetical apparatus.

There is one story from the Old Testament that is told simply and plainly, though, and that is the story of Nabal and Abigail from I Samuel 25. Grímr tells this story in response to the question of whether one should keep an oath if one has sworn to do wrong:[85]

> Svá segir Liber Regum inn fyrsti, at David konungr sór í bræði at láta drepa Nabal í Karmelo, þann mann sem áðr hafði við hann sakir gert, en fyrir sakir Abigail húsfreyju þessa manns, rauf hann þetta sœri ok gaf Nabal grið ok mælti: 'Sé blezaðr dróttinn guð Israels, sá er í dag sendi þik mér at móti, ok blezat sé þitt mál ok þú sjálf, því at þú bannaðir mér í dag at steypa út mannligum dreyra ok hefna mín með minni hendi. Ok er Nabal varð víss tiltœkja ok orða Davids, féll á hann svá mikit hugarangr, at hann var dauðr, áðr .x. dagar váru liðnir. Ok lofaði David þá enn af nýju guð, þann er hefndi hans meingerða, þeira sem hann hafði eigi hefnt. Ok eptir þat tók hann sér til eiginnar húsfreyju fyrrnefnda Abigail ins beztu konu.

> The first book of Kings says, that King David swore in anger to have Nabal in Carmel killed, the man who had previously done him wrong, but for the sake of Abigail this man's wife, he broke this oath and made peace with Nabal and said: 'May the Lord God of Israel be blessed, who today sent you to meet me, and blessed be your words and you yourself, for you have prevented me today from shedding men's blood and avenging myself by my own hand'. And when Nabal became aware of David's actions and words, he was struck by such great bitterness of heart, that he was dead before ten days had passed. And David praised God yet again, who had avenged his wrongs, the ones that he had not avenged himself. And after that he took as his own wife the aforementioned Abigail, the best of women.

The difference in style from previous passages is immediately evident: this is a well-told story. The syntax is much simpler; there are very few compound nouns, no participles, no intensifying adverbs, and only a handful of adjectives. The sequence of events is clear, and the emotions are simply but effectively drawn: David's passionate anger, soon appeased, versus Nabal's fatal bitterness of heart. It is well unified too around the idea of revenge, a word that is only

---

84 *Jóns saga baptista II*, 920.

85 *Jóns saga baptista II*, 915–16. The source for this is, again, Bede's Homily ii.23 on the Gospels, and Bede is drawing on Augustine's Sermo 308. However, neither of these include David's speech or Nabal's reaction to it; here, the homilist is translating directly from the Vulgate.

98

Types and Shadows

used once in the Latin ('ulciscerer'), but which here becomes the focus of the story: David's forbearance in taking revenge by his own hand is rewarded by God's avenging of his wrongs.[86] It is noticeable that Abigail is presented in a very positive light, both in David's prayer and by the narrator ('the best of women'), in contrast to the misogynistic diatribe against women that was cited above. Despite these 'saga' themes, the story cannot really be said to be in 'saga style': expressions like 'fyrrnefnda kona' ('aforementioned woman'), 'fyrir sakir' ('for the sake of'), are very much learned; the compound 'hugarangr' ('bitterness of heart') occurs only in romances and religious texts, and David's prayer has been carefully ornamented: 'steypa' is not used in the sagas in the sense 'to shed blood', except in the learned expression 'at steypa út blóði' ('to pour out blood'), and 'dreyri' is used only in variations on the expression 'rauðr sem dreyri' ('red as blood').[87] These words have been chosen with a keen ear for their aural effect: the rhyme between 'steypa' and 'dreyra', and the alliteration on 'd' ('dag', 'dreyra'), 'm' ('mér', 'mannligum', 'mín', 'minni') and 'h' ('hefna', 'hendi'). This short narrative is certainly in Grímr's 'plain style', but it is not really 'saga style': it remains resolutely learned.[88]

Grímr's *Jóns saga baptista* is scholarly rather than imaginative in its approach to the Old Testament; perhaps his stated distaste for 'veraldligar víkinga sǫgur' ('the secular sagas of vikings') has checked any impulse to enjoy biblical narrative for its own sake or to exploit it as a kind of pious substitute for secular romance and saga.[89] This is not the case, however, for some of the other apostles' sagas, which tend to blend their historiographical material with amusing (often extra-biblical) anecdotes and to look for ways to bridge the gap between salvation history and 'skrǫksǫgur' ('lying sagas'). There is a particularly good example of this in *Tveggja postula saga Jóns ok Jakobs*, which draws on similar sources to Grímr, including the *Speculum historiale*, but which retells biblical stories in entertaining and memorable ways. Here is its potted version of Old Testament history, reconfigured into six exciting battles between the 'city of God' and the 'city of man':[90]

> Inn fyrsti bardagi var i himinríkis hǫll millum hæsta keisara ok mesta víkings, þá er víkingrinn vildi fá ok grípa keisaravaldit ok verða líkr inum hæsta. Í þessum bardaga samþykktisk drótningin, þat er engillig náttúra, víkinginum ok fyrirlét brúðgumann en samtengdisk hórkarlinn. Ok fyrir þá sǫk var bæði hórkarlinn ok hórkerlingin rekin í myrkvastofu helvítligrar

---

[86] See 1 Sam. 25.33.

[87] *DONP*, s.v. *dreyri*, at https://onp.ku.dk/onp/onp.php?o15252 (accessed 16 December 2021).

[88] Compare what Marner says about Grímr's plain style and 'saga' style, 'glosur', 352–55.

[89] *Jóns saga baptista II*, 929 (cf. also p. 849).

[90] *Tveggja postula saga Jóns ok Jakobs*, in *Postola sögur*, 621–63.

The Old Testament in Medieval Icelandic Texts

útlegðar at eilífu [...] Annarr bardagi varð undir risum millum sona guðs ok sona mannanna, þat er at skilja millum Abel ok Seth ok hans afkvæmis ok Kain ok hans afkvæmis eða afspringis. Kallask þeir synir guðs, sem af Seth eru komnir, en þeir synir manna, sem af Chayn eru komnir. Í þessum bardaga féll Abel merkismaðr ok fekk sígr ok himneska kórónu. Lyktaðisk þessi bardagi í Nóa flóði. Þriði bardagi var undir þeim er smíðuðu stǫpulinn Babel millum frelsingja ok þræla. Þessi bardagi byrjaðisk á Cham ok Sém, ok endaðisk þá er tungnaskipti varð. Fjórða stríð var undir hǫfuðfeðrum millum þeira manna, er tóku umskurðarskírn, ok þeira, sem eigi tóku. Byrjaðisk þessi bardagi af Abraham, en endaðisk þá er Pharao konungr ok allr hans herr drukknaði í hafinu rauða. Fimti bardagi var undir gefnu lǫgmáli millum guðs þjónustumanna ok heiðingja. Þessi byrjaðisk á Josue, en endaðisk undir inum friðsama konungi Salomone. Sétta stríð var undir konungum ok spámǫnnum millum Gyðinga ok Babilonios. Þessi bardagi byrjaðisk á Roboam ok Jeroboam, en endaðisk undir inum friðsama keisara Augusto. Í þessum bardaga féllu formenn *primitive ecclesie*, þat eru spámenn, ok fengu sígr ok fagrliga kórónu.

The first battle was in the hall of heaven between the highest Emperor and the greatest Viking, when the Viking wished to acquire and seize the Emperor's power and become like the most high. In this battle, the Queen, that is angelic nature, joined with the Viking and abandoned the bridegroom, but tied herself to the adulterer. And because of that, both the adulterer and adulteress were thrown into the prison of exile in hell forever [...] The second battle took place in the time of giants between the sons of God and the sons of men, that is to say between Abel and Seth and his descendants, and Cain and his descendants or offspring. Those descended from Seth are called sons of God, and those descended from Cain [are called] sons of men. In this battle, Abel the standard-bearer fell and gained the victory and a heavenly crown. This battle ended in Noah's Flood. The third battle was in the time of those who built the tower of Babel, between freed men and slaves. This battle began with Ham and Shem and ended with the division of tongues. The fourth battle was in the time of the patriarchs between those who were circumcised and those who were not. This battle began with Abraham and ended when Pharaoh and all his army drowned in the Red Sea. The fifth battle was in the time of the Mosaic law between God's servants and heathens. It began with Joshua and ended under the peaceful king Solomon. The sixth fight was in the time of kings and prophets, between Jews and Babylonians. This battle began with Rehoboam and Jeroboam and ended under the peaceful Emperor Augustus. In this battle fell the leaders of the *primitive ecclesie*, that is prophets, and gained the victory and a beautiful crown.

He then goes on to summarise salvation history from the birth of Christ to the present in six further battles, which correspond in various ways to the

Types and Shadows

first six: the first martyr Stephen, for example, corresponds to Abel, and the passion and resurrection of Christ are described as a battle between Christ and the Viking. Collings comments that no source has been identified for this passage, but Augustine's *City of God* must be the model for how each period of history is divided between two opposing forces: I have found nothing in this passage that could not have come from a free adaptation of that source, including the understanding of 'sons of gods' as Seth's descendants, the division between 'freed men' and 'slaves', and the idea of the prophets as leaders of the 'primitive ecclesie'.[91] Perhaps the chivalric colouring is the compiler's own; it certainly corresponds closely to a variety of other lengthy chivalric metaphors in the saga, and a general delight in highly metaphorical language.[92] Above all, it is a wonderfully imaginative way of getting an audience to absorb a large quantity of Old Testament history, recast as a series of exciting battles featuring emperors, queens, adulterers, Vikings, giants and standard-bearers – precisely the content of 'skrǫksǫgur'.

Conclusion

In the homilies and saints' lives, Old Testament narrative struggles to escape the constraints of allegorical interpretation, although there are moments where it does so successfully, either because the narrative has been separated from the allegory, as in some of Gregory's *Homilies*, or because the story functioned more or less effectively as a moral exemplum, as in the case of the sacrifice of Isaac. But it is striking that, from very early on, both homilists and hagiographers clearly signal different levels of exegesis – literal or allegorical – by varying their level of style. The literal or historical level tends to be written in a 'plain' style, like that recommended by Augustine and Gregory ('sermo humilis') and in some cases this style resembles closely the style of the Icelandic sagas. We see it particularly in the homilies, where some homilists engage their audiences and keep their attention by exploiting the resources of vernacular storytelling. The style of these passages is, in many ways, close to the oldest style of the Hebrew Bible, although the Icelanders could hardly have known this. Allegorical exegesis, on the other hand, is associated with poetry, and both homilists and hagiographers draw on poetic resources, like alliteration, rhyme and assonance, when presenting allegorical interpretations of the Old Testament. In both homilies and saints' lives, then,

---

[91] Collings, 'Codex Scardensis', 114–15, 131–32; Augustine of Hippo, *De civitate Dei*, bks 15–17; *City of God*, trans. Henry Bettenson (London: Penguin, 2003), 594–760.

[92] Collings, 'Codex Scardensis', 283. See, for example, the skilful (and deliberately misleading) depiction of the saint as knight in *Tveggja postula saga Jóns ok Jakobs*, 585.

we find an alternation between 'saga-like' narrative and poetic passages of allegory. In addition, from the second half of the thirteenth century on, Icelandic hagiographers were very much aware of the competition that they faced from secular sagas, and this shaped the kinds of material they chose to include: the recensions of *Maríu saga* show an interest in extra-biblical material and Jewish traditions, while the compiler of *Tveggja postula saga Jóns ok Jakobs* goes out of his way to liven up the history of the world for an audience familiar with the legendary sagas. As biblical narrative loosens itself from the ties of patristic allegory, it starts to move into the realm of history. So, in the next chapter, I turn to the retelling of biblical stories in universal histories and encyclopaedic literature.

⤳ 4 ⤶

World History and Biblical History: Exegesis and Encyclopaedic Writing

Universal history and encyclopaedic writing were closely bound up in the Middle Ages with biblical exegesis.[1] In his *De doctrina christiana*, Augustine recommended history as an aid to biblical interpretation, since everything that has been done belongs 'to the history of time, whose creator and controller is God'.[2] He linked the six days of Creation to the six Ages of the World, giving it an organic unity, and this scheme was taken up and disseminated by Isidore of Seville and Bede the Venerable.[3] Likewise, Jerome, who translated Eusebius's world chronicle into Latin, proposed on the basis of a reading of Daniel that world history could be divided into four universal monarchies, the last of which was that of Rome.[4] In both these cases, the Bible provided a model for the schematisation of world history. The patristic interest in finding principles of unity and coherence in historical

---

[1] Mary Franklin-Brown, *Reading the World: Encyclopedic Writing in the Scholastic Age* (Chicago and London: University of Chicago Press, 2012), 46, 59; Michele Campopiano, 'Introduction', in *Universal Chronicles in the High Middle Ages*, ed. Michele Campopiano (York: York Medieval Press, 2017), 17.

[2] Augustine, *De doctrina Christiana* ii. 28, trans. Green, 56.

[3] Augustine, *De genesis contra Manichaeos*, i. 35, translated in *Saint Augustine, On Genesis: On Genesis: A Refutation of the Manichees, Unfinished Literal Commentary on Genesis, The Literal Meaning of Genesis*, trans. Edmund Hill, ed. John E. Rotell (Hyde Park, NY: New Press, 2002), 62–67.

[4] Saint Jerome, *Commentaire sur Daniel*, ed. Régis Courtray (Paris: Les Éditions du Cerf, 2019), 292; an English translation can be found in *Jerome's Commentary on Daniel: A Study of Comparative Jewish and Christian Interpretations of the Hebrew Bible*, ed. Jay Braverman (Washington, DC: Catholic Bible Association of America, 1978), 90. See Maria Ana Travassos Valdez, *Historical Interpretations of the 'fifth empire': The Dynamics of Periodization from Daniel to António Vieira, S.J.* (Leiden: Brill, 2011), 53–67, 159–66.

events was strengthened by Hugh of St Victor's development of a theology of history that embraced a sense of movement and process; his *Chronicon*, written for students of theology in Paris, includes historical and geographical information relevant not just to the Bible, but to classics like Sallust and Lucan, which were read in the cathedral schools.[5] Comestor's *Historia scholastica*, through its inclusion of non-biblical 'incidentiae', opened the way for the harmonisation of secular and sacred history and sparked off a number of universal histories in the vernacular, as discussed in Chapter 2 (p. 62). Likewise, Vincent of Beauvais's encyclopaedic *Speculum maius* follows the order of Scripture as its unifying principle: the *Speculum Naturale* is concerned with Creation and the meaning of things, the *Speculum doctrinale* with the moral consequences of the Fall, and the *Speculum historiale* with human history.[6] As Franklin-Brown has shown, its main aim was to aid in the 'spiritual interpretation of Scripture', completing the imagined project laid out by Augustine in his *De doctrina christiana*: it adheres to 'an Augustinian model in which the writing of encyclopaedias was connected to the study of Scripture'.[7] In this chapter, I examine how universal histories and other encyclopaedic works in Old Norse-Icelandic make use of Old Testament material. In particular, I want to tease out how authors select biblical stories, and how they negotiate the relationship between history and allegory.

The World's Saga

The earliest universal history in Old Norse-Icelandic is *Veraldar saga*, a history of the world in six ages which is conventionally dated to c. 1155–90 because it ends with a reference to Holy Roman Emperor Frederick I Barbaross, who reigned in 1155–90.[8] It shares some of its material with *Rómverja saga*, and so is often grouped with other secular histories, including *Rómverja saga*, *Breta sǫgur*, *Alexanders saga* and *Trójumanna saga*.[9] However, it appears not be a translation of any one source, which would make it one of the earliest original works in the vernacular. Although it is usually classified as historiography,

5 Southern, 'Aspects', 167; Mortensen, 'Hugh of St Victor', 4.
6 There is no critical edition of Vincent of Beauvais's *Speculum historiale*; however, an annotated edition based on manuscript Douai Bibliothèque municipale 797 is available online at: http://sourcencyme.irht.cnrs.fr/encyclopedie/speculum_historiale_versions_sm_trifaria_ms_douai_bm_797.
7 Franklin-Brown, *Reading the World*, 61–62. See also Monique Paulmier-Foucart, 'Vincent de Beauvais et l'histoire du *Speculum Maius*', *Journal des savants* 1–2 (1990), 107.
8 *Veraldar saga*, ed. Jakob Benediktsson (Copenhagen: Lunos, 1944), liii.
9 Stefanie Würth, 'History and Pseudo-History', in *A Companion to Old Norse-Icelandic Literature and Culture*, ed. Rory McTurk (Maldon, MA: Blackwell Publishing, 2005), 168–69.

World History and Biblical History

some manuscripts (the B-class) contain an appendix with allegorical readings of the Old Testament that seems to be integral rather than a later addition.[10] Marchand was not able to identify the source for this appendix, but it corresponds closely to part II of Richard of St Victor's *Liber exceptionum*, which circulated separately as 'Allegoriae in novum Testamentum', often alongside Comestor's *Historia scholastica*.[11] Given that much of the material in the first part of *Veraldar saga* is demonstrably from the *Historia scholastica*, it is tempting to conjecture that the model for the whole was a manuscript containing the *Historia scholastica* followed by Richard's 'Allegoriae' (which was often attributed to Hugh in medieval manuscripts). This has important consequences for how we read *Veraldar saga*: it may belong not under secular historiography but with textbooks for students and preachers that serve as an aid to biblical exegesis. Its connection with Gizurr Hallsson, who is mentioned at the very end, may suggest that it was used in the cathedral school at Skálholt which, as Bullita has shown, had close links to the abbey of St Victor in Paris from an early stage.[12]

The selection of Old Testament episodes in *Veraldar saga* certainly suggests that a major criterion was their potential for allegorical interpretation. The narratives in the first part and the allegories in the second part correspond closely to one another. So, for example, the creation of Eve out of the side of Adam translates Genesis 2.21–22: 'ór hans síðu sofanda tók guð eitt rif ok fylldi rúm rifsins með holdi; síðan samdi guð konu fagra ór rifinu' ('from his side while he was sleeping God took a rib, and filled the place of the rib with flesh, then God created a beautiful woman from the rib').[13] The allegorical explanation of this in the second part echoes the first: 'í því er Adam sofnaði ok var síðan kona samin ór rifi því er tekit var ór síðu hans sofanda, er sú jartegn at ór síðu sári dróttins várs, var heilǫg kristni saminn' ('when Adam fell asleep and a woman was made from the rib which was taken from his side while he was sleeping, this signifies that, from the wound in our Lord's side, the holy Church was made').[14] Some details only

---

[10] James W. Marchand, 'The Allegories in the Old Norse *Veraldar Saga*', *Michigan Germanic Studies* 1.1 (1975), 111. The oldest manuscript containing the allegories is AM 655 VIII 4to (c. 1175–1225).

[11] Marchand, 'Allegories', 112; Richard, *Liber exceptionum*, ed. Châtillon, 213–517. In PL 175, it is entitled 'Allegoriae in Novum Testamentum'.

[12] Dario Bullita, *Niðrstigningar saga: Sources, Transmission and Theology of the Old Norse 'Descent into Hell'* (Toronto: University of Toronto Press, 2017), 86–88.

[13] *Veraldar saga*, 5.

[14] *Veraldar saga*, 79; cf. Richard, *Liber exceptionum*, ii.I.7: 'Adam, Christus; dormitio Ade, passio Christi; conditio Eve, redemptio Ecclesie' ('Adam, Christ; Adam's sleep, the passion of Christ; the creation of Eve, the redemption of the Church').

The Old Testament in Medieval Icelandic Texts

take on their full meaning when we come to the allegories: for example, the author describes the branch carried by the dove returning to Noah's ark as 'viðsmjǫrskvist með grœnu laufi' ('an olive twig with a green leaf'). This detail is explained in the allegory: 'lauf þat it grœna er á kvistinum var merkir fagrar giptir heilags anda' ('the green leaf that was on the twig signifies the beautiful gifts of the Holy Spirit').[15] Sometimes the allegory even intrudes into the history: the author tells us that, when God commanded circumcision, Abraham 'markaði sik sjálfan því hreinlífis marki' ('marked himself with the sign of purity'). But to find out why it is a sign of purity, you need to turn to part two: 'Umskurðarskírn, sú er boðinn var Abraham, merkir hreinlífi góðra manna ok meinlæti, ok grandveri þeirra' ('Circumcision, which was commanded to Abraham, signifies the purity and abstinence of good men, and their innocence').[16] There are very few events in the first four ages of *Veraldar saga* that are not allegorised in the second part, and those events that are included without subsequent allegorisation are important originary events in their own right: the Fall of the Angels, the Fall of Man, the Tower of Babel. Likewise, the allegories contain very few details that are not present in the preceding history: the fire that Abraham and Isaac take with them for the sacrifice in Genesis 22, for example, is omitted from the first part, but included in the second. Likewise, in the first part, Rebecca plays no role in Jacob's deception of Isaac, but she does feature in the allegory. Indeed, the moral difficulty of this story is evaded in the first part, which tells us that Isaac blessed the wrong son, but not that Jacob and his mother conspired to engineer this very situation.

In the historical part of *Veraldar saga*, the author charts a clear moral course, no doubt in part because this facilitates the allegories of the second half. Abel, for example, is set up as the first martyr, a precursor to Stephen in the New Testament: 'Abel er dýrkaðr í ǫllum helgum bókum, ok er fyrir því frumváttr guðs, at hann var fyrst veginn heilagra manna fyrir guðs sakir' ('Abel is venerated in all holy books, and is God's protomartyr, because he was the first of the saints to be slain for God's sake').[17] There is a verbal echo of the Icelandic Homily Book here: 'Frumváttr guðs kallask Stephanus, því at hann tók fyrstr písl eptir Dróttin várn' ('Stephen is called God's protomartyr,

---

15   *Veraldar saga*, 12, 80. This sounds like a blend of the glosses on Gen. 8.8 and 11 from the *Glossa ordinaria*: Alcuin's identification of the dove with the Holy Spirit, and Strabo's identification of the leaf with 'munus pacis' ('the gift of peace'); see *Glossa ordinaria*, ed. Morard (Gen. 8.8, 8.11).

16   *Veraldar saga*, 17–18, 81; cf. Richard, *Liber exceptionum*, ii.II.5. Richard attributes three meanings to circumcision, which relate to the flesh, the soul and the body. The second is 'quando anima per depositionem iniquitatis circumciditur' ('when the soul is circumcised through giving up sin').

17   *Veraldar saga*, 9.

106

World History and Biblical History

because he was the first to suffer martyrdom after our Lord').[18] Likewise, the author includes the apocryphal episode about Abraham from the *Historia scholastica* in which Abraham and his brother are thrown into the Chaldean fire for refusing to sacrifice to idols: 'en eldrinn mátti ekki gera at Abraham fyrir sakir verðleika hans ok helgi' ('but the fire could not harm Abraham because of his worthiness and holiness').[19] Although this is a Jewish tradition that Jerome introduces into Latin scholarship, it is included here as evidence for Abraham's sanctity: he is described as 'svá mikill ástvinr guðs at hann er kallaðr dýrstr allra hǫfuðfeðra vára ok frá honum eru komnir allir guðs dýrlingar' ('such a dearly loved friend of God that he is called the most holy of all our patriarchs, and from him are descended all God's saints').[20] Enoch is also described as 'ástvinr' ('God's dear friend'), and Moses as 'guðs dýrlingr' ('God's holy one'), but, outside *Veraldar saga*, this first word is often and the second almost exclusively used of Christian saints.[21] The idea of the patriarchs as God's friends not only connects with the narratives of Christian saints after the birth of Christ, but also carries over into the allegorical section, where the six days of creation signify the six ages of the world 'á þeim er allir Guðs vinir skulu vinna ok fremja góð verk' ('in which all God's friends have a duty to do good works').[22] This is a unifying vision of salvation history which stretches across the incarnation, following the historical vision of Hugh of St Victor.

The strong moral stance means that the stories are well told with a clear eye for intentions and motivation. When narrating the Fall, for example, the author uses details from Comestor to specify that Eve takes the apple 'bæði af ágirni ok veggirni' ('both out of greed and pride').[23] Cain is said to act out of envy towards Abel, and cared nothing for ('hafði at engu') God's warning.[24] The builders of the Tower of Babel wish to avoid another flood:

> Þá urðu þau tiltœki nǫkkurra manna, at þeir gerðu kastala ok þat mannvirki, at þeir hugðusk mundu ganga í himin upp, því at þeir spurðu til þess, at guð hafði drekkt ǫllum heimi í Nóaflóði, er fólkit var illa siðat, ok hugðusk mundu geta sín við flóðinu, en ætluðu sér ekki bella mega.

---

[18] *Homilíubók*, 177.

[19] *Veraldar saga*, 15. On this story, see further Benjamin Williams, 'Glossa ordinaria and Glossa hebraica midrash in Rashi and the Gloss', *Traditio* 71 (2016), 179–201.

[20] *Veraldar saga*, 16.

[21] *DONP*, s.v. 'ástvinr' and 'dýrlingr', at https://onp.ku.dk/onp/onp.php?o5133 and https://onp.ku.dk/onp/onp.php?o16127 (accessed 16 December 2021).

[22] *Veraldar saga*, 79.

[23] *Veraldar saga*, 7; Comestor, *Liber Genesis*, 43–44.

[24] *Veraldar saga*, 9.

The Old Testament in Medieval Icelandic Texts

Then it was the plan of certain people to build a tower and a great monument that they intended to reach up to heaven, because they heard that God had drowned the whole world in Noah's flood, when people had evil customs, and thought they would protect themselves from the flood, and believed that nothing could bring them down.

This is a nice development of Comestor's 'timentes diluuium' ('fearing a flood') with its lively sense of how the memory of a past event might persist and the dramatic irony of the builders of the Tower of Babel thinking that 'nothing can bring them down'.[25] With more complex stories, however, the author struggles: the best that he can do with King Saul is to comment that 'hann var góðr ǫndverða æfi sína en illr ofanverða' ('he was good for the early part of his life, and evil later on').[26] Likewise, David is described as a heroic figure who suffers Saul's unjust persecution 'vel ok þolinmóðliga' ('well and patiently'), which enables his later identification with Christ: 'David konungr jarteinir Krist í lítillæti sínu, ok í þolinmœði' ('King David signifies Christ in his humility and in patience').[27] But his adultery with Bathsheba is mentioned only briefly and out of chronological order as an explanation for Absalom's rebellion; neither Bathsheba nor Uriah are named.

Perhaps the best story in the saga – and certainly the longest – is that of Joseph and his brothers, a family drama that the author clearly appreciated. It is full of complex emotions: Jacob's favouritism in loving Joseph most, his brothers' envy when they realise this, their 'óþokki' ('displeasure') when Joseph insists on telling them his dreams, Jacob's inconsolable grief when he believes Joseph to be dead, the illegitimate desire of Potiphar's wife. When Joseph's brothers arrive in Egypt, the author plays on the different levels of knowledge displayed by different characters in the story: 'þeir gengu fyrir Iosep ok lutu honum sem aðrir menn ok kenndu hann eigi. En hann kenndi þá ok hafði þó tulk á meðal þeira ('they went before Joseph and bowed to him like other men and did not recognise him. But he recognised them and yet used an interpreter to speak to them').[28] What motivates this charade on Joseph's part we are not told, nor why he holds his brothers in chains and makes them 'gagnhræddir' ('very frightened'). It is not until they return for a second time with Joseph's brother Benjamin that the emotions once again become legible: the brothers are 'stórfegnir' ('delighted') when they discover who Joseph is and there is 'fagnafundr' ('a joyful meeting') between father

---

25 Comestor, *Liber Genesis*, 75.
26 *Veraldar saga*, 31.
27 *Veraldar saga*, 32, 85.
28 *Veraldar saga*, 22–23.

World History and Biblical History

and son.[29] Perhaps the author was responding to the romance structure of the story with Joseph's dramatic rise from 'rags to riches' and the emotion of the separation and reunion scenes. It certainly receives far more attention than is necessary for the brief anti-Semitic allegory attached to it: 'Josep merkir herra Xpm í því er hann var hataðr af brœðrum sínum, svá sem dróttinn var af gyðingum' ('Joseph signifies the Lord Christ in that he was hated by his brothers, just as the Lord was by the Jews').[30] If anything, the main narrative diverts us from this allegorical interpretation by enabling us to understand the brothers' hurt feelings and experience their fear.

Many of the author's allegories are based on Richard of St Victor's, and those that diverge are paralleled in the *Glossa ordinaria*. On a couple of occasions, however, the author has developed his allegories in ways that are unique to him. On the pillar of cloud and fire, for example, Richard of St Victor simply directs us to the humanity and divinity of Christ.[31] The Gloss adds some further possibilities, including the following from Gregory's *Moralia*: 'In igne, terror. In nube, visionis lene blandimentum. Dies, vita iusti. Nox, peccatoris' ('In fire, terror; in cloud, a gentle delight to the eyes. Day, the life of the just; night, of the sinner').[32] In *Veraldar saga*, the pillar signifies Christ, who is described as 'ógurligr svá sem eldrinn vándum mǫnnum, er nóttin merkir, en blíðr ok þekkiligr svá sem bjart ský vinum sínum, er dagrinn merkir' ('terrifying as fire to evil men, signified by the night, but gentle and pleasant as a bright cloud to his friends, signified by the day').[33] The parallelism is carefully carried through and the idea of the 'bright cloud', while it may perhaps be a reminiscence of Comestor's 'nubes lucida' ('shining cloud'), captures how a brightening in the day – a single cloud illumined by the sun – leads to a lightening of one's spirits.[34] Then there is Richard's gloss on the fabrics used in the construction of the tabernacle in Exodus 38–39. He specifies that 'pelles jacintine viros celestem vitam agentes' ('the blue cloths [are] men leading a celestial life') and 'saga, quia sunt aspera penitentie, designant asperitatem' ('the sheepskins, that are rough in the same way as penitence, represent austerity of life').[35] This is beautifully developed in the Norse translation:[36]

---

29 *Veraldar saga*, 23.
30 *Veraldar saga*, 82. See Richard, *Liber exceptionum*, ii.II.15: 'Invidia decem fratrum erga Joseph innocentum et justum, est invidia Judeorum erga Christum' ('The hatred of the ten brothers for Joseph, the innocent and just, is the hatred of the Jews towards Christ').
31 Richard, *Liber exceptionum*, ii.III.2.
32 *Glossa ordinaria,* ed. Morard (Ex. 13. 22).
33 *Veraldar saga*, 83.
34 Comestor, *Liber Genesis*, 9, 15.
35 Richard, *Liber exceptionum*, ii.III.9.
36 *Veraldar saga*, 83–84.

The Old Testament in Medieval Icelandic Texts

Vefir þeir inir fǫgru, er tjaldat var innan tjaldit, merkja þá Guðs vini er sitja í skjóli kristninnar, ok hafa sitt skap eigi við veður um vandræði alþýðunnar, ok verðr af því atferð þeirra glaðfǫgr. En vaðmál ok gærur þær er tjaldit var þakit með, merkir þá menn er sitja fyrir ágangi alþýðu, ok taka svá við vandræðum manna, sem vaðmálin tóku við moldryki ok við skúrum ok skíni.

The beautiful fabrics, which were hung inside the tabernacle, signify those friends of God who sit in the shelter of the Church and have no mind to get scent of ['hafa við veður'] the troubles of the populace, and on account of this, their way of life will be happy and beautiful. But the homespun and sheepskin that the tabernacle is covered with signify those who are exposed to the aggression of the common people and absorb their troubles just as the homespun absorbed dirt and showers and sunshine.

Again, the parallelism – accentuated by alliteration on 'v' and 's' – is carefully set up: 'vefir' ('woven fabrics') versus plain 'vaðmál ok gærur' ('homespun and sheepskin'). God's friends 'sitja í skjóli' ('sit in shelter'), while others 'sitja fyrir' ('are exposed') to the elements; God's friends 'hafa sitt skap eigi við veðr um vandræði alþýðunna ('have no desire to get scent of the troubles of the populace'), while the others 'taka svá við vandræðum manna sem vaðmálin tóku við moldryki ok við skúrum ok skíni' ('absorb people's troubles just as the homespun absorbed dirt and showers and sunshine'). The wordplay depends on specifically Icelandic idioms: the polyvalence of 'sitja' ('to sit', 'to be exposed to') and the pun on 'veðr', which aurally recalls 'vefr'. Literally, it refers to weather (the 'showers and sunshine' that stain the homespun), but, metaphorically, it means something like 'to get scent of', perhaps alluding to the overpowering smell of the outsiders' dirty clothes. The contrast between shelter and exposure, together with the homely image of weather-stained homespun, infuses the allegory with realism and familiarity.

The Ages of the World

Closely related to *Veraldar saga* is a short text entitled *Heimsaldrar*, found in AM 194 8vo which dates to c. 1387. Stefán Karlsson has dated the text itself to the early twelfth century, suggesting on the basis of some parallels in phrasing that it may have been written by Ari Þorgilsson; this seems unlikely, however, in view of its dependence on the *Historia scholastica*.[37] Like *Veraldar saga*, it uses the six ages to organise biblical history, but it has

---

37 Stefán Karlsson, 'Fróðleiksgreinar frá tólftu öld', in *Afmælisrit Jóns Helgasonar 30. júní 1969*, ed. Jakob Benediktsson et al. (Reykjavík: Heimskringla, 1969), 348–49.

World History and Biblical History

no Creation and Fall narrative, and it ends abruptly with the birth of Christ at the end of the fifth age. Most of the history, by the author's own admission, takes the form of genealogy or 'langfeðgatal'.[38] While most of the stories from *Veraldar saga* are drastically reduced, there are also a few additions, which distinguish it from its close relation.

The first is the account of Cain, who as exile and city-builder commands much more interest than Abel for the author of *Heimsaldrar*. He tells us that:[39]

> Kain Adams son var rekinn frá ǫðrum mǫnnum eptir víg Abels bróður síns, sem guð bauð, ok fór hann þar til, er hann kom á Indialand, þar nam hann stað, ok gerði þar borg ok gaf henni nafn sonar síns ok kallaði hana Enos, sú var borg fyrst í heimi. Kain gaf sér konungs nafn ok girndisk fyrstr allra manna til þessa heimsmetorða. Kain tók fyrstr allra manna fyrir ofríkis sakir at rǫngu þat, er aðrir menn áttu, ok þóttisk hann af því [...] at gera, at hann mætti óhræddr um sik vera. At honum námu margir þeir, er annarra eign tóku, ok hurfu fyrir því honum til handa ok gerðu borg með honum.

> Adam's son, Cain, was driven away from other people after the killing of his brother Abel, as God commanded, and he travelled until he came to India, where he stopped and built a city and gave it the name of his son and called it Enos; that was the first city in the world. Cain called himself a king and was the first person to desire worldly rank. Cain was the first person to take wrongly by tyranny what belonged to other people, and he thought [...] so that he would not need to fear for his safety. To him resorted many of those who took others' belongings and because of this they flocked to his side and made a city with him.

Some of this information comes from the *Historia scholastica*, although it is omitted by the author of *Veraldar saga*, who is more interested in Abel as saint. According to Comestor, Cain travelled to a place called either Nayda (Josephus) or Nod (Jerome), where he built a city which he named after his son Enoch.[40] Comestor then cites Josephus on how Cain's way of life descended into robbery, violence and corruption, how he gathered other criminals who perpetuated this lifestyle, and fortified his city out of fear for his own security.[41] Some of this information may be jumbled up; elsewhere it is Nimrod who is first to call himself king. Cain's desire for worldly honour,

---

[38] 'Heimsaldrar', in *Alfræði Íslenzk: Islandsk encyclopædisk litteratur*, ed. Kristian Kålund, 3 vols (Copenhagen: Møller, 1908–18), I, 45–54.

[39] 'Heimsaldrar', 46. A few words are unreadable where the manuscript page is damaged.

[40] Comestor, *Liber Genesis*, 52–3.

[41] See Josephus, *Antiquities*, I.ii.2 at https://www.latinjosephus.org/antiquities/ (accessed 20 July 2023).

The Old Testament in Medieval Icelandic Texts

on the other hand, may be related to Jerome's well-known etymologising of his name as 'possessio uel adquisitio' ('possession or acquisition').[42] But the author's interest in this first city and the life of crime it spawns is very striking given how reticent he is about key biblical figures like Noah, Isaac and Jacob.

The author has more to say about the children of Lamech, 'vándr maðr' ('an evil man') – Jabal, Jubal, Tubal-Cain and Naamah – who wrote on tablets of marble and clay so that the knowledge and skills they had acquired would survive:[43]

> Þat er sagt, at þeir brœðr reyndu íþróttir sínar á marmarasteinum ok eldteknu leiri því, er eld mátti standask, ok ætluðu at marmarinn skyldi kenna mǫnnum íþróttirnar, þeim er síðar váru í heiminum, ef af sjóvar gangi eða vatna fœrisk mestr hluti manna, sem fyrir var spát, en ef eldr eyddi heimsbygðinni, þá skyldi nema af leirinu, því at leirinn mátti standask eldinn en eigi vatnit, en marmarinn stóðsk vatnit en eigi eldinn.

> It is said, that the brothers tried out their skills on marble stones and hardened clay that could withstand fire, and intended that the marble should teach these skills to later inhabitants of the world, if a great majority of people were to perish in the rising sea or floodwaters, as had been prophesied, and if fire laid waste to the region of the world, then they should learn from the clay, because clay could withstand fire but not water, and marble withstood water but not fire.

Again this is expanded from Comestor, who took it from Josephus.[44] According to Comestor and Josephus, Adam's prophecy, made after the deep sleep in which Eve was created, prompts the invention of two pillars or tablets, one made of marble, the other clay; elsewhere this prophecy is attributed to Enoch, who is also credited with the art of writing or 'rúnastafir' ('rune staves').[45] Whereas Josephus attributes the two tablets to the descendants of Seth, the Icelandic author follows Comestor's account, whereby the tablets are made by the descendants of Cain; for him, all technology is suspect. The final long addition is on the Tower of Babel, which is conflated with the history of Babylon:[46]

---

[42] Jerome, *Liber interpretationes hebraicorum nominum*, CCSL 72, 63.

[43] 'Heimsaldrar', 47.

[44] Comestor, *Liber Genesis*, 54–55; Josephus, *Antiquities* I.ii.3.

[45] See Andrei A. Orlov, 'Overshadowed by Enoch's Greatness: "Two Tablets" Traditions from the *Book of Giants* to the *Palaea Historica*', *Journal for the Study of Judaism* 32.1–4 (2001), 137–58.

[46] 'Heimsaldrar', 48. On Nimrod, see Karel van den Toorn and Pieter van der Horst, 'Nimrod before and after the Bible', *Harvard Theological Review* 83.1 (1990), 1–29.

World History and Biblical History

En stǫpul þann gerði Heimrod risi ok margir risar aðrir með honum. Heimrod var XXX alna hár. Borg var útan um stǫpulinn, ok var sú síðan kǫlluð Babilon, er jafnan er getit í bókum, hon var ummáls fyrir innan veggi þriggja þúsunda ins sjaunda tigar skrifa. Veggir um borgina váru L alna þykkir ok váru VII spenndar alnar, en CC alna váru háfir borgar veggir, hundrað hliða er á borginni ok eiri gert um ǫll hliðin. Í borginni stóð stǫpullinn, hann hét Babel, þat ætluðu risarnir, at hann skyldi verða svá hár, at hann tœki upp í himna, hann var fjǫgurra þúsunda [skrifa] hár.

And Heimrod the giant made that tower, and many other giants with him. Heimrod was 30 cubits high. The city surrounded the tower, and it has since been called Babylon, which is frequently mentioned in books; its circumference on the inside walls was 6,300 paces. The walls of the city were 50 cubits thick and their span 7 cubits, and the walls of the city were 200 cubits high; there were one hundred gates to the city and all the gates [were] covered in bronze. In the city stood the tower, which was called Babel, and the giants intended it to be so high that it would reach up to heaven; it was four thousand [paces] high.

The measurements of the city of Babylon are ultimately from Herodotus, but the author has probably got them from Honorius Augustodunensis's *Imago mundi*, which says that Babylon was established 'by the giant Nymrod', a tradition also found elsewhere.[47] All in all, the author of *Heimsaldrar* seems to have little or no interest in allegory or morals, but he does have a sharp eye for stories about exotic locations, arcane knowledge and technological feats. All these stories pit human invention against divine power and, unusually, in the story of the marble and clay pillars, human invention wins out. The siblings may all die in the Flood, but human knowledge – through the technology of writing – survives.

Universal History for Nuns

The most impressive 'history of the world' to survive in Old Icelandic is found in AM 764 4to, a manuscript made for (and possibly by) the nuns of Reynistaðr in the north of Iceland in c. 1362–72.[48] The Old Testament section (ages 1–5) consists mainly of abbreviated passages from the Bible interspersed with encyclopaedic material, but it does include a translation of Daniel 5 and – uniquely – the whole of the deuterocanonical book of Judith.

---

[47] Honorius Augustodunensis, *De imagine mundi libri tres*, i.15; PL 172, 125.

[48] Svanhildur Óskarsdóttir, 'What Icelandic Nuns Read: The Convent of Reynistaður and the Literary Milieu of Fourteenth-Century Iceland', in *Nuns' Literacies in Medieval Europe: The Kansas City Dialogue*, ed. Virginia Blanton, Veronica O'Mara and Patricia Stoop (Turnhout: Brepols, 2015), 235–39.

The Old Testament in Medieval Icelandic Texts

Its sources include Gregory's *Dialogues*, Isidore's *Etymologies*, Comestor's *Historia scholastica*, Honorius Augustodunensis's *Imago mundi* and possibly his *Elucidarius* and *Speculum Ecclesiae*, from which most of the cosmology comes.[49] The author seems to have used translations whenever these were available: *Stjórn III* is the source for the biblical material from Joshua to 2 Kings, and Svanhildur Óskardóttir has argued that the translation of Judith is much earlier than the manuscript, dating perhaps to the thirteenth century.[50] In fact, it looks as if the author either did not have access to Genesis in Latin, or did not feel the need to use it. When telling the story of Noah's Flood, for example, (s)he comments, at the very end, that: 'Svá segisk ok at guð hafi þessi orð talat: iðrar mik at ek hefi gert manninn' ('It is also said that God spoke these words: I regret that I made man').[51] The fact that this is out of sequence, together with the expression 'svá segisk' ('it is said'), suggests that (s)he did not know that these words come from the biblical book of Genesis, perhaps because (s)he is working primarily from a vernacular summary and/ or from secondary works.

The difference from *Veraldar saga* is striking, although the two chronicles do have one passage in common: Abraham's escape from the Chaldean fire, which is almost word for word the same. Otherwise, many of the key scenes from *Veraldar saga* are missing: the Fall of Man is radically abbreviated, as is Cain's killing of Abel; Noah's Flood is missing the raven and the dove, and Noah's drunkenness has disappeared entirely; there is no account of Abraham's sacrifice of Isaac; and Joseph's meteoric rise has been cut to a couple of sentences. The story of Moses omits all the 'wonders' of the wilderness (the rock at Horeb, the manna from Heaven, the bronze serpent), while David's lacks his persecution at the hands of Saul. On the other hand, AM 764 4to includes other details that *Veraldar saga* omits, most noticeably the names of the women in these stories: Noah's wife Poarpa (Phuapara) and his daughters-in-law Katafloa (Cataflua), Parphia (Pharphia) and Fliva; Abraham's wives Sarah, Hagar and Keturah; Isaac's wife Rebecca, Jacob's wives Leah and Rachel (together with the detail that she is 'óbyrja' or 'barren'), Joseph's wife Asenath and Moses' mother Jochebed and wife Sephora (or Zipporah).[52] Likewise, while the

---

49 Svanhildur Óskarsdóttir, 'What Icelandic Nuns Read', 240–41.
50 Svanhildur Óskarsdóttir, 'The Book of Judith: A Medieval Icelandic Translation', *Gripla* 11 (2000), 94. There is also an edition of Judith in modern Icelandic spelling in *Júdít*, ed. Svanhildur Óskarsdóttir (Reykjavík: Stofnun Árna Magnússonar í íslenskum fræðum, 2020).
51 Svanhildur Óskarsdóttir, 'Universal History in Fourteenth-Century Iceland: Studies in AM 764 4to', PhD thesis, University of London, 2000, 247; cf. Gen. 6.7 'paenitet enim me fecisse eos' ('for it repenteth me that I have made them').
52 Svanhildur Óskarsdóttir, 'Universal History', 247–49.

World History and Biblical History

burning bush is missing from Moses's story, the author has not forgotten that Pharaoh's daughter saved his life:[53]

> Ok er hann var iij mánaða gamall var hann látinn koma. Konungr bauð tortíma ǫllum sveinbǫrnum. Honum gaf nafn dóttir Pharaonis, er hon fann hann fljótanda í polli árinnar. Kenndi hon at hann var af ebresku kyni. Hon gaf honum nafn, at hann skuli Moses heita, því at Moys þýðir vatn.

> When he was three months old, he was left out to die. The king commanded that all male infants should be killed. Pharaoh's daughter gave him a name, when she found him floating in a deep part of the river. She realised that he was of Hebrew descent. She gave him the name of Moses because Mos means water.

As Svanhildur has shown, this sensitivity to the experience of women is noticeable through the compilation, and surely reflects the needs of its intended audience.[54]

Unlike *Veraldar saga*, the compilation shows no interest in reading Old Testament stories allegorically. But it does include a number of complex and difficult narratives about violence perpetrated by or against women. The most horrifying of these is the rape of the Levite's concubine from Judges 19:[55]

> Svá bar til í borg Gabaon, at sǫfnuðusk saman œskumenn ok tóku unga manns konu ok þrøngðu henni til saurlífis svá at þeir gengu at henni dauðri ok til minningar þvílíks glœps skiptu þeir [marginal note: hǫfðingjar þessa staðar] hennar líkam í xij partes, sendandi sérhvern hlut xij ættum israels lýðs.

> It happened in the town of Gibeah that some youths banded together and took a young man's wife and forced her to have sex and assaulted her until she was dead and, in memory of this crime, they [the leaders of that place] divided her body into twelve parts, sending each part to one of the twelve tribes of Israel.

---

53 Svanhildur Óskarsdóttir, 'Universal History', 249.
54 Svanhildur Óskarsdóttir, 'Arctic Garden of Delights: The Purpose of the Book of Reynistaður', in *Romance and Love in Late Medieval and Early Modern Iceland*, ed. Kirsten Wolf, Johanna Denzin and Marianne E. Kalinke (Ithaca, NY: Cornell University Press, 2008), 279–301; 'What Icelandic Nuns Read', 246.
55 Svanhildur Óskarsdóttir, 'Universal History', 250. Both AM 764 4to and *Stjórn III* take this story not directly from Judges 19, but via the retelling in Honorius Augustodunensis, *Speculum Ecclesiae* (PL 172, 837), where it is given an allegorical interpretation: the young man is Christ, his wife or concubine is the Church, riven by heretics in Gibeah, which is the world. There is no hint of this allegorical level in AM 764 4to.

The Old Testament in Medieval Icelandic Texts

The effect of this without any of the surrounding story is stark and senseless: there is nothing to explain why such a crime takes place and there appears to be no reckoning, even though *Stjórn III* – the immediate source – does include the bloodbath that follows, leading to the death of more innocent women and children. Moreover, the relocation of the story to the beginning rather than the end of Judges, as in *Stjórn III*, means that, rather than showing the extent to which society has broken down by this point, it instead sets the tone for what will follow. In AM 764 4to, it becomes the prelude to a number of violent acts perpetrated by women. The first of these, which follows immediately, is the death of Gideon's illegitimate son Abimelech: 'honum varð þat at bana at kona felldi kvernstein í hǫfuð honum' ('the cause of his death was that a woman dropped a millstone on his head'). The irony of this becomes clear when one realises what the author has (perhaps deliberately) omitted: in *Stjórn III*, Abimelech asks his servant to kill him 'at eigi segisk kona hafa veitt mér líflát' ('so that it is not said that a woman caused my death').[56] This is then followed by an account of the reason for Samson's defeat: 'Hann var svikinn ok blindaðr af einni pútu er Dalila hét' ('he was deceived and blinded by a prostitute who was called Delilah'). Although the story of Sisera and Jael is not told at this point, it is added later on in the compilation: 'þá var drepinn Sisare konungr með þeim hætti, at sú kona er Iabel hét setti nagla á vanga honum ok út um annan' ('then King Sisera was killed in this manner, that a woman called Jael put a nail through his cheek and out through the other').[57] Beginning this sequence of stories with the rape and mutilation of the anonymous woman at Gibeah poses the question of whether there is a causal relationship between atrocities against women and female violence against men. While the language of the rape is unambiguously negative, there is no such moral polarisation in the case of Jael or Abimelech's killer. The author seems all too aware that, as a rule, it is women who are the unacknowledged victims. When, in punishment for King David's sin, God sends a pestilence that kills 70,000 men, (s)he adds in a devastating aside: 'en ótaldar konur ok bǫrn' ('and uncounted women and children').[58] When Judith prays for help against Holofernes, she recalls the rape in war of 'meyjar ok konur' ('maidens and women') and the capture of 'konur' ('wives') and 'dœtr' ('daughters') as booty.[59]

This concern with women's involvement in male politics, and particularly in acts of violence, may explain the inclusion of the whole book of Judith,

---

56 *Stjórn*, 633. Cf. Judges 9.54: 'evagina gladium tuum et percute me ne forte dicatur quod a femina interfectus sim' ('draw thy sword and kill me, lest it should be said that I was slain by a woman').

57 Svanhildur Óskarsdóttir, 'Universal History', 269.

58 Svanhildur Óskarsdóttir, 'Universal History', 251.

59 Svanhildur Óskarsdóttir, 'Judith', 109.

World History and Biblical History

which is translated from the Vulgate rather than from the Old Latin or the Septuagint.[60] As elsewhere in the manuscript, the translator shows little or no interest in allegorical readings, although (s)he is aware of Judith's role as an exemplar of chastity. Svanhildur notes that the translation is very much 'saga style', with no commentary or supplementary material: speeches are abridged, the poem at the end is omitted, and the syntax is overwhelmingly paratactic, tending towards idiomatic phraseology.[61] The most common type of addition is adverbials of time that facilitate the forward movement of the narrative: 'Eptir þat' ('After that'), 'því næst' ('next'), 'nú' ('now), 'síðan' ('then'), 'nú sem' ('now that'), and 'í þann tíma' ('at that time').[62] Characteristic too are moments when the translator condenses expressions of emotion, so that 'tremor etiam et horror invasit sensus eorum' ('dread and horror seized upon their minds') becomes quite simply 'ok óttuðusk' ('and they were afraid').[63] Likewise, the powerful irony of 'gloriabatur quasi potens in potentia exercitus sui' ('he gloried as a mighty one in the force of his army') becomes the objective statement: 'var hann þá mestr konungr látinn í austrvegi af sínu ríki' ('he was esteemed as the greatest king in the East on account of his power').[64]

At the same time, there is a clear desire to replicate the stylistic effects of the Latin where this is possible in Old Norse. So, for example, when the Latin uses wordplay, as in 'tunc exaltatum est regnum Nabuchodonosor et cor eius elatum est' ('Then was the kingdom of Nabuchodonosor exalted, and his heart was elevated'), the Old Norse replicates this through anaphora: 'óx mikit ríki Nabogodonosors ok óx mjǫk ofmetnaðr hans' ('Nebuchadnezzar's kingdom expanded greatly, and so did his pride').[65] The relationship between power and arrogance is explicit here. When the Latin uses polyptoton, the Old Norse reproduces it: 'et nomen tuum nominabitur' ('thy name shall be renowned') becomes 'þitt nafn mun nefnt á hverju land' ('your name will be named in every land').[66] When the Latin uses alliteration ('sine arcu et sagitta et absque scuta et gladio' – 'without bow and arrow, and without shield and sword'), the Old Norse follows suit, sometimes even using the

---

60 Svanhildur Óskarsdóttir, 'Judith', 80. On Jerome's version, see Elena Ciletti and Henrike Lähnemann, 'Judith in the Christian Tradition', in *The Sword of Judith: Judith Studies across the Disciplines*, ed. Kevin R. Brine, Elena Ciletti and Henrike Lähnemann (Cambridge: OpenBook Publishers, 2010), 41–46; Edmon Gallagher, 'Why Did Jerome Translate Tobit and Judith?', *Harvard Theological Review* 108.3 (2015), 356–75.

61 Svanhildur Óskarsdóttir, 'Judith', 88.

62 Svanhildur Óskarsdóttir, 'Judith', 95, 96, 98, 99, 107.

63 Judith 4.2; Svanhildur Óskarsdóttir, 'Judith', 98.

64 Judith 1.4; Svanhildur Óskarsdóttir, 'Judith', 95.

65 Judith 1.7; Svanhildur Óskarsdóttir, 'Judith', 95.

66 Judith 11.21; Svanhildur Óskarsdóttir, 'Judith', 113.

The Old Testament in Medieval Icelandic Texts

same sound: 'hvárki skjǫld né skeyti eða sverð' ('neither shield nor arrow or sword').[67] The Old Norse also imitates *similiter cadens* in the Latin: 'et hinc euntem et ibi commorantem et inde huc revertentem' ('both going hence, and abiding there, and returning from thence hither') becomes 'héðan farandi ok þar verandi ok hingat aptr hverfandi' ('going hence and staying there and returning back here').[68] This careful attention to some aspects of style in the Latin shows that the translator's changes to the syntax are quite deliberate, bringing Judith in line with the storytelling tradition of the sagas.

As Svanhildur has pointed out, the translator does use some unusual terminology, particularly for jewellery, exotic goods, and clothes.[69] But it is striking that many of these are concentrated in a single chapter – the one where Judith dresses up before going to Holofernes's camp. This is a complex moment from a moral point of view: Judith is setting out to seduce Holofernes through flaunting her female beauty, which is enhanced not only through artificial means but also through the power of God. The Old Norse has:[70]

> Kastaði af sér hárklæði ok reið á sik inni beztu mirru ok reyrði hár sitt ok klæddi sik dýrligum klæðum ok setti mítr á hǫfuð sér ok sandalia á fœtr sér ok tók yfir sik virðiliga skikkju ok svá hafði hon eyrnagull ok mǫrg fingrgull ok prýddi sik allri inni beztu prýði.

> [She] cast off her sackcloth and daubed herself in the finest myrrh and put up her hair and dressed herself in expensive clothes and set a headdress on her head and sandals on her feet, and put over her shoulders a valuable cloak, and she also wore earrings and many rings and decked herself in all the best finery.

Some words – 'mirra', 'mítr', 'sandalia' – are taken directly from Latin, while others ('eyrnagull', 'fingrgull') are quite rare in Old Norse.[71] The foreignness of the vocabulary underlines the foreignness of the seduction scene, as Judith enters self-consciously and undercover into a culture that is conspicuously other. In terms of Venuti's translation theory, one could say that the translator deliberately 'foreignises' here; rather than making the scene look more familiar to his readers, (s)he reproduces what is most alien about it. The same effect is generated when Judith enters Holofernes's presence for the first

---

67 Judith 5.16; Svanhildur Óskarsdóttir, 'Judith', 101.
68 Judith 13.20; Svanhildur Óskarsdóttir, 'Judith', 116.
69 Svanhildur Óskarsdóttir, 'Judith', 93.
70 Judith 10.3; Svanhildur Óskarsdóttir, 'Judith', 110.
71 All seven instances of 'eyrnagull' are from translated texts, primarily the Bible: see *DONP*, s.v. *eyrnagull*, at https://onp.ku.dk/onp/onp.php?o18871 (accessed 17 December 2021).

118

World History and Biblical History

time:[72] 'En er Judith leit Holofernem sitjanda í hjúpi þeim, er var af purpura ok gull ofinn ok settr bæði smaragdo ok ǫðrum dýrligum steinum, þá féll hon til fóta honum' ('And when Judith saw Holofernes sitting in his canopy which was woven of purple and gold, and studded with emeralds and other precious stones, she fell to his feet'). The rare word 'hjúpr' – which elsewhere in Icelandic seems to refer to a robe or shirt – and the Latin loan-word 'smaragdus' ('emerald') create a foreign and decadent feel to the scene, but, although Judith is out of place, she knows exactly what to do.

Judith moves between these two worlds with apparent ease, but at times the translator appears genuinely baffled by allusions to her sexual appeal. When Holofernes orders Bagao to fetch her, he tells him: 'Vade et suade Hebraeam illam ut sponte consentiat habitare mecum, foedum est enim apud Assyrios si femina inrideat virum agendo ut inmunis transeat ab eo' ('Go, and persuade that Hebrew woman, to consent of her own accord to dwell with me, for it is looked upon as shameful among the Assyrians, if a woman mock a man, by doing so as to pass free from him').[73] If Holofernes fails in his intended sexual conquest, it will be a slur to his masculinity. The translator, however, has struggled with the meaning of the adjective 'foedum' ('shameful') and opts to translate it instead as the noun 'foedus' ('treaty, covenant, law'). (S)he ends up with: 'þat er lǫgmál í Assyrie, ef kona gerir mein manni sínum, at hann láti hana eina' ('It is the law in Assyria if a woman does injury to her man that he leave her alone').[74] It is not entirely clear what this means, but it seems to imply that Judith is free to refuse Holofernes's advances – in line with his earlier insincere 'sponte' ('of her own accord', translated in the Old Norse as 'sjálfkrafa'). It is certainly not, as in the Latin, a thinly veiled implication that, if necessary, Judith will be coerced.

In fact, overall it is striking how the translator has reduced the frequent allusions in the Latin to the fact that in this story a woman overcomes a man. So, in chapter 9, Judith prays in the Latin 'capiatur laqueo oculorum suorum in me' ('let him be caught in the net of his own eyes in my regard') and looks forward to the moment when 'cum manus feminea deiecerit eum' ('he shall fall by the hand of a woman').[75] The Old Norse cuts exactly these two verses, although it keeps what comes before and after them both: Judith's prayer for constancy and fortitude, and that Holofernes may be killed by his own sword.[76] In chapter 13, the Latin 'interfecit in manu mea hostem populi

---

72   Judith 10.19; Svanhildur Óskarsdóttir, 'Judith', 111–12. For the concept of 'foreigni-sation', see Lawrence Venuti, *The Scandals of Translation: Towards an Ethics of Difference* (London: Routledge, 1998).

73   Judith 12.10–11.

74   Svanhildur Óskarsdóttir, 'Judith', 114.

75   Judith 9.13–15.

76   Svanhildur Óskarsdóttir, 'Judith', 109–10.

The Old Testament in Medieval Icelandic Texts

sui in hac nocte' ('he hath killed the enemy of his people by my hand this night') becomes simply 'drap hann várn andskota á þessi nótt' ('he killed our adversary on this night').[77] Likewise, when Judith brings out Holofernes's head to show the Israelites, she declares in the Latin: 'ecce caput Holofernis principis militiae Assyriorum et ecce conopeum illius in quo recumbebat in ebrietate sua ubi et per manum feminae percussit illum Dominus Deus noster' ('Behold the head of Holofernes, the general of the army of the Assyrians, and behold his canopy, wherein he lay in his drunkenness, where the Lord our God slew him by the hand of a woman').[78] The translator has defused this by moving the direct speech into narrative description: 'Síðan tók hon ór skreppuni hǫfuð Holofernis hershǫfðingja Assire manna ok svá hjúp hans ok mælti' ('Then she took out of the bag the head of Holofernes, leader of the army of Assyrians, and also his canopy, and spoke').[79] The vivid image of a woman killing a drunken and helpless man in his bed has completely disappeared.[80] Of the three references to the 'hand of a woman' in this scene, the translator has kept just one: 'hann sneið af sjálfr hǫfuð allra trúlausra manna á þessi nótt með minni hendi' ('he cut off the head of all unbelievers this night by my hand').[81] It is worth noting that, in this case, the 'head' is not Holofernes's literal head, but Holofernes himself as the 'head' of all the enemies of God. The omission of Judith's song at the end, with its celebration of a woman's victory – 'et tradidit eum in manus feminae' ('and hath delivered him into the hands of a woman') – also has the effect of reducing the subversive power of Judith's victory: she is presented not as a ravishing beauty who has cut off Holofernes's head, but as a paragon of virtue.[82] In the final words of praise for Judith, the translator silently omits the Latin 'quia fecisti viriliter' ('for thou has done manfully') and focuses instead on her chastity: 'hon hélt hreinlífi alla sína daga í minning síns sígrs' ('she preserved chastity all her days in memory of her victory').[83] This is, after all, a more fitting model for an audience of medieval Icelandic nuns.

The King's Mirror

Konungs skuggsjá is rather different from the other works discussed in this chapter, both because it was written in Norway rather than Iceland and

---

77   Judith 13.18; Svanhildur Óskarsdóttir, 'Judith', 116.

78   Judith 13.19.

79   Svanhildur Óskarsdóttir, 'Judith', 116.

80   Perhaps this would make Judith look a bit too much like Guðrún, who kills the drunken Atli in his bed; see 'Atlakviða', st. 41–42, in *Eddukvæði*, II, 379–81.

81   Judith 13.27; Svanhildur Óskarsdóttir, 'Judith', 117.

82   Judith 16. 7–11.

83   Judith 15.11; Svanhildur Óskarsdóttir, 'Judith', 121.

World History and Biblical History

because it belongs to a specific genre known as 'advice for kings' or, more specifically, 'mirrors for princes'.[84] The form is different too: it is written as a dialogue between a father and son, which models a good pedagogical relationship.[85] The general consensus is that it was composed somewhere in Bergen in c. 1240–63; the earliest manuscripts are Norwegian, from the 1260s and 1270s, but from c. 1350 a large number of manuscripts were produced in Iceland.[86] 'Mirrors for princes' were closely associated with universal history, since history provided 'dœmi' ('examples') for instruction, and *Konungs skuggjá* uses many of the same sources as the Icelandic texts, including the *Historia scholastica*, the *Glossa ordinaria*, and possibly *Stjórn III*, although the direction of the borrowing is contested.[87] It also has close connections with encyclopaedic literature, especially in the first section, which displays a keen interest in geography and natural phenomena. Bauer describes it as a 'compilation' or 'florilegium' on a range of topics relating to medieval educational programmes.[88]

More importantly, from the point of view of biblical studies, *Konungs skuggsjá* has clear Victorine connections, as argued by Molland and Tveitane and, more recently, by Eriksen. Tveitane has explored the way in which the author develops the image of the 'arbor sapientiae' ('tree of wisdom').[89] He traces this back to Victorine writings, including Hugh of St Victor's *De archa Noe morali* and *De fructibus carnis et spiritus*, which is attributed to Hugh in some manuscripts. He suggests that tree diagrams were used in teaching at St Victor in Paris, and that the Norwegian author may have come across them there.[90] In a couple of articles, he has also explored the 'four daughters of God' allegory, which is based on Psalm 84.11.[91] This originated in Jewish *midrashim* – best represented by the Genesis Rabbah – but was adapted

---

84 Karl G. Johansson and Elise Kleivane, '*Konungs skuggsjá* and the Interplay between the Universal and the Particular', in *Speculum septentrionale*, ed. Johansson and Kleivane, 17.

85 Stefka Eriksen, 'Pedagogy and Attitudes towards Knowledge in the King's Mirror', *Viator* 45.3 (2014), 150–51.

86 Johansson and Kleivane, '*Konungs skuggsjá*', 20.

87 On the sources and direction of borrowing, see Bagge, 'Forholdet'; Eriksen, 'Pedagogy', 147.

88 Alessia Bauer, 'Encyclopaedic Tendencies and the Medieval Educational Programme', in *Speculum septentrionale*, ed. Johansson and Kleivane, 225.

89 Matthias Tveitane, 'Arbor sapientiae', in *Festskrift til Ludvig Holm-Olsen på hans 70-årsdag den 9. Juni 1984* (Øvre Ervik: Alvheim & Eide, 1984), 308–17.

90 Tveitane, 'Arbor sapientiae', 310–12.

91 Matthias Tveitane, 'The "four daughters of God" in the Old Norse King's Mirror', *Neuphilologische Mitteilungen* 73.4 (1972), 795–804, 'The Four Daughters of God: A Supplement', *Neuphilologische Mitteilungen* 81.4 (1980), 409–15. See also Einar Molland, 'Les quatres filles de Dieu', in *Épektasis: Mélanges*

The Old Testament in Medieval Icelandic Texts

by both Hugh of St Victor and Bernard of Clairvaux in the twelfth century. Tveitane suggests that the Old Norse reworking of this motif in *Konungs skuggsjá* is closest to Hugh's version of the allegory, which also appears in a sermon by Comestor. Finally, Eriksen, exploring the pedagogy of *Konungs skuggsjá*, has pointed out that the three main sources of knowledge in this work – nature, history and allegory – correspond closely to the educational programme at St Victor.[92] The house of wisdom in *Konungs skuggsjá*, for example, has seven pillars, which recall the seven liberal arts in Hugh's *Didascalicon*:[93] 'Sæll er sá, er búa skal í mínu herbergi því at í mínu herbergi eru sjau hǫfuðstólpar þeir er saman tengja allt hvolf með góðri þekju ok sjálft gólf með óþrotligum grundvǫllum ok remma þrekliga alla veggi með sterku afli' ('Happy is the one who shall dwell in my house, because in my house are seven main pillars, which join the whole vault with a good roof, and the floor itself with never-failing foundations, and robustly strengthen all the walls with great power'). The point of departure for this quotation is Proverbs 9.1, but superimposed onto it is Hugh's image of biblical exegesis as a building of which history is the foundation ('grundvǫllr'), allegory the walls ('veggir'), and tropology the roof ('þekja').[94]

The discussion of glossing the Bible in *Konungs skuggsjá* also points to Victorine influences, and here too the author uses the image of a tree:[95]

> Svá eru glósur hverrar rœðu sem limir eða kvistir af einu hverju tré. Þar vex fyrst upp einn bolr af rótunum ok kvíslask síðan með mǫrgum greinum ok limum ok hvern er þú tekr liminn ok rannsakar með réttri athygli, þá er þat jafnan fast við bolinn þann, er upp er vaxinn fyrir ǫndverðu af rótunum.

> The glosses of every word are like the limbs or branches of a certain tree. First a trunk grows up from the roots, and then it branches out into many boughs and limbs, and whichever limb you take and examine with proper care, it is always fixed to the trunk, which has grown up on top of the roots.

As Franklin-Brown has argued elsewhere of the graphic image, the tree here is 'an exegetical figure', which lends an organic unity to the enormous diversity of biblical glosses. She describes how it unites '*figura, glossa* and

---

    patristiques offerts au cardinal Jean Daniélou, ed. Jacques Fontaine and Charles Kannengiesser (Paris: Beauchesne, 1972), 155–69.

[92] Eriksen, 'Pedagogy', 157–59.

[93] *Konungs skuggsiá*, ed. Ludvig Holm-Olsen, 2nd rev. ed. (Oslo: Norske Historisk Kjeldeskrift Institutt, 1983), 99; Eriksen, 'Pedagogy', 159.

[94] See Chapter 2, p. 61; cf. Prov. 9.1 'sapientia aedificavit sibi domum excidit columnas septem' ('Wisdom hath built herself a house; she hath hewn out her seven pillars').

[95] *Konungs skuggsiá*, 84.

World History and Biblical History

ordo in the arboreal form' and enables precisely the kinds of connections between different parts of the Bible that Victorine exegesis encouraged.[96] It may even reflect the visual appearance of the *Glossa ordinaria* – for which St Victor was a centre of dissemination – in which fragments of text are organised, like the branches of a tree, around a central node or 'trunk' of biblical text.[97] The author emphasises the importance of being able to link every branch to the root:[98]

> Miskunn skilningar andans leiðir þá til þeirrar athygli at rannsaka grundvǫllu rœðnanna þeirra, sem þeir heyra. Því næst skyggna þeir um, hversu margkvíslóttar eru rœtr undir þeirri rœðu. Þat hugleiða þeir ok vandliga, hversu margar greinir vaxa á þeirri rœðu. Því næst hugsa þeir þat, hversu margir kvistir fylgja hverri grein. At því gefa þeir miklar geymdir, hverja grein, sem þeir taka, at þeir megi hana réttliga aftr leiða til þeirra róta, er hon var upp afrunnin frá ǫndverðu.

> The grace of the spirit of understanding leads them to investigate attentively the foundations of the words that they hear. Next they examine how many roots branch out beneath the words. Then they consider just as carefully how many boughs grow on the words. Next, they think about how many branches accompany each bough. They pay close attention so that, whichever branch they take, they can correctly trace it back to the roots that it grew up from at the beginning.

Again, this idea of paying careful attention to the 'foundation' – the first level of scriptural understanding – recalls the exegesis of the Victorines. The author goes on to explain how glosses work with reference to the Gloss on the Psalter and Gospels:[99]

> Þeir er glósat hafa psaltarann fram á leið, er David gerði, þá hafa þeir fleira rœtt um þat, hvat David hugði meðan, heldr en um orðin, er hann hefir mælt, því at þeir hafa langar skýringar um það gert með hverju orði, hvat David hugði, meðan hann mælti þat orð, ok sýna þeir þær með rœðum, til hverrar skýringar hugr Davids sá með hverju orði, er hann mælti í psaltaranum. Með sama hætti hafa þeir gert, er skýrt hafa rœður guðsspjallamanna. Þá hafa þeir þat mart mælt, er guðsspjallamenninir hafa þegit yfir. Ok hafa þeir í því þat sýnt, at þeir hafa þar skýrt hugrenningarinnar, sem eigi váru orð varranna, ok er sú náttúra at þeirri gjǫf, þar sem guð hefir fullan skilningaranda gefit, at sá, er hann heyrir fá orð varranna, þekktir hann mǫrg orð hugrenningarinnar. En því glósaði eigi David sjálfr

96 Franklin-Brown, *Reading the World*, 136.
97 Franklin-Brown, *Reading the World*, 59.
98 *Konungs skuggsiá*, 86.
99 *Konungs skuggsiá*, 86–87.

The Old Testament in Medieval Icelandic Texts

psaltarann, at hann vildi ǫðrum þat starf ætla at skýra með orðum alla þá hluti, er hann hugði með sjálfum sér skýringina, þá er hann ritaði rétta framgangsrœðu upphafðra psálma.

Those who glossed the Psalter, which David made, have said more about what David was thinking than about the words that he spoke, because they have given long explanations about every word as to what David was thinking when he spoke that word, and they show in words every interpretation that was present in David's mind with every word he spoke in the Psalter. Those who interpreted the accounts of the Evangelists have done the same; they have said many things that the Evangelists were silent about, and in that they have shown that they interpreted [the words] of the mind, which were not the words of the lips; and it is the property of that gift, where God has given a full spirit of understanding, that the one who hears few words on the lips has perceived many words in the mind. And that is why David did not gloss the Psalter himself, because he intended for others the work of explaining in words all those things of which he had the interpretation in mind when he was writing in correct sequence the words of the original Psalms.

The true meaning of the text lies in the mind of the author and is not identical with the words written on the page; it can be accessed only through the glosses of one who has the 'spirit of understanding'. This also instructs the reader on how to understand the author's own retellings of biblical stories, which diverge considerably from the words of the Bible itself, not least in their free use of invented speeches. The author comes back again and again to the idea of 'framgangsrœða' or 'framgangsvegr upphafðrar rœðu', compounds which are difficult to translate, but which perhaps mean something like 'the order of the words' or 'the correct sequence' – for the Victorines, the basis of all correct interpretation.[100]

One of the ways in which the author uses Old Testament stories is simply as moral exempla: he emphasises that the purpose of history is 'at allir skyldu nema og sér í nyt fœra ǫll góð dœmi, en varask in dáligu dœmi' ('that everyone should learn and put to use all good examples and beware the bad examples').[101] His first two exempla – Joseph and Esther – are united by the moral that pride comes before a fall, while humility will be rewarded; a moral that is closely associated with social status. In telling the story of Joseph and Potiphar's wife, for example, he emphasises the importance of social

---

100 Both compounds are attested only in *Konungs skuggsjá*, apart from one instance in *Thomas saga erkibiskups*, where 'framgangsvegr' seems to mean simply 'the way forward'; see *DONP* s.v. 'framgangsvegr' at https://onp.ku.dk/onp/onp. php?c167868/ (accessed 20 July 2023).

101 *Konungs skuggsiá*, 72.

124

World History and Biblical History

hierarchy. Joseph rejects her advances not just because they are immoral, but because they are socially disordered: 'Vit megum eigi vera jafnkomin saman, því at þú ert lafði mín, en ek em þræll þinn, ok er þér þat ofmikil skǫmm at leggjask undir mik' ('We two cannot come together as equals, for you are my lady, and I am your slave, and it would be too great a disgrace for you to lie under me').[102] Likewise, when she falsely accuses him to Potiphar, she declares it 'ofdramb einum þræli, at mæla slíka dirfð við lafði sína' ('the arrogance of a slave to speak so daringly to his lady'). Joseph's humility in adhering faithfully to his designated social station is eventually rewarded by his rise to wealth and power. Likewise, in Esther, the story has been adapted to emphasise the correct role of the queen and courtiers. While Queen Vastes challenges Ahasuerus's power by feasting with her own followers and refusing his request for her presence, Esther humbly submits to the king, advising only that he pay due heed to 'konungligri miskunn' ('royal mercy').[103] In the same way, Mordecai is contrasted with Haman: while Mordecai's failure to do Haman obeisance is pure oversight, caused by his anxiety for his people, Haman thinks only of himself and is condemned for his 'hóflausa yfirgirnd ok drambsamligri reiði' ('immoderate greed and arrogant rage').

These stories require only minimal adaptations to fit them to the moral: some summarising, some simplification, and the addition of imagined speeches. The account of Esther uses material from the *Glossa ordinaria*, and possibly from Josephus, but the small changes to the story of Joseph appear to be the author's own.[104] When he comes to the narrative of the Fall, the author takes a different and much more creative approach, integrating a variety of source material into a lively and dramatic narrative that allows his readers to experience this familiar story afresh. The theoretical subject under discussion between father and son at this point is how a king should balance justice and mercy in his judgements. The father begins by introducing some new characters to the Genesis account – the four daughters of God, who witness his covenant with Adam and Eve:[105]

> Til þessa sáttmáls váru kallaðar fjórar systr, guðligar meyjar þær, er heyra skyldu setning þessarra laga ok vita allt skilorð þessa sáttmáls. Ein þeirra hét sannindi, ǫnnur friðsemi, in þriðja réttvísi, in fjórða miskunn, ok mælti Guð svá við þessar meyjar: Yðr býð ek um at skyggna, at Adamr brjóti eigi lǫg þau, er nú eru sett okkar á milli. Fylgið honum vel ok gætið hans

---

102 *Konungs skuggsiá*, 68.

103 *Konungs skuggsiá*, 70.

104 The identification of Asueros with Artaxerxes and Cyrus comes either from Josephus, *Antiquities*, XI.vi.1 or, more probably, from the Gloss; see *Glossa ordinaria,* ed. Morard (Est. 1.1).

105 *Konungs skuggsiá*, 75.

125

The Old Testament in Medieval Icelandic Texts

æ vel meðan hann heldr þessa hluti, er nú eru mæltir. En ef hann brýtr þá skuluð þér í dómi sitja mót honum með feðr yðrum, með því at þér eruð dœtr dómarans sjálfs.

To this covenant were called four sisters, divine maidens, who were to listen to the establishment of these laws and know all the terms of this covenant. One of them was called Truth, the second Peace, the third Righteousness, the fourth Mercy, and God spoke thus to these maidens: 'I order you to watch closely that Adam does not break the laws which are now established between us. Accompany him well and guard him ever carefully while he keeps the things that have now been decreed, but if he breaks [them], then you must sit in judgement against him with your father, because you are daughters of the Judge himself'.

As noted above (p. 58), he is adapting Hugh of St Victor's allegory here, in which the four daughters are present at the Creation and debate whether God should make man. They then go on to provide a running commentary on the Fall. After Adam and Eve eat from the forbidden tree, Truth and Righteousness warn them to be truthful and to avoid 'lygi' ('lies') and 'ranglæti' ('wrong-doing') if they wish to receive mercy. However, each blames the other 'svá sem verjandi sína sǫk' ('as if defending their own case'). Adam even goes so far as to tell God: 'Hefðir þú eigi þessa konu mér gefna til ráðagerðar með mér, þá munda ek haldit hafa skipat lǫgmál ok eigi brotit þín boðorð' ('If you hadn't given me this woman to advise me, I would have kept the law as agreed and not have broken your commandments').[106] Augustine had pointed out that Adam's words imply God is to blame, but it is startling to have Adam state this outright.[107] God's daughters, however, reveal the real reason for Adam and Eve's actions: 'Eplin váru fǫgr ok girnilig ok sœt að bergja, en þit girntusk mjǫk at vera fróðari en ykkr var lofat' ('The apples were fair and desirable and sweet to taste, and you desired to be wiser than was permitted to you').[108] Yet Mercy and Grace, true to their names, beg for 'ván hjálpar ok líknar í dauða sínum, æ meðan hann ǫrvilnask eigi' ('hope of salvation and reconciliation in death, as long as he doesn't despair'). The scene ends with the four sisters embracing in a return to the words of Psalm 84.11: 'Allar þessar systr tóku at samþykkjask með blíðu sáttmáli, svá at miskunn ok sannindi lǫgðusk í faðma, en réttvísi og friðsemi kysstusk með blíðum hálsfǫngum' ('All these sisters were reconciled with happy accord, so that Mercy and Truth embraced one another, and Righteousness and Peace

---

106 *Konungs skuggsiá*, 76.
107 Augustine, *On Genesis*, ii.25 (trans. Hill, 88); cf. *Glossa ordinaria*, ed. Morard (Gen. 3.12); Comestor, *Liber Genesis*, 43.
108 *Konungs skuggsiá*, 77.

World History and Biblical History

kissed with happy embraces').[109] It is as if the original words of the Psalm have branched out to reveal the whole drama of salvation hidden within them, and then, true to the exegetical method detailed above, have been traced back to their roots again.

This is not the end of the matter, though, either for the daughters of God or for the story of the Fall. Responding to the son's insistent questions, the father proceeds to tell the same story a second time, this time from a different perspective. In this version, Lucifer arms himself with the seven deadly sins and sets out to take down mankind out of vengeance for his fate. He enters into a serpent with a woman's face (a detail from Comestor), who walks on two feet like a man.[110] We then get an account of how each sin is implicated in the temptation: deceit in flattering Eve, cunning in that she is fooled, pride in the desire to be like God, lust in the sweetness of the apple, covetousness in taking what was forbidden. Most interesting is the author's take on how many apples were involved. Eve, afraid of death, asks the serpent to eat first, thinking: 'Þetta aldin mun jafnvel ǫðrum kykvendum skapat til bana sem mér, ef þat hefir dauðligan krapt með sér' ('This fruit must be designed to kill other creatures as well as me, if it has the power of death in it').[111] The serpent, on the other hand, is willing to take the risk: 'Ek má vel eta eplit, því at ek em ekki at sekari né dauðligri þar sem ek em áðr í fullri reiði Guðs' ('I may as well eat the apple, because I can't be more guilty or more mortal, when I'm already subject to the full wrath of God'). The father interjects – in case we are unfamiliar with the conventions of interior monologue – that Eve does not hear his words. Then, when Eve offers an apple to Adam, he too insists that she eat first: 'Ok tók þá enn Eva tvau epli ok át þegar sjálf annat djarfliga, því at hon hafði kennt áðr sœtleik eplisins, ok girndi hana oftarri at bergja á heldr en hon skemdisk þess, er hon hafði áðr gert' ('And again Eve took two apples, and immediately ate one herself boldly, because she had previously tasted the sweetness of the apple, and she desired to taste it more often, rather than being ashamed of what she had done').[112] When Adam tastes 'lystiligan sœtleik í munni hennar' ('the delightful sweetness in her mouth'), he finally decides to eat as well. While the explicit sexual arousal described in Comestor's *Historia* is omitted, the allusions to Eve's 'boldness' and 'desire', and Adam's delight at the 'sweetness' in her mouth, make it clear that eating the apple

---

[109] *Konungs skuggsiá*, 77: 'misericordia et veritas occurrerunt; iustitia et pax deosculatae sunt' ('Mercy and truth have met each other; justice and peace have kissed').

[110] Comestor, *Liber Genesis*, 39–40. Comestor attributes this detail to Bede, but in fact it is not found anywhere in Bede's surviving works.

[111] *Konungs skuggsiá*, 81.

[112] *Konungs skuggsiá*, 81.

The Old Testament in Medieval Icelandic Texts

is as much about bodily appetite as it is about spiritual pride.[113] By giving us full access to the thoughts and feelings of all three characters in this scene, the author immerses us fully in their web of deceit and desire.

The detail that four apples were eaten is unparalleled elsewhere: Eve and the serpent consume one each, followed by Eve, then Adam. Holtsmark has suggested that the author was influenced by visual images of the Fall, which sometimes show the serpent offering Eve an apple from its mouth.[114] Medieval illuminations can combine two distinct moments in a single scene, so that Eve is shown biting into an apple herself while offering one to Adam with her other hand. In the marginal illumination in AM 227 fol. IV, for example, Adam and Eve are holding an apple each (Fig. 1). Holtsmark gives other examples, including the thirteenth-century wall-paintings in the Ål stave church, now in Oslo. Visual details such as these may have given the author the idea that Eve and the serpent each ate an apple, as well as Adam and Eve. This certainly works well with Comestor's psychological insight that Adam may have been more willing to eat when he saw that the woman did not die, even though God had said they would.[115] Yet what is striking is how seamlessly visual detail and psychological insight have been blended, creating a powerful scene in which we witness, from the inside, each character calculating the best move for themselves, as they weigh divine prohibition against their own personal (and implicitly selfish) interests. The changes to the story that this requires are followed through consistently. When God curses the serpent (which he does prior to discovering Adam and Eve), the father singles out the detail that he is to eat dust all the days of his life, making it into a punishment specifically for eating the apple: 'Beisk mold ok saurig skal vera matr þinn fyrir því at þú átzk sœtt epli þat, er þú tókt ór hendi Evu' ('Bitter filthy dirt will be your food, because you ate the sweet apple, which you took from the hand of Eve').[116] It is quite a feat to tell a story as well known as the Fall of Man twice, and to do it both times in a way that is imaginative, fresh and new.

This habit of returning to a story and retelling it from a different point of view is characteristic of this author, though. He does the same thing with the story of Aaron and the golden calf from Exodus 32, which the father tells first as an exemplum of divine judgement, and, secondly, to distinguish between lawful and unlawful killings. The first telling is influenced by Gregory's commentary on this passage, which was in the *Glossa ordinaria*: he tells us that a ruler should aim to mix 'both the authority of ruling and the kindness

---

113 Comestor, *Liber Genesis*, 41.
114 Anne Holtsmark, 'The *Speculum regale* and the apples in the garden of Eden', *Viking* 20 (1952), 141–56.
115 Comestor, *Liber Genesis*, 41.
116 *Konungs skuggsiá*, 82.

Figure 1. The Fall of Man, bottom margin, AM 227 fol. 1v.

of consoling', carefully balancing 'discipline' and 'mercy'.[117] So, when God threatens to wipe out the Israelites because of their idolatry, Moses both begs for their lives to be spared and kills thousands of those who have sinned. This is a complex narrative to comment on because Moses's intercession can appear dangerously presumptuous – he persuades God to change his mind – and because the slaughter that follows is so extreme.[118] The author manages the first of these two points by having Moses ask for 'leyfi' ('leave') to speak. Borrowing from Comestor, he adds a comment to Moses's speech to clarify that his main concern is God's reputation: 'þeir megi þat mæla, at þú sér vanafli til at leiða fólk þitt inn í þat land, er þú hafðir heitit þeim fyrir ǫndverðu' ('they may say that you are too weak to lead your people into the land you promised them at the beginning').[119] He manages the second point by having God explicitly hand over responsibility for the slaughter to Moses, so that he is acting on God's behalf. As if conjured up by Gregory's gloss,

---

[117] Gregory the Great, *Moralia*, xx.14, trans. *Morals*, 456–58; *Glossa ordinaria*, ed. Morard (Ex. 32. 10).

[118] For further discussion of the challenges posed by this story, see Phillipa Byrne, 'Exodus 32 and the Figure of Moses in Twelfth-Century Theology', *Journal of Theological Studies* 68.2 (2017), 671–89.

[119] *Konungs skuggsiá*, 90; Comestor, *Liber Exodus*, c. 73 (PL 198, 1190A): 'impotens eis dare terram, quam promiserat' ('being powerless to give them the land that he had promised').

The Old Testament in Medieval Icelandic Texts

with its focus on balancing mercy and discipline, the four daughters of God turn up to endorse this final judgement: 'Engi þeirra systra þarfnaðisk síns réttar í þessum dómi, sannindi eða réttvísi, þar sem Moyses drap mikinn her manna til þess at hógværa reiði Guðs. En þar hǫfðu þær sinn rétt, friðsemi ok miskunn, sem minna var at gert en mælt var fyrir ǫndverðu' ('None of the sisters went without their dues in this judgement, Truth and Righteousness in that Moses killed a great army of people to placate God's wrath, and Peace and Mercy had their due in that less was done than was said at the beginning'). The father then moves on to discuss other cases where God has tempered justice with mercy, including Jonah in Nineveh, and King Hezekiah with his sundial.

One of the advantages of the dialogue form is that it allows the author to articulate the potential reservations of his readers. Later on, the son comes back to this story again to question the ethics of Moses's killings: following Comestor's suggestion that Moses acted 'out of the fury of his soul, not out of reason', he suggests that Moses is culpable of failing to control his temper.[120] The father immediately counters this by explaining the distinction between lawful and unlawful killing. He argues that Moses's act was 'ástarverk en eigi ǫfundar' ('an act of love and not of envy'), because he turned the Israelites from error and evil ways: 'Hver sú refsing, er gǫr verðr fyrir ǫfundar sakar, þá er þat manndráp. En hver sú refsing, er gǫr verðr fyrir ástar sakar ok réttinda, þá er þat heilagt verk, en eigi manndráp' ('Every punishment that is done out of envy is murder, and every punishment that is done out of love and justice, is a holy deed, and not murder').[121] This echoes Augustine's views in his *Sermon on the Mount*, where he draws a contrast between those who desire to correct others 'with love' and those who want revenge 'with hatred'.[122] The son remains sceptical, questioning whether patient and peace-loving men can ever countenance killing. This gives the father an opportunity to impress yet further the king's responsibility for punishment: just as Moses 'cleanses' himself in the blood of sinners, so too 'konungr hreinsar sik í blóði ranglátra, ef hann drepr þá í réttri refsing ok gœzlu heilagra laga' ('a king cleanses himself in the blood of the wicked, if he kills them in just punishment and in keeping with holy laws').[123] This aligns with Augustine's reflection that it is permissible to kill, if you act in obedience to God's command and represent in your person 'the authority of the State in accordance with the laws of the state': if you are an 'instrument' or 'sword'.[124] The idea of the 'refsingarsverð' ('sword of punishment') becomes important later in *Konungs skuggsjá* when

---

120 Comestor, *Liber Exodus*, c. 74 (PL 198, 1190B): 'de impetu animi, non de ratione'.
121 *Konungs skuggsiá*, 106.
122 Augustine of Hippo, *De sermone domini in monte secundum Matthaeum*, i.20.
123 *Konungs skuggsiá*, 107.
124 Augustine, *De civitate Dei*, i.21, trans. Bettenson, 32. Cf. Gregory, *Moralia*, xx.7,

World History and Biblical History

the father has to explain the paradox that Saul's refusal to kill the Amalekites is condemned and yet Solomon's killing of Joab in the temple is justified.

This story needs to be told twice because it is so difficult, because no single reading can resolve the moral difficulties it presents. The same issues trouble the longest biblical story in *Konungs skuggsjá*: that of Saul and David.[125] This unfolds over multiple chapters and is not told in chronological order: it begins with David's reaction to Saul's death, then moves backwards to how Saul broke God's command to kill the Amalekites and forwards again to how David murdered Bathsheba's husband Uriah.[126] Why – asks the son – does God reject Saul for sparing the lives of his enemies and yet have mercy on David for killing an innocent man? To answer this question, we move backwards again to Saul's first encounter with David, the story of his persecutions, and finally his death. This is then linked to David's lament at the death of his son Absalom, the story of Solomon, and the bloody power struggle that follows David's death. It is a rich and complex narrative, and much of the dialogue between father and son focuses precisely on the difficulty of drawing out clear moral examples. In effect, in order to justify God's choice of David over Saul, we have to read the story backwards, against the grain of its natural development.

The starting point is the son's perception that God's actions appear biased to the point of unjust, even if he knows that this cannot be the right interpretation:[127]

> Ok veit ek eigi, hvárt meiri var sǫkin at drepa saklausan mann og at hóra konu hans, eða gefa þeim líf, er sakafullr var? Nú munu svá margir menn skilja, þeir er eigi kunnu grein á, at Guð hafi elskat meir David en Saul, ok hafi þat til gengit, at Davidi varð léttari sín sǫk. En fyrir því at Guð dœmir alla hluti eftir réttindum, en eigi eftir mismuna, þá mun þat sýnt vera, at menn skilja eigi þessa hluti rétt.

> And I don't know whether there was more guilt in killing an innocent man and making his wife a whore or in sparing the life of one who is guilty. Now many people, who cannot tell the difference, will assume that God must have loved David more than Saul, and that is the reason why David's guilt was made less. But because God judges all things according to justice

---

     trans. *Morals*, 457 for the 'uirga districtionis' ('rod of severity') and 'iudicii gladius' ('sword of judgement').

[125] On this story, see also Elizabeth Boyle, 'Biblical Kings and Kingship Theory', in *Speculum septentrionale*, ed. Johansson and Kleivane, 181–90.

[126] See Bagge, 'Kongespeilet', 168–69 for an overview of the order in which the story is told.

[127] *Konungs skuggsiá*, 108, 151.

131

The Old Testament in Medieval Icelandic Texts

and without disproportion, it must be the case that people do not understand this matter correctly.

This reworks a comment made by Comestor in the *Historia scholastica*: 'Dixerunt enim idololatrae, vel dicere potuerunt: Non est justus Deus Israel, qui Saul amovit de regno, et substituit David, cum David gravius quam Saul peccaverit' ('For idolaters said, or could have said: the God of Israel is not just, who removed Saul from the throne and substituted David, since David sinned more seriously than Saul').[128] In response to this challenge, the father tries to argue that God sees the inner nature of Saul and David, as shown by their subsequent actions. The nature of David is fundamentally good:[129]

> Nú var sú náttúra Davids, at hann var manna vaskastr til vápna í orrostum ok vel harðr í réttri refsing, en hann var maðr góðgjarn ok ásthollr hverjum manni ok aumhjartaðr yfir ófǫrum hvers manns. Hann var ok tryggr maðr í ǫllum hlutum, ráðvandr ok fastorðr í vináttu ok í ǫllum heitum, ok svá lastvarr, at hann vildi engan lǫst á sik vita, ok eigi var hans maki í Ísraels fólki.

> Now this was David's nature, that he was the bravest of men to wield weapons in battle and severe in just punishment; but he was a benevolent man, and affectionate to every man, and charitable over others' misfortunes; he was also a faithful man in all things, upright and true to his word in friendship and all promises, and so virtuous that he wished no fault to be visible in him, and none was his equal among the Israelites.

Saul's nature, on the other hand, is fundamentally bad: 'En þessi var hans náttúra, at hann var stríðr ok drambsamr í Guðs augliti, þá er hann þóttisk fullkominn í staðfestu ríkis' ('And this was his nature, that he was stubborn and prideful before God, when he thought he was perfectly established in his power').[130] Reading the two kings in line with these character portraits creates some significant challenges for the coherence of the story.

The biblical Saul, in particular, is a complex and tragic character whose personality develops and fluctuates over the course of the narrative. When he first encounters David, we are told of his fondness for this young man who can restore his sanity through music: 'elskaði hann mjǫk David og gerði hann at skjaldsveini sér. En þó hafði Samuel smurðan hann áðr til konungs leyniliga' ('he loved David very much and made him his page boy, yet Samuel had previously anointed him king in secret').[131] The tension between

---

128 Comestor, *Historia Libri II Regum*, c. 12, PL 198, 1334A.
129 *Konungs skuggsiá*, 206.
130 *Konungs skuggsiá*, 108–10.
131 *Konungs skuggsiá*, 111.

132

World History and Biblical History

Saul's love for David and David's duplicity feels uncomfortable here: David is concealing his destiny from Saul, while Saul favours him in all innocence of this. Things start to change after David kills Goliath, prompting a public outpouring of praise in which Saul is compared unfavourably with the young hero. Interior monologue reveals to us what Saul is thinking:[132]

> Ok þegar er Saul heyrði þessa hluti, þá rann á hann þegar reiði og ǫfund við David ok mælti í hugþokka sínum: 'Nú skil ek, at Guð hefir ætlat þeim manni at taka ríki eptir mik, en eigi sonum mínum. Ok skal ek við leita að fyrirkoma því ráði, ef ek má, og þó með þeirri list, at engi skal vita, at ek drepi hann at vilja mínum'.

> And when Saul heard these things, anger and envy towards David came over him, and he said in his mind: 'Now I realise that God intends this man to inherit the kingdom after me, and not my sons – and I shall seek to destroy that plan if I can, and yet with such cunning that no one shall know that I am killing him intentionally'.

On one level, this is incriminating: now Saul is the one concealing his true intentions, of which David is innocent, and we as readers – with privileged insight into his motives – can evaluate them, on a moral basis, as sinful. At the same time, what tips Saul over into anger and envy is very specifically his realisation that God has chosen David over him. We end up with the paradox – in narrative terms – that Saul's evil nature is sparked by God's rejection of him, and yet God's rejection of him is because of his evil nature.

The consequence is that the narrator has to intervene constantly to ensure that we are interpreting events correctly. On the one hand, what happens is human and understandable: Saul resents the success of the young David, which poses a threat to his heirs. Yet the more Saul forces David into situations that endanger him, in the hope that he will end up dead, the more fame David wins, and the more Saul desires his death. It is a psychological vicious circle, as the author recognises: 'Saul ǫfundaði David því meir, sem hann sá at honum tóksk betr til' ('Saul envied David all the more, the better he saw him do').[133] Saul's flaws develop over time in response to a changing situation: his accession to power, God's rejection of him, David's favour in God's eyes. At the same time, we are encouraged to see his character as static, so that faults that develop slowly as the narrative progresses are known by God from the start: 'Nú hefi ek sýnt þér grimmleiks Sauls þann, sem Guð sá í brjósti honum, þá er hann kippti honum frá ríki, ok síðan gerðisk opinberr' ('Now I have shown you Saul's ferocity, which God saw in his breast, when he deprived him of the kingdom, and which later became evident'); 'Guð sá

---

[132] *Konungs skuggsiá*, 212.
[133] *Konungs skuggsiá*, 111.

The Old Testament in Medieval Icelandic Texts

ágjarnligan grimmleik í brjósti hans þann, er síðan tók birtask' ('God saw the covetous ferocity in his breast, which was later revealed').[134]

The tension is particularly fraught at the end of Saul's life, when we are given two alternative assessments of his achievements. Unusually, for Old Norse translations, the author does not cut David's lament for Jonathan and Saul, but rewrites it in prose, reproducing its refrain ('quomodo ceciderunt fortes' – 'how are the valiant fallen'). Saul and Jonathan are praised as great warriors and leaders of the nation:[135]

> Beiskr harmr er ǫllu Ísraels fólki þetta, at svá ágætir hǫfðingjar skulu vera fallnir ífrá ráðagerðum og ríkisstjórn, sem Saul ok Ionathas váru. Mikill þrekr ok afl hefir týnzk á þeim degi, þar sem svá dýrligir hǫfðingjar hafa týnzk, sem Saul konungr ok Ionathas váru ok margr góðr riddari ok mart gott vápn ok mǫrg góð brynja sem þar hefir glatazk með þeim; varizk smælingar reiði guðs þar sem hann lofaði heiðnum þjóðum at leggja hendr á cristi sínum. Harmi allr lýðr slíka tjón, at svá dýrligir stjórnarmenn skulu falla fyrir heiðnum þjóðum.

> It is a bitter grief to all the people of Israel that such excellent chieftains should have fallen from counsel and government as Saul and Jonathan. Great courage and strength have perished on this day, where such precious chieftains have perished as King Saul and Jonathan were, and many a good horseman, and many a good weapon, and many a good mail-coat perished with them; let the poor beware the Lord's anger, that he allowed heathens to lay hands on his anointed. Let the whole people grieve this loss, that such precious rulers should fall before heathens.

Whereas in the biblical poem the public lament for the death of a king is eclipsed by David's private love for Jonathan, the Old Norse lays equal emphasis on both men as renowned 'chieftains' and 'rulers'.[136] The Vulgate's 'arma bellica' ('weapons of war') are expanded into horsemen, weapons and mail-coats, while the personal qualities of Saul and Jonathan – 'amabiles et decori' ('lovely and comely') – have disappeared. Despite this public praise, the father's final verdict makes no concessions to Saul's former glory, instead reinforcing the moral opposition pursued throughout: 'Og svá sem Guð sá í brjósti hans mildi ok miskunnsemð ok lítillæti, svá þekkti Guð í brjósti Sauls ágirnd ok grimmleik ok hóflaust dramb' ('And just as God saw in [David's]

---

134 *Konungs skuggsiá*, 112.

135 *Konungs skuggsiá*, 115; cf. 2 Sam. 1.19, 25, 27.

136 On the tendency to play down David and Jonathan's love in Comestor's *Historia* and its derivatives, see Maria Sherwood-Smith, 'Old Friends: David and Jonathan', *Oxford German Studies* 36.2 (2007), 163–83. On the balance of public and private in David's lament, see Linafelt, 'Private Poetry', 497–526.

World History and Biblical History

breast his generosity and mercy and humility, so God recognised in Saul's breast greed and ferocity and boundless pride'). The lament is a tribute to David's generosity, not praise for a great fallen hero.

David's story also needs reworking to accommodate his faults, while promoting his virtue and humility. The author argues that David repents of his adultery as soon as it has happened, but decides to hide his sin so as not to set a bad example: 'þá leitaði David þeirrar athygli, að hann mætti heldr þegja yfir og sæi Guð iðran hans, en fólkit gengi dult lǫgbrota hans, ok tœki eigi hans glœp til dœma, at þeim þœtti þá minna fyrir að falla í glœpi og lǫgbrot, ef þeir vissi hans glœp' ('then David considered that he should rather be silent and let God see his contrition, and conceal his breach of law from the people so that they would not take his fault as an example, that it would seem less serious to them to fall into sin and break the law, if they knew his error').[137] His plot to get Uriah to sleep with his wife is also justified: 'hann vildi bœta glœp hórdóms síns í leynd ok vildi aldri síðan koma nær konu hins' ('he wished to make amends for his sin of adultery in private, and never again come near the other's wife').[138] Only when this fails is David forced into murder, reckoning that it is better to compound his sin before God than to make it publicly known. When Nathan confronts him publicly, the author invents a long speech in which David says he is ready to be punished 'at eigi falli fólkit í slíkan glœp' ('so that the people do not fall into such sin'). Private sin and guilt are subordinated to appearances; this is the reality of public affairs.

As Bagge has explored in depth, these stories about biblical kings provide a way of reflecting on the responsibilities and challenges of government and the relationship between Church and State.[139] But, in doing so, they engage imaginatively with different ways of reading and glossing the Bible and with different literary forms – narrative, commentary, dialogue and lament. At the centre of *Konungs skuggsjá*, the author engages with a different biblical genre: wisdom literature. Here we are dealing not with straightforward translation nor with adaptation, but with an exercise in associative reading (or *lectio divina*) which blends poetry and prose. Here is the beginning of Wisdom's speech:[140]

---

[137] *Konungs skuggsiá*, 108.

[138] *Konungs skuggsiá*, 109.

[139] Sverre Bagge, *The Political Thought of the King's Mirror* (Odense: Odense University Press, 1987), 53–71, 98–99, 126–43; cf. Boyle, 'Biblical Kings'.

[140] *Konungs skuggsiá*, 98. On the theme of wisdom in the King's Mirror, see Andrew Hamer, 'Searching for Wisdom: The King's Mirror', in *Speculum regale: Der altnorwegische Koeningsspiegel (Konungs skuggsja) in der europaischen Tradition*, ed. Jens Eike Schnall and Rudolf Simek (Vienna: Fassbaender, 2000), 47–62.

The Old Testament in Medieval Icelandic Texts

Ek em getin af hjarta Guðs og gekk ek fram af munni hins hæsta ok skipaða ek ǫllum hlutum. En Guðs andi fluttisk yfir tómt undirdjúp, ok skildum vér ljós frá myrkrum ok skipuðum stundir ok tíma, daga ok nætr, ár og vetr og eilíflig sumur ok timbruðum vér himna konungi stirnt hásæti, og ekki gerði Guð án mína hagspakliga atvist. Því at vér vágum saman léttleik lofts ok hǫfga jarðar ok hengðum þungan jarðarbǫll í léttu lofti og styrktum festiband himins með ǫflgum krǫptum.

I was conceived in the heart of God and went forth from the mouth of the most high, and I arranged all things, and God's spirit hovered over the empty abyss, and we separated light from darkness and arranged hours and times, days and nights, years and winters and eternal summers, and we built for the king of heaven a starry high-seat, and God did nothing without the help of my crafting, because we weighed together the lightness of the air and the weight of the earth and hung the heavy orb of the earth in light air and strengthened the band of heaven with great power.

This condenses an immense amount of biblical learning: the first line translates Proverbs 8.24 ('ego iam concepta eram'), immediately followed by Sirach 24.5 ('ego ex ore Altissima prodivi'); then Prov. 8.30 ('sum eo cuncta conponens').[141] This leads into the creation narrative from Genesis, with the mention of the 'abyss' in both Proverbs 8.24 ('necdum erant abyssi') and in Sirach 24.8 ('et in profundum abyssi penetravi') evoking the 'abyss' of Genesis 1.2 over which God's spirit moves.[142] The darkness ('tenebrae') of the abyss then evokes the separation of light and darkness (Genesis 1.4) and the creation of time and seasons (Genesis 1.14: 'tempora et dies et annos') before we move back to Sirach 24.7 ('ego in altis habitavi et thronus meus in columna nubis') combined with the idea in Proverbs of Wisdom as a master-builder on whose craftmanship God himself depends (Proverbs 8.30 – 'cuncta conponens').[143] Then the idea in Proverbs 8.29 of God balancing ('adpendebat') the foundations of the earth leads into a creative rendition of Isaiah 40.12: 'Quis [...] caelos palmo ponderavit quis adpendit tribus digitis molem terrae' ('Who [...] weighed the heavens with his palm? who hath poised with three fingers the bulk of the earth?'). The last line blends the verb 'firmabat' ('established') from Proverbs 8.28 ('aethera firmabat sursum') with Sirach 24.8 ('gyrum caeli circuivi sola'); the expression 'festiband

---

141 Prov. 8.24 'I was already conceived'; Sir. 24.5 'I came out of the mouth of the most High'; Prov. 8.30 'I was with him forming all things'.

142 Prov. 8.24 'The depths were not as yet'; Sir. 24.8 'I have penetrated into the bottom of the deep'; Gen. 1.2 'and darkness was upon the face of the deep; and the spirit of God moved over the waters'.

143 Gen. 1.14 'for seasons, and for days and years'; Sir. 24.7 'I dwelt in the highest places, and my throne is in a pillar of cloud'; Prov. 8.30 'forming all things'.

World History and Biblical History

himins' ('fastening band or rope of heaven') looks like a creative translation of Latin 'gyrum caeli' ('the circuit of heaven').[144]

The passage, then, is a web of associatively linked Bible verses, a meditation on Proverbs 8.23–31 that draws on Genesis, Sirach and Isaiah. But, although we skip from one book to another within a single clause, the language and style create a unified whole. Proverbs 8.24 and Sirach 24.5 are linked together by alliteration on g and h, like two halves of a poetic line: 'Ek em **g**etin af **h**jarta **G**uðs ok **g**ekk ek fram af munni **h**ins **h**æsta'. Proverbs 8.30 is joined to the verses from Genesis and then Sirach 24.7 by both alliteration and end-rhyme: '**sk**ipa**ða** ek **ǫ**llum hlutum', '**sk**ildrum vér ljós frá myrkrunum', '**sk**ipu**ðum st**undir ok **tí**ma', '**t**imbru**ðum** vér himna konungi **st**irnt hásæti'. The blending of Isaiah and Proverbs is achieved through chiasmus and polyptoton, as well as alliteration and end-rhyme: 'vér vág*um* saman *létt*leik l*opt*s ok **h**ofga *jarð*ar ok **h**eng**ð**um þungan *jarð*arbǫll í *létt*u l*opt*i'. One can hardly tell that the two halves of the verse are from different biblical passages. In addition to this stylistic ornamentation, there is a rich use of figurative language throughout which makes connections to the poetry of the Psalms. The allusion to 'tabernaculum' ('tabernacle') in Sirach 24.12 ('qui creavit me requievit in tabernaculo meo') leads the author to the 'tabernacle' of Psalm 18.6 ('in sole posuit tabernaculum suum'): 'En ek setta landtjald mitt í skuggalausum geisla ok gekk ek fram af fǫgru herbergi sem skrýddr brúðgumi' ('And I set my tent in a shadowless sunbeam and went forth from my beautiful chamber like a bridegroom in his dress').[145] The author even uses rhyme when translating Psalm 138.7 ('quo ibo ab spiritu tuo' – 'whither shall I go from thy spirit?'): 'Hvar felr sá *sik* er flýja vill *mik*?' ('Where will he hide, who wishes to flee from me?').[146] These links are theologically inflected, as much as they are associative, for the allusion to Psalm 18.6 identifies the allegorical figure of Wisdom with Christ, moving from the Creation to the Incarnation: 'When the Word was made flesh he was like a bridegroom who found himself a bridal chamber in a virgin's womb. Once wedded to human nature, he came forth from that purest of all rooms'.[147] This piece is so carefully crafted – reflecting Wisdom's own expert craftsmanship – and so different in style from the biblical history, that even if it is not technically poetry, it is surely designed to feel as if it is.

---

[144] Prov. 8.28 'he established the sky above'; Sir. 24.8 'I alone have compassed the circuit of heaven'.

[145] *Konungs skuggsiá*, 99; cf. Sir. 24.12 'he that made me rested in my tabernacle'; Ps. 18.6 'he hath set his tabernacle in the sun: and he, as a bridegroom coming out of his bride chamber'.

[146] *Konungs skuggsiá*, 100.

[147] Augustine of Hippo, *Enarrationes in Psalmos I–L*, 18(2).6; *Expositions on the Psalms 1–32*, trans. Maria Boulding (New York: New City Press, 2000), 209.

Conclusion

In encyclopaedic writing, we find a variety of different approaches to biblical narrative, from the clear moral messages of *Veraldar saga* – already prepped for allegorisation – to the interest in the arcane and the forbidden in 'Heimsaldrar', to the universal history of AM 764 4to with its keen awareness of the untold stories of women. Longer narratives may use a variety of forms and styles: the family drama of Joseph in *Veraldar saga* is expertly told through the emotions of the protagonists, but it also uses 'gaps' and 'blanks' to hide what is happening at key moments, such as when Joseph recognises his brothers. Here the literal level of the narrative seems to pull in a different direction from the allegorical exposition that follows. The translation of Judith in AM 764 4to shows little or no interest in allegory, although, like Jerome's Latin version, it maintains a strong focus on Judith's chastity. Both style and idiom are characteristic of the Icelandic sagas, but it also retains some of the stylistic features of the Latin and, at times, deliberately deploys 'foreign' vocabulary to create particular effects. Finally, *Konungs skuggsjá* sports brilliantly imaginative retellings of biblical stories, making sophisticated use of the dialogue form, and blending narrative and allegory to reinvigorate some of the best-known stories. It even incorporates poetic passages that are stylistically quite distinct from the prose. Here we find the richest and most complex development of Old Testament narrative so far. However, far from being in the 'objective' voice of a saga author, it is written in a lively and intrusive narratorial voice, which encourages a strongly ethical mode of reading. While all these works are dependent on Comestor and the Victorine school of exegesis, they develop biblical narrative in different ways; the longer the narrative is, the more possibilities for imaginative engagement and varying of styles. In the next chapter, then, I turn to the largest corpus of Old Testament stories in Old Norse: the translations collectively known as *Stjórn*.

⤞ 5 ⤝

In the Beginning:
Primeval History in Genesis I–II

Genesis I–II has a different character from the rest of the Genesis narrative: as 'primeval history', it is often separated out from the 'ancestral history' of Genesis I2–50'.[1] There is good reason for this: the universal perspective of Genesis I–II and its closeness to Ancient Near Eastern traditions about the Creation and Flood distinguish it from later chapters, which are more narrowly focused on national and domestic concerns.[2] Its theological significance as a source for the Christian doctrines of creation, human nature and the Fall meant that it was one of the most heavily commentated parts of the Bible: Augustine wrote about the first chapters of Genesis in five of his works, including three of his commentaries.[3] Other authorities who wrote *Hexamera* on the six days of Creation include Basil the Great, Ambrose, Alcuin, Bede and, in the twelfth century, Abelard.[4] It is hardly surprising, then, that the beginning of *Stjórn I* is so heavy in commentary that the biblical text can

---

[1] Many commentaries divide at this point; see for example Claus Westermann, *Genesis I–II: A Commentary* (London: SPCK, 1984); Joseph Blenkinsopp, *Creation, Uncreation, Recreation: A Discursive Commentary on Genesis I–II* (New York: T & Clark International, 2011); John Day, *From Creation to Babel: Genesis I–II* (London: Bloomsbury, 2013); David M. Carr, *The Formation of Genesis I–II: Biblical and Other Precursors* (New York: Oxford University Press, 2020).

[2] For ANE sources, see especially Day, *Creation to Babel* and Carr, *Formation*.

[3] See Andrew Louth and Marco Conti, *Genesis I–II* (Downers Grove, IL: Intervarsity Press, 2001), xxxi; Joy A. Schroeder, *The Book of Genesis* (Grand Rapids, MI: William B. Eerdmans, 2015), I–30. Augustine's three commentaries on Genesis are all translated in *Saint Augustine, On Genesis*. He also engages with Genesis in his *Confessionum*, xi–xiii and *De civitate Dei*, xi–xvi.

[4] On *Hexamera* in the twelfth century, see Svanhildur Óskarsdóttir, 'Universal History', 225–56.

139

appear to be overshadowed. This is also the case for the beginning of Genesis in the *Glossa ordinaria*, which may have been one of the compiler's models.[5]

All of *Stjórn I* draws heavily on Comestor's *Historia scholastica* and Vincent of Beauvais's *Speculum historiale*, but the first part also makes use of Augustine's two finished commentaries on Genesis and Isidore's *Etymologiae*, which gives it a more encyclopaedic character. It incorporates etymology, natural history and geography, as well as theological discourses on angelology, human nature and sin. There is some evidence that, at an early stage, this part of *Stjórn* may have been planned around the readings for Septuagesima and Lent: Noah's Flood, for example, is introduced as 'annarr partr þessarrar gerðar' ('the second part of this work') and linked to the second Sunday in Septuagesima.[6] This would also explain the inclusion of extracts on the liturgy for Septuagesima from Durandus's *Rationale divinorum officiorum*, and the medley of sermons for 'fyrsta sunnudegi í langa föstu' ('the first Sunday of the Lenten fast'). However, if this was the plan, it appears to have been abandoned, as no 'third part' is ever marked. This chapter explores how the compilatory character of Genesis i–ii in *Stjórn I* works against any single mode of reading: we are presented not only with different ways of interpreting biblical narrative, but with differing versions of events and different styles of writing. Although one of these styles is plain and perhaps even saga-like, it is far from the only style the compiler uses and it is not – in these early chapters – the dominant one. Rather, we are encouraged to read Genesis i–ii from multiple different angles, of which the literal-historical is only one.

How to Read

The first two chapters of *Stjórn I* serve as prologue and *accessus* to Genesis and Exodus, and introduce the reader to several different lenses through which these books can be viewed.[7] The prologue, which is partly translated from the prologue to Comestor's *Historia scholastica*, includes his conceit of the Scriptures as the 'dining room' of an imperial God, where he entertains

---

[5]   The *Glossa Ordinaria* on Genesis has not been edited or translated in full, but there is an excellent electronic edition which can be accessed at https://gloss-e.irht.cnrs.fr.

[6]   *Stjórn*, 79. The extracts from Durandus are on pp. 72–79 and the homilies on pp. 213–39.

[7]   On the medieval *accessus*, see E. A. Quain, 'The Medieval *Accessus ad Auctores*', *Traditio* 3 (1945), 228–42; A. J. Minnis, *Medieval Theory of Authorship: Scholastic Literary Attitudes in the Later Middle Ages* (Philadelphia: University of Pennsylvania Press, 1988), 9–39; Zinn, '*Accessus* Treatise'.

In the Beginning

his followers so heartily as to induce a state of 'sober inebriation'.[8] As in the *Historia scholastica*, the dining hall is divided into three parts:[9]

> Sagan sjálf er grundvǫllr þessa heimuliga guðs húss ok herbergis. Sú skýring af heilagri skript sem segir hvat [er] verkit í sǫgunni hefir at merkja, er inn hæri veggrinn. En sú þyðing er þekjan sem oss skýrir þann skilning af þeim gerðum ok verkum er sagan hefir í sér, sem oss er til kennidóms, hvat er oss hœfir af þeira framferðum ok eptirdœmum at gera eða fram fara sem þá hefir frá verit sagt.

> History itself is the foundation of this private house and lodgings of God. The interpretation of holy scripture that tells what each historical deed signifies is the upper wall. And the roof is the interpretation which, from those deeds and events in history, gives us an exposition that instructs us which of the happenings and examples told about there we ought to do or carry out.

This is a fairly accurate translation of the passage in the *Historica scholastica*, with its clear distinction between *historia* ('saga'), *allegoria* and *tropologia*. Although the compiler lacks the vocabulary for technical terms like 'allegory' and 'tropology' – the words 'skýring' and 'þýðing' look like they have been chosen for the alliteration rather than for any difference in meaning – he gets round this by defining them carefully: allegory is the interpretation that tells you what an event signifies ('hefir at merkja') while tropology teaches what one should 'gera eða fram fara' ('do or carry out'). He even tries to capture the polyptoton in the Latin definition of tropology, replacing 'factum' ('what has been done') and 'faciendum' ('what is to be done') with the related words 'framferðum' and 'fram fara'. Towards the end of the Prologue in AM 227 fol., the compiler comes back to this building, describing his own compilation as beginning 'af sǫgðum guðs hallar grundvelli, þat er af ritningarinnar upphafi ok ǫndverðri Genesi' ('from the aforementioned foundation of God's hall, that is from the beginning of scripture and the start of Genesis').[10] This recalls Hugh of St Victor's recommendation that, for the historical sense of Scripture, students should start with Genesis. In AM 226 fol., the sentence runs slightly differently: its readers are to begin 'af sjálfri sǫgunni en eigi af hennar skýring, eða skilningi, ok enn heldr af upphafi þess sama grundvallar' ('with history itself, but not with its interpretation or exposition, but

---

8   *Stjórn*, 3; cf. Comestor, *Liber Genesis*, 4.

9   *Stjórn*, 3–4; Comestor, *Liber Genesis*, 4–5. See also pp. 61–62, where the Latin text and translation are given. On this passage, see also Sverrir Tómasson, *Formálar*, 114–15, where he discusses it in terms of the wordplay on *aedificium* ('edifice') and *aedificatio* ('edification').

10   *Stjórn*, 4.

The Old Testament in Medieval Icelandic Texts

rather from the beginning of this same foundation'). This appears – as in the prologue to Comestor's *Historia Scholastica* – to exclude allegory and tropology altogether to focus exclusively on the historical or literal level of interpretation.

If this is the case, though, the following chapter will come as a shock, for – despite the rubrics in AM 227 fol. that announce 'Hér byrjask upp sú bók er Biblia er kallat' ('Here begins the book that is called the Bible') – it begins not with the first words of Genesis, but with an unattributed gloss from Vincent of Beauvais's *Speculum historiale*: 'Almáttigr guð, verandi satt ljós, hverr er ljósit elskar ok gerir alla hluti með ljósi byrjandi réttliga ok vel viðrkvæmiliga heimsins skapan ok smíð af ljósinu' ('Almighty God, being true light, who loves the light and makes all things with light, beginning rightly and very fittingly the creation and crafting of the world by light').[11] Clearly whatever 'light' means in the first chapter of Genesis is not going to be straightforward or literal. After briefly citing Genesis 1.1 ('hann skapaði himin ok jǫrð') and Genesis 1.3 ('svá segjandi: 'verði ljós', ok þegar í stað varð ljósit'), the rest of the chapter proceeds to dismantle, with the help of three passages from Augustine, exactly how Genesis 1.3 should be read.[12] First, the reader is warned to beware any reading of 'God said' that construes God's words as 'líkamlig svá sem stundligt ok tímaligt tal ok orða tiltœki' ('carnal like temporal and timebound talk and turns of phrase').[13] Rather, one's reading should be guided by Christ, the Wisdom of God, who has assumed our human weakness into his divinity so that we will grow up 'í skynsemðinni ok várum skilningi' ('in reason and our understanding').[14] The compiler then moves on to a passage that is also in the *Glossa ordinaria*, which addresses the problem of scriptural verses that 'várum hugskotsaugum verði mjǫk myrkir ok fjarligir' ('are very dark and distant to the eyes of our minds').[15] Out of all the possible meanings that accord with true faith, readers are warned not to attach themselves too confidently to any one of them, lest they should be at fault: 'ok viljum vér svá víkja ok venda skriptarinnar ok sannleiksins órskurð þar eptir várum skilningi þar sem vér skyldim heldr várum órskurð ok skilningi eptir ritningarinnar órskurð vilja víkja' ('and we

---

11 *Stjórn*, 7; cf. *Speculum historiale*, 2.19: 'Prima ergo die ipse qui est vera lux lucemque diligit et omnia in luce facit, recte mundi fabricam a luce inchoavit' ('On the first day, therefore, he who is the true light and loves light and makes everything in light, appropriately began the building of the world from light').

12 Gen. 1.1 ('he created heaven and earth'); Gen. 3.1 ('saying: 'let there be light'. And at once there was light').

13 *Stjórn*, 7; Augustine, *De genesi*, i.36, trans. Hill, 185.

14 *Stjórn*, 8; the focus on 'reason and understanding' here is the compiler's own.

15 Augustine, *De genesi* i.37, trans. Hill, 185; cf. *Glossa ordinaria*, ed. Morard (Gen. Promethata laodunensia).

142

In the Beginning

wish to twist and turn scripture and the ruling of truth according to our understanding, when we ought rather wish to turn our judgement and understanding according to the ruling of scripture').[16] For those with less book-learning, the advice is simpler: one should take whatever seems most fitting 'eptir sinni skilningu ok skynsemðar manéri' ('according to one's understanding and manner of reasoning').[17]

We are already a long way from the Prologue's confident assertion that 'í heilagri ritningu skildum vér allir inn sama hlut með einu samþykki' ('in holy scripture we all understand the same thing with one accord').[18] Not only does Scripture encompass multiple meanings, but these meanings in some sense grow with our understanding, as Gregory the Great commented (p. 51). At this point, the compiler returns to Genesis 1.3 to attempt to unpack its meaning. When the Bible says that God 'spoke', it does not mean that he spoke in Hebrew, Greek, Latin or 'nǫkkura aðra líkamliga eða veraldliga tungu' ('any other carnal or worldly language'): 'heldr talaði hann þat allt með því sama ósundrskiptiliga orði ok sameiginliga eilífu sjálfum sér, sem inn heilagri Jón postuli segir af í sínu guðspjalli at í upphafi var orð, ok fyrir þat sama orð urðu allir hlutir' ('rather he spoke all this through the same unchangeable word that is co-eternal with himself, as the holy apostle John says in his Gospel that in the beginning was the Word, and by that same Word all things came into being').[19] The link between Genesis 1.1 and John 1.1 is made in the opening words of the Gloss and in the *Historia scholastica*, so it is not surprising to find it here. For Augustine, it is the proper (that is to say literal in the sense of 'ad litteram' – 'according to the letter') meaning of Genesis 1.1. For how could God speak if there was no time in which the sounds could unfold and no ears to hear them do so? Here the compiler plays on rhyming words in Old Norse, drawing attention to their temporal sequence: 'þar sem eigi beið þá enn nǫkkurs líkamligs h*eyr*n eðr *eyr*u til at h*eyr*a þar upp á' ('when there was not as yet any bodily hearing or ears to hear them with').[20] Where the Prologue gave three ways of interpreting Scripture, all of which built harmoniously one on top of the other, this section suggests rather that we must avoid turning 'til líkamligs ok veraldligs skilnings sem kirkjunnar

---

16 Augustine, *De genesi* i.37, trans. Hill, 186.

17 *Stjórn*, 9; Augustine, *De genesi* i.40 (trans. Hill, 187): 'ut pro suo modulo eligat quisque quod capere possit' ('leaving everyone ready to choose whichever they can grasp more readily in their turn').

18 *Stjórn*, 3. This is adapted from Comestor's gloss on Ps. 54.15; *Liber Genesis*, 4 ('*Ambulauimus in domo Dei cum consensu*, id est in sacra scriptura id ipsum sapientes' – '*In the house of God we walked with consent*, that is, in sacred scripture, being of one mind').

19 *Stjórn*, 9; Augustine, *De genesi contra Manichaeos* i.15; *De genesi* i.5, trans. Hill, 48, 179.

20 Augustine, *De genesi*, i.4, 16, trans. Hill, 170.

The Old Testament in Medieval Icelandic Texts

kennifeðr ok heilǫg [skrift] segir at með andligum skýringum eru skiljandi' ('to a carnal and worldly sense that which the Fathers of the Church and holy scripture says is to be understood with spiritual interpretation').[21] Both the emphasis on multiple meanings and the sharp distinction between carnal and spiritual ways of reading are typically Augustinian: the Old Testament is properly understood only through the person of Christ.

The final part of the chapter focuses on Moses as author of the Pentateuch and addresses, as an *accessus* should, the author's intention in writing. Hugh of St Victor, in his *Adnotationes*, had described Moses as a 'historiographus' ('historian') and Andrew had suggested, more audaciously, that he compiled his work through historical research.[22] I have not been able to identify the source of *Stjórn I*'s information on Moses, which Astås labels as 'eget' ('his own'), although the compiler does draw on Gregory's first homily on Ezekiel to justify how Moses could know things that had happened before anyone's lifetime: this is described as a kind of prophecy that works backwards rather than forwards.[23] Moses's intention, in asking God to reveal the past to him, is characterised as didactic: 'vildi hann opinberliga sýna Israels fólki ǫll þau dœmi at þeir mætti þaðan af auðveldliga nema viðrsýnd illra atburða en draga sér til nytsemðar ǫll þau góð dœmi sem verit hǫfðu' ('he wished openly to show the Israelites all these examples so that, from then on, they might easily take warning from the bad events and make use of all the good examples that had taken place').[24] AM 226 fol. adds that these things had to be revealed to him 'því at engin hafði þess gáð at láta skrifa sinna æfi eða minnisamlig dœmi' ('because nobody had taken the trouble to have their lives or memorable events written down'). One purpose of history, as the author of *Konungs skuggsjá* knew (p. 124), was to provide moral examples to live by. This, then, offers yet a third way in which the Old Testament might be read: as an anthology of moral exempla. All these ways of reading are entirely in accord with the methods of Victorine biblical exegesis.

The Fall of the Angels and the Creation of Woman

The first two chapters of *Stjórn I* offer multiple ways of reading without specifying whether these can or should be harmonised. In the same way, the chapters that follow accommodate more than one reading of the same event. We start with the Fall of the Angels, which is told twice, firstly from the *Speculum historiale* as a gloss on Genesis 1.1 ('God created heaven and

---

21 Cf. Augustine, *De genesi*, i.4, trans. Hill, 170.
22 Smalley, *Study of the Bible*, 131–32; cf. Hugh, *Adnotationes*, trans. van Zwieten, 61.
23 Gregory the Great, *Homiliae in Hiezechielem prophetam*, i.1.2, trans. Tomkinson, 28.
24 *Stjórn*, 11.

In the Beginning

earth'), and secondly from the *Historia scholastica* as a gloss on Genesis 1.4 ('he divided the light from the darkness'). The title in AM 227 fol. presents it as a dramatic narrative: 'hér ségir af því hversu almáttigr guð skapaði himin ok jǫrð ok hversu Lucifer braut með sínu drambi ok ǫfund í móti guði sjálfum' ('here it is told how Almighty God created heaven and earth and how Lucifer in his pride and envy rebelled against God himself').[25] But this is somewhat misleading; the compiler is far more interested in theological questions of angelology than in the narrative drama of Satan's rebellion and fall. He engages enthusiastically with some of the classic problems of angelology: angelic free will, the unchanging nature of the angels once fallen or confirmed, their ability to love God, angelic knowledge, and that staple of scholastic theology – how many angels can congregate in a single place. The fall of Lucifer is narrated in a high-flown style that has its starting point in the Latin of Vincent of Beauvais, but takes it considerably further:[26]

> Nú sem Lucifer einn af hinni fremstu engla skipun, skrýddr ok prýddr umfram aðra, þá hugleiddi ok virði fegrð ok forprísan sinnar náttúru ok djúpsetta vitru sér veitta, hóf hann sik svá hátt með sínu ofdrambi, at hann vildi jafnask ok viðrlíkjask sjálfan guð, ok fyrir þá sǫk skildi hann sik í frá sannleikinum þegar í hríðinni ok þar með í brott af ǫllum sœtleik ok eylífri sælu.

> Now when Lucifer, one of the foremost order of angels, adorned and ornamented above others, reflected and considered the beauty and excellence of his nature and the deep-set wisdom granted to him, he raised himself so high in his arrogance that he wished to be equal and comparable to God himself, and for this reason he took his leave from truth at that very moment and with it from all sweetness and eternal joy.

The rhyming word-pair 'skrýddr ok prýddr' translates and imitates the Latin 'opertus et ornatus' ('covered and adorned'), while the paired verbs 'hugleiddi' and 'virði' draw out the full strength of the Latin 'perpendens' ('to assess or to weigh carefully'). The Latin 'eminentia' ('pre-eminence, excellence') is translated with the rare loan-word 'forprísa' (from French

---

[25] *Stjórn*, 13.

[26] *Stjórn*, 14; *Speculum historiale* 2.10: 'Itaque Lucifer omni lapide precioso opertus et ornatus quia in aliorum comparatione preclarus, eminentiam nature sue perpendens et profunditate[m] scientie in tantum superbivit, quod etiam deo equare se voluit, sicque factus statim se a veritate avertit et beate vite dulcedinem non gustavit' ('And in this way, Lucifer, covered and adorned with all precious stones, because he was very bright in comparison with others, considering the excellence of his nature and the depth of his knowledge, became arrogant to such an extent that he wished to be equal even to God and, having become thus, he at once turned away from truth and did not taste the sweetness of a blessed life').

145

The Old Testament in Medieval Icelandic Texts

'pris') backed up with the more familiar 'fegrð' ('beauty'), presumably for the sake of alliteration. This tendency to duplicate or paraphrase the Latin words of the source in order to capture their full meaning and exploit the alliterative resources of Old Norse can be seen throughout this extract: 'fegrð ok forprísan' (for 'eminentiam'), 'djúpsettan vitru sér veitta' ('profunditate scientie'), 'hóf hann sik svá hátt' ('superbivit'), 'jafnask ok viðrlíkjask' ('equare'), 'sœtleikr ok eylíf sæla' ('beate vite dulcedinum'). The word-pairs take their departure from the Latin but exude a dynamic energy that is all their own. The passage that follows is so heavy in added word-pairs that it would be easy to miss the two brief references to falling: the devil is punished for his 'skaða ok glæp' ('harm and crime'), his 'glæp ok ógiptu' ('crime and ill-luck'); he and his minions are motivated by 'ǫfund ok ofbeldi' ('envy and pride'); they take pride in their 'mekt ok valdi' ('power and might'); they are parted from 'fagnað ok heiðr' ('joy and honour'), from 'sælu ok fagnaði' ('happiness and joy').[27] Instead of following the temporal movement of falling – so vividly depicted in the left-hand margin of AM 227 fol., fol. 1v (Fig. 2) – the narrative is static, enmeshed in the psychological state of the fallen angels, which is now fixed as permanent and unchanging.

When the same event is retold in Genesis 1.4, though, the style is rather different. The gloss here comes from the *Historia scholastica*: 'Intelligitur etiam hic angelorum facta diuisio: stantes lux, cadentes tenebre dicti sunt' ('Here also the division of the angels is understood to have been made, those remaining are called light, those falling are called the shadows').[28] This is the traditional understanding of the verse, which can be traced back to Augustine.[29] The compiler imitates Comestor's wording closely: 'Fyrir ljóssins nefnd merkjask þeir englar sem **st**óðu ok **st**aðfestusk i guðs **á**st ok **e**lskhuga, en fyrir myrkrinn merkisk fjándinn ok þeir sem með honum féllu' ('By the name of light are signified those angels who stood and became steadfast in God's love and affection, and by darkness is signified the devil and those who fell with him').[30] Despite the two alliterating word-pairs characterising the good angels, the style aims at precision rather than excess: the parallel clauses in the Latin are carefully reproduced and the same syntactical structure is used for each. The compiler goes on to add a detail from Day Five in the *Historia scholastica*: 'Váru þeir keyrðir brott sumir allt niðr til helvítis, en sumir í þat þokufulla lopt millum himins ok jarðar' ('They were driven away, some all the way down to hell and some into the foggy

---

27 *Stjórn*, 14. Compare: 'hann féll svá hátt' ('he fell so steeply'), 'sem hann féll' ('as he fell').

28 Comestor, *Liber Genesis*, 10.

29 Augustine, *De genesi* ii.16–18, xi.33.

30 *Stjórn*, 19.

Figure 2. The Fall of the Angels, left-hand margin, AM 227 fol. 1v.

The Old Testament in Medieval Icelandic Texts

air between heaven and earth').[31] Again, the potential for drama is passed over, but we do get a glimpse of the compiler's continuing interest in the psychology of the Fall. Whereas Comestor says that the devils are cast into hell 'ad suam penam' ('to their punishment'), the compiler adds: 'ok þó fylgir þeim ævinliga sín helvítis pína hvar sem þeir eru' ('and yet, wherever they are, each is eternally accompanied by their own torment of hell').

After the Fall of the Angels, the commentary takes on a more regular pattern, and rubrics are regularly used to identify citations from the Bible ('af genesi'), from Comestor ('af scolastica historia'), from Vincent of Beauvais ('af speculo historiale') and, finally, from Augustine ('af augustino') and Isidore ('ysidoreus'). In this way, the compilation imitates the layout of the *Glossa ordinaria* in distinguishing between text and commentary, as well as blending text and commentary in the manner of Comestor's *Historia scholastica*. There is limited scope for narrative at this stage: short extracts from the Bible are followed by long passages of commentary, and the variety of sources necessitates a fair amount of repetition and movement back and forth, signalled textually by phrases like 'fyrr sagt', 'fyrrnefndri', 'fyrir sagt', 'sem fyrr var sagt', 'fyrrsagða hluti' (all variations on 'aforesaid'); and also 'sem síðar mun heyrask' ('as will later be heard') and 'sem ofar meir mun heyrask mega' ('on which more may be heard below').[32] The biblical verses become prompts for a variety of fascinating questions: how can there be day and night without sun or moon? How do birds and fish resemble each other? Why did God create mice, flies, frogs and maggots? How can humans have dominion over animals by which they can be killed? The compiler is very fond of lists, which he borrows mainly from the *Speculum historiale*. Some of these are marked in the margins of AM 227 fol. as of particular value to the learner: the three dignities of mankind ('dignitas homine triplex'), the five ways in which mankind is in the image of God ('.v. mod.'), and the six ages of the world.[33] But there are others: the twofold danger of sin and the devil; the three enemies of the flesh, the world and the devil; the four ways in which angels bring us to paradise; the threefold image of the Trinity in the human mind.[34] Unsurprisingly, the compiler pays particular attention to the creation of humankind on Day Six and what it means for humans to be made in the image of God. This chapter ends with the allegorical significance of humans walking upright: 'svá sem sjálfan hann áminnandi at hann hafi á þann hátt sín hugskotsauga ok skilningarvit til himneskra hluta sem hans líkamlig augu ok skilningarvit ok ásjóna veit upp til himinsins' ('as if

---

31 Comestor, *Liber Genesis*, 18.
32 *Stjórn*, 18, 20, 22, 29, 31, 32, 34, 45, 47, 48, 54, 58, 59.
33 *Stjórn*, 30–32, 38–44; cf. the marginal annotations in AM 227 fol., fols 5v, 7r, 7v.
34 *Stjórn*, 15, 16, 30.

148

In the Beginning

to remind him to turn the eyes of his mind and intellect towards heavenly things to the same extent that his bodily eyes and intellect and countenance are turned up to heaven').[35]

Throughout this section, the compiler stays close to the style of his sources, often reproducing localised effects such as rhyme. For example, when translating 'signa serenitatis et tempestatis' ('signs of clear weather or stormy weather') from the *Historia scholastica*, he replaces the *similiter cadens* with rhyme: 'skír veðr eða óskír, blíð eða hríðir' ('clear weather or cloudy, sunshine or storms').[36] When Comestor speaks of how God 'creauit, disposuit et ornauit' ('created, laid out and adorned'), the compiler comes up with an alliterative equivalent: 'skapat, skipat, ok skreytt' ('created, arranged, and adorned').[37] Occasionally, the effects seem to be entirely his own, as when he speaks of how the planets 'reika ok leika lausar í loptinu' (from the Latin gloss 'id est stele erratice' in the *Speculum historiale*).[38] There are homely touches, too, although fewer than one might expect. While Comestor describes the firmament of heaven on Day Two as 'ad instar cristalli solidatam et perlucidam' ('hardened and transparent in the likeness of a crystal'), the compiler adds a more relatable simile: 'sem kristallus eða inn harðasti glerís til at jafna útan þat er þau megu lítt eða ekki bráðna af nokkurum eldshiti' ('comparable to crystal or the hardest transparent ice except that it can hardly or not at all be melted by the heat of fire').[39] When Vincent of Beauvais gives a long list of inclement weather types on Day Three (tempestuous wind, thunder and lightning, thick cloud, heavy rain, snow and hail storms), the compiler ruefully acknowledges how familiar these are: 'vindum ok vætum, þokum ok reiðarþrumum, snjóvum ok eldingum, ok öðrum þeim hlutum tilkomandi sem vér höfum fulla raun af' ('wind and rain, mist and thunder, snow-storms and lightning, and other such things that we have full experience of').[40] On Day Four, Comestor suggests that the moon and stars light up the night 'ut operantes in nocte ut naute et uiatores solatium luminis haberent' ('so that workers at night like sailors and travellers might have the consolation of light'). The compiler renders this image with an alliterative word-pair that increases its affectivity: 'at þeir menn sem á náttartímanum starfaði skyldi þar af hjálp ok huggan hafa' ('so that those people who worked at night should have help and comfort from them'). But precisely where we might expect an example from northern Europe, with its long winter nights, we are transported to Ethiopia: 'einkannliga í Blálands eyðimörkum eða

---

[35] *Stjórn*, 32; *De genesi contra Manichaeos*, i.27, trans. Hill, 57.

[36] *Stjórn*, 25; Comestor, *Liber Genesis*, 16.

[37] *Stjórn*, 44; Comestor, *Liber Genesis*, 25.

[38] *Stjórn*, 25; *Speculum historiale*, 2.25 ('That is wandering stars').

[39] *Stjórn*, 20; Comestor, *Liber Genesis*, 11; cf. *Speculum historiale* 2.25.

[40] *Stjórn*, 22; *Speculum historiale*, 2.21.

The Old Testament in Medieval Icelandic Texts

sandhǫfum, þar sem lítill vindsblær sléttir ok hylr þá vegu sem áðr hafa farnir verit' ('especially in Ethiopa's deserts and sandhills, where a small gust of wind erases and hides the paths that have previously been taken').[41]

Thus far the commentary has been primarily (though not solely) literal, justifying the statement in AM 226 fol. that this work will focus on 'history' and not allegory. However, following the 'literal' account of the six days of Creation, two long allegorical passages are inserted, both from Augustine's commentary on Genesis against the Manicheans: the six days of Creation as the six ages of the world and the six ages of man, and an allegorical interpretation of Genesis 2. These passages are characterised by vividly figurative language: the Flood which ends the First Age signifies 'óminnis gleymsku flóði' ('the flood of forgetfulness and un-remembering') in which the memories of our infancy are drowned.[42] Meanwhile, the heathens in the Fifth Age are tossed about by the great variety of their false beliefs 'sem fljúgandi fuglar renna ok reika hingat ok þangat' ('just as flying birds run and race hither and thither').[43] The rendering of Genesis 2 in particular reinforces the Augustinian idea that reading allegorically serves as a remedy for our fallen humanity: 'Spámanna bœkr ok postulanna ritningar verða mǫrgum svá myrkar ok óskiljanligar sem þær sé með nǫkkurum þokum eða skýflokum skyggðar ok huldar. En þá verða þær velskiljandum mǫnnum svá sem nýtsamlig sannleiksskúr ef þær eru með margfaldri ok vitrligri trakteran talaðar ok skynsamliga skýrðar' ('The prophets' books and the writings of the apostles are for many as dark and difficult to understand as if they are clouded and covered by mists or thick clouds. But to those who have good understanding they become like useful showers of truth if they are explained with manifold and wise exegesis and interpreted reasonably').[44] The language here recalls the *accessus* in chapter 2: the Scriptures are 'dark', but their true meaning is revealed through allegorical reading, which is accessed through understanding and reason (reproduced through the move from 'óskiljanligr' to 'velskiljandi'). The Old Norse translation incorporates into this a clever pun on 'skúr' ('shower') and 'skýra' ('to interpret'), so the metaphorical clouds ('ský') are dissipated by the 'skúr' ('showers') that are the result of 'skýring' ('interpretation'). The compiler distinguishes clearly between these allegorical reflections and the historical narrative, commenting as he moves on to the four rivers of Paradise: 'er til sǫgunnar aptr hverfanda' ('let us turn back to the history').[45]

---

41 *Stjórn*, 25; Comestor, *Liber Genesis*, 15.
42 *Stjórn*, 39; Augustine, *De genesi contra Manichaeos*, i.35.
43 *Stjórn*, 42; Augustine, *De genesi contra Manichaeos*, i.39.
44 *Stjórn*, 46, cf. pp. 8–10, 13; Augustine, *De genesi contra Manichaeos*, ii.5, trans. Hill, 73–74.
45 *Stjórn*, 47.

In the Beginning

The creation of Eve shows a similar oscillation between literal and allegorical reading. Eve is first mentioned in Genesis 1.27 ('male and female he created them'), which the compiler translates: 'skapaði hann bæði karlmann ok kvenmann ok þó síðar konuna sem ofar meir mun heyrask' ('he made both man and woman, and yet the woman later, about which more will be heard below').[46] The addition of 'ok þó síðar konuna' ('and yet the woman later') is clearly meant to smooth over the apparent contradiction between Genesis 1 and Genesis 2, where the woman is created some time after the man.[47] But, before we get to Genesis 2, the compiler adds an allegorical gloss from Augustine that depends on this later passage: 'á þeim degi varð bæði karlmaðr ok kona, með þeim hætti er á þessum aldri iHsuc xpistuc ok hans kristni' ('on that day both man and woman came to be, in the same way as in this age Jesus Christ and his Church').[48] Eve signifies the Church because she comes out of the side of the man, just as blood and water flow from Christ's side, representing the sacraments of the Church. Some time later, we arrive at Genesis 2.21–24, but even here the verses are divided up by extra-biblical glosses rather than translated continuously.[49] The compiler does not quite capture the wordplay and parallelism of the Vulgate: he translates Adam's 'os ex ossibus meis, et caro de carne mea' ('bone of my bones and flesh of my flesh') as 'Þetta bein er af mínum beinum ok þetta kjǫtin er af mínum líkam til tekit' ('this bone is from my bones, and this flesh is taken from my body'). He seems more concerned with clarifying the meaning than imitating the style. The pun on 'vir' and 'virago' in the Latin is rendered through half-rhyme and alliteration between 'karlmaðr' ('man') and 'kerling' ('old woman'), but Eve of course is not really an 'old woman', and this word-pair clashes with the earlier word-pair 'karlmaðr ok kvenmaðr' ('man and woman') found at Genesis 1.27. Though Adam's prophecy of Christ and the Church at Genesis 2.21 (from Comestor) could have been linked to Augustine's earlier reading of Adam and Eve as Christ and the Church, the compiler does not signal this, translating 'ecclesia' in the first passage as 'kristni' and in the second as 'heilǫg kirkja' ('holy church'). There is a high level of tolerance for inconsistency here, and the compiler seems unconcerned about narrative momentum and coherence. His focus is not on telling a story, but on organising his sources to convey the full range of possible interpretations.

---

[46] *Stjórn*, 30.

[47] On the two different creation accounts in Genesis, see Blenkinsopp, *Creation*, 6–8, 54–55.

[48] *Stjórn*, 43; Augustine, *De genesi contra Manichaeos*, i.40, trans. Hill, 65.

[49] *Stjórn*, 51–52; cf. Comestor, *Liber Genesis*, 35–39.

The Fall of Man

The willing accommodation of multiple interpretations also characterises the account of the Fall of Man: the theological importance of this scene overrides its considerable narrative potential. It is helpful to compare *Stjórn I* with *Konungs skuggsjá* at this point: both are using the same or similar sources, but the overall effect is different. Whereas the author of *Konungs skuggsjá* incorporates the glosses into the narrative, adapting and reshaping the biblical story to bring out the relevant moral and psychological themes, the compiler of *Stjórn I* tends to juxtapose and label different interpretations, distinguishing between text and commentary. The closest thing to a narrative sequence is the temptation and fall scene from Genesis 3.1–7, which is translated mainly from Comestor's *Historia scholastica* with some small adjustments to make it closer to the biblical text. But it is carefully framed by Augustine's theology of original sin and the beginnings of sexual arousal. The chapter starts with a passage from the *Historia scholastica*, to which the compiler has appended Augustine's gloss on the nakedness of Adam and Eve before the Fall:[50]

> Þau kenndu ǫngva þá girnd eða freistni með sér sem þau þyrfti at stǫðva, svá sem vér skammfyllumsk eigi hverr sem sér á oss hǫfuð ok fœtr, því at ótilheyrilig ok óviðrkvæmilig limanna hræring gerir þá skammfulliga. Ok sem smásveinar skammfyllask eigi þó at þeira leyndarlimir sé litnir eða sénir, því at þeir kenna eigi af gœzku síns unga aldrs með sér nǫkkura skammfulliga hræring, eða hvar af mundu þau skammfyllask, segir inn heilagi Augustinus, þar sem þeir kenndu eigi lǫgmál í sínum limum gagnstaðligt hugskotsins lǫgmáli?

> They knew no desire or temptation in themselves which they needed to control, just as we are not ashamed if someone looks at our head and feet, because the improper and inappropriate movement of limbs is what makes them shameful. And just as small boys are not ashamed if their private parts

---

[50] *Stjórn*, 52; Comestor, *Liber Genesis*, 39 'Nichil putabant uelandum, quia nichil senserant refrenandum. Sicut nec erubescimus, si quis uideat manus et caput et pedes nostros. Inordinatus enim membrorum motus ipsa facit pudenda. Sicut et pueri si uideantur pudenda eorum, non erubescunt, quia beneficio etatis motum erubesci-bilem nondum sentiunt' ('They did not think anything needed to be covered, because they had discerned nothing that needed to be held in check, just as we do not blush if anyone should see our hands and head and feet, for the inappropriate movement of these members is what makes them shameful. Just as boys, if their private parts should be seen, do not blush, because by virtue of their age they do not yet feel any movement of which to be ashamed'); Augustine, *De genesi* xi.3 'quid enim puderet, quando nullam legem senserant in membris suis repugnantem legi mentis suae' (trans. Hill, 430 'What should they be ashamed of after all, when they were aware of no law in their members fighting back against the law of their minds?').

In the Beginning

are seen or visible since they do not know on account of the goodness of their young age any shameful movement within themselves; moreover, of what would they be ashamed, says the holy Augustine, since they have not known any law in their limbs opposing the law of the mind?

Augustine's voice stands out here because the rhetorical question requires it, and his name is cited both to identify the questioner and to give authority to his words. At the end of the chapter, after Adam and Eve have both eaten the fruit, the compiler inserts a second rhetorical question from Augustine, followed by Comestor's gloss. Augustine is commenting on what it means to say that the eyes of Adam and Eve were opened:[51]

> Hversu þá útan af sjálfra þeira girnd sín í milli, upp á þann hátt at þeim þótti nǫkkleiki síns líkama harðla ljótr vera, svá sem þeir kenndu ok undirstóðu at þau váru nǫkkvið, því at þau hǫfðu áðr með sér náttúruligar girndir ok hrœringar svá hógliga stilltar ok stǫðvaðar með sjálfum sér með ungum smásveinum fyrr enn nǫkkurr girndarinnar gneisti kœmi til þeira. Váru þeira leyndarlimir þeim upp á sína náttúru svá hœgir ok eptirlátir í alla staði sem hendr eða fœtr. En síðan er þau urðu óhlýðin sínum yfirboða, þat er skaparanum, þá kenndu þau þegar nǫkkura hrœring þá í sínum leyndarlimum, sem þau skildu at í móti skynsemðinni ok andarinnar lǫgmáli váru.

In what way, then, other than their desire for one another – in that they thought the nakedness of their body very ugly when they perceived and understood that they were naked, for previously they had calmed and controlled their natural desires and arousals within themselves as easily as among young boys before any spark of desire enters them? Their private parts were naturally as obedient and docile in every respect as hands or feet. But after they were disobedient to their superior, that is the Creator, they at once felt a certain arousal in their private parts which they understood to be against reason and against the law of the mind.

Both passages are a blend of Augustine and the *Historia scholastica*, where Comestor is also drawing on Augustine. But some of the repetition has been

---

51   *Stjórn*, 54; Augustine, *De genesi* xi.40 'Quo, nisi ad invicem concupiscendum' (trans. Hill, 452 'For what, if not for lusting after each other?'); Comestor, *Liber Genesis*, 41 'quid perceperunt quod non ante, disconuenientiam scilicet nuditatis [...] Erant enim in eis naturales motus concupiscentie, sed repressi et clausi ut in pueris usque ad pubertatem [...] Et sicut inobedientes fuerunt suo superiori, sic et membra ceperunt moueri contra suum superius, id est rationem' ('they perceived – as they had not before – that their nudity was displeasing [...] for there were in them natural movements of concupiscence, but held back and closed off, as in boys up until puberty [...] and just as they were disobedient to their superior, so also their members began to be moved against their superior, that is reason').

The Old Testament in Medieval Icelandic Texts

added by the compiler: in the second passage, he has added 'hands and feet' to align with Comestor's 'head and feet' in the first passage, and he has inserted 'against the law of the mind' to refer back to the Pauline contrast in the first passage between the 'law of the flesh' and the 'law of the mind'.[52] This pattern of repetition creates a clear theological framework that guides how the biblical text should be read. The author of *Konungs skuggsjá* shares this view of the Fall as the origin of sexual arousal. But whereas he incorporates this into how he tells the story (see pp. 127–28), the compiler of *Stjórn* separates it out and marks it as commentary.

Like the author of *Konungs skuggsjá*, the compiler of *Stjórn I* is interested in psychological motivation but, rather than conveying this through direct speech, he mediates it through an omniscient narrator, who tells us what the characters are thinking and comments on their thoughts. For example, when the serpent approaches Eve rather than Adam, the compiler explains that: 'hann óttaðisk at vera kenndr af sínum svíkum af karlmanninum ok hann vissi hana veykari ok óvitrari vera en karlmanninn' ('he was afraid that he would be recognised in his deceit by the man, and he knew her to be weaker and less knowing than the man').[53] When Eve dithers over exactly what God has commanded, he criticises her sharply: 'Ok efandi maðr víkr hingat ok þangat ok er í ǫngu ǫruggr' ('and a doubter turns this way and that and is sure of nothing').[54] Before Eve takes the apple from the tree, her motivation is revealed: 'konan var metnaðargjǫrn í því, er hon vildi samlíkjask við guð af ormsins áeggjan' ('the woman was proud in that she wanted to be like God through the persuasion of the serpent'). Finally, when Adam takes the apple from Eve, we are told why he was easy to convince:

> svá sem hann sá, at hon dó eigi þegar hon hafði etit eplit af því tré, eptir því sem hann skildi Guðs orð til vera, at hon mundi deyja þegar í stað, þá trúði hann at hann hefði þat til varhygðar at eins talat ok hœtingar sem hann hafði þeim dauðanum ógnat.

> when he saw that she did not die at once after she had eaten the apple from the tree, according to what he had understood God's words to mean – that she would die on the spot – then he believed that he had only said it as a warning or threat when he had threatened them with death.[55]

In *Konungs skuggsjá*, this detail is revealed by means of narrative innovation: the serpent eats from the tree first to convince Eve that the fruit will not cause her death, and Eve then goes on to convince Adam that it will not cause

---

52 Cf. Romans 7.21–25.
53 *Stjórn*, 53; cf, Comestor, *Liber Genesis*, 39.
54 Comestor, *Liber Genesis*, 40.
55 Comestor, *Liber Genesis*, 41.

In the Beginning

his. In *Stjórn I*, a more theologically precise explanation is preferred: Adam misunderstands God's words to mean that they will die physically after eating from the tree, but in fact God's words are to be understood spiritually. The Fall hinges, therefore, on Adam's dangerously literal interpretation of God's word, and literal interpretation leads inevitably to spiritual death.[56]

This running commentary on events is even more marked in the chapter where Adam and Eve are confronted by God, where it repeatedly cuts into the biblical narrative, breaking up the dialogue. Take the rendering of Genesis 3.9–12, for example:[57]

Eptir þat kallaði guð Adam ok sagði svá til hans fyrir skepnunnar embætti í manns mynd eptir því sem heilagr Augustinus [segir] í elliftu bók yfir Genesim, eigi sem óvitandi heldr sem ásakandi ok skyldandi hann til at játa sína synd: 'Hvar ert þú, Adam?' Þat hefir svá mikit at þýða: 'Sé nú í hverja eymd ok vesǫld þú ert voltinn'. **Scolastica hystoria. Capitulum.** Fyrir þá sǫk var karlmaðrinn fyrri spurðr, at honum var fyrri boðorðit sett ok hann skyldi þat konunni kunnigt gera, sem fyrr var sagt. **Genesis. Capitulum.** Hann svaraði: 'Ek heyrða þína rǫdd hér í paradís ok óttaðisk ek fyrir þann skyld, at ek var nǫkkviðr ok því fal ek mik'. **Commestor.** Harðla heimsklig andsvǫr ok af mikilli villu ok vantrú, at maðrinn mundi fyrir nǫkkleikann guði mislíka, þar sem hann var með nǫkkleikinum skapaðr. Ok þá sagði guð svá til hans: 'Hverr sagði þér er þú værir nǫkkviðr nema þat at þu ázt af því tré, hverju er ek bauð þér at þú skyldir eigi eta?' Sjaldan eða aldrigi segir ofmetnaðarmaðrinn: 'Ek misgerða'.

After that God called Adam and said to him through the office of a created being in human form according to what St Augustine says in the eleventh book on Genesis, not as if ignorant, but rather as accusing and urging him to confess his sin: 'Where are you, Adam?' That is as much as to say: 'Now see in what distress and misery you are fallen'. **Historia Scholastica. Chapter.** The reason the man was asked first was because the commandment was given to him first, and he was supposed to make it known to the woman, as was said previously. **Genesis. Chapter.** He answered: 'I heard your voice here in Paradise and I was afraid because I

---

[56] *Stjórn*, 50: 'á þeim degi sem þú hefir af því etit munt þú andliga deyja, ok dauðligr verða' ('on the day that you have eaten of it, you will die spiritually and become mortal').

[57] *Stjórn*, 54–55; Comestor, *Liber Genesis*, 42 'et increpando, non ignorando ait: Adam, ubi es? Quasi diceret, uide in qua miseria es' ('and as a rebuke, not in ignorance, he said: Adam, where are you? As if he were to say: See in what misery you are'), 'Stulta responsio, quasi displiceret nudus qui talis fuerat factus' ('A foolish response, as if a naked man would be displeasing, when he was created this way'); Augustine, *De genesi* xi.45–47 'Superbia! Numquid dixit: Peccavi?' (trans. Hill, 455–56 'Oh, pride! Did he say: I have sinned?').

The Old Testament in Medieval Icelandic Texts

was naked and so I hid myself'. **Comestor.** A very foolish answer and with great error and unbelief, that man would displease God on account of his nakedness when he was created naked. And then God said to him: 'Who told you that you were naked unless you ate from the tree from which I told you not to eat?' The proud man seldom or never says: 'I sinned'.

The commentary – from Augustine's Literal Commentary on Genesis and the *Historia scholastica* – is wedged between question and reply and sometimes even between the verb of speaking and the speech itself: between 'God called Adam and said' and what God said; between God's first question – which is paraphrased to clarify its meaning – and Adam's reply; between Adam's reply and God's follow-up question. This is noticeable not just because the narrative is continually interrupted, but also because the rubrics visually break up the manuscript page. The compiler allows for multiple voices: the voices of God and Adam, the commentator's paraphrase ('Now see in what distress and misery you have fallen!'), Comestor's exclamation ('A very foolish answer!'), and the voice of the archetypal proud man – borrowed from Augustine – refusing to admit that 'I sinned'. The polyphony of critical voices threatens to drown out the dialogue between God and Adam.

Moreover, these different voices offer contrasting and sometimes contradictory interpretations of the biblical text. Augustine, for example, identifies the sin of pride with the man: Adam refuses to admit his fault 'eptir ofmetnaðarmanna óvana' ('according to the bad habit of proud men') and he eats the apple because 'hann vildi viðrlíkjask guði í því at vera frjáls ok liðugr af hans dróttnan' ('he wished to be like God in being free and unhindered by his lordship').[58] In contrast, Comestor attributes pride not to the man, but to the woman, commenting that the serpent sinned in three ways, the woman in two, and the man only in one. The serpent is envious, deceitful and treacherous; while Eve sinned in that 'hon eggjaði sinn bónda at eta eplit' ('she egged on her husband to eat the apple') and also 'með ofmetnaði þá er hon hugðisk ok vildi verða svá vitr sem guð' ('in pride when she purposed and wished to become as wise as God').[59] The man, however, is only at fault because 'hann át af tré því, sem honum var fyrirboðit' ('he ate from the tree which was forbidden to him'). The *Speculum historiale* also connects pride with the woman rather than the man but, unlike Comestor, Vincent of Beauvais claims that the man sinned not in one, but two ways: first, that 'hann bergði á bǫnnuðum ávexti' ('he tasted the forbidden fruit') and, second, that 'hann afsakaði sik, kennandi konunni sína sekt' ('he excused himself, blaming the woman for his guilt').[60] In one respect, however, Vincent considers Adam's

---

58 *Stjórn*, 55; Augustine, *De genesi contra Manichaeos*, ii.25, trans. Hill, 88.
59 *Stjórn*, 55–57; Comestor, *Liber Genesis*, 44.
60 *Stjórn*, 58; *Speculum historiale* 2.42.

156

In the Beginning

guilt more serious than Eve's: 'En þó misgerði karlmaðrinn enn þungligar upp á þann hátt því at hann misgerði vísvitandi þar sem hon var lokkat til með lygiligum svíkum misgerandi þar fyrir meir af nǫkkurri óvizku' ('And yet the man sinned still more heavily in that he sinned knowingly, while she was tempted with deceitful lies, sinning more out of ignorance').

If this appears to mitigate Eve's fault, it is a small pittance, for both Vincent of Beauvais and Augustine give reasons elsewhere that tend to excuse the man. From *Speculum historiale* comes the claim that Adam 'lokkaðisk [...] eptir hennar áeggjan svá sem af nǫkkurum ofmiklum vináttu góðvilja ok eptirlæti, fyrir því at hann uggði at hon mundi styggvask við ef hann æti eigi eplit, er hon bar honum' ('was tempted [...] by her persuasion as from the excessive good-will and indulgence of friendship, because he was afraid that she would get angry if he didn't eat the apple she had brought him').[61] This surprisingly domestic motive is then backed up by Augustine's longer musing: 'Ok vildi fyrir þann skyld eigi er hon styggðisk þar af eða hryggðisk, at hann hugði at hon mundi af þess háttar þeira sundrþykki mikilliga þrá eða með ǫllu helstríð fá' ('And he didn't wish her to get angry or sad about it, because he thought that she would suffer great pangs and mortal sorrow on account of their disagreement').[62] The rhyme between 'styggðisk' and 'hryggðisk' in the Old Norse suggests a certain amusement at the woman's changeable moods. Augustine clarifies that Adam's concern for Eve had nothing to do with sexual desire, which he did not feel until after the Fall, but rather is the result of overindulgent friendship: 'Af hverjum er þat verðr ok veitir oftliga, at maðrinn vinnr þat til vin hans verði eigi óvin sem guði er gagnstaðligt' ('For which reason it often comes to pass that a man will do what is displeasing to God to prevent his friend from becoming his enemy').[63] The proverbial ring to this, which fits well with the domestic context of married life, is brought out by the wordplay on 'vinna' ('to work, to do'), 'vinr' ('friend') and 'óvinr' ('enemy'). But, as elsewhere, there is little attempt to harmonise any of these different interpretations, other than the occasional 'sem fyrr var frá sagt' ('as was said about before'). Instead, a single coherent reading of the scene is subordinated to the full range of moral lessons to be learned from it.

The epilogue to the Fall – the outworking of evil in the world – is the story of Cain and Abel. Perhaps because it is shorter and more self-contained, this gives a stronger sense of narrative coherence, even though the compiler is drawing on at least three sources – Genesis, the *Historia scholastica* and the *Speculum historiale* – which are sometimes blended and sometimes separated. The introduction, which describes the different offerings made by Cain and

---

61   *Stjórn*, 57; *Speculum historiale* 2.42.
62   *Stjórn*, 57–58; Augustine, *De genesi*, xi.59, trans. Hill, 463.
63   *Stjórn*, 58; Augustine, *De genesi*, xi.59, trans. Hill, 483.

157

The Old Testament in Medieval Icelandic Texts

Abel, is from the *Speculum historiale*, probably because this source, unlike the biblical narrative, explains why Cain is at fault: it tells us that Cain took up agriculture because of his 'ágirni' ('acquisitiveness') and that he offered God 'þat korn er bitit var ok fóttroðit af þeim kvikvendum, sem víða gengu, en hélt hin sér eptir sem betra var' ('the corn that was bitten and trodden underfoot by the cattle that roamed widely, but kept back for himself the corn that was better').[64] This is then immediately balanced against an alternative possibility from the *Historia scholastica*, which is that Cain's offering of grain was correct, but that what he did wrong was to offer himself – a better offering – to the devil.[65] The compiler also provides alternatives for Cain's psychological motivation: when Cain protests at the news of his exile that anyone might kill him (Genesis 4.14), we are told that he speaks 'annathvárt af hræzlu ella fyrir því at hann œskti þess at hann væri skjótt drepinn' ('either out of fear or because he desired to be killed quickly').[66] This encourages the reader to explore different ways of interpreting the passage, but it does so at the expense of the narrative flow.

When we come to the killing of Abel, though, the commentary is much better integrated into the story (Genesis 4.8–9):

> Eptir þat talaði Kayn til síns bróður Abel: 'Gǫngum út á vǫll'. Ok sem þeir váru báðir samt á einum akri, hljóp Kain upp móti sínum brœðr ok drap hann með svíkum á þeim akri, sem nú er við borgina Damascum. Þá talaði guð til Kayns, eigi sem óvitandi, heldr ásakandi hann ok brigzlandi honum bróðurdrapit, ok sagði svá: 'Hvar er þinn bróðir Abel?' Hann vildi gjarna fela sinn glœp fyrir guð ok sagði svá: 'Ek veit eigi, minn herra, eða er ek nǫkkut skipaðr geymslumaðr bróður míns?'

> After that, Cain spoke to his brother Abel: 'Let us go out onto the plain'. And when they were both together in a field, Cain rose up against his brother and killed him with treachery in the field which is now by the city of Damascus. Then God spoke to Cain, not as ignorant, but rather accusing and upbraiding him for the death of his brother, and said this: 'Where is your brother Abel'? He wished to hide his crime from God and said this: 'I don't know, my lord, or am I appointed the keeper of my brother?'

It is noticeable that the syntax is overwhelmingly paratactic here, and there are very few compound words and no figures of speech. Although there are a couple of added comments from the *Historia scholastica* (one of which makes

---

[64] *Stjórn*, 62; *Speculum historiale* 2.56.

[65] *Stjórn*, 63; Comestor, *Liber Genesis*, 50.

[66] *Stjórn*, 64; Comestor, *Liber Genesis*, 52 'Ex timore hoc dixit, uel optando dixit, quasi: Vtinam occidat me!' ('he spoke this out of fear or desire, as if saying: If only someone would kill me!').

In the Beginning

itself felt through the run of present participles – 'óvitandi', 'ásakandi', 'brigz-landi'), they are incorporated into the passage, rather than separated out.[67] The second has been adjusted to fit the paratactic language of this section ('hann vildi fela sinn glœp [...] ok sagði svá'), although it does interrupt the otherwise externally focalised narrative by revealing Cain's thoughts. The localisation of the murder 'in the field which is now by the city of Damascus' links the biblical event to the present day by way of an identifiable place, which is a technique used frequently in the sagas. Although the location itself comes from the *Speculum historiale*, both the phrasing and the shift to the present tense ('sem nú er') are unique to the Old Norse translation.[68]

Even here, though, the historical level of interpretation is supplemented by the allegorical: just as the six days of Creation were allegorised as the six ages of the world, so the story of Cain and Abel is followed by the allegory of the two cities – the city of God and the city of man – mediated through the *Speculum historiale*. We are told that the Church has its 'upprás' ('origin') in Abel, while 'illzka guðs óvina' ('the evil of God's enemies') is turned against God's saints from the time of Cain's murder.[69] Both the Fall of Adam and Eve and the murder of Abel are reprised in the following chapter, which is translated from Durandus's *Rationale divinorum officiorum*. This chapter allegorises the liturgy of the Church during Septuagesima, which is the ninth Sunday before Easter, but which was counted (as the name suggests) as 70 days before Easter.[70] Durandus connects these 70 days with the seven days of the week and seven ages of the world, so that it signifies our exile from Paradise from the Fall to Judgement Day: 'Fyrir þenna tíma merkisk villuglapstígr, útlegð, ok þrǫngving eða endrmœðing alls mannkynsins, frá Adam allt til veraldarinnar endalyktar, er hlauzk af hans tilskyldan ok Eve, svá sem bæði þau gengu brott af Guðs boðorðum, sem fyrr var sagt' ('By this time is signified the wrong path of unbelief, exile, and the oppression or tribulation of all mankind, from Adam to the end of the world, which resulted from what was justly due to him and to

---

67 Comestor, *Liber Genesis*, 51 'Non ignorans, sed increpando improperans fratri-cidium' ('not in ignorance, but by a rebuke reproaching him for the fratricide').

68 *Speculum historiale* 2.56 'eum in agro damasceno per dolum occidit' ('he killed him treacherously in the field of Damascus').

69 *Stjórn*, 66; *Speculum historiale* 2.57.

70 On William Durandus, see Stephen Mark Holmes, 'Reading the Church: William Durandus and a New Approach to the History of Ecclesiology', *Ecclesiology* 7.1 (2011), 24–49. The critical edition of his work is *Guillelmi Duranti Rationale divinorum officiorum*, CCCM 140, 140A, 140B, ed. Anselme Davril and Timothy T. Thibodeau (Turnhout: Brepols, 1995–2000). There are translations of books 1–4 in *The Rationale Divinorum Officiorum. The Foundational Symbolism of the Early Church, its Structure, Decoration, Sacraments and Vestments by Gulielmus Durandus (1230–1296 CE)* (Louisiana: Fons Vitae, 2007).

The Old Testament in Medieval Icelandic Texts

Eve, since they both went astray from God's commands, as was said before').[71] He also points out that the responsory for the first Sunday in Septuagesima is 'In sudore uultus tui uesceris pane tuo' ('In the sweat of thy face shalt thou eat bread'), which comes from God's curse of Adam in Genesis 3.19. This is followed by a discussion of man's 'tign ok virðing' ('honour and worth'), which echoes the earlier discussion of man's threefold 'tign ok virðing' at Genesis 1.27, although with characteristic inconsistency, four points are made here, rather than three, and only one is the same.[72] Finally, Durandus explains that the psalm with which the mass for Septuagesima begins, *Circumdederunt me gemitus mortis* ('The sorrows of death surrounded me'; Psalm 17.5), can be interpreted as the cry of the early Church in the face of tribulation and martyrdom, signified by Cain's murder of Abel:[73]

> Þat er ok mikilliga merkjanda at fyrrsǫgð orð, *Circumdederunt me gemitus mortis*, eru orð ok ákall ǫndverðrar kristninnar, sýtandi ok grátandi eptir guðs frumvátt Abel, hvers blóð er af þeiri sǫmu jǫrðu kallaði til guðs sem sik rýmdi til þess at hon drakk þat sama blóð sem út var hellt með hendi sjálfs hans brœðr Kayns.

> It is also important to note that the aforesaid words *Circumdederunt me gemitus mortis* are the words and cry of the early Church, lamenting and weeping after God's first witness, Abel, whose blood called to God from the same earth that opened itself up to drink the same blood that was poured out by the hand of his brother Cain.

This is an allegorical interpretation – in which Abel signifies the early Church – but there is also a tropological interpretation relating to the individual soul: 'Fyrir it fyrsta officium *circumdederunt* megum vér skynsamliga skilja einnhvern játanda sínar syndir' ('For the first office *circumdederunt* we may reasonably understand an individual confessing his sin'). This, of course, is the very act that Adam, Eve and Cain conspicuously fail to do.[74] Durandus therefore reinforces the multiple levels on which these Old Testament stories can be read and shows how they shape the liturgy of the Church and the moral life of the individual.

Noah's Flood

The story of the Flood, which takes up Genesis 6–9, raises some formidable problems for a commentator, including the harmonisation of what appear to be two different layers of narrative, a strikingly anthropomorphic God, and

---

[71] *Stjórn*, 73.
[72] *Stjórn*, 30, 76.
[73] *Stjórn*, 75–76.
[74] *Stjórn*, 78–79.

In the Beginning

the large-scale destruction of 'every living thing' in the floodwaters.[75] So it is not surprising that, as in the Fall of Man, the narrative shifts frequently between Genesis, the *Historia scholastica* and the *Speculum historiale*, which themselves quote older authorities such as Josephus, Augustine and Methodius. The narrative takes up five chapters in *Stjórn I*: the first two are about the causes of the flood and the construction of the ark; the middle one describes the flood itself; and the final two narrate God's covenant with Noah and his descendants, symbolised by the rainbow, and tell the story of Noah's drunkenness and the division between his sons to which it leads.

The first chapter gives a variety of different reasons for the flood, but focuses on sexual behaviour.[76] Following Comestor, the compiler describes how the 'sons of god' in Genesis 6.2 (understood to be the sons of Seth) 'sá girndaraugum til dœtra Kayns ok þeirra afkvæmis' ('looked with eyes of desire on the daughters of Cain and their offspring'), who subsequently gave birth to the 'gigantes' (here translated as 'risar').[77] Following Vincent of Beauvais, he adds that the sons of Cain committed adultery with the wives of their brothers and that women 'gerðusk svá ginntar ok galnar at þær lǫgðu karlmennina undir sik til saurlífis með ljótligri ǫrskemmð' ('became so duped and frantic that they laid men under them for sexual activity in a repulsive and shameful way').[78] The sensationalising alliteration here ('gerðusk', 'ginntar', 'galnar') is a direct imitation of the Latin ('vesaniam', 'verse', 'viros'). But, amid all this colourful sexual behaviour, a strong emphasis is laid on repentance: the *Speculum historiale* reports that, 100 years before the flood, God commanded Noah to preach repentance and that he delayed his judgement to give sinners time to repent: we are told that God 'gaf þenna tíma fólkinu til iðranar' ('gave the people this time for repentance'), that Noah tried 'at snúa þeim til hjálpsamligrar iðranar' ('to turn them to saving repentance'), and that they could have avoided God's anger and punishment 'ef þeir vildi snúask til guðs með sannri iðran' ('if they wished to turn to God with true repentance').[79] Comestor even puts words into the mouth of God himself: 'Skal ek veita honum iðranartíma til þess ef hann vill iðrask af sínum syndum' ('I shall give him time for repentance to see whether he

---

[75] On the different sources of the Flood narrative in Genesis, see Carr, *Formation*, 141–52.

[76] On the background to this story, see Day, *Creation*, 77–97.

[77] *Stjórn*, 79; cf. Comestor, *Liber Genesis*, 59.

[78] *Stjórn*, 80; cf. *Speculum historiale* 2.59: 'mulieres in vesaniam verse, viros superagresse turpiter egerant' ('women turned to madness cavorted disgracefully, having clambered on top of men').

[79] *Stjórn*, 80; *Speculum historiale* 2.59.

The Old Testament in Medieval Icelandic Texts

will repent of his sins').[80] The selection of passages here suggests that the story is angled towards an audience preparing in Septuagesima for the season of repentance during Lent.

The anthropomorphisation of God is very marked in these chapters of Genesis, and nowhere more so than in the two framing passages where God declares first his intention to destroy the world, and then his intention never to destroy it again.[81] Both these passages are carefully translated in *Stjórn I* to ensure that God's apparently human behaviour is correctly understood. The first blends Genesis 6 with the *Historia scholastica*, which says explicitly that God's feelings may be 'antropospatos' ('anthropomorphic'):[82]

> Af því at guð sá, at harðla mikil ok háðulig var illzka mannanna í verǫldinni ok ǫll þeira hjartalig ástundan var allan tíman til illra hluta, þeira syndum ok sektum reiddisk guð ok angraði hann þat, at hann hafði manninn skapat upp á jǫrðina, eigi svá at hann hefði þar af nǫkkura angist, heldr eptir mannana dœmum ok viðrlíking til frásagnar.

> Because God saw that men's evil was very great and shameful in the world, and that all the desire of their hearts was at all times directed towards evil, God became angry with their sins and guilt, and he regretted that he had made man on earth, not in that that he felt any regret about it, but rather as an example for men and as an analogy.

The compiler makes it clear that the intensity of divine emotion – God's anger and regret – does not mean that God feels human emotions, but rather that he chooses to imitate human behaviour. In the same way, when God declares his intention to 'blot out' all life on earth, it is because 'guð vildi bera varhygð fyrir eptirkomanda tíma af angrsamligri mannsins tilskyldan' ('God wished to bear witness for posterity to the sorrowful deserts of man').[83] God speaks aloud not for his own sake, but for the benefit of posterity. Even God's own words are silently rephrased by Comestor: 'Skal ek þáleiðis eyða þessari minni gerð, sem sá maðr er hann iðrask sinnar gerðar ok fyrireyðir hann ok ónýtir' ('I shall destroy this my work like the man who repents of his work and who destroys and undoes it').[84] God's speeches and actions aim to model for the reader the acts of a repentant sinner.

---

80   *Stjórn*, 80; Comestor, *Liber Genesis*, 61: 'dabo ei tempus penitudinis, si uoluerit' ('I will give him time for repentance, if he should wish').

81   Gen. 6.5–6 and 8.21.

82   *Stjórn*, 90; Comestor, *Liber Genesis*, 61–62.

83   *Stjórn*, 81.

84   *Stjórn*, 81; Gen. 6.7; Comestor, *Liber Genesis*, 61 'quasi faciam quod solet facere homo penitens operis sui. Delet enim quod fecerat' ('as if he said: I will do what a man tends to do when he repents of his work. For he destroys what he had made').

In the Beginning

The corresponding passage towards the end of the flood narrative also takes care to make sure that God is not thought of as human. It avoids the implication that God can literally 'smell' the sacrifice, stating instead that he is 'appeased' by it':[85]

> Var þessi hans fórn guði svá þægilig, at hann blíðkaðisk svá með miklum sœtleiksilm, talandi svá til Nóa: 'Með engu móti mun ek upp frá þessum tíma jǫrðina banna ok bǫlva fyrir mannanna skyld, því at mannkynsins skilningarvit ok þess hjartalig hugrenning hneigja sik ok sveigja gjarna til illra hluta allt frá sínum barndómi'.

> This sacrifice of his was acceptable to God so that he was appeased with the great sweetness of the scent, saying this to Noah: 'In no way will I curse or ban the earth from this time on for men's sake, because mankind's understanding and the thoughts of his heart incline and sway readily to evil even from his childhood'.

As in Latin and Hebrew, this statement about the evil inclination of the human heart echoes – though not as closely – the one that started the flood narrative in the first place: 'ok ǫll þeira hjartalig ástundan var allan tíman til illra hluta' ('and all the desire of their hearts was all the time directed to evil'). The verbal echo is less noticeable in the Old Norse because the second statement has been stylistically ornamented with alliteration on 'b' and 'h'; word-pairs ('banna ok bǫlva'); compound noun-phrases ('mannkynsins skilningarvit', 'hjartalig hugrenning'); and the rhyme between 'hneigja' and 'sveigja'. It is tempting to see the compiler anticipating here the poetry that follows in the Hebrew, which the Vulgate captures through assonance and word-pairs: 'sementis et messis frigus et aestus aestas et hiemps nox et dies'.[86] If the switch to poetry in the Hebrew signals the end of the threat to human life and a return to the natural changing of the seasons, to a world that is predictable and conducive to human survival ('seedtime and harvest'), the high style of the Old Norse translation shifts the emphasis instead onto the persistence of human sin.

The compiler's sensitivity to poetic language is certainly evident elsewhere in the compilation, for example in the description of the floodwaters, where the figures of speech in the Vulgate imitate the poetic language in the Hebrew:[87]

---

85   *Stjórn*, 89; cf. Gen. 8.21: 'odoratusque est Dominus odorem suavitatis' ('and the Lord smelled a sweet savour').

86   Gen. 8.22 ('seedtime and harvest, cold and heat, summer and winter, night and day').

87   *Stjórn*, 85–86; Gen. 7.10–12, 8.1–4. On the poetic terminology and parallelism in the Hebrew at this point, see Gordon Wenham, *Genesis 1–15* (Grand Rapids, MI:

The Old Testament in Medieval Icelandic Texts

Ok sem næstu .vij. dagar váru liðnir, tóku vǫtnin at œsask ok yfir at fljóta alla jǫrðina [...] Þá lét guð æðar ok uppsprettur þess mikla undirdjúps sem hann hafði mestan hlut jarðríkisins vatna til samnat, sem fyrr var sagt, opnask ok upplúkask [...] Opnuðusk þá ok upplukusk þar með allar himinsins vatnrásir [...] óxu vǫtnin þá svá mjǫk at þau hófu ǫrkina af jǫrðinni ok œstusk svá akafliga at þau huldu alla jǫrðina ok hennar ásynd [...] Undirdjúps æðar ok uppsprettur ok eigi síðr himinsins vatnrásir byrgðusk þá ok aptr lukusk.

And when the next seven days had passed, the water began to swell and flood the whole earth [...] Then God caused the springs and sources of the great abyss, into which he had gathered a great part of the waters in the kingdom of earth, as was previously said, to be opened and unlocked [...] Then all the watercourses of the heaven were opened and unlocked [...] The waters swelled so much that they lifted the ark off the earth and they raged so madly that they covered all the earth and her surface [...] The springs and sources of the great abyss and no less the watercourses of the heaven were closed and locked again.

The verbs 'œsask' ('to be stirred up, swell') and 'yfir fljóta' ('to flood, overflow') translate the Latin 'inundaverunt' (overflowed'), but 'œsask' also implies violence and fury, as if the flood were personified and rages in fury ('œsing') over the face of the earth. In this sense, it captures the violent implications of the Hebrew verb בקע ('split, divide, break open'), which the Vulgate translates as 'rupti sunt' ('were broken up'). The word-pair 'æðar ok uppsprettur þess mikla undirdjúps' ('springs and sources of the great abyss') translates the Latin 'fontes abyssi' ('the fountains of the deep'), and the choice of 'æðar' ('veins, watercourses, springs') evokes the likeness of the earth to the human body, so that the flow of water is likened to a flow of blood. Both 'œsa' and 'æðr' are linked by assonance to the noun 'œði', meaning 'madness, fury, frenzy', the sense of which is intensified by the adverb 'ákafliga'. There may well be a pun too on the root meaning of 'kaf' as 'seabed' or 'sea depth'. Meanwhile, the compound 'undirdjúp' ('abyss') links what is happening in this passage to Day Three of the Creation, in which God 'safnaði' ('assembled') all the waters in 'underdjúpit' ('the abyss'); now, he returns the earth to its former state of primeval chaos.[88] Against this excess of language in the description of the flood – metaphor, word-pairs, alliteration, compounds, repetition – stands the plainness of the single, simple

---

Zondervan, 2014), 181. The Hebrew has כָּל־מַעְיְנֹת תְּהוֹם רַבָּה ('all the springs of the great deep') and אֲרֻבֹּת הַשָּׁמַיִם ('the windows of heaven'), which the Vulgate translates as 'omnes fontes abyssi magnae' ('all the fountains of the great deep') and 'cataractae caeli' ('the flood gates of heaven').

[88] *Stjórn*, 22; cf. Gen. 1.9.

In the Beginning

statement: 'dó þá ok fyrirfórsk hverr sá lifandis líkami' ('Then all living flesh died and perished').[89]

The Old Norse-Icelandic translation imitates a different aspect of biblical language in the chapter where God establishes his covenant with humans. This is a crucial moment, marked in the Hebrew by the meaningful repetition of the keyword בְּרִית ('covenant, agreement') seven times over eight verses (Genesis 9.9–17). In the Vulgate, Jerome varies this somewhat, using both 'pactus' and 'foedus', although he otherwise replicates the repetition found in the Hebrew Bible. The Old Norse translation – like the Hebrew – chooses to repeat a single term, except on its first occurrence, where it uses the word-pair 'sáttmál ok skildagi' ('words of reconciliation and terms of agreement') to bring out the full meaning of the biblical word: 'Sé hérna mitt sáttmál ok skildaga [*pactus*]', 'Svá mun ek mitt sáttmál [*pactus*] með yðr staðfesta', 'þetta er sáttmarks mark [*signum foederis*]', 'skal hann vera sáttmáls mark [*signum foederis*]', 'mun ek míns sáttmáls [*foedus*] með yðr endrminnask', 'þess eylífs sáttmáls [*foedus*]', 'þetta sáttmals mark [*signum foederis*]'.[90] By comparison, the *Historia scholastica* uses the term 'signum foederis' only once in this passage and the *Speculum historiale* not at all. The Old Norse compiler clearly understands the purpose of the repetition in the Vulgate and replicates it as closely as possible.

Just as the story of Cain and Abel serves as epilogue to the Fall of Man, so Noah's drunkenness is the epilogue to the Flood: a reminder that, although God has promised never again to destroy all life, sin remains a problem. The compiler tells this story twice, first from the *Speculum historiale* and then from the Vulgate. Vincent of Beauvais contrasts the blessing of Shem and Japheth 'sakir sœmiligrar skammfyllingar ok fǫðurligrar vegsemðar' ('on account of their respectful modesty and honour towards their father') with the cursing of Ham's son Canaan 'sakir háðuliga spotts' ('on account of his scornful mockery').[91] These strongly emotive terms imitate the Latin and provide a clear moral stance. When the compiler turns to the Vulgate, however, he adopts a plainer narrative:[92]

---

[89] *Stjórn*, 86; Gen. 7.21: 'consumptaque est omnis caro quae movebatur super terram' ('and all flesh was destroyed that moved upon the earth'). This is repeated three times in the Vulgate in verses 21–23.

[90] *Stjórn*, 91 ('see here my covenant and terms'; 'so shall I establish my covenant with you'; 'this is the sign of the covenant'; 'this shall be the sign of the covenant'; 'I will remember my covenant with you'; 'this eternal covenant'; 'the sign of the covenant').

[91] *Stjórn*, 92; *Speculum historiale* 2.61 'honesta verecundia et honore paterno' ('respectful modesty and honour towards their father'); 'impudenti patris irrisione' ('impudent mockery of his father').

[92] *Stjórn*, 93.

The Old Testament in Medieval Icelandic Texts

Nóe tók þenna tíma eptir flóðit jǫrðina at yrkja ok hana at fága, vingarð at planta ok vín at gera, ok af því at hann var þess háttar drykk ekki vanr ok vissi eigi vínsins megin ok styrk, varð hann ǫluðr. Ok sem hann var sofnaðr, hǫfðu klæðin farit af honum í sjálfs hans tjaldbúð, svá at hans getnaðarlimr varð berr. Ok sem Cham kom at feðr sínum svá liggjanda ok hann sá hversu hann lá, þá spottaði hann ok hló at honum ok gekk síðan út með skálkheið ok sagði brœðrum sínum.

At that time after the flood, Noah began to work the earth and till it, plant a vineyard and make wine. And because he was not used to that kind of drink and did not know the power and strength of wine, he became drunk. And while he was asleep in his tent, his clothes had slipped off so that his engendering limb was laid bare. And when Ham came across his father lying thus, and he saw how he lay, then he mocked him and laughed at him, and then went out with scorn and told his brothers.

There are a number of silent glosses from the *Historia scholastica* here, but they have been carefully adapted to the paratactic style of the passage.[93] Of the four present participles in Comestor's Latin ('bibens', 'ignorans', 'dormiens', 'irridens'), three have become finite verbs joined with coordination or simple subordination ('ok vissi eigi', 'sem hann var sofnaðr', 'þá spottaði hann'). The vocabulary is familiar and idiomatic, with no figures of speech or heavy noun-phrases, and there is just one rare word, found only in *Stjórn I*, 'skálkheiðr', which seems to mean 'scorn' or 'scornful laughter' and characterises Ham as a 'ruffian'.[94] There are a few word-pairs (e.g. 'megin ok styrkr') and some alliteration, but very little redundancy. Although the glosses from the *Historia scholastica* provide some moral evaluation (Noah sins through ignorance rather than debauchery, whereas Ham is disrespectful towards his father), there is no insight into the characters' inner lives: we are not told what Noah or Ham are thinking, only what they do and say. That this scene appeals to the compiler primarily on a human and a domestic level is also suggested by his addition of a proverb: 'sem forn orðskviðr kømr til, at grísir gjalda þess er gǫmul svín valda' ('as the old proverb mentions, that piglets pay for what old swine cause'). The poetic patterning of the alliteration here and the rhyme between 'gjalda' and 'valda' create an impression

---

93 Comestor, *Liber Genesis*, 72 'Bibensque uinum, sed ignorans uim eius' ('drinking wine, but not knowing its strength'), 'Et dormiens nudatus est in tabernaculo suo' ('and, while sleeping, he was naked in his tent'), 'irridens, nuntiauit hoc fratribus' ('mocking, he told this to his brothers').

94 *Stjórn*, 191, 184, 362, 397. The term 'skálkr' means 'ruffian' or 'bandit', so 'skálkheiðr' should mean something like 'the honour of/due to a ruffian', i.e. disrespect and scorn.

In the Beginning

of antiquity, whether or not this is actually a well-known proverb.[95] Still, the proverbial register suggests that the wisdom to be drawn from this passage may have less to do with filial loyalty than with the homely truth that children pay for their parents' mistakes.[96]

The use of vernacular literary tradition is even more noticeable in the account of the Tower of Babel, traditionally linked with the figure of Nimrod, the first tyrant. Nimrod is immediately familiar from the sagas: 'Hann var rammr at afli, manndrápari ok inn mesti ágangsmaðr sakir þess, at hann vildi yfir ǫðrum vald ok œgishjálm bera' ('He was physically strong, a killer, and the most aggressive man because he wished to wield power and a helmet of fear over others').[97] The expression 'rammr af afli' is very common, and the compound 'œgishjálmr' may even have mythological origins: it is the term used by Snorri Sturluson of the helmet found by Fáfnir among the treasure stolen by Loki.[98] Nimrod is later said to rule 'með ofríki ok ójafnaði' ('with tyranny and injustice'); a word-pair that links him with Egill Skalla-Grímssonar, who is accused of 'ofrkapp ok ójafnað' ('tyranny and injustice'), and with Víga-Styrr and Þorkell Eyjólfsson, who are both condemned for their 'ofsa ok ójafnaðar' ('arrogance and injustice').[99] Like Comestor, the Old Norse compiler explains the motive for the building of the tower, but his emphasis is slightly different:[100]

[95] On the compiler's use of proverbs, see Reidar Astås, 'Ordtak i *Stjórn I*', *Opuscula* 8 (1985), 126–31. It has parallels in *Saga Ólafs konungs hins helga*, ed. Oscar Albert Johnsen and Jón Helgason (Oslo: Dybwad, 1941), 217, 219: 'gagl fyrir gás, grís fyrir gamalt svín' ('a gosling for a goose, a piglet for an old swine'); *Þórðar saga hreðu*, in *Kjalnesinga saga*, ed. Jóhannes Halldórsson (Reykjavík: Hið íslenzka fornritafélag, 1959), 182: 'Rýta mun göltrinn, ef gríssinn er drepinn' ('the old swine will grunt if the piglet is killed'); and *Ragnars saga lóðbrókar*, in *Fornaldarsögur Norðurlanda*, ed. Guðni Jónsson and Bjarni Vilhjálmsson, 3 vols (Reykjavík: Bókaútgáfan,1943–44) I, 135: 'Gnyðja mundu nu grísir, ef þeir vissi, hvat inn gamli þyldi' ('the young pigs would grunt if they knew what the old one suffered').

[96] On the difficulties of interpretation in this story and the connection between the cursing of Ham and black slavery, see Day, *Creation*, 137–53.

[97] *Stjórn*, 96; cf. Comestor, *Liber Genesis*, 74.

[98] For 'rammr af afli', see for example, *Brennu-Njáls saga*, 359; *Laxdæla saga*, 109. For 'œgishjálmr', see Snorri Sturluson, *Edda: Skáldskaparmál*, ed. Anthony Faulkes (London: Viking Society, 1998), 46; *Völsunga saga*, 32, 34; *Sörla þáttr*, in *Fornaldarsögur Norðurlanda*, II, 109; it is used metaphorically in *Laxdæla saga*, 90 and *Hrafnkels saga*, 118.

[99] *Egils saga Skalla-Grímssonar*, ed. Bjarni Einarsson (London: Viking Society for Northern Research, 2003), 88; *Eyrbyggja saga, Eiríks saga rauða*, ed. Einar Ólafur Sveinsson and Matthías Þórðarson (Reykjavík: Hið íslenzka fornritafélag, 1935), 63; *Laxdæla saga*, 220.

[100] *Stjórn*, 98; Gen. 11.3–4; Comestor, *Liber Genesis*, 75–76.

The Old Testament in Medieval Icelandic Texts

Ok af því at þeir óttaðusk þá enn flóðit ok vildu ríkja yfir ǫðrum mǫnnum at ráði Nemrothe, þá talaði hverr við sinn náung. **Genesis.** Komum hér ok gerum nǫkkut ágætisverk at þaðan af frægjumsk vér fyrr en vér deyim eða viðrskilimsk eða skiptimsk til ýmissa landa. Gerum oss eina stóra ok sterka borg eða stǫpul, hvers turn eða hæð tœki allt upp til himna.

And because they were still afraid of the flood and wished to rule over other people by Nimrod's counsel, each said to his neighbour. **Genesis.** Let us come together and do some deed of renown by which we will become famous before we die or are parted from one another or dispersed into various lands. Let us make for ourselves a big and strong city or column whose tower or highest point reaches up to heaven.

The first sentence is an expansion of Comestor's 'timentes diluuium' ('fearing the flood'), but the narrative switches to Genesis just before the rubric, with the introduction of the corporate speech of the tower-builders. The Vulgate has: 'Venite faciamus nobis civitatem et turrem cuius culmen pertingat ad caelum et celebremus nomen nostrum antequam dividamur in universas terras' ('Come, let us make a city and a tower, the top whereof may reach to heaven; and let us make our name famous before we are scattered abroad into all lands'). The compiler adds to this the idea of the tower as 'ágætisverk' ('a work of renown' or 'achievement') and the pursuit of fame 'fyrr en vér deyim' ('before we die'). Neither Comestor nor Vincent of Beauvais include this speech. It connects the hubris of desiring to be like God – to reach up to heaven – with a heroic flaw that was arguably more familiar to an Old Norse-Icelandic audience: the desire to achieve fame before death.

The dispersal of Noah's sons throughout the world is the prompt for a geographical excursus, which corresponds to the geographical excursus in *Speculum historiale*, but also draws on Isidore of Seville's *Etymologiae* for its descriptions of landscape and animals. Although this temporarily pauses the historical sequence of events, it should not be thought of as a digression. Following the creation account, it affirms the divinely ordered nature of the world, and it provides important background material for the interpretation of biblical stories: it includes references to Noah and his sons, Paradise, Nimrod, the Queen of Sheba, Jerusalem, Sodom and Gomorrah, Abraham and Lot, Ishmael, Moses, and the serpent in Genesis.[101] It is also the only part of *Stjórn I* that assumes a Scandinavian outlook. It contains the only direct reference to Iceland: 'svá sem þat fjall í Sikiley er Ethna heitir eða Vesenus í Campania eða Heklufjall á Íslandi' ('like the mountain in Sicily called Etna, or Vesuvius in Campania, or the mountain Hekla in Iceland').[102] Constantinople is called

---

101 *Stjórn*, 100, 107–8,110, 112–14, 131, 148.
102 *Stjórn*, 122.

In the Beginning

by its Norse name *Miklagarðr* and Ethiopa is translated as *Bláland*.[103] There are even examples of *interpretatio norræna*: Diomedes in Ovid's *Metamorphoses* is said to have wounded the goddess Gefjon (instead of Aphrodite), and the labyrinth in which the minotaur is imprisoned is glossed as 'Vǫlundarhús' ('the house of Vǫlundr', or 'the master-smith').[104] Particular attention is paid to the lion, and the compiler comments that: 'hans miskunn ok hógleiki tésk ok auðsýnask af iðuligum dœmum ok mǫrgum merkiligum frásǫgnum' ('his mercy and gentleness are shown and made clear by frequent examples and many remarkable stories').[105] The 'many remarkable stories' is an addition to Isidore's 'frequent examples' and perhaps its sole purpose is to create a balanced pair. But the adjective 'remarkable' suggests that the compiler may be thinking of something quite specific: the helpful lion in *Ívens saga*, perhaps, or one of the many other 'grateful lions' that inhabit the Icelandic *riddarasögur* ('romances').[106]

Conclusion

The first part of *Stjórn I*, covering Genesis I–II, is a patchwork of different sources, and it seems to have been more important to the compiler to accommodate a full range of glosses than to create a continuous narrative. The six days of Creation, in particular, house a great variety of theological material, some of which is encyclopaedic and aids a literal reading and some of which is more obviously allegorical. The Fall of Man, so important for Christian doctrines of sin and human nature, is read in different ways by the Church Fathers, and the compiler is careful to preserve these differences, rather than harmonise them. This is in line with how he introduces biblical exegesis in the Prologue and *accessus* as a task that requires readers to hold in balance a number of interpretations that may all have some claim to theological truth. The compiler not only preserves differences of opinion among his sources, but also closely imitates their different styles, varying between the florid style of Vincent of Beauvais, the heavily Latinate passages from Durandus, and more homely imagery and stories. It is clear from his account of Noah and the Flood that he is sensitive to variations of biblical style in the Vulgate and can both reproduce aspects of poetic language and exploit meaningful repetition in prose. When telling some of the shorter, more self-contained stories, the compiler imitates the plain style of biblical narrative and draws out familiar themes: in the stories of Cain and Abel, Noah and Ham, and the Tower of

---

[103] *Stjórn*, 125, 145.

[104] *Stjórn*, 127, 136.

[105] *Stjórn*, 105–06; cf. Isidore, *Etymologiae* XII.ii.3 'exemplis assiduis'.

[106] Cf. Marianne Kalinke, 'The Cowherd and the Saint: The Grateful Lion in Icelandic Folktale and Legend', *Scandinavian Studies* 66.1 (1994), 1–22.

The Old Testament in Medieval Icelandic Texts

Babel, a narrative impulse has begun to emerge that showcases aspects of the style of the Icelandic sagas. In the next chapter, I show how this narrative impulse comes into its own when we turn to the stories of the biblical patriarchs and to the finely drawn novella of Joseph.

⇀ 6 ⇀

The God of Abraham, Isaac and Jacob:
Family History in Genesis 12–50

The central focus of Genesis 12–50 is kinship and the family: Steinberg has described it as 'a book whose plot is genealogy', structured around the 'toledoth' formula, usually translated as 'these are the generations of'.[1] Genealogy not only facilitates family succession and continuity but is also used to structure each family cycle: the 'toledoth' formula occurs at Genesis 11 (the Abraham cycle), Genesis 25 (the Jacob cycle) and Genesis 36 (the Joseph story). Within each cycle, Steinberg argues, we move from the 'ideal stable movement' of genealogy, to inheritance problems that threaten it, then back to the stability of genealogy.[2] Despite the difficulties around the choice of an heir, Abraham's family line continues, allowing the fulfilment of God's promises of land and descendants (the 'Abrahamic' blessings). This is important because the patriarchs are not only Israel's earliest ancestors, but also 'prefigure' the nation of Israel: Kawashima describes them as 'narrative concepts for thinking about Israel's identity', which includes its relationship with non-Israelites, such as Hagar and Ishmael.[3] Whereas Exodus shifts its focus from the family to the Israelites as a 'people', Genesis maintains its focus on the family throughout. Some scholars have suggested that we should think of it as 'family literature': Petersen, like Coats (p. 18), compares it with the Icelandic 'family' sagas, pointing out the prominence of family concerns,

---

[1] Naomi A. Steinberg, 'The World of the Family in Genesis', in *The Book of Genesis: Composition, Reception and Interpretation*, ed. Craig A. Evans, Joel N. Lohr and David L. Petersen (Leiden: Brill, 2012), 282; see also her 'The Genealogical Framework of the Stories in Genesis', *Semeia* 46 (1989), 41.

[2] Steinberg, 'Genealogical Framework', 42.

[3] Robert S. Kawashima, 'Literary Analysis', in *The Book of Genesis*, ed. Evans, Lohr and Petersen, 102.

The Old Testament in Medieval Icelandic Texts

such as births, marriages, deaths, itineraries and property.[4] Most notable is the keen interest in family strife: Steinberg comments that Genesis exemplifies 'a highly disruptive pattern of family life', while Petersen suggests that a central 'family' value in this book is the peaceful resolution of conflict between siblings.[5] Sibling rivalry and competition play an important role, and one that is theologically inflected: Kaminsky describes these ancestral narratives as 'a sustained meditation on the problems that arise when someone is mysteriously favoured by God'.[6]

When we turn to the Old Norse translation of Genesis 12–50, then, we might expect some recognition of how similar these stories are to Iceland's own ancestral narratives. It is true that the literal level of interpretation predominates in this section, although allegorical glosses continue to be present. Melchizedek, for example, is interpreted traditionally as prefiguring Christ and the sacraments, while the commentary on Jacob's prophecies in Genesis 49 points to their ultimate fulfilment in Christ.[7] Genesis 50 is followed by the Testaments of the Twelve Patriarchs, a series of 'farewell discourses' that predict the second coming of Christ. It was first composed sometime in the first two centuries CE, and is mediated here through Robert Grosseteste's Latin translation of 1242, which is included in Vincent of Beauvais's *Speculum historiale*.[8] With the move from Genesis to Exodus, the narrative refocuses on 'signs' and 'wonders' ('stórmerki') linked to the liturgy and practices of the medieval Church: the paschal lamb, the *Cantemus domino* (the 'Song of Moses' or 'Canticle of Miriam'), and Moses's prayer in Exodus 17.[9] In this respect, the compiler shows the same variety of interests as in Genesis 1–11, the same variety of styles, and the same desire to provide the fullest possible set of glosses even when these do not agree.

At the same time, the 'plain' narrative in this part of *Stjórn I* starts to exhibit much more familiar storytelling features. The titles in AM 226 fol. and AM 227

---

4 David L. Petersen, 'Genesis and Family Values', *Journal of Biblical Literature* 124.1 (2005), 12–13.

5 Steinberg, 'World of the Family', 285; Petersen, 'Family Values', 21–22.

6 Joel S. Kaminsky, 'The Theology of Genesis', in *The Book of Genesis*, ed. Evans, Lohr and Petersen, 650.

7 *Stjórn*, 346–56; there are references to Christ on pp. 346, 347, 348, 349 and 355.

8 *Stjórn*, 361–69. On the Greek Testaments of the Twelve Patriarchs, see Robert A. Kugler, *The Testaments of the Twelve Patriarchs* (Sheffield: Sheffield Academic Press, 2001); on Robert Grosseteste's translation, see Marinus de Jonge, 'Robert Grosseteste and the Testaments of the Twelve Patriarchs', *Journal of Theological Studies* 42.1 (1991), 115–25.

9 *Stjórn*, 423 (the paschal lamb), 435–37 (the *Cantemus domino*), 448 (Moses' prayer). Some of these passages are marked out in the margins of AM 227 fol.; see the references to Palm Sunday and Maundy Thursday on fol. 66r and the death of the Egyptian first-born on fol. 66v.

The God of Abraham, Isaac and Jacob

fol. foreground family concerns: 'frá því er Abram gekk út af Aram' ('about when Abram left Haran'), 'frá því er Abram gat at eiga Ysmael með Agar' ('about when Abram begat Ishmael with Hagar'), 'frá burð Isaacs' ('about the birth of Isaac'), 'af sendiferð Eliezer í Mesopotamiam ok af kvánfangi Ysaachs' ('about Eliezer's journey to Mesopotamia and Isaac's marriage'), 'frá því er Iacob fann Laban' ('about when Jacob met Laban'), 'af flótta Iacobs ok sáttmáli þeira Laban' ('about Jacob's flight and his peace treaty with Laban'), 'af dauða Rachel ok Ysaachs' ('about the death of Rachel and Isaac').[10] In addition, we start to find recognisable formulas that are used in the sagas to introduce and navigate the story: 'Þar er nú til at taka' ('Now the story is taken up'), 'skal hér nú frá hverfa' ('Now the story turns from'), 'Eptir þat' ('After that'), 'Nǫkkuru síðar' ('Somewhat later'), 'Nú er þat til máls at taka' ('Now it is to be said that'), 'Nú berr þat til eitt sinn' ('Now it happens one time'), 'Hér hefr sǫgu Iosephs' ('Here begins the story of Joseph').[11] The narrative uses the historic present increasingly often, especially at moments of high tension, such as when Laban discovers that Jacob and his daughters have fled: 'þá var Labani sagt á inum þriðja degi at Iacob hafði flýit ok brott farit. Hann bregðr við skjótt [...] ok sækir eptir þeim' ('Laban was told on the third day that Jacob had fled and gone away. He reacts quickly [...] and pursues them').[12] We also find some other familiar narrative tags, such as 'sem ván var' ('as was to be expected') and 'við svá búit' ('with matters thus'), as well as some idiomatic phrasing: 'gekksk Ysaach hugr við' ('Isaac changed his mind' or perhaps 'Isaac was moved'), 'létti sinni ferð eigi fyrr' ('did not let off his journey until'), 'þetta líkaði Laban harðla vel' ('this pleased Laban very much'), 'sem Iacob varð litit fram á skóginn' ('as Jacob happened to look towards the forest'). [13] For the Bible's overwhelming use of direct discourse, a mix of indirect and direct speech is preferred, with the occasional unmarked shift to direct discourse that is characteristic of saga narrative. In this chapter, I argue that the compiler of *Stjórn I* was highly sensitive towards the overlap between biblical stories and Icelandic sagas, and that he makes a concerted effort both to draw out some of the domestic themes and to express them in a familiar style. However, he also draws on other literary genres and is adept at exploiting different levels of style to deliberate rhetorical effect.

The Abraham Cycle

The drama of Abraham's life revolves around the conception of an heir. That his wife, Sarah, is 'óbyrja' ('barren') is mentioned at the outset of

[10] *Stjórn*, 158, 170, 192, 202, 257, 271, 286.
[11] *Stjórn*, 163, 195, 197, 239, 241, 244, 248, 265, 281, 288, 290, 299, 340, 343, 346.
[12] *Stjórn*, 272.
[13] *Stjórn*, 273, 297, 253, 255, 267, 279.

The Old Testament in Medieval Icelandic Texts

the narrative, and various heirs are put forward only to be rejected; first his nephew Lot, then his servant Eliezer, and finally Ishmael, his son by Hagar. This is a theological problem – the question of who will inherit the 'Abrahamic' promises – but it is also a social one: Sarah's status and position within Abraham's household depend upon her childbearing capacity. At the very beginning of the cycle, we are told that: 'af því at Saray var óbyrja ok átti engin bǫrn við bónda sínum Abram, þá tók hann Loth bróður hennar ok bróðurson sinn sér til óskbernis ok sér í sonar stað' ('Because Sarah was barren and had no children with her husband Abram, he adopted Lot her brother and his brother's son and took him in the place of a son').[14] This translates an unmarked addition from the *Historia scholastica*, which explains what is implicit in the biblical account: that Abraham 'Loth fratrem uxoris in filium adoptauit, quia Sarai sterilis erat' ('adopted his wife's brother Lot as a son, because Sarah was barren'). In the Old Norse, though, Lot is described consistently not as Sarah's brother, but as Abraham's brother's son, perhaps because this makes him a more obvious candidate for inheritance. He is mentioned when Abraham leaves Haran in Genesis 12 ('flutti hann með sér húsfrú sína Saray ok Loth bróðurson sinn'); when Abraham defeats King Chedorlaomer and recovers him from captivity in Genesis 14 ('flutti aptr með sér Loth bróðurson sinn'); and finally in an unmarked gloss from the *Historia*, when Abraham hears from God about the destruction of Sodom and Gomorrah ('verandi minnigr bróðursonar síns Lots').[15] Lot is out of the running for heir long before the destruction of Sodom and Gomorrah, but the episode of incest that follows it puts him out of the picture for good. It is in the context of this intense pressure to produce a viable heir that the rivalry between Sarah and Hagar is introduced.[16]

In *Stjórn I*, as in Genesis, this story comes in two parts, interrupted by chapters on the introduction of circumcision, the three angels' visit to Abraham, and the destruction of Sodom and Gomorrah. In Genesis 16,

---

14 *Stjórn*, 156; Gen. 11.30; Comestor, *Liber Genesis*, 80.

15 *Stjórn*, 158 ('he took with him his wife Sarah and Lot his brother's son'), 164 ('he took back with him Lot, his brother's son'), 181 ('being mindful of his brother's son, Lot'); cf. Gen. 12.5, 14.16; Comestor, *Liber Genesis*, 98.

16 On this story and its reception, see Phyllis Trible, *Texts of Terror: Literary-Feminist Readings of Biblical Narratives* (Philadelphia: Fortress Press, 1984), 9–35; Ruth Melinkoff, 'Sarah and Hagar: Laughter and Tears', in *Illuminating the Book: Makers and Interpreters*, ed. Michelle Brown and Scott McKendrick (Toronto: University of Toronto Press, 1998), 35–51; John Thompson, *Writing the Wrongs: Women of the Old Testament among Biblical Commentators from Philo through the Reformation* (Oxford: Oxford University Press, 2001), 17–99; Catherine Karkov, 'Hagar and Ishmael: The Uncanny and the Exile', in *Imagining the Jew in Anglo-Saxon Literature and Culture*, ed. Samantha Zacher (Toronto: University of Toronto Press, 2001), 197–218.

174

The God of Abraham, Isaac and Jacob

Sarah's slave-woman, Hagar, is given to Abraham as a wife. But, after she conceives, she is treated harshly by Sarah and flees into the desert, where an angel meets her and orders her to return. She then gives birth to Abraham's son Ishmael. In Genesis 21, after the birth of Isaac, Sarah and Abraham drive Hagar and her son back into the desert, and Ishmael is on the point of death when an angel appears to Hagar and shows her a spring of water. Both theophanies in the desert lead to promises that Hagar will be the ancestor of a great people, the Ishmaelites, whom Comestor identifies with the Saracens.

This story was interpreted allegorically as early as the first century CE both by the Jewish scholar Philo and in the Epistles of St Paul.[17] But, although the passages that surround it in *Stjórn I* are given allegorical glosses, this one is explored on a domestic level. It is Sarah's idea to give Hagar to Abraham for the purpose of providing her with a son: 'Gakk inn til minnar þjónustukonu léttliga at ek megi svá af henni syni geta' ('Go into my serving-woman, to see whether perhaps I can get a son from her').[18] With Abraham's consent, she gives Hagar 'sínum bónda í vald svá sem hans eiginkonu' ('into her husband's power as if his wife'). The 'svá sem' ('as if') is deliberately ambiguous, for while Hagar might be expected to accrue some of a wife's rights, the reality will be very different. Although Sarah clearly has the upper hand in these dealings, the relationship changes when Hagar discovers that she is pregnant: 'þá fyrirleit hon sína húsfrú Saray, en Abram lét eigi sem hann vissi hvat tíðis var' ('then she looked down on her mistress Sarah, but Abram acted as if he did not know what was going on'). The second half of this is a translation of Comestor's 'Abram dissimulabat' ('Abram feigned' or 'dissembled').[19] It draws attention to the psychological drama unfolding here: the power struggle between the two women, and Abraham's refusal to take sides. While Comestor makes it clear that Abraham chooses to ignore the women, the Old Norse leaves his inner life opaque: he may be genuinely ignorant as to what is happening or merely acting 'as if' to avoid taking responsibility for it. When Sarah complains to him that 'fyrirsmár hon mik' ('she rejects me'), he is quick to defer to her authority: 'Sé, ambátt þín er í þínu valdi' ('See, your slave-woman is in your power').[20] Hagar is transferred from Sarah's 'vald' ('power') into Abraham's, then back into Sarah's again. In the Vulgate, the term 'ancilla' ('maidservant') is used for Hagar throughout, but in the Old Norse the terminology changes: up to this point, Hagar has been described as 'þjónustukona' or 'þerna', both meaning 'servant-woman', but from this moment on she is referred to exclusively as 'ambátt' or 'female slave'. This

---

17 See Galatians 4 and, for Philo, Thompson, *Writing*, 24–27.
18 *Stjórn*, 170; Gen. 16.2 This practice is known as polycoity; see Steinberg, 'World of the Family', 283.
19 Gen. 16.4; Comestor, *Liber Genesis*, 92.
20 Gen. 16.5–6.

The Old Testament in Medieval Icelandic Texts

sudden deterioration in her social status is confirmed in the next sentence, when the Old Norse describes how Sarah 'þjáði hana ok þrøngði' ('enslaved and oppressed her'), a word-pair that is closely connected elsewhere with the slavery of the Israelites in Egypt.[21] While the Latin does not register this deterioration in social station, the Hebrew terminology does: Hagar is described throughout Genesis 16 as שִׁפְחָה ('female servant'), but after Isaac is born in Genesis 21, she is consistently referred to by the different term אָמָה ('female slave').[22] While the Old Norse compiler could not possibly have known this, both he and the biblical author are clearly sensitive, in a way that Jerome is not, to the way in which a woman's status might fluctuate in relation to her ability to bear children.

God apparently endorses Abraham and Sarah's behaviour: the angel addresses Hagar as 'Agar ambátt' ('Hagar the slave-woman') and sends her straight back into her mistress's 'vald' ('power'). However, after Sarah gives birth to Isaac, Hagar's situation deteriorates still further. When Isaac is three (the detail of his age comes from Comestor), a weaning feast is held for him, and Sarah observes the two brothers carefully:[23]

> Sem þeir léku sér báðir samt brœðrnir, Ysmael son Agar ok Ysaach, ok hinn ellri lék illa með inum yngra, þá hugsaði Sarra ok skildi eptirkomanda ófrið af leikinum þeim sem hon sá, at inn ellri mundi inum yngri dróttna vilja þann tíma sem faðir þeira er allr, ella kúgaði Ysmael hann til at dýrka líkneski þau, sem hann hafði sér af leiri gert eptir ebreskra manna sǫgn. Ok sem mœðr hans mislíkaði þetta, talaði hon til Abrahams: 'Rek í brott ambáttina ok hennar son, því at eigi mun ambáttarsonr sá erfingi þinn verða með syni mínum Ysaach'. Abraham tók þessu hennar tali heldr þungliga fyrir sonar síns skyld Ysmaels ok gaf sér ekki um.

> As the brothers were playing together, Ishmael, the son of Hagar, and Isaac, and the older played roughly with the younger, then Sarah reflected and perceived the coming conflict from the game she saw, that the older would want to dominate the younger once their father is dead, or else Ishmael forced

---

21 *Stjórn*, 171; both verbs are found in alliterative word-pairs describing the oppression of the Israelites in Egypt. See pp. 168 ('þját ok þrælkat'), 373 ('þrøngdir ok þrælkaðir'), 390 ('þrøngdir ok þrælkaðir').

22 Trible, *Texts of Terror*, 21, argues that these two Hebrew nouns have different valences.

23 *Stjórn*, 192; Comestor, *Liber Genesis*, 106–07. Compare Gen. 21.9–10 'cumque vidisset Sarra filium Agar Aegyptiae ludentem dixit ad Abraham eice ancillam hanc et filium eius non enim erit heres filius ancillae cum filio meo Isaac dure accepit hoc Abraham pro filio suo' ('And when Sara had seen the son of Agar the Egyptian playing with Isaac her son, she said to Abraham: Cast out this bondwoman, and her son: for the son of the bondwoman shall not be heir with my son Isaac. Abraham took this grievously for his son').

The God of Abraham, Isaac and Jacob

him to worship idols which he had made out of clay, according to what the Hebrews say. And as this displeased his mother, she said to Abraham: 'Drive away the slave-woman and her son, because the slave woman's son must not be your heir with my son Isaac'. Abraham took what she said rather heavily for the sake of his son Ishmael and showed no interest.

This scene blends biblical narrative with commentary from the *Historia scholastica*: the Vulgate says only that Sarah saw Ishmael 'playing' ('ludentem'), but the ambiguity of the Hebrew verb צחק led to various other interpretations, including the possibility mentioned by Comestor that Ishmael forced Isaac to worship idols.[24] The game looks innocent enough – two brothers playing together – and even the comment that the older was rather rough falls within the scope of normal sibling relations. Moreover, the bleaker interpretation of the game is positioned subjectively as what Sarah thought ('hugsaði') and perceived ('skildi') rather than as objective fact; 'what the Hebrews say' is mentioned as a possibility but is not authorially endorsed. Instead, the nouns of family relationship speak strongly of domestic tensions: Ishmael is introduced as 'son Agar' ('Hagar's son'), although Sarah previously wished to claim him as her own. Her command to Abraham sets 'the slave-woman's son' against 'my son', omitting the fact that both are Abraham's. Although Abraham is grieved 'for the sake of his son Ishmael' (which pointedly redresses Sarah's omission), his response comes across as weak and ineffective: however 'heavily' he may take Sarah's words, he does not refuse her, but merely 'gaf sér ekki um' ('showed no interest'). Again, this translates Comestor's 'dissimulabat' ('feigned' or 'dissembled'), without explaining why Abraham makes this display of indifference: does he hope that the problem will go away if he ignores it or has he already given in? Either way, his final actions, after God commands him to do what Sarah says, are described with a chilling lack of emotion: 'tók hann brauð ok einn legil með vatn ok lét upp á herðar Agar, fekk hann sveininn í hendr ok bað hana brott fara' ('he took bread and a container of water and put it on Hagar's shoulders, gave the boy into her hands and told her to go away').[25] Sarah's 'rek í brott ambáttina' echoes in that last 'bað hana brott fara', as if Abraham is merely repeating Sarah's words.[26]

It is in the two scenes in the wilderness, though, that Hagar comes into her own, and the Old Norse gives extra emphasis to the parallelism already present: in the first, Hagar is described as 'þyrst ok villzk vegar' ('thirsty

---

[24] Johnson, *Writing*, 37–38. Comestor probably borrows this conjecture from Jerome. It is based on the verb's use in Ex. 32.6, where the Israelites' 'playing' is connected to idolatry.

[25] *Stjórn*, 193; cf. Gen. 21.14.

[26] The echo here between 'drive away' ('reka í brott') and 'go away' ('brott fara') is not in the Vulgate (Gen. 21.10, 14), which has 'eice' ('cast out') and 'dimisit eam' ('sent her away').

The Old Testament in Medieval Icelandic Texts

and having lost her way'), while in the second we are told that 'villtisk hon í eyðimǫrkinni' ('she lost her way in the desert') and that 'sveininn þyrsti svá mjǫk at hann var drjúgum at dauða kominn' ('the boy was so thirsty that he was on the point of death').[27] In the Vulgate, her thirst is not mentioned in Genesis 16, and in Genesis 21 we are told only that the water was 'consumpta' ('consumed'). Both scenes, then, intensify Hagar's desperate plight and draw attention to her emotions. In the first, the word-pair 'neyð ok angist' ('distress and anguish') is used to double the Vulgate's 'adflictio' ('affliction').[28] In the second, Hagar's anticipation of her son's death is told first in indirect discourse – 'settisk þar niðr at hon sæi eigi upp á síns sonar dauða' ('sat down there so that she would not have to watch her son's death') – then repeated in direct speech: 'eigi skal ek sjá upp á þat, at sonr minn deyr' ('I shall not watch while my son dies'). The Vulgate has 'non videbo morientem puerum' ('I will not see the boy die'), but Comestor renders this in indirect speech: 'ne uideret filium morientem' ('so that she would not see [her] son die').[29] By using both, the Old Norse forces attention on Hagar's plight as a mother who refuses to witness her son's death. While the Vulgate tells us that God hears the boy's voice ('vocem pueri'), the Old Norse adds: 'ok enn heldr þína fyrir sveinsins skyld' ('or rather yours for the boy's sake'). In Comestor, it is her 'weeping' that God hears.[30] Hagar may have spoken 'fyrir sjálfri sér' ('to herself'), but her voice still carries weight with God.

A few other additions suggest that Hagar gains not just sympathy but respect in the Old Norse retelling of her story. In Genesis 16, when God announces the birth of Ishmael, the compiler adds from Comestor: 'Í þessum stað er þat fyrst lesit at nǫkkurs manns nafn hafi af guði vitrat verit' ('In this place it is first read that any person's name was revealed by God').[31] In other words, he recognises Hagar's special status as the first woman in the Bible to receive an annunciation. At the end of the same scene, after a long digression on Ishmael's descendants, he tells us that the well is named after Hagar: 'af því kallaði hon þann sama brunn sem hon fann sjánda brunn ok lifanda, fyrir þann skyld at guð dróttinn sá þá til henni þyrstandi svá sem sitt líf, sýnandi henni þann sama brunn sem vel má kallask Agar brunnr ok enn má sýnask milli Caldes ok Baraak' ('She called the same well that she found, the well of seeing and living because the Lord God saw her thirsting as if [for] her life, showing her the same well which may fittingly be called Hagar's well and can still be seen between

---

27 Gen. 21.14; Comestor, *Liber Genesis*, 92, 107.
28 *Stjórn*, 171; Gen. 16.11.
29 *Stjórn*, 193; Gen. 21.16; Comestor, *Liber Genesis*, 107.
30 Comestor, *Liber Genesis*, 107: 'id est fletum matris pro puero' ('that is the tears of the mother for the boy').
31 *Stjórn*, 171; Comestor, *Liber Genesis*, 92.

The God of Abraham, Isaac and Jacob

Cades and Bared').[32] The Vulgate has simply: 'Propterea appellavit puteum illum puteum Viventis et videntis me ipse est inter Cades et Barad' ('Therefore she called that well, the well of him that liveth and seeth me. The same is between Cades and Barad'). The idea that the well was named after Hagar may come from Comestor, who mentions that 'Adhuc puteus Agar ostenditur inter Cades et Barath' ('Hagar's well can still be seen between Cades and Barath'). Perhaps the compiler understood this comment to mean that 'Hagar's well' was its name. But, if so, he thoroughly approves: 'sem vel má kallask Agar brunnr' ('which is fittingly named Hagar's well'). Finally, while the Vulgate and Comestor say only that Ishmael grew up to be 'sagittarius' ('an archer'), the Old Norse adds: 'varð inn mesti bógmaðr ok inn bezti skyti' ('he became the greatest bowman and the best archer').[33]

In AM 227 fol., there is one more detail to add: in the capital N in the right-hand column of fol. 30r (Fig. 3), a woman's face is depicted, her eyes turned across the page towards the left-hand column, directly opposite the words: 'Rek í brott ambáttina ok hennar son' ('Drive away the slave-woman and her son'). A number of initials in the manuscript have faces sketched in them, but they are otherwise exclusively male, although some women are depicted in the marginal illuminations: Sarah in the lower margin of fol. 23v (Abraham's departure from Haran) and Rebecca in the left-hand margin of fol. 37v (the tricking of Isaac). It is possible that the face in this initial is meant to be Sarah, looking on with disapproval as Ishmael and Isaac play. However, I think it more likely that it is meant to be Hagar, because of the sadness around her eyes and mouth, and the foliage that curls not only around the initial, but also over her head, with what looks like a drop of water clinging to it – a reminder of her desperate thirst, and how she lays the dying Ishmael under a tree. If it is Hagar, it is interesting that she is not portrayed as a young and beautiful temptress, but as a sober wife and mother. But whomever the face belongs to, it communicates an emotion, perhaps the appropriate emotion with which a viewer should respond to the story. That emotion is not vindication or triumph – as Sarah may feel as she watches Hagar and Ishmael cast out – but 'neyð ok angist' ('distress and anguish'): the emotions attributed to Hagar.

After the rejection of Ishmael as heir, there is one more challenge for Abraham to overcome: God's command in Genesis 22 that he sacrifice his son Isaac. This is a particularly difficult passage because the compiler appears to be torn not only between two approaches – literal and allegorical – but also between two styles, the masterfully 'plain' style of the biblical narrative, and a florid style that foregrounds emotion and rhetoric. Abraham's sacrifice of Isaac had a well-established allegorical meaning from as early as the second

---

[32] *Stjórn*, 172; Gen. 16.14; Comestor, *Liber Genesis*, 93.
[33] *Stjórn*, 193; Gen. 21.20; Comestor, *Liber Genesis*, 107.

The Old Testament in Medieval Icelandic Texts

Figure 3. Sarah or Hagar, AM 227 fol. 30r.

century as a type of God's sacrifice of his only son.[34] This can be clearly seen in the illumination on fol. 23v of AM 227 fol. (Fig. 4). In the initial T which opens the Abraham cycle at Genesis 11, we see Isaac crouching in an attitude of prayer, not on a pile of wood but on an altar, prefiguring the Eucharistic sacrifice. Abraham stands upright, grasping Isaac's hair in one hand and his raised sword in the other, apparently unaware of the angel who has grabbed the blade from behind and the ram waiting patiently just below. Between the angel and the ram, a dove swoops downwards, its wings outstretched in alignment with the angel. This is a Trinitarian reading of Genesis 22 placed at the opening of the Abraham cycle to remind its readers that the Abrahamic promises are ultimately fulfilled in Christ. Yet the scene unfolding in the margin below (Fig. 5) shows that there is also a human drama taking place. Here we see Abraham departing from Haran, his finger gesturing towards

[34] On the reception of this story, see among others Robert L. Wilken, 'Melito, the Jewish Community at Sardis, and the Sacrifice of Isaac', *Theological Studies* 37.1 (1976), 53–69; John C. Cavadini, 'Exegetical Transformations: The Sacrifice of Isaac in Philo, Origen, and Ambrose', in *In Dominico Eloquio – In Lordly Eloquence: Essays on Patristic Exegesis in Honor of Robert Louis Wilken*, ed. Paul M. Blowers et al. (Grand Rapids, MI: Eerdmans, 2002), 35–49; Edward Kessler, *Bound by the Bible: Jews, Christians and the Sacrifice of Isaac* (Cambridge: Cambridge University Press, 2004); Schoenfeld, *Isaac*.

Figure 4. The Sacrifice of Isaac, AM 227 fol. 23v.

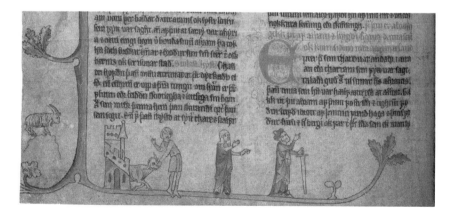

Figure 5. Abraham's Departure from Haran, AM 227 fol. 23v.

The Old Testament in Medieval Icelandic Texts

the physical words on the page where God tells him to abandon 'fǫðurhús ok herbergi' ('his father's house and home'), depicted behind him on the left.[35] While he strides ahead, carrying the same sword he will raise against Isaac, Sarah appears to remonstrate behind him, while Lot, further back still, struggles to manage a recalcitrant cow, while gesturing towards a ram in the left-hand margin who clearly has no intention of going anywhere. Sarah stands sideways, face turned to the right, but feet facing forwards, while Lot's whole body is twisted so his feet face to the right, but his face is turned fully to the left. It is an illumination that imagines a range of human responses to the divine call to leave one's house and home. It also nicely picks up on the verbal link in the Hebrew between Abraham's obedience to God in departing from Haran in Genesis 12.1 and his obedience in the sacrifice of Isaac in Genesis 22.2: in both, God commands Abraham to go (Hebrew לֶךְ־לְךָ) to a place that he will show him. The verbal echo is missing in the Vulgate, but is restored in the Old Norse, where God tells Abraham 'far til þess lands' ('go to the land') and 'far til sjónarlands' ('go to the land of vision').[36]

The interplay between literal and allegorical levels of interpretation can be seen from the very beginning of this chapter. The Old Norse starts by following the Vulgate carefully with added historical details from Comestor. It tells us Isaac's age according to Josephus (he is now 22) and then carefully translates God's command: 'Hann vitraðisk honum svá segjandi: "Abraham, Abraham". Hann svaraði: "Ek em til reiðu". "Tak þú son þinn Ysaach þann sem þu elskar", sagði guð, "ok far til sjónarlands ok offra mér hann þar með fornfœring"' ('He appeared to him, saying: "Abraham, Abraham". He answered: "I am ready". "Take your son Isaac whom you love", said God, "and go to the land of vision and offer him to me there as a sacrifice"').[37] The only noteworthy change here is the omission of 'unigenitum' ('only-begotten'), perhaps because it is difficult to reconcile with the fact that Abraham does have another son. This short passage of narrative is then followed by two blocks of commentary. Under the rubric *Scolastica hystoria*, we are provided with geographical information, identifying the mountain where Abraham is to sacrifice Isaac with the site of the Jerusalem temple, according to 'ebreskum

---

35   *Stjórn*, 158; Gen. 12.1.
36   *Stjórn*, 158, 195. The Vulgate does, though, retain the verbal echo between 'quam monstrabo tibi' and 'quem monstravero tibi' (both translated 'which I will show you' in Douay-Rheims).
37   *Stjórn*, 195; cf. Gen. 22.2. The Hebrew and Latin versions of this story are discussed on pp. 27–29 and 37–39. The compiler's 'twenty-two' is a mistake: Josephus and Comestor say that Isaac is 25.

The God of Abraham, Isaac and Jacob

mǫnnum' ('Hebrew men').[38] Under the rubric *Speculum hystoriale*, however, the compiler strikes an altogether different note:[39]

> Freistaði guð trúar ok hlýðni Abrahe í þessum sjálfs hans elskuligum ok eingetnum syni, eigi fyrir þann skyld at hann vissi eigi áðr, útan heldr til hins, at hann gerði þessa hans krapt kunniga oss til eptirdœmis, þar sem hann vildi með efanarlausum hug ok hjarta sœfa sinn son fyrir guðs boðskap af sjálfs hans samvizku.

> God tested the faith and obedience of Abraham in this his own beloved and only-begotten son, not because he did not already know, but rather in order to make this his power known as an example to us, in that he was willing with undoubting heart and mind to sacrifice his son at God's command and with his knowledge.

The difference in style is immediately noticeable: this one sentence contains three word-pairs, two of which alliterate ('**e**lskuligum ok **e**ingetnum', '**h**ug ok **h**jarta'), as well as further stretches of alliteration ('**k**rapt **k**unniga', '**s**œfa **s**inn **s**on', '**s**jálfs **h**ans **s**amvizku'). More importantly, it makes explicit what we are not told in the biblical narrative: God's reason for testing Abraham ('as an example for us') and what is inside Abraham's mind ('with undoubting heart and mind'). While the earlier translation omitted 'unigenitus', it is foregrounded here in the word-pair 'elskuligum ok eingetnum', both of which point forward to Christ as the fulfilment of this type.[40] Abraham is commended not just for his faithfulness, but specifically for his faith in the resurrection: 'af þeiri trú sem hann trúði at hann mundi síðan lifgask ok upp reisask' ('for the belief by which he believed that he [Isaac] would afterwards be resurrected and raised up').[41] We seem to have been diverted from the Hebrew traditions in Comestor and plunged straight into the New Testament.

This then merges into a florid translation of Origen's homily on Genesis 22 as preserved in the *Speculum historiale*.[42] Origen's keen interest in Abraham's inner conflict infuses the scene with all the emotion that is missing

---

[38] Comestor, *Liber Genesis*, 109. On the site of Moriah, see Kessler, *Bound by the Bible*, 82–85, 89–90.

[39] Stjórn, 196; cf. Vincent of Beauvais, *Speculum historiale*, 2.107.

[40] *Speculum historiale*, 2.107; cf. Mk 1.11 'tu es filius meus dilectus' ('thou art my beloved son'); Rom. 8.32 'qui etiam Filio suo non pepercit' ('He that spared not even his own son').

[41] Cf. Hebrews 11.17–19 'fide obtulit Abraham Isaac cum temptaretur [...] arbitrans quia et a mortuis suscitare potens est Deus' ('By faith Abraham, when he was tried, offered Isaac [...] accounting that God is able to raise up even from the dead').

[42] *Speculum historiale* 2.107. On Origen's Homily, see pp. 45–46.

The Old Testament in Medieval Icelandic Texts

in the biblical account. The reader is encouraged to use their imagination to enter into the story and live out Abraham's dilemma:

> Má vel hugsa hversu hættliga feðrins ástúð ok elskhugi mundi kveykjask ok upp vekjask til síns sonar af svá mǫrgum sœtum nafnagiptum til þess at hans hǫnd yrði léttliga því seinni at sœfa sjálfs síns son sem elskhugans ok kjærleiksins minni vaknaði meir með honum af þess háttar sonarnǫfnum ok sœtum áminningum, ef hann hefði eigi þvílíka trú ok staðfestu haft til guðs.

> It may well be imagined how dangerously the father's love and affection for his son would have been kindled and awakened by so many sweet names, so that his hand would perhaps have been slower to sacrifice his son, the more the memory of love and affection was awakened within him by these names for his son and sweet reminders, if he had not had such faith and steadfastness in God.

This skilfully opens up the possibility that Abraham's paternal love for Isaac might overwhelm his faith, before shutting it down at the end: it is not how Abraham feels, but how he might have felt 'if he had not had such faith and steadfastness in God'. It is even more fiercely emotional in Old Norse than in the Latin, with four references to love ('ástúð', 'elskhugi', 'elskhugans', 'kjærleiksins') where Vincent has only two ('affectus', 'amoris'), repeated evocations of sweetness ('sœtum nafnagiftum', 'sœtum áminningum'), where Vincent has only one ('dulcibus appellationibus'), and its appeal to a parent's fond memories of their beloved child. While the opening of the narrative blanked Abraham's emotions, the compiler here appears to luxuriate in the emotional expansiveness of his style.

This deliberate contrast between the terseness of the Bible and the extravagance of Origen's commentary continues throughout the chapter. When the compiler translates from Genesis 22.3–4, he follows the Vulgate closely, if anything simplifying the syntax:[43] 'Abraham reis upp þegar á náttartíma ok sagði engum manni sína fyrirætlan, klæddi með reiða einn sinn asna, kallandi með sér .ij. sveina ok son sinn inn þriðja. Ok sem hann hafði hǫggvit þau tré sem hann þurfti til fornfœringarinnar at hafa, þá fór hann á .iij. dǫgum' ('Abraham rose up at once during the night and told no one his intention. He put a saddle on a donkey, calling to him two young men and his son the third. And when he had cut the wood which he needed for the sacrifice, he travelled for three days'). The first present participle 'consurgens' has been changed to the finite 'reis upp', although the second ('ducens' or 'kallandi') remains. More importantly, there is no sense at all at this point of how Abraham might feel, and his problematic opaqueness is evoked particularly

---

[43] *Stjórn*, 197; cf. Comestor, *Liber Genesis*, 109 'nemini quod facturus erat indicans' ('telling no one what was to be done'). See also Chapter 1, pp. 27–28.

184

The God of Abraham, Isaac and Jacob

well in the unmarked gloss from Comestor that 'he told no one his intention'. Instead, the focus is on the series of actions Abraham must undertake: he gets up, saddles the donkey, calls his servants, cuts the wood, and travels for three days – three days that we are told nothing about in the Bible. The only potential moment of pathos is in the placement of 'his son' as Abraham's third and final companion – 'son sinn inn þriðja' – which just barely hints at reluctance on Abraham's part. Then, just as abruptly as we moved back into the biblical narrative, we return to Origen's evocation of Abraham's inner conflict, in which the three days that were blanked are filled to the brim with emotions:[44]

> Allan þriggja daga tíma vannsk þeira vegr, á hverjum er fǫðurligr hugr ok hjarta þjáðisk ok pínaðisk af angrsamligum áhyggjum, því at á ǫllum þessum tíma, svá lǫngum leit hann ok sá upp á sinn son ok átu báðir samt, á svá mǫrgum náttum hálsspenti sveinninn með sœtum blíðskap sinn fǫður ok lá við hans brjóst með fǫðurligu faðmlagi.

> Their journey lasted for the whole span of three days, in which the father's heart and mind was oppressed and tortured by anxious thoughts because, in this whole time, for as long as he watched and looked upon his son and they ate both together, for just as many nights the boy embraced his father with sweet affection and lay on his chest in a father's embrace.

Again, the word-pairs, alliteration, and *similiter cadens* are used to intensify Abraham's feelings: 'fǫðurligr **h**ugr ok **h**jarta þjáð*isk* ok pínað*isk*' ('the father's heart and mind were oppressed and tortured'), '**a**ngrsamlig*um* **á**hyggj*um*' ('anxious thoughts'), fǫðurligu fa*ð*mlagi' ('father's embrace').[45] The longer he gazes at Isaac and the longer Isaac embraces him, the more difficult becomes his task. In this deeply affective reimagining of the three-day journey, Isaac is no longer Comestor's young man of 22 years, but the small boy imagined by the Church fathers, nestled within Abraham's loving arms.[46]

There is a similar inconsistency in the two different versions of the dialogue between father and son. The first comes directly from Genesis 22 without any additions:[47]

> Ok sem þeir fóru .ij. samt talaði sveinninn til síns feðr: 'Faðir minn', sagði hann. 'Hvat viltu, son minn?' sagði Abraham. 'Sé, faðir minn', sagði

---

[44] *Stjórn*, 198.

[45] Cf. *Speculum historiale* 2.170 'paterna viscera crucianter' ('the father's inward parts were tormented'), where the verb 'crucio' ('to torment, to crucify') may direct an attentive reader towards the passion of Christ; 'in amplexibus patris' ('in his father's embrace').

[46] On Isaac's age, see Kessler, *Bound by the Bible*, 102–08, 125.

[47] *Stjórn*, 198; Gen. 22.7–8.

The Old Testament in Medieval Icelandic Texts

sveinninn. 'Eldrinn ok tréin eru hér til reiðu. En hvar er þat er offrask skal?' Hann svaraði: 'Guð sjálfr mun sjá sér fórn til handa, son minn'. Fóru síðan báðir samt.

And as they went, the two of them together, the boy said to his father: 'My father', he said. 'What do you want, my son?' said Abraham. 'See, my father', said the boy, 'the fire and the wood are ready here, but where is what is to be sacrificed?' He answered: 'God himself will provide the sacrifice, my son'. They went on both together.

This preserves almost perfectly the stylistic features of the Hebrew: the verbal echo of 'the two of them together' and 'both together' that frames the dialogue, the repetition of 'my father' and 'my son', and the playing off of limited perspectives.[48] Isaac, speaking with all the innocence of childhood, cannot possibly understand that he is the sacrifice, while Abraham does not yet know that what he says is true: God will provide a sacrifice, and it will not be his son. But the compiler also provides an alternative to this conversation, which he translates from Comestor, but which ultimately derives from Josephus:[49]

Sem hann sagði: 'Faðir minn, hvar er sú fórn sem offrask skal?', hafi faðir hans á þessa leið svarat, at svá sem hann var með guðs vilja dásamliga hingat í heiminn fæddr, mundi hann ok eptir því sem viðrkvæmiligt ok nauðsynligt væri með guðs vilja dásamliga af heiminum fara, hvern er guð dróttinn hafði makligan gert at lykta sitt líf, eigi með sjúkdómi eða krankleika, eigi í bardaga eða vápnskiptum eða af nøkkurri mannligri pínu, útan heldr at kalla sjálfs hans ønd ok sál til sín með bœnum ok fornfœringum ok reisa hann síðan upp.

When he said, 'My father, where is the sacrifice to be offered?', his father may have answered in this way: that just as by God's will he had been miraculously born into this world, so he would also, as was fitting and necessary, by God's will, miraculously leave the world again, whom the Lord God had made worthy to end his life, not with sickness or disease, not in battle or skirmishes or from any human torment, but rather by calling his very spirit and soul to himself with prayers and sacrifices and by raising him to life again.

This sounds more like a conversation with a consenting adult than a small child and, armed with this foreknowledge, Isaac makes an active choice to go 'gjarnsamliga' ('eagerly') to his death. But, in the very next sentence, we are

---

48 See pp. 28–29.
49 *Stjórn*, 198; Comestor, *Liber Genesis*, 110; *Speculum historiale*, 2.170; and cf. pp. 63–64.

The God of Abraham, Isaac and Jacob

back in Genesis again:[50] 'Eptir þat batt Abraham son sinn ok lét hann upp á viðarbulung, þann sem hann hafði yfir altarinu gert, greip síðan sverðit með annarri hendi ok ætlaði at hǫggva hann' ('After that Abraham bound his son and put him on the pile of wood he had made over the altar, then grasped the sword with his other hand and intended to kill him'). The moment is full of tension, with the verse ending at the very moment depicted in the initial on fol. 23v when Abraham raises his sword to strike – the only moment, of course, when we can be absolutely sure that Abraham does intend to kill his son.

If, in the story of Hagar, the compiler chose to dwell on the domestic drama between two women, the sacrifice of Isaac shows something rather different. Here it looks as if the compiler is deliberately alternating between two styles: a 'plain' style that replicates the style of the Vulgate itself and a more florid style that is used for commentary of an emotional or rhetorical nature. It is the movement back and forth between these two styles that makes them so noticeable in this chapter; the compiler even signals that he is moving between different levels of interpretation when he finishes a passage from Vincent of Beauvais with the words 'skal hér nú um eina stund frá snúa ok til sǫgunnar aptr hverfa' ('now we shall turn from this for a while and go back to the story' i.e. the *historia*).[51] Nor can the differences between these two styles be attributed entirely to the sources the compiler is using: although he does sometimes imitate Vincent's style, the addition of word-pairs and alliteration is largely his own. When translating the Vulgate, on the other hand, he routinely simplifies the syntax and carefully avoids any heavy compound phrases. The result, in the case of Isaac, is an oddly bifurcated narrative which makes us uncomfortably aware of how the drama between father and son is overburdened by the weight of allegorical interpretation.

The Jacob Cycle

The sacrifice of Isaac is the only scene that is handled in this way, presumably because of its theological importance as a type of Christ's sacrifice. Although the compiler continues to provide allegorical interpretations – of Jacob's ladder, for example – the focus of the Jacob cycle is very much on family relationships and on the various tricks played in the fulfilment of God's promises by Rebecca, Laban and Jacob.[52] The terms used repeatedly by the compiler throughout this section are 'klokr' ('skilled' 'competent', 'clever', 'cunning', 'deceitful') and 'klokskapr' ('skill' or 'cunning'), which nicely

---

[50] *Stjórn*, 199; Gen. 22.9–10.

[51] *Stjórn*, 198.

[52] For Jacob's ladder, see *Stjórn*, 256–57: 'píning ihsu xpisti er himinríkis port ok upplokning' ('the passion of Jesus Christ is the gate of heaven and its opening').

187

The Old Testament in Medieval Icelandic Texts

capture the moral ambiguity of Jacob's character.[53] At the beginning, Esau is described as 'klokr veiðimaðr' ('a skilled hunter'), translating the Vulgate's 'gnarus', while Jacob is 'einfaldr' ('simple, innocent'), translating 'simplex', but exactly what we are meant to understand by this becomes increasingly less clear as the story progresses.[54] After Jacob has tricked his father and stolen Esau's blessing, Isaac tells his older son that 'þinn samborinn bróðir kom nǫkkut svá klokliga ok tók þína blezan' ('your twin brother came with cunning and took your blessing'), here translating the Vulgate's 'fraudulenter' ('fraudulently').[55] Yet in a passage of moral commentary from the *Historia scholastica*, Jacob is excused for what Comestor calls 'pia fraus' ('pious fraud'), which translates into Old Norse as 'sú milda flærð ok klokskapr' ('that mild deceit and cunning').[56] Later, when Jacob devises an elaborate trick to increase his wealth and property at Laban's expense, the compiler uses the term 'klokskapr' three times in a row: 'Jacob fann ok fekk eina klokskaparlist nýja' ('Jacob found and came up with a new trick'), 'varð þetta allt með hans klokskap ok tilstilli framgengt' ('this all came to pass by his skill and agency'), 'þá hafði hann þessa klokskaparlist' ('then he used this skilful artifice').[57] The first of these translates Comestor's 'nouam nature stropham' ('a new trick of nature'), but the other two are only in the Old Norse. Elsewhere in the compilation, 'klokr' has a variety of uses: the serpent in Genesis I is 'klokastr ok slœgastr af ǫllum kvikvendum' ('the most cunning and slyest of all creatures'), but later when Joseph advises Pharaoh on the famine in Egypt, he recommends that Pharaoh choose 'vitran mann ok vel klokan' ('a wise and industrious man').[58] By repeatedly using the terms 'klokr' and 'klokskapr' of Jacob, the brother favoured by God, the compiler not only raises questions about the moral status of his actions, but also highlights the ambiguous relationship between human initiative and divine grace. Laban's sons complain that Jacob 'tekr ok dregr undir sik allt þat sem várt ok várs feðr eign er eða var' ('takes and appropriates for himself everything that is or was our property and our father's'). Jacob sees it differently. He tells his wives: 'tók guð feðr ykkars eign ok gaf mér' ('God took

---

53 On Jacob as a trickster figure, see Susan Niditch, *A Prelude to Biblical Folklore: Underdogs and Tricksters* (San Francisco: Harper & Row, 1987); Nicholas Andrew Dean, *The Trickster Revisited: Deception as a Motif in the Pentateuch* (Oxford: Peter Lang, 2009); John Anderson, *Jacob and the Divine Trickster: A Theology of Deception and Yhwh's Fidelity to the Ancestral Promise in the Jacob Cycle* (University Park, PA: Penn State University Press, 2021).

54 *Stjórn*, 241–42; Gen. 25.27. Abel is also described as 'einfaldr' (p. 62).

55 *Stjórn*, 252; Gen. 27.35.

56 Comestor, *Liber Genesis*, 128.

57 *Stjórn*, 268–69; Comestor, *Liber Genesis*, 136.

58 *Stjórn*, 52, 306; Gen. 3.1 (translating 'callidior'), Gen. 41.33 (translating 'industrium').

The God of Abraham, Isaac and Jacob

your father's property and gave it to me').[59] The narrative manages to accommodate both perspectives without a steer as to which is right.

Moreover, the conflict between family members that was such a prominent aspect of Abraham's life continues here, first in the sibling rivalry between Jacob and Esau, and then in the childbearing competition between Rachel and Leah, which replays the rivalry between Sarah and Hagar. Just as the childish game between Isaac and Ishmael alerted Sarah to 'komanda ófrið' ('coming strife'), so Rebecca's difficult pregnancy with Jacob and Esau foreshadows the division between them 'sem síðarr kom fram' ('which later came to pass').[60] Parental favouritism plays a significant role in this: we are told that 'Ysaac elskaði meirr Esau' ('Isaac loved Esau more'), while 'Rebecca elskaði framarr Iacob' ('Rebecca loved Jacob most').[61] This pattern is repeated with Jacob's two wives, Leah and Rachel: we are told that 'lagði hann ok meira kjærleik ok elskhuga til hennar síðarri heldr en innar fyrri' ('he had more love and affection for the second than for the first').[62] In fact, we are told that 'Iacob fyrirleit sína húsfrú Lyam' ('Jacob looked down on his wife, Leah') in exactly the way that Hagar 'fyrirleit' ('looked down on') her mistress Sarah.[63] As a consolation, God blesses Leah with four sons, while Rachel – like Sarah – remains barren.

Predictably, this leads to a childbearing competition in which each woman vies with the other for a son who will increase her status. With each son she bears, Leah rejoices that her husband will now love her: 'Mun minn húsbóndi nú elska mik' ('Now my husband will love me'), 'Nú mun minn bóndi vísliga mér samtengjask' ('now my husband will surely be joined to me').[64] In response, Rachel – like Sarah – seeks to bear Jacob sons through her slave-woman Bilhah: to her, the birth of Bilhah's two sons proves that God is 'samvirðandi mik systur minni' ('valuing me as equal to my sister') and that 'samvirði guð mik systur minni' ('God has valued me equally to my sister').[65] Each new son brings a shift in their relative social standing. The contest ends with the two sisters bargaining over who will sleep with Jacob in exchange for mandrake root, reputed to aid fertility. When Jacob comes home from the fields that evening, Leah announces: 'Til minnar sængr átt

---

[59] *Stjórn*, 270–71; Gen 31.1. 9.

[60] *Stjórn*, 192, 239; cf. Comestor, *Liber Genesis*, 119–20.

[61] *Stjórn*, 242; cf. Gen. 25.28 'Isaac amabat Esau [...] et Rebecca diligebat Isaac' ('Isaac loved Esau [...] and Rebecca loved Jacob'); the comparatives 'meirr' and 'framarr' are added by the compiler.

[62] *Stjórn*, 261; cf. Gen. 29.30.

[63] *Stjórn*, 170, 262; Gen. 16.4 and 29.31. 'Fyrirleit' is the reading of AM 226 fol. at this point; AM 227 fol. has 'fyrirlét' ('rejected' or perhaps 'neglected').

[64] *Stjórn*, 262; Gen. 29. 32, 34.

[65] *Stjórn*, 263; this blends Gen. 30.6–8 and Comestor, *Liber Genesis*, 133.

The Old Testament in Medieval Icelandic Texts

þú í kveld at ganga, því at með kaupi leigða ek þik' ('You must go to my bed tonight, because I have hired you at a price').[66] The shock of this – the verb 'leiga' is used more often of animals or land than people – hinges on how it reverses the bargain by which Jacob acquired Leah and Rachel as his 'verkkaup' ('wages') for 14 years of labour: we are told that 'hann þóttisk svá elskuligan ok ástsamligan hlut við litlu verði keypt hafa sem Rachel var' ('he thought that in Rachel he had bought a loveable and precious thing at a small price').[67] The compiler even jokes about this happy conjunction of work and pleasure, commenting that: 'féll honum ok létt lystisamligt verk', which has the proverbial ring of 'love makes light work'.[68] Jacob bargained with Laban over the price of his two wives, and now they are bargaining over the price of sex with him. Although both women side firmly with Jacob in his dispute with their father Laban, Jacob's favouritism towards Rachel continues. When, in Genesis 33, he divides all his wealth and possessions into convoys in preparation for meeting a potentially violent Esau, he uses the women as a kind of human buffer: he puts the two slave-women up front, Leah and her sons in the middle, and Rachel and Joseph right at the back 'svá sem kærast sér af ǫllum þeim' ('as the most beloved to him of them all').[69]

Love, favouritism, social standing: the Old Norse compiler deals extraordinarily sensitively with these problematic aspects of Jacob's story. Although he is keen to justify morally the process by which Jacob usurps Esau's blessings, he does not (like the Icelandic Homily Book) divide his characters into good and evil but shows a keen appreciation for the social pressures that drive them and the domestic tensions within the family. He uses keywords and verbal echoes to connect scenes and draw attention to generational patterns, sometimes – but not always – taking his lead from key terms in the Vulgate: the punning on Jacob's 'verkkaup' ('wages'), the price he pays ('kaupa') for his two wives, and their 'kaup' ('bargain') over him is entirely the compiler's own. Just as Jacob's wives are not averse to bargaining over their husband, so too they are prepared to cheat their father if it benefits them. They complain that Laban has treated them like disposable property: 'sem óskyldar konu ok með ǫllu venzlalausar' ('like unrelated women and bound by no family ties').[70] Have they received anything of value from their father's

---

66 Stjórn, 265; Gen. 30.16 'mercede conduxi te' ('I have hired thee'). This is omitted in Comestor.

67 Stjórn, 260, 265; Gen. 29.29.

68 This translates the proverb in Comestor, Liber Genesis, 132 'laborem leuigabat amor' ('love lightened work') and even alliterates on the same letter. However, it is possible that it is also a proverb in Old Norse; compare 'létt eru lustverk' ('light are the works of lust' or 'pleasurable work is easy') in Homilíubók, 24.

69 Stjórn, 279; Gen. 33.2; Comestor, Liber Genesis, 141.

70 Stjórn, 271; Gen. 31.15 (translating 'quasi alienas' – 'as strangers').

The God of Abraham, Isaac and Jacob

house? Their answer is emphatic: 'nei og eigi' ('no and not at all').[71] It seems fitting, given how Laban has 'setit' (literally 'sat') in wait for Jacob's wealth, that when Rachel leaves, she puts the household idols under the saddle of her camel and hides them by sitting ('settisk') on them.[72]

These complex family tensions play an important role in what is perhaps the most saga-like scene in the whole of *Stjórn I*: the rape of Dinah in Genesis 34.[73] In this unpleasant episode, Jacob's daughter by Leah, Dinah, is abducted and raped by the son of the prince of Shechem, who subsequently falls in love with her. He and his father go to Jacob to ask permission for Shechem to marry Dinah, but Jacob's sons insist that this can only happen if the men of Shechem are circumcised. The father and son agree to this condition, and the circumcision takes place. On the third day, while the men are still incapacitated, Jacob's sons Levi and Simeon take up weapons and kill all the male inhabitants of the town, taking back their sister Dinah. The other sons join forces, destroy the town, and enslave the women and children. When Jacob questions the wisdom of their actions, they answer: 'Should they abuse our sister as a whore?'[74]

The Old Norse retelling of this story pays careful attention both to social relations within the family and to the legal ramifications of Dinah's rape. Some scholars have suggested that it is not clear in the Hebrew Bible whether Dinah is raped or whether we are dealing with an abduction marriage to which she might theoretically have consented: we are told that Shechem took (וַיִּקַּח) her and lay with her (וַיִּשְׁכַּב) and 'violated' (וַיְעַנֶּהָ) her, but this last verb – it has been argued – is better understood to mean a lowering in social status, something more like 'debased' her. Only after this is Shechem said to

---

[71] There is no equivalent to this lively response in either the Vulgate or in Comestor.

[72] *Stjórn*, 270, 273; Gen. 31.7 ('circumvenit' – 'beset') and 31.34 ('sedit' – 'sat'). The pun on *sitja um* (literally, 'to sit over/around'; metaphorically 'to waylay, plot against') is the compiler's own.

[73] Astås, *Studies in Stjórn*, 92.

[74] On the interpretation of this story in the Hebrew Bible, see among others Ellen J. van Wolde, 'Love and Hatred in a Multi-Racial Society: The Dinah and Shechem Story in Genesis 34 in the Context of Genesis 28–35', in *Reading from Right to Left: Essays on the Hebrew Bible in Honour of David J.A. Clines*, ed. Cheryl J. Williamson and Hugh G. M. Williamson (London: Sheffield Academic Press, 2003), 435–49; Yael Shemesh, 'Rape is rape is rape: The Story of Dinah and Shechem (Genesis 34)', *Zeitschrift für die Alttestamentliche Wissenschaft* 199.1 (2007), 2–21; Caroline Blyth, 'Redeemed by His Love? The Characterization of Shechem in Genesis 34', *Journal for the Study of Old Testament* 33.1 (2008), 3–18; Yitzhaq Feder, 'The Defilement of Dinah: Uncontrolled Passions, Textual Violence and the Search for Moral Foundations', *Biblical Interpretation* 24.3 (2016), 281–309; Janell Johnson, 'Negotiating Masculinities in Dinah's Story: Honor and Outrage in Genesis 34', *Review and Expositor* 115.4 (2018), 529–41.

The Old Testament in Medieval Icelandic Texts

fall in love with Dinah: his soul 'cleaved' to her (וַתִּדְבַּק) – the same verb used in Genesis 2.24 – and he loved her (וַיֶּאֱהַב) and spoke to her heart (לֵב). In the Vulgate, the order of these events has changed. We are told first that Shechem fell in love with Dinah ('adamavit'), then that he 'rapuit et dormivit cum illa vi opprimens virginem' ('took her away, and lay with her, ravishing the virgin'), where 'opprimens', translating the Hebrew verb 'debase', certainly can refer to rape. In the Old Norse, however, Dinah's lack of consent is explicit. Instead of following the lead of Jerome's 'adamavit' ('loved'), the compiler replaces it with 'leit hann girndaraugum til hennar' ('he looked at her with eyes of desire'), a phrase that clearly denotes illicit desire rather than love.[75] It is the same expression used for the sons of Seth who sleep with the daughters of Cain, and for how the Egyptians look upon Sarah, Abraham's wife. The Vulgate 'rapuit' is translated with two present participles: 'grípandi hana ok takandi með valdi' ('grabbing her and taking her by force'). The Vulgate's 'opprimens' is then paraphrased in a way that clearly indicates rape: 'ok svaf síðan með henni at hennar óvilja' ('and then slept with her against her will'). As in the Hebrew, it is only now that Shechem's desire turns to love, but this is clearly presented as a continuation of his earlier violence: the series of actions that began with 'grípandi hana ok takandi' ('grabbing and taking her') is continued in 'leggjandi hjartaligan ástarhug til hennar ok huggandi hana hrygga með mǫrgum blíðkanum' ('setting his heart's love on her and comforting her sadness with many endearments').[76] Shechem's apparent change of heart serves as a retrospective justification of his wrong-doing.

The compiler shows a strong interest in the legal consequences of this case. Shechem's father, Hamor, goes directly to Jacob and his sons to make a formal marriage proposal: 'þá gengu Emmor oc Sichem til þeira feðga; bar Emmor upp þeira erendi' ('Hamor and Shechem went to the father and sons; Hamor made known their business').[77] Without mentioning the rape, Hamor explains that Shechem is in love with Dinah and suggests that they make their 'samlag' ('cohabitation') honourable. This is an addition in the Old Norse – the Vulgate has simply 'date eam illi uxorem' ('give her him to wife') – and, although it seems woefully inadequate to describe rape as 'samlag', it shows a good understanding of what some Hebrew scholars have pointed out: that marriage to her rapist – something we now would consider monstrous – is the only outcome to the situation that will restore Dinah's

---

75   *Stjórn*, 281; cf. pp. 79, 189, 191.

76   None of these present participles occur in the Latin; compare Gen. 34.2–3. The one present participle in the Latin ('opprimens') is translated as a finite verb 'svaf síðan með henni' ('then slept with her'). In other words, this is a deliberate effect on the part of the compiler to make the sequence of verbs stand out.

77   Cf. Gen. 34.8 'locutus est itaque Emor ad eos' ('Hamor spoke to them').

The God of Abraham, Isaac and Jacob

social standing.[78] Viewed purely in terms of a marriage offer, it is a generous one: Shechem proposes to pay for the dowry ('heimanferð') and whatever else the brothers wish. However, Jacob's sons – although they play along – are all too aware of what is unspoken: that Dinah is already in Shechem's home. They are described as 'grimmhugaðir af legorðssǫk systur sinna, þó at þeir léti þat lítt á sjásk þá at sinni' ('angry-minded because of the seduction of their sister, though they let little of this be seen for the time being').[79] The term 'legorðssǫk' here (which translates the Vulgate's 'stuprum', meaning 'defilement, dishonour, disgrace') is a legal term attested in numerous Old Norse law-codes, for which the penalty can be full outlawry in the most serious cases, effectively a death sentence.[80] The legal language picks up on the implications of 'inlicitum' ('an unlawful act') in the Vulgate, which has no parallel in the Hebrew, where the emphasis is rather on pollution and ritual impurity, signalled by the repetition of the verb טמא (piel: 'to make impure, defile').[81] But, acting 'með prett ok undirhyggju' ('with deceit and cunning'), the brothers agree to settle ('sættask': another legal term) if all the men of Shechem will be circumcised.

The legal terminology continues into the following scene, where Hamor and Shechem persuade the townsmen to be circumcised. There appears to be some sympathy for Shechem at this point, however repellent we may find this: he is described as a young man, deeply in love, and both 'frægr ok framr' ('famous and prominent').[82] Again, the speech is presented much more formally in the Old Norse: while the Vulgate has simply 'locuti sunt populo' ('they spoke to the people'), this is translated as 'hǫfðu þeir feðgar þetta nýmæli frammi fyrir ǫllu sínu fólki' ('the father and son presented this new law in front of all their people'). The term 'nýmæli' is attested in numerous law-codes; it is the term used for changes to the law during Gizurr's episcopate in *Íslendingabók* and *Kristni saga*.[83] While the speech of Hamor and Shechem is in direct discourse in the Vulgate, the compiler moves most of it into indirect discourse, skimming over repetitions with 'lǫgðu þar

---

78 Johnson, 'Negotiating Masculinities', 533; van Wolde, 'Love and Hatred', 438.

79 Cf. Gen. 34.13 'saevientes ob stuprum sororis' ('being enraged at the deflowering of their sister').

80 *DONP*, s.v. 'legorðssǫk' at https://onp.ku.dk/onp/onp.php?o48457 (accessed 24 July 2023). For the penalties in Iceland, see *Grágás: Lagasafn íslenska þjóðveld-isins*, ed. Gunnar Karlsson, Kristján Sveinsson and Mörður Árnason (Reykjavík: Mál og menning, 1992), 124–30.

81 Van Wolde, 'Love and Hatred', 443; Feder, 'Defilement of Dinah', 293–94.

82 *Stjórn*, 283; Gen. 34.19 (translating the Vulgate 'inclitus': 'renowned, famous').

83 *Grágás*, 34–35, 337, 424; *Íslendingabók, Landnámabók*, ed. Jakob Benediktsson (Reykjavík: Hið íslenzka fornritafélag, 1968), 23; *Biskupa sögur I*, ed. Sigurgeir Steingrímsson, Ólafur Halldórsson and Peter Foote (Reykjavík: Hið íslenzka fornritafélag, 2003), 42.

The Old Testament in Medieval Icelandic Texts

til mǫrg orð' ('they added many words'). At the end, however, there is an unmarked shift into direct discourse which highlights the most persuasive part of their argument: 'en þeir hafa eignir miklar ok margar hjarðir ok mun þat allt skjótliga vár eign verða' ('but they have great possessions and many herds, and it will all quickly become our property'). This contradicts what Hamor and Shechem earlier promised to Jacob and his sons: 'eignisk slíkt af sem yðr er vel viljat' ('you take possession of whatever you wish'). Ever the consummate politicians, Hamor and Shechem tell each side what it wants to hear – but the echo of 'eignisk', 'eignir' and 'eign' suggests that there is more than love at stake: this is about wealth and property. Most striking are the parallels with the speech at the Althing in *Íslendingabók* in which Þorgeirr persuades the Icelanders to accept Christianity.[84] Hamor and Shechem's speech is introduced with the verb 'hafa frammi/uppi' ('to promote, put forward'); Þorgeirr's speech is introduced with 'hefja upp'. Hamor and Shechem's speech concludes: 'lúku þeir svá sinni tǫlu at allir samþykktusk' ('they ended their speech so that all were in accord'). Þorgeirr's speech ends: 'Hann lauk svá máli sínu, at hvárirtveggju játtu því' ('He ended his speech so that both sides agreed'). Both speeches begin in indirect discourse but switch to direct discourse to make their final point. If these echoes are deliberate, rather than a shared use of the same literary conventions, then perhaps the link between these two stories was suggested to the compiler by the typological relationship between 'skurðarskírn' ('circumcision') and 'skírn' ('baptism'). While the speech in *Íslendingabók* ends with the Icelanders accepting baptism, the one in *Stjórn I* ends with the townsmen accepting circumcision.

As so often, though, legal settlement provides little defence against blood vengeance. In the Vulgate, the massacre begins with Simeon and Levi, 'fratres Dinae' ('brothers of Dinah') taking up weapons to kill the newly circumcised Shechemites while they are still weak with pain. The Old Norse makes a small but significant change: it describes Simeon and Levi as 'sammœddir brœðr Dyne' ('brothers of Dinah by the same mother'). This draws out what is implicit in the Hebrew: that Jacob's apparent indifference to Dinah's rape and abduction may have something to do with the fact that she is the daughter of Leah, the wife whom he does not love. In the Vulgate, Dinah is described right up to the end as the 'daughter of Jacob', as if to draw attention to his failed obligations, but the Old Norse tends to prefer 'systir' ('sister') or 'frændkona' ('relative'): it is Dinah's brothers who are obliged to avenge her shame.[85] The appropriateness of their vengeance is suggested by the way

---

84 *Íslendingabók*, 17.

85 *Stjórn*, 282–83. In Gen. 34.7, 'filia Iacob' is translated as 'þeira systur' ('their sister') and at Gen. 34.8 and 17, 'filia' is translated 'frændkonu yðarrar' ('your kinswoman') and 'frændkona vára' ('our kinswoman').

194

The God of Abraham, Isaac and Jacob

in which it reverses Shechem's wrongdoing: he is described as 'grípandi hana ok takandi með valdi' ('grabbing and taking her by force'), while the brothers are described as 'takandi systur sína Dynam í brott' ('taking their sister Dinah away') and 'hefnandi svá svívirðingar systur sinnar' ('avenging thus the dishonouring of their sister').[86] Both the repeated verb 'takandi' and the sequence of present participles stand out at the beginning and end of the chapter. This verbal echo is also present in the Hebrew (which uses וַיִּקַּח and וַיִּקְחוּ), but is obscured in the Vulgate, which varies 'rapuit' ('took') with 'tollentes' ('taking').

The compiler not only understands the logic of the brothers' revenge but includes a further critique of Jacob's weakness. Once the massacre is completed, the Vulgate tells us that: 'quibus patratis audacter Iacob dixit ad Symeon et Levi' ('when they had boldly perpetrated these things, Jacob said to Simeon and Levi').[87] The Old Norse compiler appears to have misunderstood this and applies the adverb 'audacter' ('boldly') to Jacob's words instead: 'þá talaði hann djarfliga við Simeonem ok Leui' ('then he spoke boldly to Simeon and Levi').[88] But applied to Jacob, this adverb can only be ironic, for earlier the brothers were described as acting 'djarfliga' ('boldly') in attacking the town, but here the same adverb is applied to a speech in which Jacob expresses his fear that he and his family will be killed by the surrounding tribes, a fear that is immediately afterwards shown to be groundless.[89] The repetition is not present in the Vulgate, which uses two different adverbs ('confidenter' and 'audacter'), so the irony is entirely the compiler's own.

The Old Norse compiler's understanding of this story has been shaped by his own literary tradition. He is most sensitive to the familial aspects of the crisis: the relationship between father and daughter, between father and sons, and between brothers and sister. Although Leah is absent from the story, she is evoked in the first verse, which describes Dinah as 'dóttir Iacob ok Lye' ('daughter of Jacob and Leah').[90] However, the focus in the Hebrew on the defilement of Dinah – the ritual pollution of Shechem sleeping with 'Jacob's daughter' – is missing from the Old Norse; there is no sense there of Israel's distinctive and separate identity, which must be maintained at all costs, even that of massacring every male inhabitant of Shechem.[91] Instead, in the Old Norse, the story has become a drama of honour and revenge that

---

[86] *Stjórn*, 283; cf. Gen. 34.27. The Hebrew has טִמְּאוּ אֲחוֹתָם 'because their sister had been defiled'.

[87] Gen. 34.30.

[88] *Stjórn*, 284; cf. Gen. 34.30.

[89] *Stjórn*, 285; cf. Gen. 35.5.

[90] *Stjórn*, 281; cf. Gen. 34.1 which describes her only as 'filia Liae' ('Leah's daughter').

[91] Van Wolde, 'Love and Hatred', 444–47; Feder, 'Defilement of Dinah', 307–9.

The Old Testament in Medieval Icelandic Texts

showcases sharp divisions within the family and illustrates the failure of legal settlements in the face of strongly held ideals. This may take its prompt from the Vulgate's 'in ultionem stupri' ('in revenge for their dishonour') and Latin 'stuprum' may itself be an attempt to render the Hebrew נְבָלָה ('outrage, disgrace'). But in the Norse retelling, the rape of Dinah has become a tightly structured feud narrative, in which the law fails to hold back the strong cultural imperative of revenge.

The Joseph Story

With Joseph, for the first time, a biblical narrative is described as a saga: 'hér hefr sǫgu Iosephs' ('here begins the saga of Joseph') is the title in AM 227 fol.[92] This reflects, perhaps, a recognition of the clear structure and movement of Joseph's story: from childhood to old age and death, from Canaan to Egypt, and, most importantly, from shepherd boy and slave to the top of the Egyptian social hierarchy. While some might consider it properly still to be part of the story of Jacob, it is clear that it has its own logic, which is the logic of romance: Joseph is the kind of person who will always rise to the top, no matter how low he has been cast down.[93] The compiler recognises this quality in him as 'gipta' or 'gæfa', which might be thought of as the *leitmotiv* of his story in the Norse retelling. It is referenced repeatedly: 'allar sinar gerðir tókusk honum giptusamliga' ('all his doings went favourably'), 'fekk hann síns herra giptu ok vináttu' ('he acquired his lord's favour and friendship'), 'hann gaf honum þá giptu ok gæfu' ('he gave him favour and good fortune'), 'greiddi guð þá giptusamliga allar hans gerðir ok framferðir' ('God caused all his doings and undertakings to go favourably'), 'mun guð giptusamlig andsvǫr ok farsællig veita Pharaoni' ('God will give a favourable and prosperous answer to Pharaoh').[94] Its last occurrence is in the mouth of Pharaoh himself: 'Munum vér nǫkkurn þann mann fá annan á jǫrðinni sem svá sé fullr af guðs anda gipt ok gæfu sem þessi?' ('Will we be able to get any other man on earth who is so full of the grace of God's spirit and favour as this?').[95] The Old Norse terms are notoriously difficult to translate, and they correspond to a range of words in the Latin: 'erat vir in cunctis prospere'

---

92   *Stjórn*, 288.

93   See R. J. Clifford, 'Genesis 37–50: Joseph Story or Jacob Story?', in *The Book of Genesis*, ed. Evans, Lohr and Petersen, 213–29. On the Joseph story as 'novella' or indeed 'family saga', see André LaCocque, 'An Ancestral Narrative: The Joseph Story', in André LaCocque and Paul Ricœur, *Thinking Biblically: Exegetical and Hermeneutical Studies*, trans. David Pellauer (Chicago: University of Chicago Press, 1998), 365–97.

94   *Stjórn*, 299, 301, 305.

95   *Stjórn*, 306.

The God of Abraham, Isaac and Jacob

('he was a prosperous man in all things'), 'invenitque Ioseph gratiam coram domino suo' ('Joseph found favour in the sight of his master'), 'omnia eius opera dirigebat' ('made all that he did to prosper'), 'virum qui spiritu Dei plenus sit' ('a man that is full of the spirit of God').[96] In the *Dictionary of Old Norse*, the primary meaning of 'gifta' is given as '(good) luck, fortune' and, secondarily as 'gift, grace', while 'gæfa' is translated as 'good luck, good fortune, success'.[97] Both words are far more frequent in the sagas of Icelanders than in religious literature. It seems that, in characterising Joseph, the compiler has recognised from his own literary tradition that he is the embodiment of a 'gæfumaðr' or 'giptumaðr': the kind of man for whom things always turn out for the best.[98]

Joseph's ability to interpret dreams also links him with saga tradition. When Joseph's brothers mockingly call him 'somniator' ('one who dreams' or 'puts faith in dreams'), the Norse translates it as 'draumamaðrinn' ('dreamer' or 'interpreter of dreams').[99] This is the term used of Gísli in *Gísla saga* and of Þórhaddr in *Þorsteins saga Síðu-Hallssonar* and both senses are relevant to the biblical Joseph.[100] The introductory formulas used of his many dreams are familiar from the sagas too: 'Mér sýndisk í svefninum' ('it seemed to me in the dream'), 'ek þóttisk sjá' ('I thought that I saw'), 'sýndisk mer' ('it seemed to me'), 'þat dreymdi mik' ('I dreamed'), 'hann þóttisk vera staddr' ('he thought that he was standing'), 'honum sýndisk sem' ('it seemed to him as if'), 'svá at honum sýndisk' ('as it seemed to him').[101] Most of these have no equivalent in the Latin, which tends to introduce dreams with 'vidi per somnium' ('I saw in a dream') or 'videbam' ('I saw'), although occasionally it does use 'puto' ('to think, imagine'). Astås has suggested that the Norse

---

[96] Gen. 39.2, 4, 21, 23; 41.38.

[97] *DONP*, s.v. *gipta, gæfa* at https://onp.ku.dk/onp/onp.php?027024 and https://onp.ku.dk/onp/onp.php?029958 (accessed 25 July 2023). See also Hermann Pálsson, 'Um gæfumenn ok ógæfu í íslenzkum fornsögum', in *Festskrift til Björn Sigfússon*, ed. Björn Teitsson et al. (Reykjavík: Sögufélag, 1975), 135–53; Peter Hallberg, 'The concept of *gipta-gæfa-hamingja* in Old Norse Literature', in *Proceedings of the First International Saga Conference*, ed. Peter Foote et al. (London: Viking Society for Northern Research, 1973), 143–83.

[98] Probably the best-known *gæfumaðr* or *giptumaðr* in Old Norse is Auðunn; see *Auðunar þáttr vestfirzka* in *Vestfirðinga sǫgur*, ed. Björn K. Þórólfsson and Guðni Jónsson (Reykjavík: Hið íslenzka fornritafélag, 1943), 368; cf. also *Vatnsdæla saga, Hallfreðar saga, Kormáks saga*, ed. Einar Ólafur Sveinsson (Reykjavík: Hið íslenzka fornritafélag, 1939), 10 and *Hungrvaka*, in *Biskupa sǫgur II*, 5.

[99] *Stjórn*, 291; cf. Gen. 37.19. This is to be distinguished from *draummaðr*, which means 'a person who appears in a dream'.

[100] *Gísla saga*, in *Vestfirðinga sǫgur*, 70; *Þorsteins saga Síðu-Hallssonar*, in *Austfirðinga sǫgur*, 314.

[101] *Stjórn*, 290, 302–04; cf. Gen. 37.7, 9; 39.9, 16; 41.1–6.

The Old Testament in Medieval Icelandic Texts

formulae suggest scepticism as to dreams on the part of the compiler.[102] However, if this is so, it remains that case that Joseph's interpretations all turn out to be true: 'Gekk hvárum rétt eptir því sem Ioseph hafði draumana ráðit' ('It went for each exactly as Joseph had interpreted the dreams').[103] It seems more likely that the compiler is couching the dream narratives of the Bible in the language of the sagas, validating the high worth and wisdom of one who both himself dreams true dreams and can interpret the dreams of others.

The compiler continues to focus on the family relationships that are so central to the stories so far. The harmful effects of favouritism are very much evident among Joseph's brothers, who hate him precisely because his father loves him best, a situation that we are told repeatedly leads to envy and hatred, as well as to suspicion and deceit.[104] Jacob's grief for the son whom he believes to be dead is vividly depicted through word-pairs, rhyme and alliteration: 'Sneið hann þá ok reif klæði af sér' ('he tore and ripped off his clothes'), 'sýtandi son sinn ok þráandi eptir honum' ('grieving for his son and weeping for him').[105] The division between Jacob's sons by Rachel and his sons by Leah is recognised by all parties and drawn out by the compiler's repeated use of 'samborinn' and 'sammœddr', prompted by the Latin 'uterinus'. When Jacob's sons ask to take Benjamin to Egypt with them, Jacob replies, rather heartlessly: 'Bróðir hans samborinn er allr, en hann einn eptir' ('his brother by the same mother is dead, and he is left alone').[106] Likewise, Joseph can barely restrain his emotion when he sees 'sinn samborinn bróður' ('his brother born of the same mother') and feels deep compassion for his 'sammœddum brœðr' ('his brother by the same mother').[107] When the brothers plead with Joseph to let Benjamin go home, they acknowledge that their father's love for Benjamin springs from the fact that 'hans sammœddr bróðir' ('his brother by the same mother') is dead.[108] Jacob's favouritism casts a long shadow here.

The story of Joseph, though, is a 'comedy' that ends happily with the reconciliation of the brothers and Jacob reunited with his son.[109] Like a romance, it depends heavily on the theme of recognition (anagnorisis),

---

102 Astås, *Studies in Stjórn*, 135.

103 *Stjórn*, 303; cf. Gen. 40.22.

104 *Stjórn*, 289–90: 'brœðr hans hǫtuðu hann' ('his brothers hated him'), 'lǫgðu þeir svá mikit hatr upp á hann' ('they directed such great hatred towards him'), 'meiri hatrs sǫk ok sundrlyndis sáð ok kveykja' ('a greater cause of hatred, and the seed and kindling of discord'), 'mikil œsing ok auki þeirar ǫfundar ok hatrs' ('great incitement and increase to their envy and hatred'); cf. Gen. 37.4, 5 and 8.

105 *Stjórn*, 294; cf. Gen. 37.34–35.

106 *Stjórn* p. 323; cf. Gen. 42.38.

107 *Stjórn*, 327; cf. Gen. 43.29–30.

108 *Stjórn*, 330; cf. Gen. 44.20.

109 LaCocque, 'Ancestral Narrative', 389, 396.

The God of Abraham, Isaac and Jacob

conveyed in the Vulgate by the repeated use of 'agnosco' and 'cognosco' and in the Old Norse by the verb 'kenna' ('to know, to recognise').[110] The plot is launched with Jacob's recognition of Joseph's coat of many colours ('Iacob kenndi kyrtilinn' – 'Jacob recognised the robe') and his misinterpretation of what has happened to him.[111] Likewise, the inset story of Judah and Tamar in Genesis 38 hinges on disguise and recognition – the 'faldr' ('hood') with which Tamar conceals her identity and the ring and staff that prove at the end that Tamar is pregnant by Judah: 'kenn sjálfr hvers eign gullit er' ('recognise yourself to whom the gold belongs'), 'hann kenndi gripina' ('he recognised the gifts').[112] When Joseph's brothers arrive in Egypt, we are told twice that Joseph recognises them, but they do not recognise him: 'hann kenndi þá gjǫrla en þeir kenndu hann með engu móti' ('he recognised them clearly, but they did not recognise him at all'), 'hann kenndi þá, en þeir kenndu hann eigi' ('he recognised them, but they did not recognise him').[113] It is not until Judah is prepared to trade his own life for Benjamin's, that Joseph is finally ready to recognise them as brothers and to allow them to recognise him: 'hann vildi at hans brœðr kenndi hann' ('he wished for his brothers to recognise him').[114]

As with the Jacob cycle, the biblical story is well told with a keen eye for family relations as well as the role of dreams and the prominence of 'gæfa' ('luck, good fortune'). But the compiler also interpolates into the biblical narrative of Joseph two passages from the *Speculum historiale*, which Vincent of Beauvais entitles 'hystoria Assenech': the story of Joseph and Asenath, which is otherwise known in Old Norse only in an early modern translation from Danish.[115] Asenath is mentioned once in Genesis as Joseph's Egyptian wife, where she is described as the daughter of Putiphare, priest of Heliopolis and mother of Joseph's two sons, Ephraim and Manasseh.[116] In the 'history of Asenath', she has become the daughter of the same Potiphar whose wife landed Joseph in prison by falsely accusing him. The genre of Joseph and Asenath has been debated, but it is clearly influenced by Greek

---

[110] See Piero Boitani, *Anagnorisis: Scenes and Themes of Recognition and Revelation in Western Literature* (Leiden: Brill, 2021), 185–98; Alter, *Art*, 9–10, 118.

[111] *Stjórn*, 294–95; cf. Gen. 37.33.

[112] *Stjórn*, 298; cf. Gen. 38.25–26.

[113] *Stjórn*, 320; cf. Gen. 42.7–8 'et agnovisset eos' ('and he knew them'), 'et tamen fratres ipse cognoscens non est agnitus ab eis' ('and though he knew his brethren, he was not known by them').

[114] *Stjórn*, 331; cf. Gen. 45.1.

[115] See Richard Cole, 'An Edition and Translation of the Icelandic Book of Joseph and Asenath', *Journal for the Study of the Pseudepigrapha* 26.3 (2017), 167–200; and on the possible influence of this story, 'Echoes of the Book of Joseph and Asenath, Particularly in *Yngvars saga víðfǫrla*', *Saga-Book* 41 (2017), 5–34.

[116] *Stjórn*, 307; Gen. 41.50.

The Old Testament in Medieval Icelandic Texts

romance and represents a sort of 'hybrid' of biblical source material and novelistic genre.[117] Although in its original form, it may have been the work of a Jewish author in Graeco-Roman Egypt (between 100 BCE and 115 CE), in its current form it is deeply indebted to Christian allegory, in which Joseph is a type of Christ and his marriage to Asenath a type of the marriage between Christ and the Church.[118] This is certainly implied in *Stjórn*, where the first part of the book is inserted immediately after Pharaoh describes Joseph as 'heimsins hjálpari' ('saviour of the world').[119] Later on, Joseph is described as 'guðs sonr' ('God's son') and Asenath as 'dóttir ins háleitasta' ('daughter of the most sublime').[120] The Christological implications are registered explicitly in what may be a scribal error in AM 226 fol.: while in AM 227 fol., the Archangel Michael anoints Asenath 'með heilagri krismu' ('with holy chrism'), in AM 226 fol., he anoints her with 'kristni' ('Christianity'), transforming her into a convert to Christianity.[121]

As with the sacrifice of Isaac, the compiler's style and vocabulary change significantly as he launches into Asenath's story. The opening description roots us firmly within the genre of romance and specifically the romance of the 'maiden-king': 'Hann átti sér þá dóttur sem Asenech hét; ǫllum Egiptalands ungfrúm var hon fegri ok frjálsligri [...] hon var hæversk ok háttsǫm ok bar sik heiðrs sœmiliga, metnaðarsǫm ok mikillát svá at engi karlmaðr þótti henni sér jafnkosta' ('He had a daughter called Asenath. She was more beautiful and had more freedom than all the virgins in the land of Egypt [...] She was courtly and well-mannered and conducted herself properly with honour, and so proud and grand that she thought no man an equal match for her').[122] This self-consciously employs the language and style of romance: the word-pairs translate single words in the *Speculum historiale* ('pulcra', 'elata' and 'superba'), the vocabulary is stylised, and the alliteration is all added. The translation of the last line (from the Latin 'despiciens omnem virum') is particularly interesting. Elsewhere, the verb 'despicio' is

---

[117] Tim Whitmarsh, *Dirty Love: The Genealogy of the Ancient Greek Novel* (New York: Oxford University Press, 2018), 105–10; Michael Kochenash, 'Trojan Horses: The Counter-Intuitive Use of Dinah, Helen and Goliath in Joseph and Asenath', *Journal for the Study of Judaism* 52 (2021), 417–41.

[118] See the discussion in Jill Hicks-Keeton, *Arguing with Asenath: Gentile Access to Israel's Living God in Jewish Antiquity* (New York: Oxford University Press, 2018), 22–39.

[119] *Stjórn*, 307; cf. Gen. 41.45.

[120] *Stjórn*, 318; cf. *Speculum historiale*, II.122.

[121] *Stjórn*, 314; see AM 226 fol. 44r.

[122] *Stjórn*, 308. *Speculum historiale* 2.118: 'Huius filia erat Asenech pulcra super omnes virgines terre [...] elata et superba despiciens omnem virum' ('His [Pharaoh's] daughter was Asenath, beautiful over all the virgins of the land [...] exalted and proud, despising every man').

The God of Abraham, Isaac and Jacob

translated with 'fyrirlíta', as in the four other occurrences in this chapter.[123] But when Asenath here thinks that no man is 'jafnkosta' ('an equal match') for her, she is speaking specifically of marriage: her attitude is that of the 'maiden-king', characterised as a strong and arrogant woman who refuses all love matches until she is finally – usually violently – overcome.[124] So, in *Fornkonunga saga*, King Helga 'kvað engan konungsson þann, er henni þœtti sér fullkosta' ('said that there was no king's son who seemed to her an equal match') while, in *Rémundar saga*, the king's daughter declares that 'eigi veit ek þann mann, sem mér þykki mér fullkosta' ('I don't know any man who seems to me an equal match for me').[125] When Potiphar tells Asenath that she should marry Joseph, she responds with anger, saying: 'hon hugðisk heldr skyldu giptask konungs syni en herteknum kotkarls syni ok henni þótti þat meir eptir sinni mekt ok manéri' ('she thought she should be married to a king's son rather than to the enslaved son of a farmer, and she thought that more befitting her honour and conduct').[126] The Latin has only: 'respondit se nolle dari viro captivo, sed filio regis' ('she said that she did not wish to be given to a captive man, but to the son of a king'). Asenath sounds here quite like Þorgerðr Egilsdóttir in *Laxdæla saga*, when she declares that her father cannot love her as much as she has heard 'ef þú vill gipta mik ambáttarsyni' ('if you wish to marry me to the son of a slave') or Hallgerðr in *Njáls saga*, when she objects that her kinsmen cannot love her, since they have organised a marriage that is not 'svá mikils háttar' ('as prestigious') as she was promised.[127] Whereas in the Latin, the hatred of men is proof of Asenath's purity and virginity, in the Old Norse it signals a dangerous pagan arrogance that will eventually be overcome by her conversion and marriage.

The insult of 'kotkarl' ('farmer') is used later by Joseph when he accuses his 11 brothers of lying: he observes that it is unlikely for 'einum kotkarli' ('a farmer') to have so many fine sons when 'varla kunnu konungar jafnmarga syni svá mannvænliga' ('kings could hardly have so many handsome sons').[128] The social distance between the Egyptian ruling classes and the inhabitants of Canaan appears to be imagined here along the lines of the

---

[123] *Stjórn*, 311 ('fyrirlitið', 'fyrirleit', 'fyrirlítr', 'fyrirlítr').

[124] See Marianne Kalinke, *Bridal-Quest Romance in Medieval Iceland* (Ithaca, NY: Cornell University Press, 1990), 66; Jóhanna Friðriksdóttir, *Women in Old Norse Literature: Bodies, Words, and Power* (New York: Palgrave Macmillan, 2013), 107–33.

[125] *Sögur Danakonunga*, ed. Carl af Petersens and Emil Olsen, 2 vols (Copenhagen, 1919–25), I, 3; *Rémundar saga keisarasonar*, ed. Sven Grén Broberg (Copenhagen: Møller, 1909–12), 332.

[126] *Stjórn*, 310; *Speculum historiale*, 2.119.

[127] *Laxdæla saga*, 63; *Brennu-Njáls saga*, 31.

[128] *Stjórn*, 321; Comestor, *Liber Genesis*, 162. The Latin has 'idiota' ('commoner', 'uneducated person').

The Old Testament in Medieval Icelandic Texts

relationship between the Norwegian aristocracy and the Icelandic farmer. When King Óláfr Haraldsson is defied by Þorkell in *Laxdœla saga*, he describes it as 'ofsi einum bóndasyni' ('the arrogance of a farmer's son').[129] Likewise, when Vermundr asks Earl Hákon for two berserkers in *Eyrbyggja saga*, he is warned that it would require 'flestum bóndasonum ofrefli, at stýra þeim' ('too much brute force for most farmers' sons to control them').[130] Just as Icelanders abroad tend to be characterised as independent and stubborn in the face of royal power, so in Exodus the Israelites are described not only as 'too independent' ('of frjálsir', translating 'vacant'), but more importantly as self-willed ('sjálfráðir').[131]

The second episode that is borrowed from 'historia Assenech' is a fascinating episode that rewrites Genesis 34 (the rape of Dinah) and is entitled in AM 227 fol. 'af vélræðum konungs sonar við Ioseph' ('about the plot of the king's son against Joseph').[132] It starts, like the first extract from Asenath, in the romance genre with a flamboyant description of Jacob after his arrival in Egypt when Asenath sees him for the first time:[133]

> Skeggit var ok snjóhvítt ok svá síðt at þat breiddisk niðr um brjóstit ok bringuna. Hann var svá snareygr sem hans augu væri glóandi eða gneistar flýgi út af þeim, hans sinar ok axlir, herðar ok armleggir váru þá enn stórligans sterkligir. Kné hans ok lærleggir, fœtr ok fótleggir, váru þvílíkir sem risa fœtr væri eða leggir.

> His beard was also snow-white and so wide that it spread out over his chest and bosom. He was as sharp-eyed as if his eyes were glowing or sparks flew out of them. His sinews and shoulders, upper back and arms were also enormously strong; his knees and thighs, feet and legs, were like the feet or legs of giants.

If there were any lingering doubts that Jacob really was no more than a 'kotkarl', this description lays them to rest. To be 'snareygr' ('sharp-eyed') is a trait of the finest and highest-ranking saga heroes: King Óláfr Haraldsson, Gunnarr Hámundarson, Bolli Bollason.[134] The Latin states only that Jacob's eyes are 'fulgurantes' ('flashing'); the rest is all in the

---

[129] *Laxdœla saga*, 217.

[130] *Eyrbyggja saga*, 62.

[131] *Stjórn*, 397; Ex. 5.8 ('vacant enim' – 'for they are idle').

[132] On its relationship to Genesis 34, see Kochenash, 'Trojan Horses', 420–23.

[133] *Stjórn*, 339; cf. *Speculum historiale*, 2.123: 'oculi eius fulgurantes et nervi eius et humeri et brachia firma, genua et crura et pedes ut gygantis' ('his eyes were flashing and his sinews and shoulders and arms were strong, his knees and legs and feet were like a giant's').

[134] *Saga Óláfs konungs hins helga*, 34; *Njáls saga*, 53; *Laxdœla saga*, 187.

The God of Abraham, Isaac and Jacob

translation. The word-pairs, alliteration and similes (all added) signal that we are in a romance, and the veneer of romance therefore lingers over what comes next: when Pharaoh's son sees Asenath, 'hann fýstisk svá með miklum girndarhita til hennar fegrðar' ('he yearned with the heat of desire for her beauty').[135] The compound 'girndarhiti' ('heat of desire') recalls the 'girndaraugar' ('eyes of desire') with which Shechem looked at Dinah: this is an illicit love. The king's son speaks to Dinah's brothers, Simeon and Levi, asking them to kill Joseph and give him Asenath as wife. These are the same two brothers who killed all the Shechemites to retrieve Dinah from Shechem's house. But, this time, they refuse their help, and the prince turns instead to Dan and Gad, Jacob's sons by the slave-women Bilhah and Zilpah. He arouses their suspicions of what they must surely already fear: that, after Jacob's death, Joseph will have them killed, for 'aldrigi skyldu þeir ambáttasynirnir arfgengr verða með eiginkvenna sonum' ('they, the sons of slaves, should never be heirs together with the sons of lawful wives').[136] In the light of what happened to Hagar and Ishmael, this is a plausible threat, and it reprises Sarah's words: 'eigi mun ambáttarsonr sá erfingi þinn verða' ('the slave-woman's son will not be your heir').

From romance, then, we dive back into saga narrative, as the plotting results in a fierce and vividly evoked battle which makes effective use of the historic present. Asenath walks straight into an ambush in which all but one of her men are killed: 'slær þar þegar í bardaga sem þeir mœtask ok lýkr svá at þeir sem í fyrirsátinni váru drápu hvert mannsbarn af mǫnnum Aseneth' ('a battle breaks out as soon as they meet, and it ends in such a way that those in the ambush killed every living soul of Asenath's men').[137] The escapee bears the news to Simeon and Levi who, in a heroic flourish, quickly summon 'alla sína menn þá sem vápnum máttu valda' ('all their men who could wield weapons') and launch a fierce counter attack. Meanwhile, Benjamin, who is with Asenath, sees Pharaoh's son approaching 'at taka hans bróðurkona' ('to take his brother's wife') – the family relationship has been added in the Old Norse – and he reacts at speed: 'hann hleypr ór kerrunni ok grípr einn stein upp ór forsinum hjá hverjum er þau óku ok slær konungs son með inn vinstra megin á hálsinn svá at hann féll þegar í óvit niðr af sínum hesti, svá sem hann væri dauðr' ('he leaps out of the chariot and grabs a stone up from the ditch that they had driven past and hits the king's son on the left side of his neck so that he fell unconscious down from his horse as if he were

---

[135] *Stjórn*, 340; cf. *Speculum historiale*, 2.123. The metaphor of heat is borrowed from Vincent of Beauvais, who says that 'exarsit in pulcritudine eius' ('he was inflamed in the presence of her beauty').

[136] Cf. *Speculum historiale*, 2.123.

[137] *Stjórn*, 341; cf. *Speculum historiale*, 2. 123.

The Old Testament in Medieval Icelandic Texts

dead').[138] He then prevents 'brœðr sína' ('his brothers') Simeon and Levi from killing 'brœðr sína' ('his brothers') Dan and Gad, narrowly averting fratricide.[139] Instead, Pharaoh's son dies from his wound, and Pharaoh then dies of grief, leaving Joseph to rule until Pharaoh's youngest son is ready to take the throne. It is a politically astute episode that recognises the risks of holding a high-ranking position at a foreign court – a story of some interest, perhaps, to Icelanders serving at the court of Norway. But it also continues to explore – and ultimately to contain – the sibling rivalry that has been such a prominent theme of the book of Genesis.

Moses's Wives

With Moses, we move away from the family themes that are characteristic of Genesis: Moses is not, like the patriarchs, a family man, but a national hero whose task is to deliver God's people from slavery in Egypt. The central importance of the Exodus in Christian allegory has left its mark on this part of the story: particular attention is paid to the liturgical resonances of events, not just within the text, but also in the margins of AM 227 fol. The focus is on 'jartegnir' ('miracles') and 'stórmerki' ('signs'): the paschal lamb prefigures Christ; the crossing of the Red Sea foreshadows the Easter procession to the baptismal font; Moses's prayer points forward to Christ's arms opened wide on the cross and the priest's raising of the host during mass.[140] This chapter, then, considers just two early episodes from Moses's life: his marriage to the Ethiopian queen Tharbis, and the mysterious episode involving his Midianite wife Zipporah, when Moses sets out to return to Egypt with his family.

The beginning of Moses's story lends itself easily to the genre of romance: Moses is a foundling who is brought up at the Egyptian court by a princess, a 'fair unknown' who rises to power and influence until a chance event gives his true identity away. So it is not surprising that many apocryphal tales are woven into this period of this life: the baby Moses's refusal to drink breastmilk from any of the Egyptian wet-nurses, for example, and the young boy's violent response when Pharaoh places a golden crown on his head with the image of an Egyptian god on it.[141] As is characteristic of romance, Moses's heroic career is enabled by the women who surround him: the midwives who disobey Pharaoh, his mother and sister Miriam, and the Egyptian princess who looks upon him 'miskunnaraugum' ('with eyes of mercy'), draws him

---

138 *Stjórn*, 341–42; cf. *Speculum historiale*, 2.124.
139 *Stjórn*, 342; cf. *Speculum historiale* 2.124.
140 See the references to signs and miracles at *Stjórn*, 389, 391, 393, 438, 445, 499.
141 *Stjórn*, 379–80; both stories are found in Comestor (*Liber Exodus*, c. 5; PL 198, 1143D-1144A), and the second is also in *Speculum historiale* 3.1.

The God of Abraham, Isaac and Jacob

out of the Nile, and gives him his name.[142] To this number, one might add the Egyptian Queen Tharbis, who was probably invented to make sense of the cryptic mention in Numbers 12 of Moses's 'Cushite' wife.[143] The story appears in a fragment of Irenaeus on Numbers and is also in Josephus's *Antiquities*; it circulated among the Alexandrian Jews of the second century BCE and may be of Hellenistic or Palestinian origin.[144]

The standard allegorical reading of this story appears in Jerome and identifies Tharbis as a type of the Church, opposed by Miriam as a type of the Synagogue and Aaron as a priest after the flesh.[145] However, there is little sign of this in the Norse retelling, which comes from Vincent of Beauvais, and presents Moses as a successful military leader as well as a hero with a mission.[146] When the Ethiopians attack Egypt, he is appointed to lead them and is described as 'inn frægasti ok inn klokasti bardagamaðr' ('the most famous and skilled man of war').[147] The adjective 'klokasti' as elsewhere encompasses both skill and cunning: Moses twice manages through elaborate and fantastical schemes to come upon the Ethiopian army 'á óvart' ('unaware'). The city of Cambyses, however, proves impossible to overcome, until a chance meeting with the Ethiopian princess, who 'kom augum á Moysen ok kastaði svá framt girndarhug til hans at hon gaf honum borgina' ('cast her eyes on Moses and developed so great a desire for him that she gave him the town').[148] The relationship between the woman and the city here has been compared to that between Dido and Carthage, or Lavinia and Rome.[149] However, the compound 'girndarhugr' gives a negative twist to the sexual conquest, which proves important in evaluating what

---

[142] *Stjórn*, 379; cf. Ex. 2.6.

[143] Numbers 12.1 ('uxorem eius aethiopissam'); *Stjórn II*, 488, names this wife Poekilla, which Kirby, *Bible Translation* (p. 59) suggests is a corruption of the Vulgate 'Æthiopissam'.

[144] See Tessa Rajak, 'Moses in Ethiopia: Legend and Literature', *Journal of Jewish Studies* 29 (1978), 111–22; Donna Runnalls, 'Moses' Ethiopian Campaign', *Journal for the Study of Judaism* 14.2 (1983), 135–56; Mark Balfour, 'Moses and the Princess: Josephus's "Antiquitates Judaicae" and the "Chansons de Geste"', *Medium Ævum* 64.1 (1995), 1–16; Elizabeth McGraph, 'Jacob Jordaens and Moses' Ethiopian Wife', *Journal of the Warburg and Courtauld Institutes* 70 (2007), 247–85.

[145] Jerome, *In Sophoniam*, ed. M. Adriaen, CCSL 76 (Turnhout: Brepols, 1970), 690.

[146] The rubrics in AM 227 fol. indicate that this story comes from the *Speculum historiale*, but it is also in the *Historia scholastica* (*Liber Exodus*, c. 6; PL 198, 1144B–1144D).

[147] *Stjórn*, 381; *Speculum historiale* 3.2. The adjective 'klokr' here links him to Jacob, as does his trickery ('klokskapr') at pp. 382–83.

[148] *Stjórn*, 382; cf. *Speculum historiale* 3.2.

[149] Balfour, 'Moses and the Princess', 5.

205

The Old Testament in Medieval Icelandic Texts

happens next. Tharbis loves Moses so greatly that she refuses to let him leave, rather like Dido with Aeneas. So, Moses makes two rings, one that aids the memory and one that erases it: he keeps 'minnisgullit' ('the ring of memory') for himself, and gives 'gleymskugullit' ('the ring of forgetting') to Tharbis.[150] She immediately forgets 'allri þeiri elsku ok ástúð' ('all that love and affection') and gives Moses permission to leave. Moses comes out of this as a great warrior and lover, although one who succeeds by sleight rather than by strength. This goes some way towards vindicating him from some later insults, such as when Pharaoh describes him as 'sinn hræddan and flóttagjarnan þræll' ('his frightened and prone-to-take-flight slave').[151] The adjectives 'hræddr' and 'flóttagjarn' are particularly cutting here: Comestor has only 'servum suum fugitivum' ('his run-away slave'). Unlike the story of Asenath, though, romance in this episode is not positive and enabling, nor is there any conversion theme; rather, as Dido for Aeneas, Tharbis is a distraction from a higher calling that Moses must lay aside.

Moses marries again while in exile in Midian, after killing an Egyptian slave-owner. When God tells him to go back to Egypt, he sets out with his wife and two sons – 'útan guðs boðskap' ('against God's command'), the compiler specifies.[152] What happens next is something of a mystery for biblical scholars, as God appears to try to kill Moses almost immediately after his dispatch: 'þá kom guðs engill með brugðnu sverði honum í mót svá sem búinn til at vilja drepa hann' ('then God's angel came to meet him with drawn sword as if fully intending to kill him'). The angel and the drawn sword come from Comestor; the Vulgate has 'occurrit ei Dominus et volebat occidere eum' ('The Lord met him and would have killed him') from the Hebrew 'sought to kill him' (וַיְבַקֵּשׁ הֲמִיתוֹ), where it is not clear that the object is necessarily Moses. This scene has been variously explained as a reworking of Jacob's wrestling with the angel, a reflex of God's earlier anger with Moses for his reluctance to speak, or (if it is Moses's son rather than Moses whom God seeks to kill) a foreshadowing of the killing of the Egyptian first-born.[153] The compiler, however, follows Comestor in identifying the threat as directed towards Moses because he has taken his family with him: 'hvar af er honum mátti leiða mikit hindr ok tálman' ('from which great hindrance and difficulty might result for him'). In other words, this is the moment where Moses must leave family concerns behind in order for the nation of Israel to emerge.

---

[150] Stjórn, 383; cf. Speculum historiale 3.2.

[151] Stjórn, 397; Comestor, Liber Exodus, c. II; PL 198, 1148A.

[152] Stjórn, 394; cf. Ex. 4.20.

[153] See Ilana Pardes, 'Zipporah and the Struggle for Deliverance', in Countertraditions in the Bible: A Feminist Approach (Cambridge, MA: Harvard University Press, 1992), 80–97; David Pettit, 'When the Lord seeks to kill Moses', Journal for the Study of the Old Testament 40.2 (2015), 163–77.

The God of Abraham, Isaac and Jacob

Zipporah, then, could be read as another Hagar, a woman who is introduced into the narrative only to be rejected. Despite this, she proves both active and outspoken:[154]

> Fyrrnefnd húsfrú hans Sephora brá við skjótt [...] ok tók einn harðla hvassan stein með hverjum er hon af sneið inn fremsta part getnaðarlim síns sons eftir því sem í skurðarskírninni var skipat, því at Moyses var svá þrøngðr af englinum at hann mátti þat eigi gera, hvaðan af er hon reiddisk, grípandi sveinsins fœtr ella engilsins, ok talaði svá til síns bónda: 'Hvárt ert þú mér blóða brúðgumi eða eigi?'

> His aforenamed wife Zipporah reacted quickly [...] and took a very sharp stone with which she cut off the foremost part of her son's penis as is prescribed in circumcision, because Moses was so hard-pressed by the angel that he couldn't do it, at which she became angry, taking hold of the boy's feet or the angel's, and said to her husband: 'Are you a bridegroom of blood to me or not?'

There is some expansion and some explanation here: Zipporah's quick reaction expands the adverb 'ilico' ('immediately') in the Vulgate, while the comment that Moses was too busy holding off the angel to help appears to be the compiler's own. It provides a reason for her sudden turn to anger against Moses, which is developed out of Comestor's adjective 'irata'. The phrasing of her statement in the Vulgate ('A bloody spouse thou art to me') as a question in Old Norse is inspired by one of Comestor's glosses and comes across here as a challenge to Moses, perhaps to sting him into action.[155] Later, under the rubric *scolastica historia*, Zipporah's words are paraphrased to suggest that Moses has forced her into bloodshed: 'Hvárt skyldumk ek af þínum hjúskap til þess at gera svá mikinn glœp at hella út míns sonar blóði' ('Am I obliged by marriage to you to do so great a crime as to pour out my own son's blood?'). In the Hebrew, the bloody foreskin plays an apotropaic role, although it is not clear whose feet Zipporah touches with it: those of her son or of the angel or of Moses.[156] But in the Old Norse, as in most commentary on the scene, the apotropaic function has disappeared, and the grasping of the feet is either defensive (if it is the feet of her

---

[154] *Stjórn*, 394–95; cf. Ex. 4.24–26.

[155] The Hebrew is חֲתַן דָּמִים which is translated in the Vulgate as 'sponsus sanguinum tu mihi est' ('A bloody spouse thou art to me'). Comestor, *Liber Exodus*, c. 10 (PL 198, 1147B) develops this into a question: 'Esne mihi vir sanguinum, id est an ex conjugio tuo tantum scelus teneor agere, ut fundam sanguinem filii mei' ('Are you not to me a bloody spouse, that is, am I obliged by marriage to you to do such an evil deed as to pour out the blood of my son?').

[156] The Hebrew simply has: וַתַּגַּע לְרַגְלָיו ('and touched his feet') without specifying to whom the feet belong.

207

The Old Testament in Medieval Icelandic Texts

son) or propitiatory (if it is the feet of the angel). Rather than interrupt the narrative, the compiler includes these as alternatives, but he also provides, from Comestor, the Hebrew interpretation that it is Moses' feet that Zipporah touches, paraphrasing her speech for a third time: 'Mitt blóð helltisk út í míns sonar blóði til þess at mýkja ok stọðva engilinn er þér ógnaði dráp ok dauða' ('My blood was poured out in my son's blood to placate and calm the angel who threatened you with slaughter and death'). There is a real interest here in understanding exactly what Zipporah's cryptic words mean despite her peripheral role in Moses's story; she is mentioned only one more time, when Jethro brings her and her two sons back to Moses after he has successfully crossed the Red Sea.[157] Although one of the purposes of this story is to show that Moses must leave his family behind in order to fulfil his national destiny, Zipporah nevertheless comes across as a formidable character, strong and capable in the face of divine threat and unafraid to challenge her husband.

Conclusion

This chapter shows a range of different responses to the biblical material that is compiled in *Stjórn I* and which corresponds to Genesis 12–50. The compiler is clearly interested in doing a variety of different things, including translating the Vulgate, providing a range of possible glosses, and including extra-biblical material where this is available, especially material that lends itself to allegorical reading or is of an entertaining character. In managing this material, he shows himself to be adept in mobilising a variety of different styles. While the universal character of Genesis 1–11 lent itself well to allegorical interpretation and theological reflection, the strong focus on the family in Genesis 12–50 has steered him in a different direction – towards the themes, style, and idiom of the sagas of Icelanders. This is seen not only in the use of storytelling formulae, but also in the careful reshaping of some stories to draw out the family dynamics and to situate them in relation to vernacular literary tradition. At the same time, the sagas of Icelanders are not the only genre the compiler evokes: he is also clearly influenced by romance. If the rape of Dinah becomes in his hands a classic feud narrative, the story of Asenath has become something more like a bridal quest romance. If Tharbis is a negative, moralised version of the romance heroine, holding back the hero from his destiny by her possessive and irrational love, Zipporah is more like a saga heroine, unafraid to take matters into her own hands and, if necessary, shed blood. In the story of the sacrifice of Isaac, uniquely, we see the compiler pulled in both directions at once, drawn on the one hand towards

---

[157] *Stjórn*, 449; Ex. 18.2–3: 'tullet Sefforam uxorem Mosi quam remiserat et duos filios eius' ('He took Sephora the wife of Moses whom he had sent back: and her two sons').

The God of Abraham, Isaac and Jacob

the laconic style of the biblical story and, on the other, towards the emotional extremes and imaginative fervour of Origen's powerful rhetoric. The result is a deeply hybrid narrative that eschews a unified perspective and gives a rich and multi-dimensional character to the world of the Old Testament.

→ 7 ←

Heroes, Heroines and Royal Biography:
From Judges to 2 Kings

The books of Joshua, Judges, 1 and 2 Samuel and 1 and 2 Kings (known in the Middle Ages as the four books of Kings or 'Kingdoms') are grouped together in the Hebrew Bible as the 'Former Prophets'. They chronicle the history of Israel and Judah from the conquest of Canaan to the Babylonian Exile in 560 BCE. Their history of composition is complex: while Noth argued in 1943 that Deuteronomy–2 Kings was the work of a single redactor writing shortly after 560 BCE, it is now generally agreed that there are multiple layers to this redaction, and that each book can be thought of as having its own distinct identity.[1] At the same time, it is clear that the historical books do cohere by means of a 'narrative arc' that runs from the settlement in Canaan to the establishment of the monarchy and ends with its dissolution and the destruction of Jerusalem.[2] The book of Ruth, which is among the 'Writings' in the Hebrew Bible, was placed between Judges and 1 Samuel in the LXX, where it belongs chronologically, as it is set in the time of the Judges.[3] However, it was probably written later than the other books, and is different in genre, best described as 'a finely crafted short story' or even 'a narrative text in poetic form'.[4] Within this larger unit – sometimes known

---

1   Thomas Römer, 'The Narrative Books of the Hebrew Bible', in *The Hebrew Bible: A Critical Companion*, ed. John Barton (Princeton, NJ: Princeton University Press, 2016), 125–26.

2   Susan Niditch, 'The Role of Orality and Textuality, Folklore and Scribalism in the Historical Books', in *The Oxford Handbook of the Historical Books of the Hebrew Bible*, ed. Brad E. Kelle and Brent E. Strawn (Oxford: Oxford University Press, 2020), 398.

3   Timothy J. Stone, 'The Search for Order: The Compilational History of Ruth', in *The Shape of the Writings*, ed. Julius Steinberg and Rachel Marie Stone (Winona Lake, IN: Eisenbrauns, 2015), 175–85.

4   A. Graham Auld, 'Ruth: A Reading of Scripture?', in *The Oxford Handbook of the*

Heroes, Heroines and Royal Biography

as the Deuteronomistic History – is 'the David story', which runs from 1 Samuel to 1 Kings 2 and is one of the most masterful narratives in the Hebrew Bible: von Rad considered it the beginning of 'genuine historical writing' in Israel, while Alter describes it as a reimagining of history of Shakespearean stature and breadth.[5] Most notable is its close focus on human concerns and individuals: Nelson lists the main themes as 'political tensions, family dysfunction, the relationship between the sexes, and the use and preservation of power'.[6] There is much here to interest medieval Icelandic readers, who themselves had an ambivalent relationship to the institution of kingship and whose own storytelling tradition shares many of the same themes and the same 'secular' or 'history-like' style.

This pre-existing resemblance may explain why a mid-thirteenth century Icelander chose to translate into Old Norse-Icelandic the books from Joshua to 2 Kings (including Ruth) which are now known as *Stjórn III*. Although in AM 226 and AM 227 fol., these books form a continuation of the Pentateuch, they are also transmitted independently and seem to have been written as a continuous history of Israel from the Conquest to the Exile. In this respect, they are not unlike other historical compilations from thirteenth-century Iceland: *Heimskringla*, for example, begins with the prehistoric past and runs up to c. 1177 with the reign of Saint Óláfr Haraldsson at its centre. A compilation like this may well have provided the model or stimulus for the translations in *Stjórn III*, although it could be argued, of course, that *Heimskringla* is itself indebted to biblical models. Still, a historical compilation that began with settlement and detailed the chaos preceding the establishment of the monarchy would hardly have seemed strange to the Icelanders, whose own sagas are typically set between the settlement of Iceland in c. 870 and the end of the Republic in 1262/64. Nor would the critical perspective on kingship in these books have surprised anyone familiar with the Icelandic *konungasǫgur*. Other material would also look familiar: there are stories based on place-names and features of the landscape, local hero tales, poems and riddles, as well as regnal notices, lists and genealogies.[7] It is not surprising that we find the closest ties to the Icelandic sagas in the translation of precisely these biblical books.

Writings of the Hebrew Bible, ed. Donn F. Morgan (Oxford: Oxford University Press, 2018), 215; Marjo C. A. Korpel, *The Structure of the Book of Ruth* (Leiden: Brill, 2001), 223.

5   von Rad, 'Beginnings of Historical Writing', 192; Robert Alter, *The David Story: A Translation with Commentary of 1 and 2 Samuel* (London: Norton, 2000), xxvii.

6   Richard D. Nelson, 'The Former Prophets and Historiography', in *The Cambridge Companion to the Hebrew Bible/Old Testament*, ed. Stephen B. Chapman and Marvin A. Sweeney (Cambridge: Cambridge University Press, 2016), 221.

7   Richard D. Nelson, 'Historiography and History-Writing in the Ancient World', in *The Oxford Handbook of the Historical Books of the Bible*, ed. Brad E. Kelle and Brent A. Strawn (Oxford: Oxford University Press, 2020), 13.

The Old Testament in Medieval Icelandic Texts

The translator of *Stjórn III* had a very different approach from the compiler of *Stjórn I*. There are much fewer interpolations from extra-biblical sources, and very few additions are marked out. At the same time, the translator has felt much freer to rearrange and even rewrite the biblical text to improve its coherence and narrative flow, whether by filling in gaps or blanks in the Bible, or by giving a more pronounced shape and character to individual scenes. Allegorical interpretations – taken from Richard of St Victor's *Liber exceptionum* – tend to be separated from the narrative and placed either at the end of each book (as in the case of Joshua and Ruth) or at the end of each episode (as in Judges). From 1 Samuel on, however, the allegory peters out and, at the end of the story of David, we are told only: 'En þat er vel trúanda at þessi hinn dýrðarfulli David konungr mun nú gleðjask í eylífri sælu útan enda með þenna guðs syni lifanda sem hann bar merking um marga hluti í þessum heimi' ('And it is fitting to believe that this glorious King David is now rejoicing in eternal happiness without end with the living Son of God whom he signified in many ways in this world').[8] The focus is firmly on history and narrative, and there are many close parallels with the sagas, as well as some direct loans. This chapter focuses on the stories in *Stjórn III* that engage most closely with the traditions of saga literature: the story of Samson in Judges, the 'women's history' in Ruth, and the story of David as it is told in the books of Samuel and Kings.

Samson the Strong

The book of Judges is set before the monarchy was established, as its refrain points out: 'In those days there was no king in Israel' (Judges 18.1, 21.25). It offers, then, a close parallel to the Icelandic *söguöld* ('age of the sagas'): the 'Golden Age' of the Icelandic Republic. Webb describes its contents as 'a cycle of stories depicting the exploits of hero figures from Israel's heroic age', a statement that could just as easily be applied to the sagas of Icelanders.[9] The figure of Samson, in particular, offers a parallel with Icelandic heroes such as Gísli, Egill and Grettir: he is a complex character, on the one hand capable of immense feats of strength and verbally dexterous, but on the other emotionally vulnerable, liable to unpredictable and uncontrolled fits of rage. Unlike the other heroes of Judges, he pursues personal vendettas rather than leading armies into battle, and he has been variously described as 'freedom fighter', 'terrorist', 'trickster' or 'bandit'.[10] Exum describes him as 'a man of

---

8   *Stjórn*, 1003–04.
9   Barry G. Well, *The Book of Judges* (Grand Rapids, MI: Eerdmans, 2012), 60.
10   J. Cheryl Exum, 'The Many Faces of Samson', in *Samson: Hero or Fool? The Many Faces of Samson*, ed. Erik M. M. Eynikel and Tobias Nicklas (Leiden: Brill, 2014), 17–18, 25–26.

Heroes, Heroines and Royal Biography

contradictions, who combines opposites': he has enormous 'creative powers', but is profoundly 'anti-social', a marginal figure who consistently violates social boundaries.[11] Samson's is the only story in Judges to be identified as a saga in the rubrics of AM 227 fol.: 'Her byrjask saga frá Samson inum sterka dómanda sonar Manue ok Dalida' ('Here begins the saga of Samson the Strong, a judge, son of Manoah and Delilah').[12] He is also the only character to have the nickname 'inn sterki' ('the strong'), which links him with many saga characters, including Styrbjǫrn 'inn sterki' in *Eyrbyggja saga*, Ari 'inn sterki' in *Laxdœla saga*, and Grettir 'inn sterki' in *Grettis saga.*[13] As well as forming part of the translation of Judges in *Stjórn III*, his 'saga' is found independently in AM 617 4to (dating to the sixteenth century) and is also included in a collection of mythic-heroic sagas in AM 335 4to (c. 1390–1410).

The beginning of Samson's story provides an excellent example of how the translator shapes and adapts biblical narrative to the conventions of the saga. He begins at Judges 13.2 ('erat autem vir') with a classical saga formula: 'Maðr er nefndr Manue' ('There was a man named Manoah') in AM 227 fol. or 'Maðr hét Manue' ('There was a man called Manoah') in AM 226 fol.[14] While the Vulgate tells us only that he was 'de stirpe Dan' ('of the tribe of Dan'), the Old Norse adds a brief genealogy – 'af kyni Dan sonar Jacobs ins gamla' ('of the kin of Dan, son of Jacob the old') – and while the Vulgate tells us only that he had a barren wife, the Old Norse introduces her properly: 'Manue var kvæntr. Kona hans var óbyrja ok er eigi nefnd' ('Manoah was married. His wife was barren, and she is not named'). The last comment suggests that one would expect her to be named, although the biblical narrative takes it for granted that she is not. While the Vulgate moves straight from this introduction to the beginning of the narrative with 'cui apparuit angelus Domini' ('to whom an angel of the Lord appeared'), the Old Norse separates the genealogical setting from the first scene by prefacing it with: 'Svá bar til einn dag' ('It happened one day').

All sorts of small additions and rearrangements are made in the scene that follows, which narrates Manoah's and his wife's interaction with the angel of the Lord who has come to announce Samson's birth. When Manoah's wife tells her husband about the encounter, she launches straight into the story: 'quae cum venisset ad maritum dixit ei vir Dei venit ad me' ('And when she was come to her husband she said to him: A man of God came to me'). In the Old Norse, she prefaces this with a familiar idiom: 'Ek hefi þér ný tíðindi at segja' ('I have some fresh news for you').[15] When she describes how the

---

[11]   Exum, 'Faces of Samson', 25.
[12]   *Stjórn*, 645.
[13]   *Eyrbyggja saga*, 80; *Laxdœla saga*, 288; *Grettis saga*, 289.
[14]   *Stjórn*, 645; cf. Judges 13.2–3.
[15]   *Stjórn*, 646; cf. Jdg. 13.5.

The Old Testament in Medieval Icelandic Texts

angel has told her that Samson will be 'puer nazareus Dei ab infantia sua' ('a Nazarite of God from his infancy'), the Old Norse rephrases this as 'hann kvað þenna svein myndu verða mikinn fyrir sér snemmindis' ('he said that this boy would be impressive from early on'). As well as the move to indirect speech, this means something rather different; 'mikill fyrir sér' is a common expression in the sagas and not necessarily a positive one, for it can imply arrogance and abuse of power.[16] Elsewhere, too, the translator prefers indirect speech to direct and varies the tense between past and present. For example, 'festinavit et cucurrit ad virum suum nuntiavitque ei dicens ecce apparuit mihi vir quem ante videram' ('she made haste and ran to her husband: and told him, saying: Behold the man hath appeared to me, whom I saw before') becomes: 'rann hon sem skjótask ok segir bónda sínum, at nú birtisk henni sá inn sami drengr er hon hafði fyrr sét' ('she ran as fast as she could and tells her husband that now the same man has appeared to her whom she had seen before'). AM 226 fol. moves this even closer to saga narrative by avoiding any unnecessary repetition, leaving us with: 'En hon sagði þat bónda sínum' ('and she told her husband this').[17]

A different sort of gap-filling can be seen in the scene where Samson kills the lion while accompanying his parents to make a marriage proposal on his behalf. The biblical narrative at this point is highly economic, leaving out all non-essentials: 'descendit itaque Samson cum patre suo et matre in Thamnatha cumque venissent ad vineas oppidi apparuit catulus leonis saevus rugiens et occurrit ei. Inruit autem spiritus Domini in Samson et dilaceravit leonum quasi hedum in frustra concerperet nihil omnino habens in manu et hoc patri et matri noluit indicare' ('Then Samson went down with his father and mother to Thamnatha, and when they were come to the vineyards of the town, behold a young lion met him, raging and roaring. And the Spirit of the Lord came upon Samson, and he tore the lion as he would have torn a kid in pieces, having nothing at all in his hand; and he would not tell this to his father and mother'). Where are Samson's father and mother when he kills the lion? They are clearly not present, and this detail is important because later, when Samson makes up a riddle based on this incident, he will tell his wife that not even his parents know the answer. But why they are not present is clearly not important to the biblical writer. It does matter to the translator, however, who does his best to resolve this unsatisfactory state of affairs:[18]

---

16 See, for example, *Heiðarvíga saga*, in *Borgfirðinga sǫgur*, ed. Sigurður Nordal and Guðni Jónsson (Reykjavík: Hið íslenzka fornritafélag, 1938), 93; *Víga-Glúms saga*, in *Eyfirðinga sǫgur*, ed. Jónas Kristjánsson (Reykjavík: Hið íslenzka fornritafélag, 1956), 16.

17 *Stjórn*, 647; cf. Jdg. 13.10.

18 *Stjórn*, 650–51; cf. Jdg. 14.5–6.

Heroes, Heroines and Royal Biography

Fara þau með honum í borg Thamnath. Nú sem þau kómu at vingǫrðum borgarinnar rann í móti þeim einn léo, grimmr ok gráðugr, þó at ungr væri, hræðiliga emjandi. Við þessa sýn flýðu með mikilli hræzlu Manue ok kona hans. En andi dróttins kom yfir Samson með miklu kappi ok afli. Snýr hann þegar at dýrinu svá at hann hafði ekki í hendi. Hann ræðr á ok léttir eigi fyrr en hann hefir drepit dýrit ok svá lamit ok smátt í sundr slitit sem hann hefði brytjað eitt kið til ketils. Síðan fór hann at leita fǫður síns ok móður. Ok fann þau þar sem þau hǫfðu fólgizk. En eigi vildi hann segja þeim þetta þrekvirki er hann hafði unnit.

They go with him to the town of Thamnatha. Now when they came to the vineyards of the town, a lion ran towards them, grim and greedy, though it was young, howling terrifyingly. At this sight, Manoah and his wife fled in great fear. But the spirit of the Lord came over Samson with great fervour and power. He turns at once to the animal, though he had nothing in his hand. He attacks and doesn't stop until he has killed the animal and beaten it and torn it to pieces as if he had chopped up a kid for the pot. Then he went to seek his father and mother, and found them where they had hidden. But he didn't wish to tell them this impressive deed that he had done.

Here the scene has been fully fleshed out: Samson's parents flee in terror and, after he has killed the lion, he has to search for them before he locates their hiding-place. As well as explaining why they were not present, this also raises Samson's heroic stature through contrasting his courage with his parents' fear. There are other nice details too: the alliteration of 'grimmr ok gráðugr' ('grim and greedy'), describing the lion, contrasts pointedly with the alliteration in 'kið til ketils' ('a kid for the pot'), an expression with a proverbial ring that emphasises just how effortlessly Samson dispatches the lion. The fight itself is lent some extra drama: while the Vulgate says only that Samson 'dilaceravit' ('tore') the lion, the Old Norse adds that he 'turns' to it, 'attacks it' and 'doesn't stop until he has killed' it; he tears it to bits with some added triumphal alliteration ('smátt í sundr slitit'). The Vulgate says that the 'Spirit of the Lord came upon Samson', but the Old Norse adds 'með miklu kappi ok afli' ('with great fervour and power'), connecting it explicitly with his physical strength. The scene ends with praise of Samson's first 'þrekvirki' ('deed of strength'), a term that is also used of Þórr's feats against the giants and of the exploits of legendary heroes.[19]

The Old Norse translator is particularly interested in those scenes where Samson fights against the odds. When the Philistines burn his wife and in-laws

---

[19] Snorri Sturluson, *Edda: Prologue and Gylfaginning*, ed. Anthony Faulkes (London: Viking Society for Northern Research, 1988), 63, 105; *Heimskringla*, ed. Bjarni Aðalbjarnarson, 3 vols (Reykjavík: Hið íslenzka fornritafélag, 1941–51), I, 90; *Brennu-Njáls saga*, 303.

The Old Testament in Medieval Icelandic Texts

in their house, Samson tells them: 'Nú þykkizk þér vel hafa sýst ok hefnt skaða yðars, en þér munuð þó þessu eigi lengi fagna, því at ek skal sannliga hefna yðr mínar svívirðingar' ('Now you must think you've done a good job and avenged your injury, but you won't rejoice at this for long, because I will truly avenge my dishonour on you').[20] The Vulgate has: 'licet haec feceritis tamen adhuc ex vobis expetam ultionem' ('although you have done this, yet will I be revenged of you') – the drama of revenge and dishonour in the Old Norse grows out of a single word ('ultio') in the Vulgate. The irony is also added: the Philistines may think that they have 'done a good job' ('vel hafa sýst'), but their joy will be short-lived. The Vulgate concludes: 'percussitque eos ingenti plaga' ('and he made a great slaughter of them'), but the Old Norse is more dramatic: Samson 'brá þá sverði sínu ok hjó bæði hart ok títt' ('drew his sword and struck both hard and often'). Even more exciting is the episode where Samson bursts the ropes with which he is bound and kills a thousand Philistines with the jawbone of an ass. Again, the translator adds irony, commenting as Samson breaks free: 'váru þá þegar hans óvinir eigi jafn ákafir at honum at ganga er hann var lauss orðinn' ('his enemies were not half so eager to attack him once he got loose').[21] The Vulgate tells us that, finding a jawbone, Samson 'interfecit ea mille viros' ('slew therewith a thousand men'). In the Old Norse, he 'grípr' ('grabs') it, 'hleypr þá þegar á alvápnaðan óvina her, ok berr á tvær hendr' ('immediately attacks the fully armed troop of enemies and strikes on both side') until all who are not dead have fled. The present tense creates a sense of immediacy, and the fact that Samson attacks men who are 'fully armed' accentuates his raw physical strength. In the Hebrew, we are told that the jawbone is 'fresh' (טְרִיָּה), a detail that is left out of the Vulgate. Curiously, the Old Norse translator describes it as 'forn' ('ancient'), perhaps thinking of the value of ancient weapons in the heroic world.

Samson's feats of strength also come in for some special treatment at the hands of the Old Norse translator. While spending the night with a prostitute in Gaza, Samson is discovered by the Philistines who surround the city and lock the gate. Enjoying the irony of this, the translator comments: 'þóttusk þeir nú fullkomliga hafa ráð hans í hendi' ('they thought that now they had him fully in their power').[22] As they wait for sunrise, Samson quietly gets up, picks up the gate, posts and all, and carries it up the mountain: 'adprehendit ambas portae fores cum postibus suis' ('he took both doors of the gate, with the posts thereof'). The Old Norse translator tries to imagine the mechanics of this:[23]

20 *Stjórn*, 656; Jgd. 15.7.
21 *Stjórn*, 660; cf. Jdg. 15.15.
22 *Stjórn*, 662; cf. Jdg. 16.2.
23 *Stjórn*, 663; cf. Jdg. 16.3.

216

Heroes, Heroines and Royal Biography

Nú varð hann varr við umsátina, ok snýr út at borgarhliði, ok sér þat með styrkum lásum lukt. Hann gengr þó til ok faðmar portit með því móti at hann tekr með sinni hendi hváru megin ok spennir um svá undir stólpa hliðsins. En hann setr háls ok herðar undir yfirportit, treystir á síðan, þar til er losnar allt saman.

Now he became aware of the ambush, and turns to the city gate, and sees it fastened with strong padlocks. However, he goes up and embraces the gate in such a way that he puts one hand on either side and clasps the posts of the gate and sets his neck and shoulders under the lintel of the gate, puts pressure on it until it loosens altogether.

The detail here is striking: the verb 'faðma' ('to embrace') is not used elsewhere in this sense and it recalls the prostitute whom Samson was embracing not so long ago. It links his physical and sexual prowess and perhaps foreshadows Delilah's embrace, which will bring about his final downfall. Likewise, the verb 'spenna' ('to clasp') – which one might use of clasping a sword or an arm ring – emphasises the huge span of Samson's arms, which can fully encircle the gate. While the biblical Samson lifts the gate effortlessly, the Old Norse translator gives a strong impression of muscular strength. The scene as a whole foreshadows 'inn síðasti sígr Samsons' ('Samson's last victory') when he pulls down the pillars of the Philistine hall, killing himself and 3,000 others: 'Í þessu bili sviptir hann stólpunum styrkliga undan svá at allt herbergit hrapar svá skjótt niðr á þá sem inni váru, at engi maðr komsk heill undan' ('In that moment, he shakes the pillars so strongly from beneath that the whole building collapses so fast that no one got away alive').[24]

Samson is not just physically strong, though; he is also gifted with words. Taciturn and uncommunicative when it comes to his parents, Samson is perfectly capable of poetic eloquence when it serves his purpose. At his wedding, he proposes a riddle competition with 30 of his guests to win 30 suits of linen clothes. In Hebrew, the riddle is poetry, and its parallelism survives into the Vulgate, where the Norse translator picks up on it: 'Matr fór út af etanda, ok af styrkum stórmikill sœtleikr' ('Food came out of the eater, and from the strong great sweetness').[25] This feels poetic in Old Norse: although the first half-line lacks alliteration, it uses half-rhymes ('matr', 'út' and 'etanda') to create a rhymical pattern, while the second half-line has both alliteration and half-rhyme ('styr-', 'stor'). In addition, the translator creates a chiasmus with 'matr' and 'sœtleikr' at either end of the poetic line and 'af etanda' and 'af styrkum' in the middle. Unfortunately, the riddle has not fared well in AM 227 fol. (84v), where the scribe wrote 'maðr' ('man') instead of 'matr' ('food'), which must have confused the readers. While the Vulgate

---

[24] Stjórn, 677–78; cf. Jdg. 16.30.
[25] Stjórn, 652; Jdg. 14.14.

The Old Testament in Medieval Icelandic Texts

leaves us to imagine Samson's self-satisfaction at coming up with this riddle, in the Old Norse he cannot resist rubbing it in: 'eigi er meiri, segir Samson, min gáta' ('there's no more, says Samson, to my riddle'). There's a dangerously complacent ring to this that suggests his self-confidence is misplaced – as turns out to be the case. When the Philistines find out the answer, Samson again resorts to enigmatic language: 'enn hefði þér eigi fundit djúpan grafning gátu minnar útan þér hefðið arit til með minni kvígu' ('You would not have found the underlying meaning of my riddle if you hadn't ploughed with my heifer').[26] The second part of this is closely translated from the Vulgate, but the metaphor has been extended, so that Samson imagines the Philistines as having dug up ('grafa upp') the buried meaning ('grafning') of his riddle. Perhaps there is even a poetic pun: 'grafningr' occurs only here in prose, but in poetry it is used as a *heiti* for 'snake' in kennings for gold ('one who buries itself in the ground').[27]

The most overwritten part of Samson's story is, predictably, the love affair between Samson and Delilah, at which point the translator becomes outraged and unusually outspoken, despite the fact that Delilah in no way tries to deceive Samson as to what she will do once she knows the secret of his strength. The moment that she has discovered it, she summons the Philistines, and the translator launches into a long tirade:[28]

En sú in bannsetta ok bitra naðra, er alla vega var útan á at sjá tigurlig ok lystilig, því at hon var allra kvenna fríðust sýnum, en innan ljót ok leiðilig, full eitrs ok ólyfjans, plagar sik nú alla vega við skraut ok skart, klæðisk inni beztu gangverju ok ǫllum inum bezta ok fegrsta búnaði, gengr síðan inn fyrir Samson, byrlar ok berr honum inn styrkasta drykk ok lokkar hann mjǫk til at drekka með blíðum hálsfǫngum ok blautligum kossum. Með þeim hætti sem nú megi þér heyra sveik ok sigraði þessi prettafull púta með eitri sinnar illsku þann ágæta kappa sem aldri áðr varð yfirstiginn af sínum óvinum.

But that cursed and bitter snake – who was in every way noble and delightful to gaze at from the outside, because she was the most beautiful of all women in appearance, but inside ugly and hateful, full of venom and poison – now adorns herself in every way with finery and splendour, dresses in the finest clothes and all the best and fairest attire, then goes in to Samson, serves and bears him the strongest drink and lures him to drink excessively with tender embraces and soft kisses. In this way that you can now hear, this deceitful whore deceived and conquered with the poison of her evil the excellent hero who had never before been overcome by his enemies.

---

26 *Stjórn*, 653; Jdg. 14.15.

27 Anonymous, *Orma heiti* 2, ed. Elena Gurevich, in *Poetry from Treatises on Poetics*, ed. Kari Ellen Gade and Edith Marold (Turnhout: Brepols, 2017), 929.

28 *Stjórn*, 670–71; there is no equivalent in the biblical Judges.

Heroes, Heroines and Royal Biography

This is a marked departure from the translator's style up to this point; it sounds more like a sermon than a saga, with its exhortation as to what 'you can now hear'. Delilah is not actually described as a prostitute in Judges, although arguably we are encouraged to conflate her with the prostitute at Gaza in the previous episode.[29] And there is nothing about her dressing up, serving drink, or using sexual allure to overcome Samson, though such methods are used by other biblical women, including Judith and Ruth. The reference to Delilah as a 'snake' suggests that the figure of Eve is behind the translator's caricature, and perhaps the idea of her luring Samson to drink from her cup of 'poison' derives from the homiletic metaphor of Eve bearing the 'drink of death'.[30] Yet the description of Samson as an 'excellent hero' whose downfall is the fault of women seems to be a wilful misunderstanding of the story as it has been told so far. Perhaps the translator is drawing on an actual sermon at this point, but it is also possible that he is thinking of Eddic poetry, and woman as cupbearer in heroic legend. There is a parallel with, for example, Guðrún in *Atlakviða* coming out to meet Atli with a cup, luring him to destruction with food and drink, and murdering him as he lies drunk in their marriage bed.[31] Likewise, in *Heimskringla*, Snæfríðr serves drink to King Haraldr the Fair-haired, only to drive him mad with desire; and, in Oddr's *Óláfs saga Tryggvasonar*, the role of female cupbearer is taken by a devil, who tries to serve poison to King Óláfr.[32] The biblical narrative has been conflated not only with homily, but also with heroic legend, resulting in a strong condemnation of Delilah.

According to the Vulgate, Delilah 'dormire eum fecit super genua sua et in sine suo reclinare caput' ('made him sleep upon her knees, and lay his head in her bosom') before she calls a barber to shave off his hair. She then 'coepit abicere eum et a se repellere' ('began to drive him away, and thrust him from her') and calls for the Philistines. The Old Norse, however, is subtly different. We are told that: 'nú sem Dalila sér at drykkr mœðir Samson ok svefn sígr á hann, settisk hon niðr hjá honum, ok leggr hann sitt hǫfuð í kné henni, sofnar bæði skjótt ok fast' ('now, when Delilah sees that the drink is tiring Samson and sleep is overcoming him, she sat down by him, and he puts his head on her knee, falls asleep both quickly and soundly'). After shaving Samson, 'skreiðisk hon undan hǫfði honum' ('she slips out from under his head')

---

[29] Cheryl J. Exum, *Fragmented Women: Feminist (Sub)versions of Biblical Narratives* (London: Bloomsbury, 2016), 49.

[30] *Homilíubók*, 85: 'Eva byrlaði dauðadrykk ǫllu mannkyni' ('Eve served the drink of death to all mankind').

[31] *Eddukvæði*, II, 379–81.

[32] *Heimskringla*, I, 126; Oddr Snorrason, *Óláfs saga Tryggvasonar*, in *Færeyinga saga, Óláfs saga Tryggvasonar eptir Odd munk Snorrason*, ed. Ólafur Halldórsson (Reykjavík: Hið íslenzka fornritafélag, 2006), 292.

The Old Testament in Medieval Icelandic Texts

and shouts for the Philistines.[33] The wording here closely echoes a scene in *Laxdœla saga*. Óláfr Hǫskuldsson offers an unnamed serving-woman money to bring the outlaw Stígandi, her lover, into his grasp. When Stígandi comes to see her, she welcomes him and offers to pick lice from his hair. We are told that: 'Hann leggr hǫfuðit í kné henni ok sofnar skjótliga. Þá skreiðisk hon undan hǫfði honum' ('He lays his head on her knee and falls asleep quickly. Then she slips out from under his head').[34] The verbal correspondences here seem too close to be accidental. The easier solution is that *Laxdœla saga* is borrowing from *Stjórn III*, and perhaps the idea of female betrayal does come from the biblical story of Samson. However, in every case where there is a verbal parallel between *Laxdœla saga* and *Stjórn III*, it is lacking in the Vulgate: according to the Vulgate, Samson's head is not on Delilah's knee but in her bosom, and she does not slip out from under his head, but pushes him away; there is not much point in slipping away when she is about to wake him anyway. On the other hand, these details make perfect sense in *Laxdœla saga*: Stígandi puts his head on his lover's lap so she can examine it for lice, and she slips out from under him so that she can get away and tell Óláfr where he is. It looks at least as likely that the translator of *Stjórn III* is remembering a scene in *Laxdœla saga* as that the author of *Laxdœla saga* had read *Stjórn III*. While one might not expect a saga to influence a biblical translation, this is far from the only occurrence in *Stjórn III*, as will be shown below.

The attraction of Samson for a medieval Icelandic audience is clear: his extraordinary strength, his verbal dexterity, and his anti-social behaviour all make him a hero whose story is instantly recognisable. His ability to kill with his bare hands and to lift heavy objects puts him into the same category as Egill Skalla-Grímsson and Grettir the Strong – and there are some tantalising connections with Gísli Súrsson as well, which are explored in the Epilogue (see pp. 250–54). He is comfortably at home alongside the other heroes, outlaws and poets celebrated in Old Norse-Icelandic literature.

Ruth and Naomi

While the story of Samson is easily saga-like, the same cannot be said about the book of Ruth, which has at its core the story of two women and the bond of friendship between them. As van Deusen has shown, the sagas of Icelanders have little to say about friendship between women, although there are some notable instances of female rivalry, which recall the competition between women in Genesis.[35] Rather, Ruth's place in this compilation is

---

33 *Stjórn*, 671–72; Jdg. 16.19.

34 *Laxdœla saga*, 109.

35 Natalie van Deusen, 'Sworn Sisterhood?: On the (Near-)Absence of Female Friendship from the *Íslendingasögur*', *Scandinavian Studies* 86.1 (2014), 52–71.

Heroes, Heroines and Royal Biography

guaranteed by her descendants: the genealogy with which her book ends runs from Obed, her son by Boaz, to Jesse, the father of David. It therefore creates a link between the time of the Judges – when it is set – and the beginning of David's story. In what follows, I look at how the Icelandic translator handles what could be described as 'women's history'. While he strives to make some aspects of the story recognisable, he also either misunderstands or reworks some of the ways in which the biblical Ruth subverts expectations.

The 'saga' starts with a brave move on Ruth's part: faced with the choice to return to her kin and country, following the death of her husband, she chooses instead to follow her mother-in-law Naomi to a place where she has never been before. When Naomi encourages her two daughters-in-law to leave her and return home, she speaks in familiar terms, urging them to return 'í ykkra ættleifð' ('to your patrimony'): to the land and property passed down ('leifð') among their own kin ('ætt'). Orpha duly turns back to 'fǫðurhúss síns' ('her father's house'), but Ruth chooses instead to follow Naomi: 'Fyrir útan af skal ek þér fylgja ok þik aldri fyrirláta, hvar sem þú ferr eða dvelsk skal er þar vera, þinn lýðr skal vera minn lýðr héðan af ok þinn guð minn guð' ('From now on I shall follow you and never leave you; wherever you go or stay, there I shall be; your people shall be my people from now on and your god my god').[36] This is poetry in Hebrew, and some of its lyricism is carried over into the Old Norse through parallelism, rhyme and alliteration. Ruth is determined that only death will separate her from Naomi 'ef ek má ráða' ('if I have my way'). This last phrase is the translator's addition, and it captures something of how daring, even stubborn, Ruth is in this small bid to exercise some agency over her future, rather than simply return to be under her father's authority. Boaz echoes her words when he commends Ruth for her kindness to her mother-in-law: 'nú [þú hefir] fyrirlátit frændr þína ok fǫðurhús ok ert nú komin hér með ókunnum lýð' ('now [you have] left your kin and your father's house, and have come here among an unknown people').[37] Her refusal to abandon Naomi, to whom she has no blood relationship, is at the cost of abandoning all her other familial ties.

Ruth's relationship to Naomi causes problems for the translator, depending as it does on a relationship by marriage between two women, which is tricky to translate into Old Norse. The translator is forced to use vocabulary that is rare in the sagas, even the translated ones, such as words for one's son's

---

[36] *Stjórn*, 683; cf. Ruth 1.16: 'quocumque perrexeris pergam ubi morata fueris et ego partier morabor populus tuus populus meus et Deus tuus Deus meus' ('for whithersoever thou shalt go, I will go; and where thou shalt dwell, I also will dwell. Thy people shall be my people, and thy God my God').

[37] *Stjórn*, 685; cf. Ruth 2.11. The Vulgate has 'parentes' ('parents') here, translating the Hebrew אָבִיךְ וְאִמֵּךְ ('your father and your mother'); the translator expands it to include relations and household.

221

The Old Testament in Medieval Icelandic Texts

wife ('sonarkván', 'sonarkona' and 'snør') and words for one's husband's mother ('sværa'). These simply do not occur in the sagas of Icelanders: the *Dictionary of Old Norse Prose* lists 16 occurrences in total of 'sonarkván' and 'sonarkona', of which nine come from legal texts or letters (most of which list the prohibited degrees of kinship), three are in lists of *heiti* and kennings in *Snorra Edda*, and the rest are all from *Stjórn I* and *Stjórn III*.[38] Similarly, there are only four occurrences of the term 'snør' ('daughter-in-law'), two of which are from Ruth, one from *Snorra Edda* and the final one from the *Dialogues* of Gregory the Great. Meanwhile, 'sværa' ('mother-in-law') is found three times in *Snorra Edda*, once in the same passage of the *Dialogues* as 'snør' and once in *Vǫlsunga saga* – its only occurrence within a saga.[39] Atli accuses Guðrún of making her mother-in-law weep, but this character is not otherwise mentioned.[40] The association of these terms with laws and poetic *heiti* means that they inevitably feel formal and legalistic in contrast to, for example, 'mágkona', which can also mean 'mother-in-law, sister-in-law, or daughter-in-law', but of which every recorded occurrence refers to a woman's relation to a man.[41] Naomi, for example, is described as Boaz's 'mágkona' to indicate that he is a close relation of her dead husband.[42] It is notable, then, that on two occasions, the translator resorts to the terminology of a much more familiar relationship: foster parent and child. When Boaz provides Ruth with lunch, we are told that she saves her left-overs 'at fœra fóstru sinni' ('to bring to her foster-mother') and, later, she tells Naomi how Boaz gave her extra corn because he did not wish her to return empty-handed 'til fóstru minnar' ('to my foster-mother').[43] The first of these is an addition on the part of the translator, and the second is a translation of 'ad socrum tuum' ('to your mother-in-law') in the Vulgate. Perhaps they are used here with a delicate sense of irony: to foster is to provide 'fóstr' ('sustenance, provisions'), yet here it is Ruth who provides for Naomi, rather than Naomi who provides for Ruth. Yet the terminology of 'fostering' draws the relationship into the sphere of emotions: in the sagas of Icelanders, foster-relations between women are warm and affectionate, binding together women of different generations who live together. In *Egils saga Skalla-Grímssonar*,

---

38 *DONP*, s.v. 'sonarkván', 'sonarkona' at https://onp.ku.dk/onp/onp.php?074027 and https://onp.ku.dk/onp/onp.php?074026 (accessed 24 July 2023).

39 *DONP*, s.v. 'snør', 'sværa' at https://onp.ku.dk/onp/onp.php?073699 and https://onp.ku.dk/onp/onp.php?077974 (accessed 24 July 2023).

40 *Vǫlsunga saga*, in *The Saga of the Volsungs*, ed. and trans. Ronald G. Finch (London: Nelson, 1955), 73.

41 *DONP*, s.v. 'mágkona' at https://onp.ku.dk/onp/onp.php?051628 (accessed 24 July 2023).

42 *Stjórn*, 684.

43 *Stjórn*, 685, 688; cf. Ruth 2.14, 3.17.

Heroes, Heroines and Royal Biography

Bera does not wish to be separated from her foster-daughter Ásgerðr while, in *Laxdœla saga*, Melkorka's foster-mother weeps for joy to hear that her foster-daughter is safe and well.[44] One also thinks of the close relationship between Guðrún and her granddaughter Herdís at the end of that same saga; *Laxdœla saga* comes closest to Ruth of all the sagas in its focus on nurturing relationships between women. The switch from 'sværa' to 'fóstra', then, allows the translator to capture something of Ruth's love and devotion to Naomi, although it does not necessarily imply that this is returned.

In the Hebrew, Ruth's foreignness is a significant factor, but this has little meaning for the Old Norse translator, who emphasises instead her poverty.[45] When Naomi tells her daughters-in-law to go home, she insists that: 'ykkr skortir ekki með frændum ykkrum en mik sœkir mikit fátœki' ('you will lack for nothing amongst your kin, while great poverty pursues me').[46] There is no parallel to this in the Vulgate. It reveals that Ruth's choice to follow Naomi is not just a rejection of her family but means forgoing their material support. Her poverty is repeatedly referenced as she gleans in Boaz's fields: when Boaz first speaks to her, Ruth expresses her gratitude 'at þú virðisk at kynnask við mik auma konu ok útlenda' ('that you think to become acquainted with me, a poor and foreign woman').[47] One wonders whether the verb 'kynna' here ('to get to know') carries an echo of 'kyn' ('kin') – which is what Ruth now lacks and Boaz is in a position to provide. She thanks him 'at þú virðisk at gleðja mína fatœkt með mǫrgum hugganarorðum' ('that you think to gladden my poverty with words of comfort'), while he warns his men not to shame or embarrass her 'þó at hon fari fátœkliga' ('even though she goes in poverty').[48] At the same time, the translator clearly feels the need to dissociate Ruth from unbecoming or forward behaviour. When she goes out to glean in the field, we are told that she 'gekk heldr ódjarfliga' ('went rather timidly') – which seems to counter the possible negative connotations of 'djarfliga' as 'rashly', 'impudently', or 'immoderately'.[49] This is repeated a few lines later in the words of Boaz's servant: 'ekki get ek at hon sálug sé mjǫk djarftœk' ('I don't think the poor wretch is very bold in gathering up [grain]'). The *Dictionary of Old Norse Prose* translates this last word as

---

[44] *Egils saga*, 48; *Laxdœla saga*, 58.

[45] Laura Quick, 'The Book of Ruth and the Limits of Female Wisdom', *Journal of Biblical Literature* 139.1 (2020), 61.

[46] *Stjórn*, 682; cf. Ruth 1.13.

[47] *Stjórn*, 685; cf. Ruth 2.10. The Vulgate has only 'peregrinam mulierem' ('a woman of another country').

[48] Cf. Ruth 2.13 and 2.16, where there is no reference to poverty in either Hebrew or Latin.

[49] *Stjórn*, 684; cf. Quick, 'Book of Ruth' p. 63, who points out that Ruth's activities are 'masculine' in the sense that they put her in the public sphere.

The Old Testament in Medieval Icelandic Texts

'quick to snatch (up)', but the related noun 'djarftœki' is translated as 'greed' or 'covetousness', so the implication seems to be that Ruth is not acting inappropriately or immoderately, but is sparing in taking only what she needs.[50] Again, these are both additions to the narrative. Ruth is positioned not as a foreigner who knowingly puts herself in danger, but as a poor relation of Boaz whose virtue and excellence are recognisable from how she behaves despite the poverty of her situation.

The scene in which Ruth goes to Boaz on the threshing floor is a particular challenge for the translator, since it is dangerously close to the scene where Delilah seduces Samson, to which he has reacted so strongly. Naomi tells Ruth to dress up: 'nú skalt þú laugask ok smyrja þik ágætum jurtum, síðan klæð þú þik sœmiligri gangverju ok gakk leyniliga í láfagarðinn' ('now you must wash and anoint yourself with excellent perfumes, then dress in suitable garments and go secretly to the barn').[51] There is a direct echo here of Delilah's preparations, when she 'klæðisk inni beztu gangverju' ('dressed in the best garments').[52] Ruth waits until Boaz goes to bed 'gleðikenndr af drykk' ('cheerful from drink'), just as Delilah waits until 'drykkr mœðir Samson' ('drink wearies Samson'). Everything is set for a scene of seduction, as Naomi advises Ruth: 'Gakk þú þar til ok létt upp á breizlinu at fótum honum ok ligg þar undir, síðan mun hann segja þér hvat þú skalt at hafask' ('Go to him and lift up the bedcover by his feet and lie down underneath it, then he will tell you what you should do'). Ruth follows these instructions exactly: 'kom þar Ruth leyniliga ok kastaði sér undir klæðin at fótum honum' ('Ruth came there secretly and settled herself under the bedclothes at his feet'). Both occurrences of the adverb 'leyniliga' ('secretly') are added by the translator and suggest an illicit sexual encounter.[53] The translator also increases Boaz's confusion when he discovers her: the Vulgate has 'conturbatus est' ('he was disturbed'), which the Old Norse expands to: 'slær í fyrstu á hann ótta ok undran mikilli, vissi hann eigi gjǫrla hverju fá myndi' ('fear and great wonder strikes him, he did not know for sure what would happen').[54] This jars with Naomi's earlier certainty that Boaz will know exactly what to do. Although 'feet' do not have the same connotations as in Hebrew (see pp. 255–56), the implications of Ruth's behaviour were not lost on the compiler of AM 227 fol., who gave this chapter the title: 'Ruth lagðisk undir klæðin hjá Booz'

---

50 *DONP*, s.v. 'djarftœkr', 'djarftœki' at https://onp.ku.dk/onp/onp.php?o14640 and https://onp.ku.dk/onp/onp.php?o14639 (accessed 24 July 2023).

51 *Stjórn*, 687; cf. Ruth 3.3–4.

52 *Stjórn*, 671.

53 Ruth 3.3 and 3.7. The first may be inferred from 'non te videat homo' ('let not the man see thee'), while the second corresponds to Vulgate 'abscondite', which translates Hebrew בַּלָּט ('softly, gently').

54 *Stjórn*, 687, cf. Ruth 3.8.

Heroes, Heroines and Royal Biography

('Ruth lay down under the bedclothes with Boaz').[55] The idiom 'leggjask hjá' certainly means 'to have sex with' in at least two other occurrences.[56] The translator must also have found her behaviour suspect, for he puts two additional comments in the mouth of Boaz to offset any possible criticism. Boaz praises her 'í þessi þinni mætu meðferð er þú sveimar eigi úti um nætr með geðlausum gárungum' ('in this your excellent conduct, that you don't roam about at night with fickle jokers').[57] This is a rather odd interpretation of the Vulgate's 'quia non es secuta iuvenes' ('because thou hast not followed youths') and arguably a backhanded compliment given that Ruth has indeed been 'roaming about at night'. He then adds that 'þessi þín meðferð mun þér snúask til fullkominnar farsælu' ('this your conduct will bring you to full prosperity'), which replaces the Vulgate's 'quicquid dixeris mihi faciam tibi' ('whatsoever thou shalt say to me I will do to thee').[58] Perhaps the translator felt uncomfortable with how Boaz here explicitly follows Ruth's lead.[59] Instead, he has Boaz identify Ruth's virtue as the cause of her success.

Perhaps the most subversive moment, though, comes after Boaz and Ruth marry, when Ruth gives birth to Obed. Although throughout the book her remarriage has been positioned as a way of ensuring the continuity of her dead husband's family line, when she does give birth to an heir he is described as Naomi's son and successor: 'Nú er Noemi fœddr son' ('Now a son is born to Naomi').[60] Even more strikingly, the source of Naomi's happiness is identified by her female friends as Ruth: 'de nuru enim tua natus est quae te diligit et multo tibi est melior quam si septem haberes filios' ('he is born of thy daughter-in-law, who loveth thee and is much better to thee than if thou hadst seven sons').[61] Since 'seven' is the number of perfection

---

55 *Stjórn*, 686. For a discussion of this scene, see André LaCocque, *The Feminine Unconventional: Four Subversive Figures in Israel's Tradition* (Minneapolis: Fortree, 1990), 106–7; Ellen J. van Wolde, *Ruth and Naomi* (London: SCM, 1997), 70; Tod Linafelt and T. K. Beal, *Ruth and Esther* (Collegeville: Liturgical, 1999), 80–81; Lillian R. Klein, *From Deborah to Esther: Sexual Politics in the Hebrew Bible* (Minneapolis: Fortress, 2003), 62–64; Laura Quick, 'Decorated Women: A Sociological Approach to the Function of Cosmetics in the Books of Esther and Ruth', *Biblical Interpretation* 27.3 (2019), 354–71.

56 *Þiðriks saga af Bern*, ed. Henrik Bertelsen (Copenhagen: Møller, 1905–11), 58; *Heimskringla*, I, 349.

57 *Stjórn*, 687; Ruth 3.10.

58 *Stjórn*, 688; Ruth 3.11.

59 Cf. Linafelt and Beal, *Ruth and Esther*, 91: 'Against the reader's expectations, Ruth is the one who drives the plot of the story, not Boaz'.

60 Cf. Ruth 4.17: 'natus est filius Noemi' ('there is a son born to Naomi'), cf. Quick, 'Book of Ruth', 65: 'At every point, our expectations for the successful continuity of the house of Elimelech are subverted'.

61 Ruth 4.15.

The Old Testament in Medieval Icelandic Texts

in Hebrew, this is quite a claim. The Norse translator keeps the idea of Obed as Naomi's son and 'erfingi' ('heir'), but adds as a counterweight that she 'fóstraði við mikla ást ok elsku sem hann væri hennar eigin son' ('fostered [him] with great love and affection as if he were her own son').[62] This shifts the focus from Naomi as progenitor of a genealogical line to her affection for her foster-child. However, what is most noticeable is that the translator misunderstands – perhaps deliberately – the comment on the seven sons, resulting in the following translation in AM 227 fol.: 'Nú er sá fœddr af þinni sværu er þik elskaði, ok þér einn betri heldr en þú ættir sjálf vij. sonu' ('Now is born of your mother-in-law who loved you, one who is far better for you than if you had seven sons of your own'). This is rather a mess, since 'sværa' ('mother-in-law') must be a mistake for 'snør' ('daughter-in-law'), but what is clear is that it is Obed, not Ruth, who is better for Naomi than seven sons. In other versions, it is not even Ruth who loved Naomi: AM 226 fol. has 'hann mun þik elska ok þér einn betri vera' ('he will love you and be far better for you'), as does AM 228 fol.: it is the newly adopted son and not the daughter-in-law who restores Naomi to her former happiness. So, the foster-relationship between the two women is replaced at the end of the story by something more conventional: Naomi's fostering of her grandson Obed, who alone engages her 'love and affection'.

Ruth is the least saga-like of the stories described in this chapter, at least in its focus on the close and loving relationship between two women, which has few parallels in saga literature. Moreover, the translator clearly felt uneasy about aspects of Ruth's behaviour and did his best to tone down some of the ways in which she takes the initiative, not only in providing for Naomi, but also in arranging her marriage to Boaz. At the same time, the story's investment in the importance of genealogy is something any saga author would appreciate, and it justifies Ruth's place as a prelude to the reign of David. In the end, Ruth's purpose is to give birth to a son, who will be the ancestor of Israel's greatest king.

The David Story

The greatest of the 'sagas' within *Stjórn III* is the story of King David, and in AM 227 fol. it is formally marked out at the beginning and end. On fol. 96r, I Samuel 17 is prefaced by the title 'upphaf sǫgu Davids' ('the beginning of David's saga') beside a late illuminated initial that appears to show David and his father Jesse.[63] It runs until the end of I Kings 2, the last chapter of

---

62   *Stjórn*, 692; Ruth 4.16 where the Vulgate has 'et nutricis' ('and she was a nurse unto it').

63   *Stjórn*, 777. AM 226 fol. has instead: 'er David konungr reif kjapta á óarga dýri' ('when David ripped off the lion's jaw'), which echoes *Veraldar saga*, 31.

226

Heroes, Heroines and Royal Biography

which is entitled 'andlát ins blezaða David' ('death of the blessed David') and
the following chapter 'hér hefr iii bók liber regum. Upphaf ríkis Salamonis'
('here begins the third book of kings. The beginning of Solomon's reign').[64]
It therefore takes us from David's childhood to his death, ending with the
succession of his son. David's story bears a close likeness to saga narrative
– both *Íslendingasǫgur* and *konungasǫgur* – and this likeness is drawn out
and elaborated by the translator in a variety of ways. In what follows, I will
focus on scenes that raise the possibility of direct borrowing from the sagas.

In the Hebrew Bible, the story of David is closely intertwined with the
fall of Saul: it unfolds in a recognisable world in which political power is
hardwon and shortlived, and in which divine favour is unreliable. Saul's loss
of divine favour is dramatically told in the chapter immediately preceding
the introduction of David: it begins with Saul's disobedience to the divine
command and ends with Samuel's pronouncement that God has rejected him:
'fyrir þat sama er þú kastaðir í brottu dróttins boðskap, þá kastar hann þér af
hendi at þú sér eigi konungr yfir hans lýð' ('because you cast away the Lord's
command, so he will cast you from his hand so that you will not be king over
his people').[65] This is then given a visual illustration: as Samuel gets up to
leave, Saul grabs his cloak in desperation 'svá at rifnaði' ('so that it tore').
Samuel declares: 'svá slítr dróttinn af þér á þeim degi ríki gyðinga' ('so
the Lord will tear from you this day the kingdom of the Jews').[66] Both the
wordplay on *rifna* and *slíta* (Latin *scindo*) and the visual image of the ripped
cloak are reminiscent of a famous and repeated scene in Old Norse historiography: the defeat of Óláfr Tryggvason – also king by divine election – at the
battle of Svǫlðr. Óláfr Tryggvason is standing in his ship, the *Long Serpent*,
alongside his best bowman, Einarr *þambarskelfir*, when Einarr's bowstring
bursts before he can shoot Óláfr's enemy. Óláfr asks: 'Hvat brast þar svá hátt'
('What broke there so loudly?'), to which Einarr replies: 'Nóregr ór hendi
þér' ('Norway from your hand').[67] A version of this also occurs in the saga of
Óláfr Haraldsson, when Áslákr *fitjaskalli* strikes Erlingr Skjálgsson his death
blow. Óláfr responds: 'Nú hjóttu Nóreg ór hendi mér' ('Now you have struck
Norway out of my hand').[68] It is striking that all these variants are placed

---

64   *Stjórn*, 1003, 1005.

65   *Stjórn*, 776; cf. I Sam. 15.26.

66   I Sam. 15.28. In the Latin, the cloak 'scissa est' ('rent') and 'scidit Dominus
regnum Israel a te hodie' ('the Lord hath rent the kingdom of Israel from thee
today'). The Hebrew verb is קרע ('to tear, rend').

67   *Heimskringla*, I, 362–63; cf. Oddr Snorrason, *Óláfs saga Tryggvasonar*, 342–43.

68   *Heimskringla*, II, 317; cf. *Ágrip af Nóregskonunga. A Twelfth-century Synoptic
History of the Kings of Norway*, ed. Matthew Driscoll (London: Viking Society for
Northern Research, 1995), 38–39; *Fagrskinna*, ed. Finnur Jónsson (Copenhagen:
Møller, 1902–3), 176. Compare *Víga-Glúms saga*, 41 and the discussion in

The Old Testament in Medieval Icelandic Texts

at exactly the same moment: the passing of the 'mantle' of political power from one king to another. It is tempting to conjecture that the saga authors have been influenced by the combination of word and image in 1 Samuel 15, although they have chosen to use the breaking of a bowstring or the strike of an axe rather than the tearing of a cloak. At the same time, it is possible that the translator's addition of 'þér af hendi' to Samuel's warning that God will 'cast you aside' ('proiecit te') is influenced by the idiom 'ór hendi þér/mér' ('from your/my hand') in these sagas of kings. It is certainly used later in *Stjórn III* in an addition to 2 Kings 13.19, in which Elisha tells Joash: 'Nú draptu mikinn sígr ór hendi þér' ('Now you have struck a great victory from your hand').[69] Whichever way the loan goes, it is clear that the world of power looks the same: whether Iceland or Israel, kings deal with the same unpredictable mix of divine power and political manoeuvring.

In this context, the translator is careful to make sure that David's story begins like a saga. He kicks off with a genealogical notice about Jesse and his eight sons borrowed from later in 1 Samuel 17.12–13, which allows him to begin in the expected manner with: 'Isay eða Iesse hét einn ríkr maðr' ('Isai or Jesse was the name of a powerful man').[70] He then names his three oldest sons in order, before commenting about the youngest, David, that 'hann var virðr minnst af þeim' ('he was esteemed least of them'). This may well be inferred from the story that follows, but it coheres well with the folktale pattern of the youngest son and the saga tradition of the *kolbítr* ('coal-biter').[71] Rather than start from David's anointing, as in the Vulgate, the translator instead pulls together material on David's youth, using as his basis David's speech to Saul in 1 Samuel 17 alongside some extra-biblical sources. Most interesting, from the point of view of the sagas, is the way that David's youthful adventures are transformed. In the Vulgate, David tells them to prove that he can fight Goliath: 'Pascebat servus tuus patris sui gregem et veniebat leo vel ursus tollebatque arietem de medio gregis et sequebar eos et percutiebam eruebamque de ore eorum et illi consurgebant adversum me et adprehendebam mentum eorum et suffocabam interficiebamque eos nam et leonem et ursum interfeci ego servus tuus' ('Thy servant kept his father's sheep, and there came a lion, or a bear, and took a ram out of the midst of the flock. And I pursued after them, and struck them, and delivered it out of their mouth: and they rose up against me, and I caught them by the throat, and I strangled and killed them. For I thy servant

---

Hermann Pálsson, 'På leting etter røttene til Víga-Glúms saga', *Maal og Minne* (1979), 18–26.

69 *Stjórn*, 1175; 2 Kgs 13.19.

70 *Stjórn*, 778.

71 Ásdís Egilsdóttir, 'Kolbítr verður karlmaður', in *Miðaldabörn*, ed. Ármann Jakobsson and Torfi Tulinius (Reykjavík: Hugvísindastofnun Háskóla Íslands, 2005), 87–100.

Heroes, Heroines and Royal Biography

have killed both a lion and a bear').[72] The translator turns this into a third-person narrative situated at the beginning of David's life. He divides it into two separate events, beginning with a bear coming 'ór skógi' ('out of the forest') and taking a kid from the flock. David pursues it: 'ferr svá leikr með þeim at hann lemr leggi bjarnarins ok drepr hann en frelsar kiðit' ('the game between them goes such that he breaks the bear's legs and kills him and frees the kid'). The details here are slightly changed – David breaks the bear's legs rather than strangling it – and the idea of 'leikr' ('game, contest') is added, but otherwise it is not too different from the Vulgate. But things hot up considerably when the lion arrives on the scene:[73]

Annan tíma kemr af mǫrkinni sér matar at leita leó með miklum grimmleik ok greip einn hrút af hjǫrðinni. David sneri þegar eptir honum. En er dýrit fann sér eptirfǫr veitta snarask hann þegar móti ok ógnaði manninum með grimmligri asjónu ok grettisk reiðuliga en vildi þó eigi laust láta sitt ránfengi. David var vápnlauss ok rennr þó at djarfliga, þrífr báðum hǫndum faxit á dýrinu ok kastar sér upp á hálsinn, spennir saman báðum fótum undir kverkina en tekr sinni hendi hvárn kjǫptinn ok rífr frá niðr kjalkana. Ferr svá hrútr feginn til hjarðar en David gengr af dauðum leóni.

Another time a lion comes from the wilderness to seek its food with great ferocity and seized a ram from the flock. David immediately pursued it. And when the animal saw that it was pursued, it immediately turns round and threatened the human with a fierce countenance and growled angrily, but refused to let go of its prey. David was without a weapon, and yet runs boldly at it, seizes with both hands the lion's mane and throws himself up onto its neck, braces with both feet under its chin, puts a hand on either side of the jaw and rips out the jawbone from underneath. Thus the ram returns happily to the flock, and David parts from the dead lion.

This has turned into a full-blown heroic incident with exciting shifts of perspective between David and the lion, a dramatic confrontation, plenty of detail about David's actions, and a conclusion that ironically juxtaposes the 'happy' ram returning to the flock with David's taking leave of the 'dead lion' – the final two words of the chapter. The detail about David using the lion's mane to catapult onto its back is imaginative and easy to visualise; it is not unlike Þóroddr's fight with the wild bull in *Eyrbyggja saga*, where he too leaps onto its back and clasps his arms around its neck, hoping to wear it out.[74] Meanwhile, the bracing with the feet and the ripping of the jaw might recall for some readers Víðarr's struggle with Fenrir in *Snorra Edda*, where

---

[72] 1 Sam. 17. 34–36.
[73] *Stjórn*, 778–79.
[74] *Eyrbyggja saga*, 175: 'þá hljóp hann upp á háls griðunginum ok spennti hǫndum

The Old Testament in Medieval Icelandic Texts

Víðarr also braces himself and then tears ('rífr') the wolf's jaw apart.[75] The translator puts David's short retrospective to excellent use in constructing a heroic biography for David with the expected prodigious exploits.

David's fight against Goliath in his youth, as one might expect, is a high point for the translator. In the Vulgate, the description of Goliath spans four verses (I Samuel 17.4–7), which cover his height, his armour, his helmet, shield and spear. The translator follows this description closely, until he gets to the spear: 'Spjót í hendi af inu harðasti járni svá tungt at skaptit vá .vi. hundrað skillinga; þat var svá vaxit at fjǫðrin var breið upp at falnum, en slegit ferstrent fram, slíkt er nú kallat bryntrǫll. Hann var gyrðr sverði því, er bæði var mikit ok hvast' ('[He had] a spear in his hand of the hardest iron, so heavy that it weighed six hundred shillings; it was shaped so that the blade was broad up at the neck-joint and beaten into four edges at the other end, such as is now called *bryntrǫll*. He was also girded with a sword which was both big and sharp').[76] A weapon called a *bryntrǫll* is mentioned in *Laxdæla saga* and *Færeyinga saga*, and the *Dictionary of Old Norse Prose* describes it as a 'double-sided axe (with a spike at the tip of the shaft?)'.[77] But the closest parallel to *Stjórn III* is in *Egils saga*, where Þórólfr is said to be carrying a weapon called a 'brynþvari' ('chain-mail borer'?):[78]

> Þórólfr var svá búinn: hann hafði skjǫld víðan ok þykkvan, hjálm á hǫfði allsterkan, gyrðr sverði því er hann kallaði Lang, mikit vápn ok gott, kesju hafði hann í hendi, fjǫðrin var tveggja álna lǫng ok sleginn fram broddr ferstrendr, en upp var fjǫðrin breið, falrinn bæði langr ok digr [...] Járnteinn var í falnum, ok skaptið allt járnvafit. Þau spjót váru kǫlluð brynþvarar.

> Þórólfr was equipped like this: he had a wide and thick shield, a very strong helmet on his head, he was girded with a sword which he called Long, a big fine weapon, he had a spear in his hand, the blade was two ells long and beaten into a four-edged point at the top, and the blade was broad at one end, and the neck-joint was both long and thick [...] There was an

---

 niðr undir kverkina' ('then he leaped up onto the bull's back and clasped with his hands down under the chin').

75 Snorri Sturluson, *Edda: Prologue and Gylfaginning*, ed. Faulkes, 72–73: 'Annarri hendi tekr hann en efra keypt úlfsins ok rífr sundr gin hans' ('With one hand he took hold of the upper jaw and tore apart his jaws').

76 *Stjórn*, 787; cf. I Sam 17.7: 'hastile autem hastae eius erat quasi liciatorium texentium ipsum autem ferrum hastae eius sescentos siclos habebat ferri' ('the staff of his spear was like a weaver's beam, and the head of his spear weighed six hundred sicles of iron').

77 *Laxdæla saga*, 105; *Egils saga*, 36; *Færeyinga saga*, 65; DONP, s.v. 'bryntroll' at https://onp.ku.dk/onp/onp.php?011796 (accessed 26 July 2023).

78 *Egils saga*, 76. Cf. DONP, s.v. 'brynþvari' at https://onp.ku.dk/onp/onp.php?011801 (accessed 26 July 2023).

Heroes, Heroines and Royal Biography

iron rod in the neck, and the shaft was covered in iron. Those spears were called *brynþvarar*.

The verbal echoes between this passage and the one in *Stjórn III* suggest a dependence of some sort, and it makes more sense for *Stjórn III* to be borrowing from *Egils saga*, not only so that Goliath's spear can be identified by an Icelandic audience, but also so that David can be recognised as a hero of Þórólfr's calibre. In fact, the translator appears to have liked this description so much that he also uses it elsewhere: when describing how one of David's champions fought a different Goliath, he comments that his spear is 'ferstrent fram en fjǫðrin breið upp' ('four-edged at the top and the blade broad at the other end').[79] He also equips Saul, uniquely, with a *kesja* ('spear'), which is what the author of *Egils saga* calls the weapon carried by Þórólfr. This is the spear over which Saul lies slumped after his defeat in battle: 'þar lá Saul á grúfu yfir kesju sína' ('Saul lay face down there over his spear').[80] It looks as if *Stjórn III* is borrowing from *Egils saga* here to 'domesticate' the biblical story and draw out its resemblance to saga narrative. In fact, it is noticeable that Goliath is described as 'sá inn grimmi heiðingi' ('that grim heathen') and 'inn vándi víkingr' ('that evil Viking'), but never – as in the biblical account – as 'uncircumcised'.[81]

The duel itself is an odd mixture of religious polemic and characteristic heroic understatement. On the one hand, Goliath is described in morally loaded language as 'merciless', 'cursed' and 'miserable'.[82] On the other, the duel is framed not as religious warfare, but as a matter of honour: Goliath whets the Israelites in typical fashion, declaring that 'engi af ǫllum þeim mun þora at stríða við mik' ('not one of all of them will dare to fight me').[83] The translator confirms that Goliath continued 'at spotta gyðinga er engi af þeim þorði at berjask við hann' ('to mock the Jews that none of them dared to fight with him').[84] When Goliath is confronted with the young David, he challenges him to come forward 'ef þú þorir' ('if you dare'); these verbs of daring are all additions to the Vulgate, although it does speak of the 'obprobrium' of Goliath's taunts, translated into Old Norse as 'svívirðing' ('dishonour').[85] In the midst of this discourse of honour and shame, the translator slips in a couple of effective understatements. When Saul questions

---

79 *Stjórn*, 985; 2 Sam. 21.19.
80 *Stjórn*, 873; 2 Sam 1.6.
81 *Stjórn*, 791, 795, 797; cf. 1 Sam. 17.26; 'hic Philistheus incircumcisus' ('this uncircumcised Philistine'); 1 Sam. 17.36 'Philistheus hic incircumcisus' ('this incircumcised Philistine').
82 *Stjórn*, 793–94; cf. 1 Sam. 17. 31, 36–37.
83 *Stjórn*, 788; cf. 1 Sam. 17.10.
84 *Stjórn*, 789, cf. 1 Sam 17.16
85 *Stjórn*, 792, 796; cf. 1 Sam 17.44, 26.

The Old Testament in Medieval Icelandic Texts

whether a 'smásveinn' ('small boy') can really fight a giant like Goliath, David replies: 'Eigi em ek mikill, en þó hefir þinn þjónustumaðr orðit skógdýrum heldr harðleikinn' ('I am not big, and yet your servant has played somewhat roughly with the beasts of the forest').[86] The effect of this understatement depends on our memory of the previous chapter, in which David's heroic exploits were described as a 'leikr' ('game'). Later, when David boasts to Goliath that he will give the Philistines' corpses to 'hræfuglum himins ok skógdýrum jarðar' ('carrion birds of the air and forest beasts of the earth'), we are told that: 'Goliath þótti David heldr vera stórorðr' ('Goliath thought that David was rather big-mouthed').[87] This plays on the irony of the situation: it may seem to Goliath that David's words are bigger than this 'smásveinn' ('small boy'), but in fact it turns out that they are perfectly sized to his actions.

David is set up as the ideal hero in his youth, but this does not mean that the translator is unaware of the ambiguities of his character. A much more problematic story is David's escape to the court of King Achish of Gath in 1 Samuel 21, after his relationship with Saul has broken down. Afraid of being recognised by Achish as a great warrior, he protects himself by feigning madness.[88] The Vulgate tells us that 'inmutavit os suum coram eis et conlabebatur inter manus eorum et inpingebat in ostia portae defluebanque salivae eius in barbam' ('he changed his countenance before them, and slipped down between their hands; and he stumbled against the doors of the gate, and his spittle ran down upon his beard'). The translator pays particular attention to the art of David's disguise: 'Hann breytir sem mest má hann sinni ásjónu ok torkennir sik, svá at hann kastar moldu í augu sér ok andlit, en þenr út hvarmana ok líkir sik gǫmlum karli. Hann hostar mjǫk ok hrækir í skegg sér' ('He changes his appearance as best he can and disguises himself in such a way that he smears dirt on his eyes and face and turns his eyelids inside out and makes himself look like an old man; he coughs repeatedly and spits into his beard').[89] The details about the dirt on his face, the turning inside out of his eyelids, the coughing, and the appearance of an 'old man' are all added to the Vulgate. Perhaps the translator is extrapolating from the biblical scene, but there is a close parallel in *Hallfreðar saga*, when Hallfreðr reluctantly sets out at Óláfr Tryggvason's command to convert the heathen Þorleifr to Christianity. In AM 61 fol., his disguise is described at length:[90]

---

86 *Stjórn*, 793–94; cf. 1 Sam 17.34.
87 *Stjórn*, 797.
88 Jan P. Fokkelman, *Narrative Art and Poetry in the Books of Samuel: A Full Interpretation Based on Stylistic and Structural Analyses* (Assen: Van Gorcum, 1986), 367–71.
89 *Stjórn*, 823; cf. 1 Sam 21.13.
90 *Hallfreðar saga*, in *Vatnsdæla saga*, 164. Cf. *Gísla saga*, 82–84, where Gísli, also

Hallfreðr tók sér stafkarls gervi ok lét breyta sem mest ásjónu sinni. Hann lét leggja lit í augu sér en sneri um hvǫrmunum ok lét ríða leiri ok kólum í andlit sér. Hann gerði sér mikit skegg ok lét þat lima við hǫku sér ok kjálka. Var hann þá með ǫllu ókenniligr ok gamaligr.

Hallfreðr wore the clothes of a beggar and changed his countenance as much as he could. He put colour on his eyes and turned his eyelids inside out, and smeared mud and coal on his face. He made himself a big beard and glued it to his chin and jaw; he was in every respect unrecognisable and old-looking.

He acts like an old man too: 'fór hann heldr seint ok stumraði mjǫk, hafði karl þrǫngð mikla ok hrækti mjǫk í skeggit' ('he walked rather slowly and stumbled greatly; the old man was short of breath and spat repeatedly into his beard').[91] The verbal echoes here seem too extensive to be coincidental, especially the detail about turning one's eyelids inside out. Although either text might theoretically have influenced the other, what the two have in common is precisely what the translator has added to the Vulgate: the attempt to 'colour' the face with dirt, the turning inside out of the eyelids, the spitting into the beard, and the appearance of an old man or 'karl'. This suggests that *Stjórn III* is borrowing from the saga, and this impression is reinforced by the fact that disguise, poor eyesight, and old age are traits associated with the god Óðinn in Old Norse literature: in *Hallfreðar saga*, Hallfreðr's disguise makes perfect sense in view of his past devotion to Óðinn, and his continuing ambivalence towards Christianity.[92] Transferring these traits to David, if it is deliberate, is an interesting touch on the part of the translator: it suggests that David's behaviour is also ambivalent, more what one might expect of an Odinic hero than of a type of Christ. To an audience familiar with the sagas, it signals that David is more complex and less ideal a character than one might initially have thought.

We see David at his least ideal and most ambivalent in the scene where he has Uriah killed to cover up his adultery with Bathsheba (2 Samuel 11). Here his disguise is verbal. He orders Joab to put Uriah in the forefront of the fighting and arrange it 'svá til, at víst sé at hann komisk eigi með lífi á brott' ('in such a way that it is certain he will not get away alive').[93] This is slightly less shocking than the Latin, which has 'leave ye him there, that he may be wounded and die'. However, the Old Norse is much more forthcoming on Uriah's heroic defence: while the Vulgate has simply 'Urias the Hethite was

---

on the run, successfully acts as if he were mad in order to avoid pursuit by his enemies.

[91] *Hallfreðar saga*, 69.

[92] Cf. *Vǫlsunga saga*, 4, 20, 78.

[93] *Stjórn*, 916; 2 Sam. 11.15.

The Old Testament in Medieval Icelandic Texts

killed', the Old Norse adds that he 'lét sitt líf með hreysti ok góðum orðstír' ('lost his life with bravery and good renown').[94] Likewise, when Joab reports back to David, where the Vulgate says simply that Uriah is 'dead', the Old Norse tells us that the men fought 'fulldrengiliga' ('very bravely') and that Uriah was 'reyndr at allri dygð ok drengskap' ('proven in all virtue and bravery').[95] David responds to this message with a proverb: 'Opt kann þat henda sem mælt er at fall er farar heill' ('It can often happen, as it is said, that a fall is a good omen'). This is linked with a particular story in Old Norse-Icelandic tradition: the fall of Haraldr Sigurðarson from his horse as he prepares for the battle of Stamford Bridge.[96] It is double-edged: as Harold Godwineson more accurately sees, Haraldr's fall is a 'good omen' not for Haraldr but for him. The doubleness of the proverb – the ambivalence as to whom the 'good omen' applies – is mirrored by the doubleness with which David uses it in *Stjórn III*: under the guise of encouraging his disspirited men, he passes off an intentional strategy as a temporary misfortune, and covers up his murder by construing Uriah's fall as an sign of future luck. However, as for Haraldr, the opposite proves true: Uriah's murder will be punished by conflict within David's family, culminating in the death of two of his sons.

These stories of feuding and revenge, treachery and betrayal, are among the best in *Stjórn III*. They cluster particularly around Joab and the struggle for power at David's court. The death of Abner (2 Samuel 3) is a good example. In an earlier chapter, Abner has unwillingly killed Joab's brother Asael, knowing that to do so was effectively a death sentence. Later, however, he makes peace with David in Joab's absence. When Joab finds out, he goes straight to David to accuse Abner of spying. In the Vulgate, this scene consists purely of Joab's speech which begins: 'ingressus est Ioab ad regem et ait quid fecisti ecce venit Abner ad te quare dimisisti eum et abiit et recessit' ('And Joab went into the king and said: 'What has thou done? Behold Abner came to thee: Why didst thou send him away and he is gone and departed').[97] The translator appears to understand intuitively what is missing here, pointing out both that Joab has failed to greet David, and that David does not respond to his speech: 'ok kvaddi hann ekki nema með reiði ok ásakanarorðum' ('and did not greet him except with anger and words of blame'); 'Konungr svaraði ǫngu' ('The king gave no answer').[98] This is a

---

94 *Stjórn*, 917; 2 Sam 11.17 'et mortuus est etiam Urias Hetheus'.

95 *Stjórn*, 918; 2 Sam. 11.23–24 'servus tuus Urias Hetheus mortuus est'.

96 *Morkinskinna*, 2 vols, ed. Ármann Jakobsson and Þórður Ingi Guðjónsson (Reykjavík: Hið íslenzka fornritafélag, 2011), I, 314; *Fagrskinna*, 288; *Heimskringla*, III, 186.

97 *Stjórn*, 883; 2 Sam. 3.24.

98 Cf. Barbara Green, 'Joab's Coherence and Incoherence: Character and Characterization', in *Characters and Characterisation in the Book of Samuel*,

Heroes, Heroines and Royal Biography

silence that is strategic, leaving deliberately open what David wishes Joab to do. What happens next is told briefly in the Vulgate: 'cumque redisset Abner in Hebron seorsum abduxit eum Ioab ad medium portae ut loqueretur ei in dolo et percussit illum ibi in inguine et mortuus est in ultionum sanguinis Asahel fratris eius' ('And when Abner was returned to Hebron, Joab took him aside to the middle of the gate, to speak to him treacherously; and he stabbed him there in the groin, and he died in revenge for the blood of Asael his brother').[99] The Old Norse translator reimagines this:

> Sem Abner kom aptr í borgina, settisk hann niðr í einshverjum stað með sveit sína ok gekk eigi þegar inn fyrir konung, því at hann vissi sér engis ótta vánir. Þá gekk Joab at honum ok leiddi hann á eintal frá sínum mǫnnum í mitt hlið borgarinnar. Hann hafði brugðit sverð undir yfirhǫfninni, ok lagði í gegnum hann svá at hann féll jafn skjótt dauðr niðr á jǫrðina. Joab mælti við er hann lagði hann: 'Svá hefni ek Asael bróður míns'.

> When Abner returned to the town, he sat down in a certain place with his troop and did not go straight to the king, because he knew of no reason to be afraid. Then Joab went to him and led him away from his men for a private talk in the middle of the town gate. He had a drawn sword under his cloak and stabbed him with it so that he at once fell dead to the ground. Joab said as he stabbed him: 'Thus I avenge my brother Asahel'.

Abner's complete lack of suspicion – which might be considered naïve in the circumstances – draws him into fatal error, both in failing to seek out the king at once and in agreeing to a private talk. Whereas the Vulgate tells us directly that Joab's intentions are 'treacherous', the Old Norse relies on a visual signifier: the 'drawn sword' under his cloak. Most interesting is the way that the authorial comment ('he died in revenge for the blood of Asael his brother') has been put into the mouth of Joab himself, making it part of his revenge: Abner dies knowing that Joab has avenged his brother. The sword under the cloak recalls the killing of Eglon in Judges 3, but it is also strikingly like the scene where Áslákr kills Erlingr, the enemy of Óláfr Haraldsson, just after Óláfr has granted him quarters. Áslákr strikes Erlingr his death-blow with a 'handøxi er hann hafði undir yfirhǫfn sinni' ('a handaxe which he had under his cloak') and, like Joab, he makes sure that Erlingr knows why: 'Svá merkjum vér dróttins svíkaran' ('This is how we mark a betrayer

---

ed. Keith Bodner (London: T&T Clark, 2019), 188, who characterises Joab's discourse here as 'blunt, shorn of courtesy and honorific language typically used to address kings' and notes that 'David makes no reply to Joab's words, with the impact of his silence unclear'.

[99] 2 Sam. 3.27.

The Old Testament in Medieval Icelandic Texts

of his lord').[100] The two scenes are so alike in character and wording that it is difficult to tell whether the legendary saga has borrowed from 2 Samuel 3, whether *Stjórn III* has borrowed from the legendary saga, or whether each has influenced the other at some stage. Both writers are working with a shared understanding of the imperatives of revenge and the pragmatics of power.

The longest and most dramatic story of treachery and betrayal is that of David's own son, Absalom (2 Samuel 13–19). It begins with the rape of David's daughter Tamar by her half-brother Ammon, then the murder of Ammon by his half-brother Absalom, and finally Absalom's rebellion against his father, David's enforced flight, and Absalom's death in battle at the hands of Joab and his men. David finds himself in that most intolerable of situations in heroic legend: he is caught up in the midst of 'ættvíg' ('killings within the family'), where to avenge one son inevitably means to lose another.[101] The dramatic climax to this series of killings is the battle fought at the forest of Ephraim, in which Absalom's forces are defeated and he takes flight:[102]

> Absalon konungssonr reið einum múl um daginn, en svá bar til at allr herrinn dreifðisk frá honum, en hann hleypti hart um skóginn undan mǫnnum David konungs. En svá bar til, sem múllinn undir honum rann fram at einni eik mikilli ok margkvíslóttri, þá snart hǫfuð hans eikina ok brásk hárit um einn kvist svá at honum lypti upp ór sǫðlinum en múllinn rann fram undan honum ok hekk hann svá í loptinu.

> Absalom the king's son rode a mule during the day, but it came to pass that the whole army was scattered away from him, and he rode hard through the forest away from King David's men. And it came to pass that the mule beneath him ran under a big oak-tree with many branches, and his head touched the oak and his hair tangled around a branch so that it lifted him up out of the saddle, but the mule ran on from beneath him, and thus he was suspended in the air.

As Absalom hangs there, Joab thrusts three spears into his heart, before his soldiers finish him off.[103] It is difficult when reading this scene not to recall Óðinn hanging from the world-tree, especially since Odinic sacrifices are

---

100 *Óláfs saga hins helga*, ed. Oscar Albert Johnsen (Oslo: Dybwad, 1922), 66; cf. *Heimskringla*, II, 317, where the wording is not so close.

101 *Stjórn*, 936; cf. 2 Sam. 14.11, where 'ættvíg' translates the Vulgate 'proximi sanguinis' ('next of kin') and cf. *Heimskringa*, I, 31 'ættvíg skyldu ávalt vera í ætt þeira Ynglinga síðan' ('there should always be killings in the family among the descendants of the Ynglings from then on').

102 *Stjórn*, 962; 2 Sam. 18.9.

103 *Stjórn*, 963; 2 Sam. 18.14. Old Norse 'spjót' follows the Vulgate 'lanceas' ('spears'); the Hebrew is שְׁבָטִים ('sticks'), which are probably not meant to kill Absalom, but to wound him. See Alter, *Story of David*, 306.

Heroes, Heroines and Royal Biography

often marked by the combination of hanging and wounding by a spear.[104] One word in the Old Norse suggests that the translator may also have made this link. After Joab stabs Absalom in the Vulgate, we are told that 'palpitaret herens in quercu' ('he yet panted for life, sticking on the oak'). The Old Norse translates this: 'Absalon spornaði enn á eikinni' ('Absalom was still kicking on the tree').[105] The verb 'sporna' is an interesting one and relatively rare. The *Dictionary of Old Norse Prose* lists only one other occurrence in this sense: the death of Svanhildr, daughter of Sigurðr and Guðrún, who is trampled to death by horses at the command of Jǫrmunrekkr in another story about killings within the family.[106] However, it is also used in the idiom 'sporna gálga' ('to kick the gallows'), which may be what the translator is thinking of here; and the idiom 'sporna við' is used in the sense 'to struggle against' or 'to withstand', which may colour our sense of Absalom still struggling, despite everything, for his life. But 'sporna' has poetic uses that tie in more closely with mythology: in *Vǫluspá*, in the first battle between the Æsir and the Vanir, the Vanir are said to 'vǫllu sporna' ('kick the plains?'), while in *Oddrúnargrátr*, babies are said to 'moldveg sporna' ('kick the earth') when they are born.[107] Dronke has suggested that these two expressions are connected and that 'sporna' alludes to the Vanir's power of rebirth as fertility gods: as fast as the Æsir kill them, they are reborn again.[108] So, at the moment of Absalom's death, the translator evokes the mythic complex of death and rebirth, which is at the heart of the myth of Óðinn and Baldr. It is a complex that is beautifully and evocatively captured in the Old Norse version of David's lament for Absalom: 'hvat skyldi mér gǫmlum karli at lifa hrǫrnandi á hverjum degi, en þú, sonr minn, Absalom, skyldir deyja í blóma aldrs þíns' ('what good it is to me, an old man, to live wilting every day, while you, my son Absalom, must die in the bloom of your youth?').[109]

Despite the tragedy of David's personal life, he remains a successful military leader who treats his men well and, throughout his life, inspires loyalty and devotion in others. When Abiathar, the sole survivor of Saul's

---

[104] *Hávamál*, st. 138, in *Eddukvæði*, I, 138; *Hamðismál*, st. 17, in *Eddukvæði*, II, 410; *Gautreks saga*, in *Fornaldarsögur Norðurlanda*, III, 26–27.

[105] *Stjórn*, 963; 2 Sam. 18.14.

[106] *Vǫlsunga saga*, 76; *DONP*, s.v. 'sporna' at https://onp.ku.dk/onp/onp.php?o74579 (accessed 26 July 2023).

[107] *Vǫluspá*, st. 24, and *Oddrúnargrátr*, st. 8, in *Eddukvæði*, I, 297, II, 366.

[108] *The Poetic Edda, Vol. II Mythological Poems*, ed. Ursula Dronke (Oxford: Clarendon Press, 1997), 42–43.

[109] *Stjórn*, 966; this may be borrowed from *Konungs skuggsiá*, 115. It has no equivalent in the Vulgate, where David famously and poignantly laments: 'fili mi Absalom, fili mi Absalom quis mihi tribuat ut ego moriar pro te Absalom fili mi fili mi' ('My son Absalom, Absalom my son: would to God that I might die for thee, Absalom my son, my son, Absalom').

The Old Testament in Medieval Icelandic Texts

massacre at Noe, comes to the young David, David promises him that 'eitt skal yfir okkr ganga báða' ('one fate will befall us both').[110] This is what Kolbeinn promises Kári in *Njáls saga*, and what Bjǫrn tells his friend Þórólfr in *Egils saga*: it places David within a familiar heroic context of male bonds of friendship and love.[111] Much later, when David goes into exile, he urges the foreigner Ethai to turn back, wishing to spare him from trouble. Ethai refuses: 'Ek þræll þinn skal þar vera sem þú ert ok þér fylgja, minn herra, hvárt sem þú ert lífs eðr dauðr, ok engum ǫðrum konungi þjóna undir heimsólu' ('I your servant shall be where you are and follow you, my lord, whether you are alive or dead, and serve no other king under the sun').[112] The first part of this (which translates the Vulgate's 'in morte sive in vita') recalls Þormóðr *Kolbrúnarskáld*'s desire not to be separated from Óláfr Haraldsson 'lífs né dauðr' ('alive or dead'), but the expression 'undir heimsólu' ('under the world's sun') has been added by the translator.[113] It is rare and learned, perhaps imitating the skaldic idiom 'und sólu' ('under the sun') or 'und veg sólar' ('beneath the path of the sun') in poetry about the fame of kings:[114]

> Skjǫldungr mun þér annarr aldri
> œðri gramr und sólu fœðask.

King, another lord loftier than you will never be born under the sun.

This skaldic lexis may have been suggested to the translator by the traditional heroic sentiment of following one's lord in life or death: as Arnórr says elsewhere, 'gott's fylgja vel dróttni' ('it is good to follow one's lord loyally').[115] The most closely related use of *heimssól* is in *Hulda-Hrokkinskinna*, where the poet Arnórr gives a summary of one of his verses about Haraldr Sigurðarson: 'Arnórr kallar sér óvíst at nǫkkurr konungr undir heimssólu muni með slíkri hugprýði ok hreysti barizk hafa' ('Arnórr says he's not sure whether any king under the sun would have fought with such pride and courage').[116] David's followers relate to him as a retainer to his lord. Finally, when David returns to Jerusalem after Absalom's death, he asks his faithful servant Barzillai to come with him. Barzillai asks to be spared,

---

110 *Stjórn*, 828; cf. 1 Sam. 22.23, where there is no equivalent.

111 *Brennu-Njáls saga*, 437; *Egils saga*, 49.

112 *Stjórn*, 945; cf. 2 Sam. 15.21.

113 *Heimskringla*, II, 362.

114 Arnórr jarlaskáld Þórðarson, 'Hrynhenda, Magnúsdrápa 20', ed. Diana Whaley, in *Poetry from the Kings' Sagas 2: From c. 1035 to c. 1300*, ed. Kari Ellen Gade (Turnhout: Brepols, 2009), 206.

115 Arnórr, 'Lausavísa 1', 280.

116 *DONP*, s.v. *heimssól* at https://onp.ku.dk/onp/onp.php?o32841 (accessed 4 August 2022); cf. Arnórr, 'Haraldsdrápa', 276.

Heroes, Heroines and Royal Biography

saying: 'falls er ván at fornu tré' ('an aged tree can be expected to fall').[117] Perhaps Barzillai speaks only of himself, but it seems at least possible that the old tree about to fall is David, who is reaching the end of his life. The young man who tore apart lions in his youth has become the old man who must be kept away from battles, because he is a liability rather than an asset: 'oss þykkir alls gætt ef þín er' ('we think all is well if you are'), his men tell him.[118] In the final stages of his life, he is an old man who lies helpless in bed and cannot keep himself warm, just as Egill at the end of his saga cannot keep his feet warm.

The story of David gives a remarkable sense of the span of a whole life, from the young man who wrestled with lions and bears to the elderly king who lies impotent in bed while his sons engage in a bloody struggle for the succession. The translator responds to this account of a life in which the personal and political are inextricably linked on multiple levels, seeing in David a heroic leader, a flawed king, and a bereaved father: a figure who can be readily understood through the lens of saga literature with its keen interest in complex character and the interplay between heroic values and political power. Although the end of the saga reminds us that David is a 'figure' of Christ, the focus throughout is on the human dimension of his story: the dense web of family feuding and political compromise beneath which divine providence can be difficult to locate.

Kings and Skaldic Verse

As we move into the two books of Kings, the long narrative sequences of David's saga are replaced with sequences of regnal reports on the kings of Judah and Israel. While the translator continues to retell and rearrange the narrative, adding familiar idioms and phrases, there is less opportunity for saga-length stories, although there are some fabulous set-pieces, including the defeat of Ahab (1 Kings 22.29–36) – who fights all day standing in his chariot while mortally wounded – and the reign of Queen Athaliah (2 Kings 11), the evil step-mother *par excellence*.[119] While battles, treachery and plots are always vividly depicted, elsewhere the translator has more trouble. The description of Solomon's palace and temple in 1 Kings 7 is a real challenge, and the translator comments: 'þetta hús var smiðat með meira vitrleik ok vísdóm margháttaðra lista ok háleitum hagleik, segir sá er sǫgunni hefir snúit til sinnar tungu af latínu, en mín fáfrœði kunni skilja eðr skýra' ('this house was built with more knowledge and wisdom of multiple skills and

---

[117] *Stjórn*, 973; 2 Sam. 19.37.

[118] *Stjórn*, 959, 984; cf. 2 Sam. 18.3, 21.17; in both verses, it is an addition. See also Epilogue, p. 255.

[119] *Stjórn*, 1113–14, 1168–71.

The Old Testament in Medieval Icelandic Texts

sublime workmanship, says the one who turned the saga from Latin into his own language, than my ignorance can understand or explain').[120] This sounds like a modesty topos, but disguises genuine bafflement over how to describe the master-craftsman's work: the translator leaves out verses 3–12, 16–22 (avoiding 'nets of chequer work', 'lattice-work', 'pomegranates' and 'lily work'), 24–38 ('wreaths of bevelled work'), and 40–47 ('the cords of the chapiters'). When he comes to translate verse 50, he runs into trouble again, being confronted with: 'forcipes aureos, et hydrias, et fuscinulas, et fialias, et mortariola, et turibula' ('golden snuffers, and pots, and flesh-hooks, and bowls, and mortars and censers'). He renders this: 'reykelsisker af hreinu gulli ok mart annat miklu fleira en ek kunni greina gerði Hyram af gulli *in templo domini* til þjónustu' ('Hiram made censers out of pure gold, and much else, far more than I am able to describe, out of gold for service in the temple of the Lord').[121] He is at his most disarmingly honest, though, in 2 Kings 4, when Elisha's servant goes out and gathers 'wild gourds of the field' ('colocyntidas agri'). The translator writes: 'þar af las hann sem hann mátti mest hafa í mǫtli sínum, þat veit ek eigi hvat þat heitir, þat var því líkast vaxit sem akrdái' ('from there he gathered as much as he could in his cloak – I don't know what it's called but it was most likely something like *akrdái*').[122] The term *akrdái* may be related to New Norwegian *då* ('hemp nettle'; modern Icelandic *hjálmgras*), but 'akr' simply copies the Vulgate's 'agri'. One gets a good sense from passages like this of the limits of the translator's capacity.

The *tour de force* of these two books, though, is the scene in 2 Kings 3 in which the kings of Israel and Judah set out to fight the Moabites. Here the translator draws not only on the style of the sagas, but also on the style and diction of skaldic poetry. Stranded in the wilderness, the two kings take the prophet Elisha's advice to dig channels, which are miraculously filled with water: 'þetta fór svá at um morgininn árla dundu vǫtn svá at drjúgum flaut ǫll jǫrð af' ('it came to pass that early in the morning, waters gushed forth so that almost the whole land was flowing with them').[123] As the sun rises, the water shines red like blood, tricking the Moabites into believing that their enemies have slaughtered each other:[124]

---

[120] *Stjórn*, 1025.

[121] *Stjórn*, 1026.

[122] *Stjórn*, 1138; cf. 2 Kgs 4.39.

[123] *Stjórn*, 1130; 2 Kgs 3.20.

[124] *Stjórn*, 1130–31; 2 Kgs 3.22–23 'primoque mane surgentes et orto iam sole ex adverso aquarum viderunt Moabitae contra aquas rubras quasi sanguinem dixeruntque sanguis est gladii pugnaverunt reges contra se et caesi sunt mutuo' ('And they rose early in the morning, and the sun being now up, and shining upon the water, the Moabites saw the waters over against them red, like blood, and they said: It is the blood of the sword; the kings have fought among themselves and they have killed one another').

Heroes, Heroines and Royal Biography

þat var snimma um morgininn, er Moabite váru klæddir, at vǫtn flutu um alla vǫllu. Þá rann sól upp ok skein í vǫtnin ok sýndusk þeim mjǫk rauð vǫtnin er þeir áttu at sjá við morginskininu. Þeir mæltu þá sín í milli: 'þetta er eigi vatn, heldr blóð er hér rennr. Nú munu konungar þessir hafa barizk ok drepizk niðr ok er þetta þeira sára lǫgr er hér rennr um vǫlluna'.

It was early in the morning, when the Moabites were armed, that water flowed over all the plains. Then the sun rose and shone on the waters and the waters that they could see in the light of the morning seemed very red to them. They said to each other: 'This isn't water but blood flowing here. These kings must have fought and killed each other, and it is the sea of their wounds which flows over the plain'.

However, when they enter the camp to plunder, they are surprised by the Israelites, who attack them and slaughter them like cattle. The translator enjoys the irony of this turn-around, commenting: 'varð þar ǫðruvís en þeir ætluðu; átti þeir heldr vápnum at mœta en val at ræna' ('It did not go as they had expected; they had weapons to meet rather than corpses to rob').[125] The result is the wholesale destruction of the area: 'þar váru nú margstaðar eptir grýttar grundir sem áðr hǫfðu verit eng ok akrar inir beztu' ('there were now stony slopes in many places where there had previously been pastures and the best fields').[126]

Clearly this scene appealed to the translator, and it is not difficult to see why, given the striking visual image of the water shining red as blood in the glow of the early morning sun – blood which the Moabites assume is the Israelites' but which, in a cruel twist of fate, turns out to presage their own. But what is interesting is how the translator reads this scene through the lens of skaldic poetry. The Moabites describe the reddened water as 'sára lǫgr' ('a sea of wounds'), a skaldic kenning for 'blood' that is not otherwise found in prose. It may have been inspired, though, by the Vulgate's 'blood of the sword', which sounds strikingly skaldic, although it is probably a misreading of the Hebrew text, which simply has: 'This is blood'.[127] There is only one other occurrence of exactly this kenning, in the twelfth-century poem *Líknarbraut*, where it refers to the blood of the Lamb of God; but there are many other kennings for

---

[125] *Stjórn*, 1131; this is an addition to 2 Kgs 3.24.

[126] This is an addition to 2 Kgs 3.25.

[127] 2 Kgs 3.23. The Hebrew has: דָּם זֶה הָחֳרֵב נֶחֶרְבוּ הַמְּלָכִים, which is usually translated as something like 'This is blood; the kings must have fought together' (NRSV). Jerome's 'sanguis gladii' follows the Septuagint reading αἷμα τοῦτο τῆς ῥομφαίας ('this is blood of the sword'). This is not impossible as a translation of the unpointed Hebrew text, but it is much more plausible that הָחֳרֵב is an infinitive absolute of the verb חרב (niphal: 'smite, attack') rather than the noun חֶרֶב ('sword'). With thanks to Hywel Clifford for advice on this passage.

241

The Old Testament in Medieval Icelandic Texts

'blood' that use the same model of a base-word for sea and a qualifying word referring to wounds: 'benja lǫgr' ('sea of wounds'), 'hrælǫgr' ('corpse-sea'), 'sǫgn sára' ('fjord of wounds'), 'sárfljóð' ('wound-flood'), and so on.[128] In Eyvindr *skáldaspillir*'s *Hákonarmál*, Eyvindr describes how:[129]

> Svarraði sárgymir   á sverða nesi
> fell flóð fleina   í fjǫru Storðar

The wound-sea [BLOOD] roared on the headland of swords [SHIELD], the flood of barbs [BLOOD] fell on the shore of Stord.

This creates, in the midst of battle, a seascape where waves crash against the exposed headlands, except the incoming tide is a tide of blood battering against men's shields. Likewise, in *Hákonarkviða*, Sturla Þórðarson writes that:[130]

> Þar baugsegl
> í brimis vindi
> branda byrr
> blása knátti,
> en hrælǫgr
> af hjarar borðum
> geiguligr
> glymjandi fell

There the fair breeze of swords [BATTLE] blew at shield-boss sails [SHIELDS] in the wind of the sword [BATTLE], and the frightful corpse-sea [BLOOD] fell foaming from the planks of the swords [SHIELDS].

Again, battle is reimagined as the sails of a fleet setting out in a 'fair breeze' ('byrr') only for this to turn to nightmare as the sea resounding against the sides of the ship turns out to be a sea of blood from the corpses of the fallen. The use of the kenning in *Stjórn III* is particularly clever in that it relies on familiarity with this type of kenning to make it work in the opposite direction:

---

128   'Líknarbraut', ed. George S. Tate, in *Poetry on Christian Subjects: 1. The Twelfth and Thirteenth Centuries*, ed. Margaret Clunies Ross (Turnhout: Brepols, 2007), 271–73; Einarr Skúlason, 'Eysteinsdrápa' and 'Sigurðardrápa II', ed. Kari Ellen Gade, *Poetry from the Kings' Sagas 2*, 550–51, 559–60; Arnórr, 'Hrynhenda, Magnússdrápa', 200–01; Snorri Sturluson, *Háttatal*, ed. Kari Ellen Gade, in *Poetry from Treatises on Poetics*, ed. Kari Ellen Gade and Edith Marold (Turnhout: Brepols, 2017), 1169.

129   Eyvindr skáldaspillir Finsson, 'Hákonarmál', ed. R. D. Fulk, in *Poetry from the Kings' Sagas 1: From Mythical Times to c. 1035*, ed. Diana Whaley (Turnhout: Brepols, 2012), 181.

130   Sturla Þórðarson, 'Hákonarkviða', in *Poetry from the Kings' Sagas 2*, 713–14.

Heroes, Heroines and Royal Biography

the Moabites think that they see a 'sea of wounds' – a metaphor in which blood is likened to water – but in fact they just see water.

The translator has chosen this kenning carefully to underline the irony of the Moabites' mistake, but the connection to skaldic poetry has coloured other aspects of the translation as well. In the skaldic conceit of sea as blood, the noise of battle is often evoked as the roar of the ocean, as in the verbs 'svarra' ('to roar') in *Hákonarmál* and 'glymja' ('to resound') in *Hákonarkviða*. Elsewhere, this noise of waves/battle is captured in the term 'dynr', as in the kenning 'sára dynbára' ('the resounding wave of wounds') in Þormóðr Trefilsson's *Hrafnsmál* or 'hræs dynbrunnar' ('resounding fountains of corpse') in Snorri Sturluson's *Háttatal*.[131] It is notable, then, that while the Vulgate speaks of the channel being filled ('replebitur') with water or water coming ('veniebant') by way of Edom, the Old Norse translation uses the verb 'dynja' ('to resound, gush') –'mun þó vatn dynja um farveg þenna' ('water will resound/gush along this channel'), 'um morgininn árla dundu vǫtn' ('early in the morning waters resounded/gushed'). It prefigures the noise of the battle in which the Moabites will be killed. In addition, the translator makes frequent use of rhyme and alliteration in this passage: the Moabites gather 'þegn ok þræl' ('thane and thrall'), all who 'vápnum mátti valda' ('could wield weapons'), and they find 'vápnum at mœta en val at ræna' ('weapons to meet rather than dead bodies to rob'), which combines alliteration and rhyme. Meanwhile, the Israelites 'hjuggu þá niðr sem naut er næstir þeim váru' ('struck down like cattle those who were nearest') and 'brutu borgir ok brendu herbergi' ('broke cities and burned dwellings'), 'eyddu akra ok aldinskóga' ('laid waste fields and orchards'), leaving stony slopes 'sem áðr hǫfðu verit eng ok akrar' ('where there was previously pasture and fields'). All these phrases use threefold patterns of alliteration not unlike the three alliterating syllables one finds across two lines of skaldic verse. Working from the single image of blood-red water, captured in the kenning 'sára lǫgr', the translator has infused the whole of the biblical scene with the texture of skaldic verse.

Conclusion

Stjórn III is a remarkable translation that reimagines the historical books of the Hebrew Bible/Old Testament in the style and idiom of the Icelandic sagas. Whereas the compiler of *Stjórn I* was primarily concerned with providing full and accurate glosses, the translator of *Stjórn III* was more interested in narrative coherence: rather than interpolate information from elsewhere,

---

[131] Þormóðr Trefilsson, 'Hrafnsmál', in *Den Norsk-Islandske Skjaldedigtning,* ed. Finnur Jonsson (Copenhagen: Nordisk Forlag, 1912), B. I, 196; Snorri Sturluson, *Háttatal*, ed. Gade, 1139.

The Old Testament in Medieval Icelandic Texts

he fills in the gaps and imagines the details, shaping his material into scenes his audience would recognise. He not only perceived the likeness of biblical stories to the Icelandic sagas, but developed this further, though idiomatic language, careful stylistic choices and, in places, through direct loans. There is a particularly close link to early sagas about Óláfr Tryggvason and Óláfr Haraldsson, and the early compilations of kings' sagas in Old Norse-Icelandic may have provided an impetus for the translation of precisely these biblical books. It is not implausible that, as Kleivane has suggested, the title 'Stjórn' may originally have applied to this part of the translation, characterising its interest in leadership and the use and preservation of political power. There are also, however, links to early sagas of Icelanders including *Egils saga Skalla-Grímssonar*, *Gísla saga*, *Hallfreðar saga* and *Laxdœla saga*, and it may be relevant that these sagas are connected to the west of Iceland and are attested in manuscripts from Helgafell, where one of the main manuscripts of *Stjórn* was produced. For the Icelandic translator, Samson and David provided familiar and well-loved models of male heroism: the outlaw-poet whose downfall is a woman, and the charismatic leader dogged by problems at home. The book of Ruth, on the other hand, offered something new and different – a vision of history through the eyes of women. From proverbial diction to poetic conceit, the translator makes use of a vernacular tradition of storytelling in order to render his translation idiomatic, vivid and gripping. This rich and artful retelling of Judges–2 Kings deserves to be much better known.

EPILOGUE: BIBLICAL LITERATURE
AND SAGA LITERATURE

Medieval Icelanders drew richly on their own storytelling tradition when translating stories from the Old Testament, and this was facilitated by the significant overlap between biblical stories and sagas. The translator of *Stjórn III* might even be thought of as a saga author in his own right, recreating the world of the Hebrew Bible/Old Testament in the style of an Icelandic saga. But what can be said about the opposite scenario: it is possible that any of the Icelandic sagas were influenced by the Hebrew Bible/Old Testament? Although the translations into Old Norse-Icelandic are relatively late, stories from the Old Testament must have circulated early in order for some of the allusive references in the Old Icelandic Homily Book to make sense. Most monastery and cathedral libraries would have had copies of the Pentateuch with Joshua and Judges and the *Libri regnum*, so those well versed in Latin could have read the historical books of the Old Testament, especially in Augustinian monasteries that followed the educational programme recommended by Hugh of St Victor. Any Icelanders who studied abroad after 1215 would also know Comestor's *Historia scholastica*, since this was prescribed reading for the first year of university study.

Although there is no overview of material in the sagas borrowed from the Bible, a number of individual studies have found possible loans in *Sverris saga*, Oddr's *Óláfs saga Tryggvasonar*, *Hrafnkels saga*, *Egils saga Skalla-Grímssonar*, *Eyrbyggja saga*, *Laxdœla saga*, *Njáls saga*, *Flóamanna saga*, *Bárðar saga Snæfellsáss* and *Yngvars saga viðfǫrla*.[1] Some of these are New

---

[1] Lars Lönnroth, 'Sverrir's Dreams', *Scripta Islandica* 57 (2006), 97–110; Hermann Pálsson, *Art and Ethics in Hrafnkel's Saga* (Copenhagen: Munksgaard, 1971); Torfi Tulinius, *The Enigma of Egill: the Saga, the Viking Poet, and Snorri Sturluson*, trans. Victoria Cribb (Ithaca, NY: Cornell University Press, 2014); Kevin Wanner, 'Purity and Danger: Excrement, Blood, Sacred Space and Society in *Eyrbyggja saga*', *Viking and Medieval Scandinavia* 5 (2009), 213–50; Grønlie, 'Hagar and Ishmael'; Andrew Hamer, *Njáls saga and its Christian Background: A Study of Narrative Method* (Leuven: Peters, 2014); Richard Perkins, 'An Edition of *Flóamanna saga* with a Study of its Sources and Analogues', PhD

The Old Testament in Medieval Icelandic Texts

Testament loans: the nativity and the transfiguration in Oddr's *Óláfs saga Tryggvasonar* or the temptation of Christ in *Flóamanna saga*.[2] These are easily visible, and there can be little doubt that they are borrowed, since they stand out in the saga world. The same cannot be said for borrowings from the Old Testament. While *Sverris saga* and Oddr's *Óláfs saga Tryggvasonar*, both written at the Benedictine monastery of Þingeyrar, make direct references to biblical characters or verses, this is not the case in the sagas of Icelanders and most of the possible loans could be disputed.[3] Many would question Torfi Tulinius's typological interpretation of *Egils saga* – ingenious and insightful though it is – and Hermann Pálsson's moralised reading of *Hrafnkels saga*.[4] Others are cautious about claiming direct influence. In an excellent article on *Eyrbyggja saga* and the purity laws in the Pentateuch, Wanner stops short of claiming that the numerous parallels 'demonstrate influence of the Bible', suggesting merely that there is 'no reason to think such influence impossible'.[5] Cole, in a fascinating article on the influence of the Joseph and Asenath story, is wary of suggesting that Snorri Sturluson might have been able to read it in Latin, although he does point out that Snorri moved in a learned, Latinate milieu.[6]

My contention is that these Old Testament loans are difficult to spot not because they are any rarer than other types of loan, but because the closeness of the two storytelling traditions renders them effectively invisible. The problem with readings like those of Hermann Pálsson and Torfi Tulinius is not the fact of borrowing itself, but the typological or moralistic meaning attached to it. It is entirely plausible to posit a parallel with King David when Egill grieves the deaths of his two sons or pays poetic tribute to his close friend Arnkell, especially given the popularity of Carolingian complaints voicing David's losses.[7] It seems likely, too, that an educated audience might have thought of

---

thesis, Oxford University, 1972; Annette Lassen, 'The Old Norse Contextuality of *Bárðar saga Snæfellsáss*: A Synoptic Reading with *Óláfs saga Tryggvasonar*', in *Folklore in Old Norse – Old Norse in Folklore*, ed. Daniel Sävborg and Karen Bek-Pedersen (Tartu: University Press of Tartu, 2014), 102–19; Cole, 'Echoes of the Book of Joseph and Asenath'.

2   Oddr Snorrason, *Óláfs saga Tryggvasonar*, 131, 267–69; *Flóamanna saga*, in *Harðar saga*, 278–79.

3   *Sverris saga*, ed. Þorleifur Hauksson (Reykjavík: Hið íslenzka fornritafélag, 2007), 17, 152; Oddr Snorrason, *Óláfs saga Tryggvasonar*, 147, 252.

4   See, for example, Wellendorf, 'Ecclesiastical Literature', 52–53 and references in n. 940.

5   Wanner, 'Purity and Danger', 239.

6   Cole, 'Joseph and Asenath', 28–29.

7   See Janthia Yearley, 'A Bibliography of *Planctus* in Latin, Provencal, French, German, English, Italian, Catalan and Galician-Portuguese from the Time of Bede to the Early Fifteenth Century', *Journal of the Plainsong and Mediaeval*

Epilogue

the aged David when Egill, at the end of his life, complains about the coldness of his feet.[8] What is unlikely is that the saga author is trying to make Egill into a type of Christ. Like the translator of *Stjórn III*, he is not thinking allegorically: his interest is in complex character, of which David is a notable example. Some recent studies may support the idea that the primary function of Old Testament loans in the sagas is not typological. While Wanner acknowledges the possibility of reading *Eyrbyggja saga* 'typologically', he prefers the suggestion that loans from the Bible made the pagan past seem 'less foreign to the sagas producers and audience than might be assumed to have been the case'.[9] Cole argues that, while *Yngvars saga* takes the themes of the Joseph and Asenath story seriously, this is not the case in *Kormáks saga* and *Snorra Edda*, where the borrowed motifs 'appear to be chosen more for their aesthetic appeal than their typological appropriateness'.[10] In my own study of the story of Hagar and Ishmael, I found that it was the power of Hagar's story as story – the themes of childbearing and social status, jealousy and competition – that sparked the interest of the saga authors.[11] The Old Testament lends to the sagas as one story-telling tradition to another, because of a shared interest in character, motivation and narrative art.

A full discussion of biblical influence on the Icelandic sagas is beyond the scope of this book. However, in what follows, I want to explore just three cases where loans from the Old Testament – including its glosses – may have been overlooked. The sagas in question are deliberately taken from different stages in the saga's development and different areas of the country. They are: Oddr's *Ólafs saga Tryggvasonar*, first written in Latin at the monastery of Þingeyrar in c. 1190 and translated into Old Norse before c. 1220; *Gísla saga Súrssonar*, which is roughly dated to c. 1225–50 and is set in the west of Iceland; and, finally, *Hrafnkels saga*, set in the east of Iceland and written c. 1300.[12]

Oddr's *Ólafs saga Tryggvasonar* is, as Wellendorf has put it, 'crown witness' for the influence of learned literature on the sagas and, given that it was first written in Latin by a Benedictine monk, there is no particular reason to doubt that Oddr was familiar with the Latin Vulgate and possibly commentary on it.[13] He refers directly to Genesis 41, Psalm 7, John 3.30, and 1 Peter 2.17

 Music Society 4 (1981), 17; for Abelard's *Planctus David*, see Peter Dronke, *Poetic Individuality in the Middle Ages: New Departures in Poetry* (Oxford: Clarendon, 1970), 203–09.

8 1 Kings 1.1; *Egils saga*, 179–80.

9 Wanner, 'Purity and Danger', 240.

10 Cole, 'Joseph and Asenath', 27.

11 Grønlie, 'Hagar and Ishmael', 45.

12 Oddr Snorrason, *Ólafs saga Tryggvasonar*, clxxxiii–iv; *Gísla saga*, xxxix–xli; *Hrafnkels saga*, lvi.

13 Wellendorf, 'Ecclesiastical Literature', 51.

The Old Testament in Medieval Icelandic Texts

as well as events in the life of Christ. The episode that interests me, though, is the account of Óláfr's childhood in Garðaríki and particularly his marriage to Geira. Andersson has suggested that this episode is based on the story of Dido and Aeneas,[14] but a closer parallel can be found in the story of Moses and Tharbis; in fact, the extra-biblical material about Moses's childhood found in Josephus's *Antiquitates* may provide a model for much of this part of the saga.[15] In both, women play the leading roles: Queen Allogia is deeply impressed by Óláfr's wisdom and beauty and treats him 'sem eiginligan sinn son' ('as her own son'), just as Pharaoh's daughter Thermutis is struck by Moses's beauty and 'sibi filium adoptauit' ('adopted him as her son').[16] Valdamarr soon appoints Óláfr as a chieftain of his court and 'at stjórna hermǫnnum' ('to lead warriors'), while Moses is appointed 'dux' ('leader') of the Egyptian army.[17] Both are successful in military operations on behalf of the king, until they are arrested by the love of a woman. Tharbis sees Moses in action and realises that he is behind the Egyptians' unexpected success; she falls 'crudeliter' ('cruelly') in love and sends her faithful servant to fetch him.[18] This servant seems to be the inspiration for Geira's servant Dixin, who goes between Óláfr and Geira, and convinces them that the marriage is 'girniligt' ('desirable').[19] Oddr tells us that 'er hann hafði þessi orðasáði sáit í brjóst þeim, þá tók þat at rœtask ok festask með þeim báðum' ('when he had sown the seed of his words in their breasts, it began to take root and to establish itself in them both'). This looks like an elaboration of the Latin 'effectus uerba praeuenit' ('the effect came before/anticipated the words' or 'the words took immediate effect'). According to Josephus, Moses simply departs once the marriage is consummated, and he has successfully completed his military expedition.[20] Óláfr carries out various military expeditions on behalf of Geira and leaves only after her death in order to distract himself from grief.

There are a number of other parallels as well, which might have been verbal echoes in the Latin. Two prophecies tell of Moses's birth and arrival in

14 Oddr Snorrason *The Saga of Olaf Tryggvason*, trans. Theodore Andersson (Ithaca, NY: Cornell University Press, 2018), 14–15.

15 Josephus's *Antiquitates* was translated into Latin in the sixth century, but it is not clear that his work was known in Iceland directly. However, much of the material on Moses's childhood is also in the *Glossa ordinaria* and in Comestor's *Historia scholastica*.

16 Oddr Snorrason, *Óláfs saga Tryggvasonar*, 151; Josephus, *Antiquitates*, II.ix.7.

17 Oddr Snorrason, *Óláfs saga Tryggvasonar*, 152; Josephus, *Antiquitates*, II.x.2.

18 Josephus, *Antiquitates*, II.x.2.

19 Oddr Snorrason, *Óláfs saga Tryggvasonar*, 157. Ólafur Halldórsson suggests that this name is invented, but it is (like Alvini) English, which may suggest that Oddr got this story from an English intermediary.

20 Comestor, *Exodus*, c. 6 (PL 198, 1144D) has a different ending, involving magic rings. See p. 206.

Epilogue

Egypt and his future glory ('gloriam in perpetuum' – 'glory in perpetuity').[21] Two prophecies tell of Óláfr's birth and arrival in Garðaríki and his future glory ('miklu meiri dýrð en ek kunna um at tala' – 'much more glory than I can say').[22] It is interesting to note that the prophecies about Óláfr stress that he will bring no harm ('skaða') to the kingdom, almost as if they are resisting the pull of the Latin source in which Moses will bring about the 'humiliation' of the Egyptians and the 'increase' of the Israelites. Thermutis describes Moses to her father as having 'forma diuina, et prudentia ualde fortissimum' ('a divine form and very great wisdom'), while Dixin tells Geira that Óláfr is 'umfram mannligan hátt ok øðli' ('beyond human manner and nature') and has 'vit mikit ok ágæta speki' ('great intelligence and excellent wisdom').[23] Both emphasise the extraordinary effect of the hero's appearance. In Josephus, Moses is eventually driven from the Egyptian court by hatred ('odium') and envy ('invidia'), while Óláfr departs with his army 'fyrir ǫfund margra gǫfugra manna' ('because of the envy of many noble men').[24] It is difficult, between languages, to be sure about verbal echoes, but one guesses that these would have been more evident in the Latin. If Cole is right that the monks at Þingeyrar also had the story of Joseph and Asenath to hand, then there is good evidence for a strong interest in and knowledge of extra-biblical stories in the north of Iceland by c. 1200.[25]

What is striking, though, is that, although this story was interpreted allegorically in the Middle Ages, there is no sign of this in Oddr's rendition, even though a parallel between Moses and Óláfr would contribute to the idea of Óláfr as a type of Christ. Rather, Oddr seems interested in the potential of the story to establish Óláfr as a young warrior of great promise, a future leader, and a passionate (if perhaps rash) lover. The only hint of an allegorical interpretation relates to the rejection of idolatry. In Josephus, Pharaoh places a crown on the young Moses's head, which he dashes to the floor, a symbol of how he will crush the Egyptians.[26] In the Gloss and in the *Historia scholastica*, it is interpreted as a rejection of idolatry.[27] One wonders whether it lies behind the scene in Oddr's saga where Óláfr refuses to accompany King Valdamarr to the temple, rejecting his adopted father's idolatry.[28] In both cases, it leads to the first expressions among the courtiers of envy and suspicion.

---

[21] Josephus, *Antiquitates*, II.ix.2.

[22] Oddr Snorrason, *Óláfs saga Tryggvasonar*, 145 (the S-text).

[23] Josephus, *Antiquitates*, II.ix.7; Oddr Snorrason, *Óláfs saga Tryggvasonar*, 155.

[24] Josephus, *Antiquitates*, II.x.1; Oddr Snorrason, *Óláfs saga Tryggvasonar*, 153.

[25] Cole, 'Echoes of the Book of Joseph and Asenath'.

[26] Josephus, *Antiquitates*, IX.vii.232.

[27] *Glossa ordinaria*, ed. Morard (Ex. 2.9); Comestor, *Exodus*, c. 5 (PL 198, 1144A).

[28] Oddr Snorrason, *Óláfs saga Tryggvasonar*, 153.

The Old Testament in Medieval Icelandic Texts

Two more episodes in the saga show Oddr's in-depth knowledge of the historical books of the Old Testament. In an unpleasant episode in 2 Kings 10, King Jehu of Judah uses guile and deceit to clean the land of sorcerers and idolaters. He gathers 'all the prophets of Baal, and all his servants, and all his priests', claiming that Ahab worshipped Baal 'a little' ('parum') but he will worship him 'more' ('amplius') and that he has 'a great sacrifice to offer to Baal'. The biblical author adds, lest we take this at face value: 'porro hieu faciebat hoc insidiose ut disperderet cultores Baal' ('now Jehu did this craftily, that he might destroy the worshippers of Baal').[29] Of course, the great sacrifice turns out to be the idolaters: once they are all gathered in the temple, he sends in his men to slaughter them before destroying the temple and burning Baal's pillar. This seems to be the source for two incidents in Oddr's saga, in the first of which Óláfr gathers 'ǫllum seiðmǫnnum ok fjǫlkunngum mǫnnum' ('all the sorcerers and magicians') and invites them to a feast.[30] Once they are nicely drunk, he sets fire to the hall, and burns them all to death. The second is when Óláfr attends an assembly in Trondheim and finds that he cannot convert the people. He changes tack and declares that 'sýnisk mér þat konungligra at auka heldr blótin en þverra' ('it seems to me more royal to increase the sacrifice than to decrease it').[31] The 'auka' ('increase') and 'þverra' ('decrease') echo the 'parum' ('little') and 'amplius' ('more') in 2 Kings 10. Like the biblical author, the saga author follows this up with a spoiler: 'Konungr var þá blíðr í máli, en mikill í skapi' ('The king was gracious in speech but had much in mind'). Óláfr then enters the temple and takes an axe to Þórr, before commanding that the worshippers remember 'at auka blótin, en þverrum eigi' ('to increase the sacrifice, and let us not decrease it'), by which it becomes clear that he means to sacrifice them. The pagans hastily agree to be baptised after all and, with the exception of their leader Járn-Skeggi, the threatened bloodshed is averted. These scenes may not seem particularly moral or Christian. But Oddr's idea of kingship is forged in an Old Testament world, and the idea that one can justifiably use deceit to impose religious uniformity is indisputably biblical.

Oddr is clearly steeped in the historical books of the Old Testament, and even across languages the parallels make themselves felt. *Gísla saga Súrssonar* is a very different work and, to my knowledge, no link to the Old Testament has been made, other than in the dream verses of Gísli, where there is an allusion to 2 Esdras.[32] But there is a curious coincidence between

---

29 2 Kgs 10.18–19.

30 Oddr Snorrason, *Óláfs saga Tryggvasonar*, 232–34.

31 Oddr Snorrason, *Óláfs saga Tryggvasonar*, 279–80.

32 Fredrik Paasche, 'Esras aabenbaring og Pseudo-Cyprianus i norrön litteratur', in *Festskrift til Finnur Jónsson*, ed. Johns. Brondum-Nielsen et al. (Copenhagen: Levin & Munksgaard, 1928), 199–205. See also Bergljót Soffía Kristjánsdóttir,

Epilogue

Samson tying together the tails of 300 foxes in Judges and Gísli tying together the tails of 30 cows – if it is a coincidence. Both men are pursuing a private vendetta: Samson to avenge his wife's remarriage, and Gísli to avenge the murder of his wife's brother. In Judges, Samson captures 300 foxes, ties torches to their backs, and sends them out to burn the cornfields of the Philistines. The consequences are dire: when the Philistines find out, they burn his in-laws to death in their home, as the killings spiral out of control. In the saga, likewise, Gísli's murder of his sister's husband leads to the breakdown of his family. Gísli ties together the cows' tails when he reaches his sister's farmhouse, fastening the doors securely before killing his brother-in-law, and then passing through the cowshed to go home. But we never find out what the function of the tied tails is.[33] It presents itself as an enigma, a kind of riddle that has never been satisfactorily solved.

Both the story of Samson and that of Gísli hinge around riddles, both literally and metaphorically.[34] At his wedding, Samson speaks a poetic riddle that no one could possibly guess, wagering on it 30 sets of new clothes. But the wedding guests badger his wife until she finds out the answer and Samson loses the bet. In *Gísla saga*, the riddle is the verse that Gísli speaks before an audience of women, presumably because he thinks that they will not understand it.[35] The verse reveals that he has murdered his brother-in-law, and his sister not only memorises it, but tells her new husband what it means. In both stories, the unanticipated initiative of a woman leads to the hero's downfall.

These parallels are close but inconclusive, and there are no verbal echoes that allow a more secure identification to be made. If it were not for the cows' tails, the connection would be entirely obscure. But, once made, it is teasingly plausible: both Samson and Gísli are great heroes, driven by honour and revenge, but they are also trickster figures, who implausibly evade and outwit their enemies until they are finally hunted down. Both end their lives with a suicidal display of heroics, killing others as they die. There is one more

---

'Hinn seki túlkandi: Um tákn, túlkun og sekt í styttri gerð Gísla sögu Súrssonar', *Gripla* 12 (2001), 7–21, where *Gísla saga* is read through the lens of an Augustinian understanding of the Fall of Man and its effects on language and interpretation.

[33] Theodore Andersson suggests that it is a 'necessary precaution' lest Gísli should be pursued through the barn; see 'Some Ambiguities in *Gísla saga*: A Balance Sheet', *BONIS* 1968 (1969), 33. The same motif occurs in *Droplaugarsona saga*, where it also appears to serve no purpose, but it is likely to have been borrowed from *Gísla saga*; see *Austfirðinga sǫgur*, 170.

[34] Joseph Harris, 'Obscure Styles (Old English and Old Norse) and the Enigma of *Gísla saga*', *Mediaevalia* 19 (1993), 75–99 (Samson is mentioned on p. 89); Bergljót Kristjánsdóttir, 'Hinn seki túlkandi', 14.

[35] Harris, 'Obscure Styles', 86. Harris also comments (p. 75) on how the setting for this riddle resembles 'some contest or agonistic game', which is certainly true of Samson's riddle setting.

The Old Testament in Medieval Icelandic Texts

possible link, although it comes in the form of a contrast. The final betrayal for Samson is that of Delilah, who makes a financially beneficial deal with the Philistines to find out the secret of Samson's strength: 'Nú viljum vér gera kaup við þik' ('Now we wish to make a deal with you'), it is translated in *Stjórn III*.[36] Gísli's enemies attempt to do the same: 'Ek vil eiga kaup við þik, Auðr' ('I want to make a deal with you, Auðr'), Eyjólfr offers.[37] When Eyjólfr pours the money 'í kné henni' ('on her knee'), there is a faint reminiscence of Samson laying his head on Delilah's knee ('í kné henni') before she shaves his head.[38] In fact, Gísli's foster-daughter runs to Gísli to warn him that Auðr is about to betray ('svíkja') him, as Delilah 'sveik' ('betrayed') Samson. For an audience who have recognised the parallels with Samson, the suspense at this point is compounded by the knowledge that, in Auðr's situation, Delilah took the money. Yet Auðr acts unexpectedly. She puts the money in a purse and swings it at Eyjólfr's face, drawing blood and shaming him for thinking (as we too perhaps thought) that there was any hope that 'ek myndi selja bónda minn í hendr illmenni þínu' ('I would sell my husband into the hands of a wretch like you').[39]

In the Hebrew, the Philistines offer Delilah 1,100 pieces of silver each ('mille centum argenteos'), but in *Stjórn III*, the compiler translates this as 300 silver pennies ('.iijiu. hundrað silfr peninga').[40] This is interesting because, in *Gísla saga*, Auðr is also offered 300 pieces of silver ('þrjú hundruð silfurs') in exchange for Gísli's betrayal.[41] Like the cows' tails, it is difficult to tell whether or not this is just a coincidence – and, if not, whether *Stjórn III* is borrowing from *Gísla saga* at this point or whether *Gísla saga* is borrowing from an earlier version of *Stjórn III*. Either way, there seems to be a connection between Delilah and Auðr that adds to the narrative suspense and sets one woman's deep love and commitment against the other's deceit and betrayal. Delilah jibes Samson with the taunt that, if he loved her, he would tell her everything.[42] Gísli's quiet confidence in the love of his wife needs no spoken assurances.

Thirty cows tied back-to-back by their tails, and 300 pieces of silver – perhaps this is not much to connect an Israelite freedom fighter with a

---

36   *Stjórn*, 664; cf. Jdg. 16.5.

37   *Gísla saga*, 99.

38   *Stjórn*, 671; cf. Jdg. 16.19.

39   *Gísla saga*, 101.

40   *Stjórn*, 664; Jdg. 16.5.

41   *Gísla saga*, 99.

42   *Stjórn*, 668: 'harðla mjǫk hryggir mik þat er þú segisk elska mik, en þat er þó ekki útan hégómi þinn, því at hugr þinn er mér hvar fjarri' ('it saddens me greatly that you say you love me, but it is nothing but your own nonsense, because your heart is very far from me'); cf. Jdg. 16.15.

Epilogue

celebrated Icelandic outlaw. Yet it seems entirely appropriate for a saga that hinges around 'ambiguity' and 'enigma' to shroud this connection in mystery. If the tying of the cows' tails is not just a narrative loose end (forgive the pun), if it is there for a reason, then perhaps it is a clue to some of the murkier and potentially incestuous aspects of this story: for anyone familiar with the story of Samson, it associates Gísli's murder of his brother-in-law with Samson's jealousy of his wife and his frustration at being barred from her bed.[43] For both men, sexual jealousy explodes into violence with disastrous consequences. Like Gísli's verse, the cows' tails are a riddle that leads us more deeply into the characters' psychology.

If the author of *Gísla saga* is, as I suggest here, riddling around the biblical Samson, then he may have got this idea from two of Gísli's verses. Gísli's 'worse' dream woman washes his hair in blood, transforming what should be a tender image into horror:[44]

> Hugðak þvá mér Þrúði
> þremja hlunns ór brunni
> Óðins elda lauðri
> auðs mína skǫr rauða

I felt Þrúðr <goddess> of wealth [WOMAN] wash my cut hair red in the lather of Óðinn's fire [SWORD>BLOOD] from the well of the roller of blades [SWORD>WOUND].

The word that interests me here is the word for hair, 'skǫr', which comes from the verb 'skera' ('to cut'); the cognate in English is 'to shear'. So the 'worse' dream woman washes Gísli's 'sheared' head in blood, an act that might well recall how Delilah sheared off Samson's locks while he slept in her lap, another tender image cruelly inverted. In the sagas of Icelanders, the term 'skǫr' occurs in one other context in which a woman betrays a man: in *Laxdæla saga*, when Þorgerðr exults in the death of Bolli, who has brought about the death of her son Kjartan. When Bolli's head is cut off, she comments: 'nú Guðrúnu mundu eiga at búa um rauða skǫr Bolla' ('now Guðrún will have to manage Bolli's red haircut').[45] In view of the other

---

[43] Hermann Pálsson, 'Death in Autumn: Tragic Elements in Early Icelandic Fiction', *BONIS* 1973 (1974), 19; Andersson, 'Some Ambiguities in *Gísla saga*', 37–39; Preben Meulengracht Sørensen, 'Murder in Marital Bed: An Attempt at Understanding a Crucial Scene in *Gísla saga*', trans. Judith Jesch, in *Structure and Meaning in Old Norse Literature: New Approaches to Textual Analysis and Literary Criticism*, ed. John Lindow et al. (Odense: Odense University Press, 1986), 235–63.

[44] *Gísla saga*, 103.

[45] *Laxdæla saga*, 168.

The Old Testament in Medieval Icelandic Texts

echoes of Samson and Delilah in *Laxdœla saga*, this may be an allusion to Samson's hair-cut, and Guðrún might certainly be thought of as having betrayed Bolli in the sense that she goads him into taking the life of her lover Kjartan, knowing that it will bring about his death. The next verse in *Gísla saga* is even more striking:[46]

> Hugðak geymi-Gǫndul
> gunnǫld mér falda
> of rakskorinn reikar
> rúf dreyrugri húfu,
> væri hendr á henni
> í hjǫrregni þvegnar;
> svá vakði mik Sága,
> saums ór mínum draumi

I felt the war-like Valkyrie [WOMAN] place a bloody hood on my close-shaven head. Her hands were washed in sword-rain [BLOOD], so the goddess of seams [WOMAN] woke me from my dream.

Cleasby-Vigfússon translates 'rakskorinn' as 'clean-shaven'; 'skorinn' is the past participle of 'skera', and 'rak' here appears to mean the 'hay left in the meadow after stacking' or 'the rakings of hay in a field'. It recalls, though, the verb used for Samson's hair-cut in *Stjórn III*: 'rakar hon af Samson .vij. hans lokka' ('she shaves' – literally 'rakes' – 'off Samson's seven locks').[47] After Delilah has shaved him, she wakes him from sleep, just as Sága wakes Gísli from his dream: 'hann vaknaði ok reis upp skjótt' ('he woke and got up quickly'). Perhaps the allusions to Samson and Delilah in *Gísla saga* can be traced back to these early verses in which Gísli dreams of a woman who washed his close-shaven head in blood.

Hrafnkels saga is from around the same time as *Stjórn*, and Hermann Pálsson has written extensively about the parallels between these two works, which I do not intend to go over here.[48] I note only that the author of *Hrafnkels saga* might well have known the biblical translations in *Stjórn III* and might have thought of the pagan Hrafnkell as belonging to the same sort of kingless society that is depicted in the book of Judges: 'Í þann tíma var engi konungr yfir Israel ok lifði þá hverr sem sýndisk' ('In that time there was no king in Israel, and everybody lived as they pleased').[49] There

---

46 *Gísla saga*, 104.
47 Richard Cleasby and Gudbrand Vigfusson, *An Icelandic-English Dictionary*, 2nd ed. with a supplement by Sir William A. Craigie (Oxford: Clarendon Press, 1957), s.v. 'rakskorinn'; *Stjórn*, 672 ; cf. Jdg. 16.19.
48 Pálsson, '*Hrafnkels saga* ok *Stjórn*'.
49 *Stjórn*, 678 ; cf. Jdg. 17.6.

Epilogue

is some overlap in vocabulary and phrasing between these works. The way Sámr dredges up a band of 'einhleypingar' ('tramps') to accompany him to the assembly, for example, recalls the bunch of dissolutes whose loyalty Abimelech buys: 'ok keypti hann sér þar með lið einhleypingja félausa' ('and with it he bought himself a group of destitute tramps').[50] The way Hrafnkell's 'ofsi' ('pride') leads to his downfall reflects how 'ofsi' is a constant attribute of the Philistines in *Stjórn III* as well as of failed Israelite leaders like Abimelech.[51] Both texts make use of the expression 'forn orðskviðr' ('an old proverb') and, in one case, both use the same proverb: 'er þá alls gætt ef þín er' ('everything is taken care of if you are'), 'oss þykkir alls gætt ef þín er' ('It seems to us that everything is taken care of if you are').[52] When Hrafnkell declares that: 'Mǫrgum mundi betr þykkja skjótr dauði en slíkar hrakningar' ('to many a quick death would seem better than such humiliations'), the saga author might just be thinking of those many occasions in *Stjórn III* where a quick death is advocated as better than everlasting damnation: 'er þér betra at taka hér skjóta hefnd fyrir' ('it is better that you suffer a quick punishment for this here'), 'er betr at þú látir hann taka hér skjóta hefnd' ('it is better to make him suffer a quick punishment here'), 'heldr vil ek at hann taki hér skjóta hefnd' ('I would rather he suffered a quick punishment here').[53] The difference is that, in *Stjórn III*, the aim is avoid eternal punishment, while in *Hrafnkels saga*, the aim is to avoid perpetual shame. But Hrafnkell's words might be construed as a wry comment on the ideology of *Stjórn III*: 'kjósa mun ek líf, ef kostr er' ('I will choose life, if it is offered').

The scene that interests me, though, is the toe-pulling scene in Þorgeirr's booth at the Althing. This strikes me as having an ironic – perhaps a parodic – likeness to the scene in the book of Ruth where Naomi instructs her on how to approach Boaz.[54] In both cases, someone of lower social standing (Sámr, Ruth) needs legal support from someone of higher social standing (Þorgeirr, Boaz) and in both cases a third party (Þorkell, Naomi) prepares on their behalf an elaborate charade involving feet. This seems too unusual to be a coincidence. Naomi offers Ruth 'gott ráð' ('good advice') and Sámr rather doubtfully commends Þorkell for being 'heilráðr' ('generous with his advice'), while suspecting that his plan is not 'ráðligt' ('advisable'). Naomi tells Ruth: 'gakk leyniliga í laufagarðinn' ('Go secretly into the barn'), while Þorkell tells Sámr and Þorgils: 'gangið inn í búðina' ('Go into the booth'). Naomi then advises Ruth to wait until Boaz 'er sofnaðr' ('is asleep'), while

---

50 *Hrafnkels saga*, 109; *Stjórn*, 626; cf. Jdg. 9.4 'qui conduxit sibi ex eo viros inopes et vagos' ('he hired to himself men that were needy and vagabonds').
51 *Hrafnkels saga*, 122; *Stjórn*, 630, 636, 650.
52 *Hrafnkels saga*, 122, 128; *Stjórn*, 837, 959, 984.
53 *Hrafnkels saga*, 121; *Stjórn*, 874, 1002, 1008.
54 *Stjórn*, 686–87; *Hrafnkels saga*, 112–13.

The Old Testament in Medieval Icelandic Texts

Þorkell asserts confidently that 'er mannfólk í svefni' ('everyone will be asleep'). Naomi instructs Ruth: 'Gakk þú þar til ok létt upp á breizlini at fótum honum ok ligg þar undir' ('Go up to him and lift up the cover over his feet and lie down under it'). Þorkell's instructions are more elaborate: Þorgeirr, he tells his astonished auditors, has a huge boil on his toe and has stretched his foot out from under the covers. Þorbjǫrn must go to the hammock, stumble over it, fall onto the footboard, and pull hard on the toe. Both Naomi and Þorkell leave their puppets in the dark as to what might happen next: 'síðan mun hann segja þér hvat þu skalt at hafizk' ('then he'll tell you what you must do'), 'ok vit, hversu hann verðr við' ('and find out how he'll respond'). In both cases, the charade is carefully acted out: Sámr agrees that 'svá skal gera sem hann gefr ráð' ('it must be done as he advises'), while Ruth 'gerir alla hluti sem sværa hennar hefir fyrir sagt' ('does everything as her mother-in-law has told her').

This is not to suggest that the two scenes have one and the same moral; quite the contrary. In the Bible, Naomi's plan is not entirely obscure, but depends on the knowledge that 'place of the feet' (מַרְגְּלֹת) in Hebrew can be a euphemism for the genital area, as it is in Isaiah 7.20 (where pubic hair is translated literally and rather nonsensically in the NRSV as 'the hair of the feet').[55] So too the seraphs in Isaiah 6.2 are covering not their 'feet', but their genitals with their wings, and the besieged woman in Deuteronomy 28.57 will eat the afterbirth that passes through not her 'thighs' but through her genitals. Although in the event it is not what happens, it is at least possible that what Naomi envisages when Ruth uncovers Boaz's 'feet' in the middle of the night is some sort of sexual encounter that will then oblige him to marry her. However, in the absence of this understanding of 'feet', the scene appears odd in the extreme. In this case, it is not unlikely that an Icelander reading it might appreciate not Naomi's cunning and Ruth's daring, but the sheer comedy of it all: the farcical quality of the charade that is acted out, and the humour of Boaz waking with a jump and finding himself lost for words when he discovers a strange woman clutching his feet. From here, it is only a small jump to the scene in *Hrafnkels saga* with the same farcical qualities, which are only enhanced by the large and undignified boil on Þorgeirr's foot and the total cluelessness of Sámr and Þorbjǫrn. So, I would argue, the scene in *Hrafnkels saga* – whatever its final meaning – took shape as a parody of

---

55 On the different ways of interpreting this passage in Ruth, see Jeremy Schipper, *Ruth: A New Translation with Introduction and Commentary* (New Haven, CT: Yale University Press, 2016), 143–44. A better translation of the Hebrew might be 'she undressed at his feet and lay down'. However, the Vulgate translates 'discoperto a pedibus eius' ('uncovering his feet'). On readings of the passage in *Hrafnkels saga*, see William Ian Miller, 'Feeling Another's Pain: Sympathy and Psychology Saga Style', *European Review* 22.1 (2014), 55–63.

Epilogue

the biblical book of Ruth by an Icelander who saw the potential in it for some biblically infused comedy.

Tracing biblical influence in the Icelandic sagas is a topic for another book. But I hope I have shown with these few examples that there is still much to be discovered, and much enjoyment to be had in the discovery. After all, we are talking about two superlative storytelling traditions, both of which are characterised by a 'vigorous' economy of means, a policy of 'self-effacement' and a narrative art that depends on ambiguity and indirection, which encourages the reader to fill in gaps and silences, to negotiate events as if encountering them at first hand. I have argued that this 'astounding' kinship between the two traditions has shaped the history of biblical translation and adaptation in Old Norse-Icelandic: that the translators of biblical stories recognised their saga-like qualities and allowed these to emerge in their retelling. Likewise, saga authors encountering the Old Testament, whether in Latin or in Old Norse-Icelandic, recognised its value not just as a symbolic language that pointed forward to the New Testament, but as a reservoir of stories that shared many characteristics with their own. We may think of the Hebrew Bible/Old Testament as being irreducibly alien, but the historical books at least were in many ways familiar to the Icelanders, depicting a world that was recognisably like theirs. It is high time that we recognised biblical translation and adaptation as an essential part of the wider history of Old Norse-Icelandic literature.

ACKNOWLEDGEMENTS

The origins of this book lie in a seminar on medieval narrative that I attended as a graduate student. It was convened by Heather O'Donoghue and Thomas Charles-Edwards, and every week there was a presentation on a short passage from a medieval narrative, which everybody read in advance. We read an extraordinary range of texts in different medieval languages, including Irish, Welsh, Old Norse and French. It was one of the richest experiences that I had as a graduate. But the presentation I remember most clearly was the very first one, for which we read 2 Samuel 11: the story of David's adultery with Bathsheba. As the presenter talked us through various aspects of Hebrew style – the avoidance of direct judgement, the use of meaningful repetition, the impression of verisimilitude – those of us present who worked on Old Norse became increasingly astonished by the sheer level of likeness to what we all knew as 'saga style'. I think – although this was a long time ago – that Heather described herself as 'astounded'. Could there be a link between biblical style and saga style? This is the question out of which this book has taken shape.

I have always felt that, in a hypothetical other life, I would have liked to study Theology and become a scholar of biblical Hebrew; in the last few years, I am lucky to have had the opportunity to do the first (if not the second) of these two things. I am grateful to Stephen Herring for teaching me the basics of biblical Hebrew and for helping me to read parts of Genesis, Judges, Ruth and 1 Samuel in Hebrew. Likewise, I am indebted to Hywel Clifford for his lectures on Old Testament history and his encyclopaedic knowledge of biblical commentaries, as well as for his help with citations of biblical Hebrew. My biblical and patristic Greek has been much improved by the teaching of Michael Dormandy, although I am afraid I was by far the least accomplished pupil in the small Greek reading class he ran. Finally, I am thankful to Andrew Sillett for helping me with the – sometimes peculiar – medieval Latin of Peter Comestor's *Historia scholastica* and Vincent of Beauvais's *Speculum historiale*, which have not yet been translated into English, let alone properly edited. It has been a real challenge – albeit an enjoyable one – to manage so many texts in different languages, and it goes without saying that any errors are entirely my own.

Acknowledgements

Others have contributed significantly to my thinking about the Victorine order and its influence on biblical exegesis in medieval Iceland and Scandinavia. I would like to extend thanks particularly to Christian Etheridge, Karl-Gunnar Johansson, Hilde Bliksrud, Roger Andersson and Samu Niskanen for inviting me to be part of the organising committee for a series of conferences on the Victorine order in Iceland and Scandinavia. These conferences introduced me to the work of Juliet Mousseau and Frans van Liere on the Victorines, and Dario Bullita and Gottskálk Jensen on the various links between Iceland and St Victor. Gunnar Harðarson was kind enough to send me scans of material from the book catalogues in Skálholt, and his article on music and manuscripts in Þingeyrar and Skálholt.

At an early stage in my work on this book, I was awarded a Snorri Sturluson scholarship to live in Iceland for three months and work at the Árni Magnússon Institute in Iceland. While my children initially had mixed feelings about this, we all had a wonderful time living in an ancient and dusty apartment next to Kringlan. While the children attended Landakotsskóli, where they learned to play chess and the ukulele, I sat in the dróttninga dyngja at Árnastofnun immediately in front of Margaret Cormack, who was welcoming and interested from the start. She not only took all my children out for pancakes (a brave undertaking!) and came to hear Benji sing in *Tosca*, but also read through the first draft of this book when I was too scared to show it to anyone else. I am deeply grateful to her.

There are so many other people I could thank. Heather O'Donoghue, Carolyne Larrington, Gareth Evans and Brittany Schorn have been kind and supportive colleagues. George Manning covered my teaching over my last sabbatical so that I could write without interruption. Eugenia Vorobeva has been invaluable in providing research assistance. For keeping me going when I was flagging, and reminding me that Old Norse is fun, I am grateful to all my students, especially Hollie, Thorsteinn, Elena, Eloise, Iannah, Chantale, Rachel, Finn, George and Amy. Of the many, many people I could thank for their encouragement and support over the past few years, I think of Martin Henig, Anne Holmes, Peter Groves, Noam Reisner, Sif Rikharðsdóttir, Matthew Reynolds and Laura Seymour.

My dear friend Melanie Florence accompanied me throughout the writing of this book, but did not live to see its completion. She was an inspiration to me as a scholar, a friend, and a person of faith. I miss her unspeakably.

Finally, my family. Tom, Sunniva, Benji and James: I am so very proud of you. Andy: thank you, thank you, thank you. You probably never imagined that you would marry someone who wrote books on medieval Icelandic translations of texts from the Ancient Near East. Still, this one is for you.

BIBLIOGRAPHY

Manuscripts

Copenhagen, Den Arnamagnæanske Samling, AM 225 fol.
Copenhagen, Den Arnamagnæanske Samling, AM 226 fol.
Reykjavík, Stofnun Árna Magnússonar í íslenzkum fræðum, AM 227 fol.

Primary Sources

Ágrip af Nóregskonunga. A Twelfth-century Synoptic History of the Kings of Norway, ed. Matthew Driscoll (London: Viking Society for Northern Research, 1995)

Alfræði Íslenzk: Islandsk encyclopædisk litteratur, ed. Kristian Kålund, 3 vols (Copenhagen: Møller, 1908–18)

Anonymous, *Orma heiti*, ed. Elena Gurevich, in *Poetry from Treatises on Poetics*, ed. Kari Ellen Gade and Edith Marold (Turnhout: Brepols, 2017), 927–34

Arnórr jarlaskáld Þórðarson, 'Hrynhenda, Magnúsdrápa', ed. Diana Whaley, in *Poetry from the Kings' Sagas 2: From c. 1035 to c. 1300*, ed. Kari Ellen Gade (Turnhout: Brepols, 2009), 181–206

——, 'Lausavísur 1', ed. Diana Whaley, in *Poetry from the Kings' Sagas 2*, 280–81

——, 'Haraldsdrápa', ed. Diana Whaley, in *Poetry from the Kings' Sagas 2*, 260–80

Auðunar þáttr vestfirzka, in *Vestfirðinga sǫgur*, 359–68

Augustine of Hippo, *In Iohannis evangelius tractatus CXXIV*, ed. R. Willems, CCSL 36 (Turnhout: Brepols, 1954)

——, *De civitate dei*, 2 vols, ed. B. Dombart and A. Kalb, CCSL 47–48 (Turnhout: Brepols, 1955)

——, *Enarrationes in Psalmos I–L*, ed. E. Ekkers and J. Fraipoint, CCSL 38 (Turnhout: Brepols, 1956)

——, *De doctrina christiana*, ed. K. D. Daur and J. Martin, CCSL 32 (Turnhout: Brepols, 1962)

Bibliography

——, *De sermone domini in monte*, ed. A. Mutzenbecher, CCSL 35 (Turnhout: Brepols, 1967)

——, *Confessionum librum XIII*, ed. Lucas Verheijen and Martin Skutella, CCSL 27 (Turnhout: Brepols, 1981)

——, *Tractates on the Gospel of John 1–10* (Washington, DC: Catholic University of America Press, 1988–95)

——, *Confessions*, trans. Henry Chadwick (Oxford: OUP, 1991)

——, *Expositions on the Psalms 1–32*, trans. Maria Boulding (New York: New City Press, 2000)

——, *Saint Augustine, On Genesis: On Genesis: A Refutation of the Manichees, Unfinished Literal Commentary on Genesis, The Literal Meaning of Genesis*, trans. Edmund Hill (Hyde Park, NY: New Press, 2002)

——, *City of God*, trans. Henry Bettenson (London: Penguin, 2003)

——, *Answer to Faustus, a Manichean*, trans. Roland Teske (Hyde Park, NY: New City Press, 2007)

——, *On Christian Teaching*, trans. R. P. H. Green (Oxford: Oxford University Press, 2008)

——, *De Genesi ad litteram*, ed. J. Zycha, CSEL 28

——, *Contra Faustum manichaeum*, ed. J. Zycha, CSEL 25

——, *De Genesi contra Manichaeos*, ed. D. Weber, CSEL 90

Austfirðinga sǫgur, ed. Jón Jóhannesson (Reykjavík: Hið íslenzka fornritafélag, 1950)

Bárðar saga Snæfellsáss, in *Harðar saga*, 99–172

Biblia Hebraica Stuttgartensia (Stuttgart: Deutsche Bibelgesellschaft, 1997)

Biblia sacra iuxta vulgatam versionem, ed. Roger Gryson et al., 4th ed. (Stuttgart: Deutsche Bibelgesellschaft, 1994)

Biskupa sögur I, ed. Sigurgeir Steingrímsson, Ólafur Halldórsson and Peter Foote (Reykjavík: Hið íslenzka fornritafélag, 2003)

Biskupa sögur II, ed. Ásdís Egilsdóttir (Reykjavík: Hið íslenzka fornritafélag, 1998)

Brennu-Njáls saga, ed. Einar Ólafur Sveinsson (Reykjavík: Hið íslenzka fornritafélag, 1954)

Cantus Index: Online Catalogue for Mass and Office Chants at https://cantusindex.org

Cleasby, Richard and Vigfusson, Gudbrand, *An Icelandic–English Dictionary*, 2nd ed. with a supplement by Sir William A. Craigie (Oxford: Clarendon Press, 1957)

Comestor, Peter, *Historia scholastica*, PL 198, 1045–1721

——, *Petri Comestori Scolastica historia. Liber Genesis*, ed. Agneta Sylwan, CCCM 191 (Turnhout: Brepols, 2005)

Cursor Mundi, *The Southern Version of Cursor mundi*, vol. 1, ed. Sarah M. Horral (Ottawa: University of Ottawa Press, 1978)

262

Bibliography

Droplaugarsona saga, in *Austfirðinga sǫgur*, 135–80

Diplomatarium Islandicum, ed. Jón Sigurðsson, 16 vols (Copenhagen: Hið íslenzka bókmentafélag, 1857–1972)

Durandus, William, *Guillelmi Duranti Rationale divinorum officiorum*, CCCM 140, 140A, 140B, ed. Anselme Davril and Timothy T. Thibodeau (Turnhout: Brepols, 1995–2000)

——, *The Rationale Divinorum Officiorum. The Foundational Symbolism of the Early Church, its Structure, Decoration, Sacraments and Vestments by Gulielmus Durandus (1230–1296 CE)* (Louisiana: Fons Vitae, 2007)

Eddukvæði, ed. Jónas Kristjánsson and Vésteinn Ólason, 2 vols (Reykjavík: Hið íslenzka fornritafélag, 2014)

Egils saga Skalla-Grímssonar, ed. Bjarni Einarsson (London: Viking Society for Northern Research, 2003)

Einarr Skúlason, 'Eysteinsdrápa', ed. Kari Ellen Gade, in *Poetry from the Kings' Sagas 2*, ed. Kari Ellen Gade (Turnhout: Brepols, 2009), 559–61

——, 'Sigurðardrápa II', ed. Kari Ellen Gade, in *Poetry from the Kings' Sagas 2*, ed. Kari Ellen Gade (Turnhout: Brepols, 2009), 550–51

Eyrbyggja saga, Eiríks saga rauða, ed. Einar Ólafur Sveinsson and Matthías Þórðarson (Reykjavík: Hið íslenzka fornritafélag, 1935)

Fagrskinna, ed. Finnur Jónsson (Copenhagen: Møller, 1902–03)

Finnson, Eyvindr skáldaspillir, 'Hákonarmál', ed. R. D. Fulk, in *Poetry from the Kings' Sagas 1: From Mythical Times to c. 1035*, ed. Diana Whaley (Turnhout: Brepols, 2012), 171–95

Flóamanna saga, in *Harðar saga*, 229–327

Færeyinga saga, Óláfs saga Tryggvasonar eptir Odd munk Snorrason, ed. Ólafur Halldórsson (Reykjavík: Hið íslenzka fornritafélag, 2006)

Fornaldarsögur Norðurlanda, ed. Guðni Jónsson and Bjarni Vilhjálmsson, 3 vols (Reykjavík: Bókaútgáfan, 1943–44)

Gísla saga Súrssonar, in *Vestfirðinga sǫgur*, 1–118

Glossae Scripturae Sacrae electronicae, IRHT-CNRS, 2023, available at: http://gloss-e.irht.cnrs.fr/php/livres-liste.php?id=glo

Grágás: Lagasafn íslenska þjóðveldisins, ed. Gunnar Karlsson, Kristján Sveinsson and Mörður Árnason (Reykjavík: Mál og menning, 1992)

Gregory the Great, *Morals on the Book of Job*, 3 volumes (Oxford: John Henry Parker, 1844–1850)

——, *Homiliae in Hiezechielem prophetam*, ed. M. Adriaen, CCSL 142 (1971)

——, *Sancti Gregorii Magni Moralia in Iob*, ed. Marcus Adriaen, CCSL 143–143B (Turnhout: Brepols, 1979–85)

——, *Forty Gospel Homilies*, trans. Dom David Hurst (Kalamazoo, MI: Cistercian Publications, 1990)

——, *Homélies sur l'évangile*, 2 vols, ed. Raymond Étaix, Charles Morel and Bruno Judic (Paris: Cerf, 2005–08)

Bibliography

——, *Homilies on the Book of the Prophet Ezekiel*, trans. Theodosia Tomkinson, 2nd ed. (Etna, CA: Centre for Traditionalist Orthodox Studies, 2008)

Grettis saga Ásmundarsonar, ed. Guðni Jónsson (Reykjavík: Hið íslenzka fornritafélag, 1936)

Hallfreðar saga, ed. Bjarni Einarsson (Reykjavík: Stofnun Árna Magnússonar, 1977)

Harðar saga, Bárðar saga, Þorskfirðinga saga, Flóamanna saga, ed. Þórhallur Vilmundarson and Bjarni Vilhjálmsson (Reykjavík: Hið íslenzka fornritafélag, 1991)

Heiðarvíga saga, in *Borgfirðinga sǫgur*, ed. Sigurður Nordal and Guðni Jónsson (Reykjavík: Hið íslenzka fornritafélag, 1938), 213–326

The Historye of the Patriarks, ed. Mayumi Taguchi (Heidelberg: Winter, 2010)

Homilíubók: Isländska homilier efter en handskrift från tolfte århundradet: Isländska skinnboken 15 qu. å Kungl. Biblioteket i Stockholm, ed. Theodor Wisén (Lund: Gleerup, 1872)

Honorius Augustodunensis, *De imagine mundi libri tres*, PL 172, 115–88

——, *Speculum Ecclesiae*, PL 172, 807–1107

Hrafnkels saga, in *Austfirðinga sǫgur*, ed. Jón Jóhannesson (Reykjavík: Hið íslenzka fornritafélag, 1950), 95–113

Hugh of St Victor, *Didascalicon de Studio Legendi. A Critical Text*, ed. Charles Henry Buttimer (Washington, DC: Catholic University of America, 1939)

——, *Didascalicon*, in *The Didascalicon of Hugh of St Victor: A Medieval Guide to the Arts,* trans. Jerome Taylor (New York: Columbia University Press, 1991)

——, *Hugh of St Victor on the Sacraments of the Christian Faith*, trans. Roy J. Deferrari (Eugene, OR: Wipf & Stock, 2007)

——, 'On Sacred Scripture and its Authors', in *Interpretation of Scripture: Theory: A Selection of Works by Hugh, Andrew Godfrey and Richard of St Victor*, ed. Franklin T. Harkins and Frans van Liere (Turnhout: Brepols, 2012), 213–30

——, 'Notes on Genesis', trans. Jan van Zwieten, in *Interpretation of Scripture: Practice. A selection of works of Hugh, Andrew, and Richard of St Victor, Peter Comestor, Robert of Melun, Maurice of Sully and Leonius of Paris*, ed. Frans van Liere and Franklin T. Harkins (Turnhout: Brepols, 2015), 53–117

——, *De scripturis et scripturibus*, PL 175, 9–28

——, *Adnotationes in Pentateuchem*, PL 175, 29–86D

——, *De sacramentis christiane fidei*, PL 176, 173–618B

The Icelandic Homily Book: Perg. 15 4to in the Royal Library Stockholm, ed. Andrea de Leeuw van Weenen (Reykjavík: Stofnun Árna Magnússonar á Íslandi, 1993)

Bibliography

Isidore of Seville, *Etymologiae*, PL 82, 73–728C

Íslendingabók, Landnámabók, ed. Jakob Benediktsson (Reykjavík: Hið íslenzka fornritafélag, 1968)

Jerome, *The Letters of St Jerome*, in *A Select Library of the Nicene and Post-Nicene Fathers: Second Series*, ed. Philip Shaff and Henry Wace, 14 vols (Oxford: Parker, 1890–1900), VI, 50–692

——, *Tractatus sive homiliae in psalmos*, ed. G. Morin, B. Capelle and J. Fraipont, CCSL 78 (1958)

——, *Hebraicae quaestiones in libro Geneseos. Liber interpretationis hebraicorum nominum. Commentarioli in psalmos. Commentarius in Ecclesiasten*, ed. P. de Lagarde, C. Morin and M. Adriaen, CCSL 72 (Turnhout: Brepols, 1959)

——, *Homilies of Saint Jerome Volume 1 (1–59 On the Psalms)*, trans. Sister Marie Liguori Ewald (Washington, DC: Catholic University of America Press, 1964)

——, *In Sophoniam*, ed. M. Adriaen, CCSL 76A (Turnhout: Brepols, 1970)

——, *Jerome's Commentary on Daniel: A Study of Comparative Jewish and Christian Interpretations of the Hebrew Bible*, ed. Jay Braverman (Washington, DC: Catholic Bible Association of America, 1978)

——, *Commentaire sur Daniel*, ed. Régis Courtray (Paris: Les Éditions du Cerf, 2019)

——, *Epistolae*, ed. I. Hilberg, CSEL 54–56

——, *Liber de situ et nominibus locorum Hebraicorum*, PL 23, 859–928

Josephus, Flavius, *Antiquities*, ed. R. M. Pollard et al., 2013–19, available online at https://www.latinjosephus.org/.

Júdit, ed. Svanhildur Óskarsdóttir (Reykjavík: Stofnun Árna Magnússonar í íslenskum fræðum, 2020)

Klaeber's Beowulf and The Fight at Finnsburg, ed. Robert D. Fulk and John D. Niles, 4th ed. (Toronto: University of Toronto Press, 2008)

Konungs skuggsiá, ed. Ludvig Holm-Olsen, 2nd rev. ed. (Oslo: Norske Historisk Kjeldeskrift Institutt, 1983)

Laxdœla saga, ed. Einar Ólafur Sveinsson (Reykjavík: Hið íslenzka fornritafélag, 1934)

Leifar fornra kristinna frœða íslenzkra: Codex Arna-Magnœanus 677 4to auk annara enna elztu brota af íslenzkum guðfrœðisritum, ed. Þorvaldur Bjarnarson (Denmark: Hagerup, 1878)

'Líknarbraut', ed. George S. Tate, in *Poetry on Christian Subjects: 1. The Twelfth and Thirteenth Centuries*, ed. Margaret Clunies Ross (Turnhout: Brepols, 2007), 228–86

Makkabear, ed. Karl Óskar Ólafsson and Svanhildur Óskarsdóttir (Reykjavík: Stofnun Árna Magnússonar í íslenskum fræðum, 2020)

Maríu saga: Legender om jomfru Maria og hendes jertegn, ed. Carl R. Unger (Oslo: Brögger & Christie, 1871)

Bibliography

Morkinskinna, 2 vols, ed. Ármann Jakobsson and Þórður Ingi Guðjónsson (Reykjavík: Hið íslenzka fornritafélag, 2011)

Necrologium abbatiae Sancti Victoris Parisiensis, ed. Ursula Vones-Liebenstein, Monika Seifert and Rainer Berndt (Aschendorff: Monasterii Westfalorum, 2012)

Njal's Saga, trans. Magnús Magnússon and Hermann Pálsson (Harmondsworth: Penguin, 1960)

Oddr Snorrason, *Óláfs saga Tryggvasonar*, in *Færeyinga saga*, 123–362

——, *The Saga of Olaf Tryggvason*, trans. Theodore Andersson (Ithaca, NY: Cornell University Press, 2018)

Óláfs saga hins helga, ed. Oscar Albert Johnsen (Oslo: Dybwad, 1922)

Origen, *Origenes Werke: Band 6, Homilien zum Hexateuch in Rufins Übersetzung, Teil 1: Die Homilien zu Genesis, Exodus und Leviticus*, ed. W. Baehrens (Leipzig: J. C. Hinrichs'sche Buchhandlung, 1920)

——, *Homilies on Genesis and Exodus*, trans. Ronald Heine (Washington, DC: Catholic University of America Press, 1982)

Philo, 'On Mating with the Preliminary Studies', in *Philo*, trans. F. H. Colson and G. H. Whitaker, vol. 4 (Cambridge, MA: Harvard University Press, 1932), 458–51

The Poetic Edda, Vol. II Mythological Poems, ed. Ursula Dronke (Oxford: Clarendon Press, 1997)

Postola sögur: Legendariske fortællinger om apostlernes liv, deres camp for kristendommens udbredelse, samt deres martyrdöd, ed. Carl R. Unger (Oslo: Bentzen, 1874)

Pseudo-Jerome, *Quaestiones Hebraicae in libros Regum et Paralipomenon*, in PL 23, 1327–1402

Rémundar saga keisarasonar, ed. Sven Grén Broberg (Copenhagen: Møller, 1909–12)

Richard of St Victor, *Liber exceptionum: texte critique avec introd., notes et tables*, ed. Jean Châtillon (Paris: Vrin, 1958)

——, *Benjamin Minor*, in *The Twelve Patriarchs, The Mystical Ark, Book III of the Trinity*, trans. Grover A. Zinn (New York: Paulist Press, 1979), 53–147

——, 'The Book of Notes (selections)', in *Interpretation of Scripture: Theory: A Selection of Works by Hugh, Andrew Godfrey and Richard of St Victor*, ed. Franklin T. Harkins and Frans van Liere (Turnhout: Brepols, 2012), 297–326

Saga Óláfs konungs hins helga: Den store saga om Olav den hellige, ed. Oscar Albert Johnsen and Jón Helgason (Oslo: Dybwad, 1941)

Snorri Sturluson, *Heimskringla*, ed. Bjarni Aðalbjarnarson, 3 vols (Reykjavík: Hið íslenzka fornritafélag, 1941–51)

——, *Edda: Prologue and Gylfaginning*, ed. Anthony Faulkes (London: Viking Society for Northern Research, 1988)

Bibliography

——, *Edda: Skáldskaparmál*, ed. Anthony Faulkes (London: Viking Society, 1998)

——, *Háttatal*, ed. Kari Ellen Gade, in *Poetry from Treatises on Poetics*, ed. Kari Ellen Gade and Edith Marold (Turnhout: Brepols, 2017), 1094–210

Sögur Danakonunga, ed. Carl af Petersens and Emil Olsen, 2 vols (Copenhagen, 1919–25)

Stjorn: Gammelnorsk bibelhistorie fra verdens skabelse til det babyloniske fangenskab, ed. Carl Rikard Unger (Christiania: Feilberg & Landmark, 1862)

Stjórn: Tekst etter håndskriftene, ed. Reidar Astås, Norrøne Tekster 8 (Oslo: Riksarkivet, 2009)

Sturla Þórðarson, 'Hákonarkviða', in *Poetry from the Kings' Sagas 2*, ed. Kari Ellen Gade (Turnhout: Brepols, 2009), 669–724

Sverris saga, ed. Þorleifur Hauksson (Reykjavík: Hið íslenzka fornritafélag, 2007)

Vatnsdœla saga, Hallfreðar saga, Kormáks saga, ed. Einar Ólafur Sveinsson (Reykjavík: Hið íslenzka fornritafélag, 1939)

Veraldar saga, ed. Jakob Benediktsson (Copenhagen: Lunos, 1944)

Vestfirðinga sǫgur, ed. Björn K. Þórólfsson and Guðni Jónsson (Reykjavík: Hið íslenzka fornritafélag, 1943)

Víga-Glúms saga, in *Eyfirðinga sǫgur*, ed. Jónas Kristjánsson (Reykjavík: Hið íslenzka fornritafélag, 1956), 1–98

Vincent of Beauvais, *Speculum historiale*, annotated edition based on manuscript Douai Bibliothèque municipale 797, available online at: http://sourcencyme.irht.cnrs.fr/encyclopedie/speculum_historiale_version_sm_trifaria_ms_douai_bm_797

Vǫlsunga saga, in *The Saga of the Volsungs*, ed. and trans. Ronald G. Finch (London: Nelson, 1955)

Þiðriks saga af Bern, ed. Henrik Bertelsen (Copenhagen: Møller, 1905–11)

Þormóðr Trefilsson, 'Hrafnsmál', in *Den Norsk-Islandske Skjaldedigtning*, ed. Finnur Jonsson (Copenhagen: Nordisk Forlag, 1912), 196–97 *Þórðar saga hreðu*, in *Kjalnesinga saga*, ed. Jóhannes Halldórsson (Reykjavík: Hið íslenzka fornritafélag, 1959), 161–226

Þorsteins saga Síðu-Hallssonar, in *Austfirðinga sǫgur*, 297–320

Secondary Sources

Abram, Christopher, 'Anglo-Saxon Influence in the Old Norwegian Homily Book', *Mediaeval Scandinavia* 14 (2004), 1–35

——, 'Anglo-Saxon Homilies in their Scandinavian Context', in *The Old English Homily: Precedent, Practice and Appropriation*, ed. Aaron J Kleist (Turnhout: Brepols, 2007), 425–44

Bibliography

Alter, Robert, *The Art of Biblical Narrative* (London: Allen & Unwin, 1981)

——, *Genesis: Translation and Commentary* (New York and London: Norton, 1996)

——, *The David Story: A Translation with Commentary of 1 and 2 Samuel* (London: Norton, 2000)

Anderson, John, *Jacob and the Divine Trickster: A Theology of Deception and Yhwh's Fidelity to the Ancestral Promise in the Jacob Cycle* (University Park, PA: Penn State University Press, 2021)

Andersson, Theodore, *The Problem of Icelandic Saga Origins: A Historical Survey* (New Haven, CT: Yale University Press, 1964)

——, 'Some Ambiguities in *Gisla saga*: A Balance Sheet', *BONIS* 1968 (1969), 7–42

——, *The Growth of the Medieval Icelandic Saga (1180–1280)* (Ithaca, NY: Cornell University Press, 2006)

Andresen, Merete Geert, *Katalog over AM Accessoria. De latinske fragmenter*, ed. Jonna Louis-Jensen (Copenhagen: C. A. Reitzels forlag, 2008)

Anlezark, Daniel, *Water and Fire: The Myth of the Flood in Anglo-Saxon England* (Manchester: Manchester University Press, 2006)

Ásdís Egilsdóttir, 'Kolbítr verður karlmaður', in *Miðaldabörn*, ed. Ármann Jakobsson and Torfi Tulinius (Reykjavík: Hugvísindastofnun Háskola Íslands, 2005), 87–100

Asplund Ingemark, Camilla, 'The Trolls in *Bárðar saga* – Playing with the Conventions of Oral Texts?', in *Folklore in Old Norse – Old Norse in Folklore*, ed. Daniel Sävborg and Karen Bek-Pedersen (Tartu: University of Tartu Press, 2014), 120–38

Astås, Reidar, 'Ordtak i *Stjórn I*', *Opuscula* 8 (1985), 126–31

——, *An Old Norse Biblical Compilation: Studies in Stjórn* (New York: Peter Lang, 1991)

——, 'Kilder for og særtrekk ved *Stjórn IV*', *Alvíssmál* 1 (1992), 55–64

Auerbach, Erich, *Mimesis: The Representation of Reality in Western Literature*, trans. Willard R. Trask (Princeton, NJ: Princeton University Press, 2013)

Auld, A. Graham, 'Ruth: A Reading of Scripture?', in *The Oxford Handbook of the Writings of the Hebrew Bible*, ed. Donn F. Morgan (Oxford: Oxford University Press, 2018), 215–28

Aðalheiður Guðmundsdóttir, 'The Other World in the *Fornaldarsögur* and in Folklore', in *Folklore in Old Norse – Old Norse in Folklore*, ed. Daniel Sävborg and Karen Bek-Pedersen (Tartu: University of Tartu Press, 2014), 14–40

Bagge, Sverre, 'Forholdet mellom Kongespeilet og Stjórn', *Arkiv for nordisk filologi* 89 (1974), 163–202

——, *The Political Thought of the King's Mirror* (Odense: Odense University Press, 1987)

268

Bibliography

——, 'The Old Norse Kings' Sagas and European Latin Historiography', *Journal of English and Germanic Philology* 115.1 (2016), 1–38

Balfour, Mark, 'Moses and the Princess: Josephus's "Antiquitates Judaicae" and the "Chansons de Geste"', *Medium Ævum* 64.1 (1995), 1–16

Barthes, Roland, 'The Struggle with the Angel: Textual Analysis of Genesis 32:23–33', in *Structural Analysis and Biblical Exegesis: Interpretational Essays*, trans. Alfred M. Johnson (Pittsburgh, PA: Pickwick, 1974), 21–33

Barton, John, *Reading the Old Testament: Method in Biblical Study* (London: Darton, Longman & Todd, 1984)

——, 'Old Testament or Hebrew Bible?', in *The Old Testament: Canon, Literature and Theology* (Aldershot: Routledge, 2007), 83–89

——, *A History of the Bible: The Book and its Faiths* (London: Penguin, 2019)

Battista, Simonetta, 'The "Compilator" and Contemporary Literary Culture in Old Norse Hagiography', *Viking and Medieval Scandinavia* 1 (2005), 1–13

Battles, Paul, 'Dying for a Drink: "Sleeping after the Feast" Scenes in *Beowulf, Andreas*, and the Old English Poetic Tradition', *Modern Philology* 112.3 (2015), 435–57

Bauer, Alessia, 'Encyclopaedic Tendencies and the Medieval Educational Programme', in *Speculum septentrionale: Konungs skuggsjá and the European Encyclopedia of the Middle Ages*, ed. Karl G. Johansson and Elise Kleivane (Oslo: Novus Forlag, 2018), 217–44

Bekker-Nielsen, Hans and Widding, Ole, 'Fra ordbogens værksted', *Opuscula* 1 (1960), 341–49

——, 'The Fifteen Steps of the Temple: A Problem in the *Maríu saga*', *Opuscula* 2.1 (1961), 80–91

Berg, Kirsten M., 'Homilieboka – for hvem og til hva?', in *Vår eldste bok: Skrift, miljø og biletbruk i den norske homiliebok*, ed. Odd Einar Haugen and Åslaug Ommundsen (Oslo: Novus, 2000), 35–76

Bergljót Soffía Kristjánsdóttir, 'Hinn seki túlkandi: Um tákn, túlkun og sekt í styttri gerð Gísla sögu Súrssonar', *Gripla* 12 (2001), 7–21

Berndt, Rainer, *André de Saint-Victor (d. 1175): Exegète et Théologien* (Paris: Brepols, 1991)

——, 'The School of St Victor in Paris', in *Hebrew Bible/Old Testament: The History of its Interpretation, Volume 1 From the Beginnings to the Middle Ages (until 1300). Part 2 The Middle Ages*, ed. Magne Sæbø (Göttingen: Vandenhoeck & Ruprecht, 2000), 467–95

Besserman, Lawrence L., *The Legend of Job in the Middle Ages* (Cambridge, MA: Harvard University, 2014)

Blenkinsopp, Joseph, *Creation, Uncreation, Recreation: A Discursive Commentary on Genesis 1–11* (New York: T & Clark International, 2011)

Bibliography

Blyth, Caroline, 'Redeemed by His Love? The Characterization of Shechem in Genesis 34', *Journal for the Study of Old Testament* 33.1 (2008), 3–18

Bohak, Gideon, 'Classica et Rabbinica I: The Bull of Phalaris and the Tophet', *Journal for the Study of Judaism in the Persian, Hellenistic and Roman Period* 31.1–4 (2000), 203–16

Boitani, Piero, *Anagnorisis: Scenes and Themes of Recognition and Revelation in Western Literature* (Leiden: Brill, 2021)

Bonnard, Fourier, *Historie de l'abbaye royale et de l'ordre de chanoines réguliers de Saint-Victor de Paris*, 2 vols (Paris: A. Savaète, 1905–07)

Bouman, A. C., 'An Aspect of Style in Icelandic Sagas', *Neophilologus* 42.1 (1958), 50–67

Boyle, Elizabeth, 'Biblical Kings and Kingship Theory', in *Speculum septentrionale: Konungs skuggsjá and the European Encyclopedia of the Middle Ages*, ed. Karl G. Johansson and Elise Kleivane (Oslo: Novus Forlag, 2018), 173–99

Bullita, Dario, *Niðrstigningar saga: Sources, Transmission and Theology of the Old Norse 'Descent into Hell'* (Toronto: University of Toronto Press, 2017)

Byrne, Phillipa, 'Exodus 32 and the Figure of Moses in Twelfth-Century Theology', *Journal of Theological Studies* 68.2 (2017), 671–89

Campopiano, Michele, 'Introduction', in *Universal Chronicles in the High Middle Ages*, ed. Michele Campopiano (York: York Medieval Press, 2017), 1–18

Carr, David M., *The Formation of Genesis 1–11: Biblical and Other Precursors* (New York: Oxford University Press, 2020)

Cavadini, John C., 'Exegetical Transformations: The Sacrifice of Isaac in Philo, Origen, and Ambrose', in *In Dominico Eloquio – In Lordly Eloquence: Essays on Patristic Exegesis in Honor of Robert Louis Wilken*, ed. Paul M. Blowers et al. (Grand Rapids, MI: Eerdmans, 2002), 35–49

Ceulemans, Reinhart, 'The Septuagint and Other Translations', in *The Oxford Handbook of Early Christian Biblical Interpretation*, ed. Paul M. Blowers and Peter W. Martens (Oxford: Oxford University Press, 2019), 33–54

Ciletti, Elena and Lähnemann, Henrike, 'Judith in the Christian Tradition', in *The Sword of Judith: Judith Studies across the Disciplines*, ed. Kevin R. Brine, Elena Ciletti and Henrike Lähnemann (Cambridge: OpenBook Publishers, 2010), 41–68

Clark, Mark J., *The Making of the Historia scholastica, 1150–1200* (Toronto: Pontifical Institute of Mediaeval Studies, 2015)

Clifford, R. J., 'Genesis 37–50: Joseph Story or Jacob Story?', in *The Book of Genesis: Composition, Reception and Interpretation*, ed. Craig A. Evans, Joel N. Lohr and David L. Petersen (Leiden: Brill, 2012), 213–29

Clunies Ross, Margaret, *The Cambridge Introduction to the Old Norse-Icelandic Saga* (Cambridge: Cambridge University Press, 2010)

Bibliography

Coats, George W., *Genesis with an Introduction to Narrative Literature* (Grand Rapids, MI: W. B. Eerdmans, 1983)

——, *Moses: Heroic Man, Man of God* (Sheffield: JSOT Press, 1988)

Cohen, Jeremy, *Living Letters of the Law: Ideas of the Jews in Medieval Christianity* (Berkeley: University of California Press, 1999)

Cole, Richard, 'The French Connection, or Þórr versus the Golem', in *Medieval Encounters: Jewish, Christian and Muslim Culture in Confluence and Dialogue* 20.3 (2014), 238–60

——, 'Hebrew in Runic Inscriptions and Elsewhere', *Viking and Medieval Scandinavia* 11 (2015), 33–78

——, 'An Edition and Translation of the Icelandic Book of Joseph and Asenath', *Journal for the Study of the Pseudepigrapha* 26.3 (2017), 167–200

——, 'Echoes of the Book of Joseph and Asenath, Particularly in *Yngvars saga víðfǫrla*', *Saga-Book* 41 (2017), 5–34

Collings, Lucy, 'Codex Scardensis: Studies in Icelandic Hagiography', PhD thesis, Cornell University, 1979

Conti, Aidan, 'Gamalt og nytt i homiliebokens prekeunivers', in *Vår eldste bok: Skrift, miljø og biletbruk i den norske homiliebok*, ed. Odd Einar Haugen and Åslaug Ommundsen (Oslo: Novus, 2000), 165–86

Coulter, Dale M., *Per visibilia ad invisibilia: Theological Method in Richard of St Victor (d. 1173)* (Turnhout: Brepols, 2006)

——, 'Introduction to Richard of St Victor, *The Book of Notes* (selections)', in *Interpretation of Scripture: Theory: A Selection of Works by Hugh, Andrew Godfrey and Richard of St Victor*, ed. Franklin T. Harkins and Frans van Liere (Turnhout: Brepols, 2012), 289–95

Crocker, Christopher, 'All I Do the Whole Night Through: On the Dreams of Gísli Súrsson', *Scandinavian Studies* 84.2 (2012), 143–62

Dahan, Gilbert, 'La méthode critique dans l'étude de la Bible (XII–XIIIe siècles)', in *La méthode critique au Moyen Âge*, ed. Mireille Chazan and Gilbert Dahan (Turnhout: Brepols, 2006), 103–28

——, 'Les pères dans l'exégèse mediévale de la Bible', *Revue des Sciences Philosophiques et Théologiques* 91.1 (2007), 109–27

Daly, Saralyn, R., 'Peter Comestor: Master of Histories', *Speculum* 32.1 (1957), 62–73

Damrosch, David, *The Narrative Covenant: Transformations of Genre in the Growth of Biblical Literature* (London: Harper & Row, 1987)

Dawson, David, *Christian Figural Reading and the Fashioning of Identity* (Berkeley: University of California Press, 2002)

Day, John, *From Creation to Babel: Genesis 1–11* (London: Bloomsbury, 2013)

Dean, Nicholas Andrew, *The Trickster Revisited: Deception as a Motif in the Pentateuch* (Oxford: Peter Lang, 2009)

Bibliography

De Andrado, Paba Nidhani, '"A Model of Christ": Melito's Re-Vision of Jewish Akedah Exegeses', *Studies in Christian-Jewish Relations* 12.1 (2017), 1–18

DeGregorio, Scott, 'Gregory's Exegesis: Old and New Ways of Approaching the Scriptural Text', in *A Companion to Gregory the Great*, ed. Bronwen Neil and Matthew Dal Santo (Boston: Brill, 2013), 269–90

de Jonge, Marinus, 'Robert Grosseteste and the Testaments of the Twelve Patriarchs', *Journal of Theological Studies* 42.1 (1991), 115–25

de Lubac, Henri, *History and Spirit: The Understanding of Scripture according to Origen*, trans. Anne Englund Nash (San Francisco, CA: Ignatius Press, 2007)

De Troyer, Kristin, 'The Septuagint', in *The New Cambridge History of the Bible,* ed. James Carleton Paget and Joachim Schaper, 4 vols (Cambridge: Cambridge University Press, 2012–15), I (2013), 267–88

Dolezalova, Lucie, 'The Dining Room of God: Petrus Comestor's "Historia scholastica" and Retelling the Bible as Feasting', in *Retelling the Bible: Literary, Historical and Social Contexts*, ed. Lucie Dolezalova and Tamas Visi (Frankfurt am Main: Peter Lang, 2011), 229–44

Dorival, Gilles, 'Origen', in *The New Cambridge History of the Bible*, ed. James Carleton Paget and Joachim Schaper, 4 vols (Cambridge: Cambridge University Press, 2012–2015), I (2013), 605–28

Drechsler, Stefan, *Illuminated Manuscript Production in Medieval Iceland: Literary and Artistic Activities of the Monastery at Helgafell in the Fourteenth Century* (Turnhout: Brepols, 2021)

Dronke, Peter, *Poetic Individuality in the Middle Ages: New Departures in Poetry* (Oxford: Clarendon, 1970)

Edstam, Torsten K., 'The Reception of the Victorines', in *A Companion to the Abbey of St Victor in Paris*, ed. Hugh Feiss and Juliet Mousseau (Leiden: Brill, 2017), 547–78

Einar G. Pétursson, 'Guðbrandur Þorláksson og bókaútgáfa hans', in *Hulin pláss. Ritgerðasafn* (Reykjavík: Stofnun Árna Magnússonar í íslenskum fræðum, 2011), 93–109

Einar Ólafur Sveinsson, 'Athugasemdir um *Stjórn*', in *Studia Centenalia. In honorem memoriae Benedikt S. Þórarinsson*, ed. B. S. Benedikz (Reykjavík: Typis Ísafoldianis, 1961), 17–32

——, *Njáls saga: A Literary Masterpiece* (Lincoln: University of Nebraska Press, 1971)

Eldjárn, Kristján and Hörður Ágústsson, *Skálholt: Skrúði og áhöld* (Reykjavík: Hið íslenska bókmenntafélag, 1992)

Eriksen, Stefka, 'Pedagogy and Attitudes towards Knowledge in the King's Mirror', *Viator* 45.3 (2014), 143–68

Evans, Gillian R., *The Language and Logic of the Bible: The Earlier Middle Ages* (Cambridge: Cambridge University Press, 1984)

Bibliography

Exum, J. Cheryl, 'The Many Faces of Samson', in *Samson: Hero or Fool? The Many Faces of Samson*, ed. Erik M. M. Eynikel and Tobias Nicklas (Leiden: Brill, 2014), 13–31

——, *Fragmented Women: Feminist (Sub)versions of Biblical Narratives* (London: Bloomsbury, 2016)

Fairise, Christelle, 'Relating Mary's Life in Medieval Iceland: Similarities and Differences with the Continental Lives of the Virgin', *Arkiv for nordisk filologi* 129 (2014), 165–96

Feder, Yitzhaq, 'The Defilement of Dinah: Uncontrolled Passions, Textual Violence and the Search for Moral Foundations', *Biblical Interpretation* 24.3 (2016), 281–309

Feldman, Louis, 'The Jewish Sources of Peter Comestor's Commentary on Genesis', *in Begegnungen zwischen Christentum und Judentum in Antike und Mittelalter: Festschrift für Heinz Schreckenberg*, ed. Dietrich-Alex Koch et al. (Göttingen: Vandenhoek & Ruprecht, 1993), 93–122

Ferreiro, Alberto, 'Job in the Sermons of Caesarius of Arles', *Recherches du théologie ancienne et médiévale* 54 (1987), 13–26

Fokkelman, Jan P., *Narrative Art and Poetry in the Books of Samuel: A Full Interpretation Based on Stylistic and Structural Analyses* (Assen: Van Gorcum, 1986)

——, *Reading Biblical Narrative: A Practical Guide* (Leiden, Boston: Brill, 1999)

Fox, Michael and Sharma, Manish (eds), *Old English Literature and the Old Testament* (Toronto: University of Toronto Press, 2017)

Franklin-Brown, Mary, *Reading the World: Encyclopedic Writing in the Scholastic Age* (Chicago and London: University of Chicago Press, 2012)

Fredricksen, Paul, *Augustine and the Jews: A Christian Defence of Jews and Judaism* (New York and London: Doubleday, 2008)

Gallagher, Edmon, 'Why Did Jerome Translate Tobit and Judith?', *Harvard Theological Review* 108.3 (2015), 356–75

Geiger, Ari, '*Historia Judaica*: Petrus Comestor and His Jewish Sources', in *Pierre le mangeur ou Pierre de Troyes, maître du XIIe siècle*, ed. Gilbert Dahan (Turnhout: Brepols, 2013), 125–45

Green, Barbara, 'Joab's Coherence and Incoherence: Character and Characterization', in *Characters and Characterisation in the Book of Samuel*, ed. Keith Bodner (London: T&T Clark, 2019), 183–204

Green, William M., 'Hugo of St Victor: *De tribus maximis circumstantiis gestorum*', *Speculum* 18 (1943), 483–93

Grønlie, Siân, '"Cast out this bondwoman": Hagar and Ishmael in Old Norse-Icelandic Literature', *Arkiv for nordisk filologi* 134 (2019), 25–48

Gunkel, Hermann, *The Legends of Genesis: The Biblical Saga and History*, trans. William Foxwell Albright (New York: Schocken, 1964)

Bibliography

——, *Genesis*, trans. Mark E. Biddle (Macon, GA: Mercer University Press, 1997)

Gunn, David M., *Story of King David: Genre and Interpretation* (Sheffield: JSOT, 1978)

Gunnar Harðarson, *Littérature et spiritualité en Scandinave médiévale : La traduction norroise du De arrha animae de Hugues de Saint-Victor* (Paris: Brepols, 1995)

——, 'Music and Manuscripts in Skálholt and Þingeyrar', in *Dominican Resonances in Medieval Iceland: The Legacy of Bishop Jón Halldórsson of Skálholt*, ed. Gunnar Harðarson and Karl-Gunnar Johansson (Leiden: Brill, 2021), 260–89

Guðbjörg Kristjánsdóttir, 'Handritalýsingar í benediktínasklaustrinu á Þingeyrum', in *Íslensk klausturmenning á miðöldum*, ed. Haraldur Bernharðsson (Reykjavík: Miðaldastofa Háskóla Íslands, 2016), 241–50

Hailperin, Herman, *Rashi and the Christian Scholars* (Pittsburgh: University of Pittsburgh Press, 1963)

Hall, Thomas N., 'Old Norse-Icelandic Sermons', in *The Sermon*, ed. Beverly Mayne Kienzle (Turnhout: Brepols, 2000), 661–709

Hallberg, Peter, 'Some Observations on the Language of *Dunstanus saga*: With an Appendix on the Bible Translation *Stjórn*', *Saga-Book* 18 (1973), 346–53

——, 'The concept of *gipta-gæfa-hamingja* in Old Norse Literature', in *Proceedings of the First International Saga Conference, University of Edinburgh, 1971*, ed. Peter Foote et al. (London: Viking Society for Northern Research, 1973), 143–83

Hamer, Andrew, 'Searching for Wisdom: The King's Mirror', in *Speculum regale: Der altnorwegische Koeningsspiegel (Konungs skuggsja) in der europaischen Tradition*, ed. Jens Eike Schnall and Rudolf Simek (Vienna: Fassbaender, 2000), 47–62

——, *Njáls saga and its Christian Background: A Study of Narrative Method* (Leuven: Peters, 2014)

Harkins, Franklin T., *Reading and the Work of Restoration: History and Scripture in the Theology of Hugh of St Victor* (Toronto: Pontifical Institute of Medieval Studies, 2009)

Harris, Joseph, 'Obscure Styles (Old English and Old Norse) and the Enigma of *Gísla saga*', *Mediaevalia* 19 (1993), 75–99

Harris, Robert A., 'Jewish biblical exegesis', in *The New Cambridge History of the Bible*, ed. James Carleton Paget and Joachim Schaper, 4 vols (Cambridge: Cambridge University Press, 2012–15), II (2012), 596–611

Haugen, Odd Einar, 'Om tidsforholdet mellom *Stjórn* ok *Barlaams ok Josaphats saga*', *Maal og Minne* (1983), 18–28

Bibliography

Haugen, Odd Einar and Ommundsen, Åslaug, 'Nye blikk på homilieboka', in *Vår eldste bok: Skrift, miljø og biletbruk i den norske homiliebok*, ed. Odd Einar Haugen and Åslaug Ommundsen (Oslo: Novus, 2000), 9–33

Heine, Ronald, *Origen: Scholarship in the Service of the Church* (Oxford: Oxford University Press, 2010)

Henze, Matthias, 'King Manasseh of Judah in Early Judaism and Christianity', in *On Prophets, Warriors and Kings: Former Prophets through the Eyes of their Interpreters*, ed. George J. Brooke and Ariel Feldman (Berlin and Boston: De Gruyter, 2016), 181–228

Hermann Pálsson, 'På leting etter røttene til Víga-Glúms saga', *Maal og Minne* (1959), 18–26

——, *Art and Ethics in Hrafnkel's Saga* (Copenhagen: Munksgaard, 1971)

——, 'Death in Autumn: Tragic Elements in Early Icelandic Fiction', *BONIS* 1973 (1974), 7–39

——, 'Um gæfumenn ok ógæfu í íslenzkum fornsögum', in *Festskrift til Björns Sigfússonar*, ed. Björn Teitsson (Reykjavík: Sögufélag, 1975), 135–53

——, '*Hrafnkels saga* og *Stjórn*', in *Sjötíu ritgerðir helgaðar Jakobi Benediktssyni, 20 júlí 1977*, ed. Einar G. Pétursson and Jónas Kristjánsson, 2 vols (Reykjavík: Stofnun Árna Magnússonar á Íslandi, 1977), I, 335–43

Hicks-Keeton, Jill, *Arguing with Asenath: Gentile Access to Israel's Living God in Jewish Antiquity* (New York: Oxford University Press, 2018)

Hofmann, Dietrich, 'Die Königsspiegel-Zitate in der Stiorn', *Skandinavistik* 3 (1973), 1–40

Holmes, Stephen Mark, 'Reading the Church: William Durandus and a New Approach to the History of Ecclesiology', *Ecclesiology* 7.1 (2011), 24–49

Holtsmark, Anne, 'The *Speculum regale* and the apples in the garden of Eden', *Viking* 20 (1952), 141–56

Hooguliet, Margriet, 'The Medieval Vernacular Bible in French as a Flexible Text: Selective and Discontinuous Reading Practices', in *Form and Function in the Late Medieval Bible*, ed. Eyal Poleg and Laura Light (Leiden: Brill, 2013), 283–306

Jakob Benediktsson, 'Some Observations on *Stjórn* and the Manuscript AM 227 fol.', *Gripla* 15 (2004), 7–42

Jóhanna Friðriksdóttir, *Women in Old Norse Literature: Bodies, Words, and Power* (New York: Palgrave Macmillan, 2013)

Johannessen, Ole-Jörgen, 'Litt om kildene til Jóns saga baptista II', in *Opuscula septentrionalia: Festskrift til Ole Widding*, ed. Bent Christian Jacobsen et al. (Copenhagen: C. A. Reitzel forlag, 1977), 100–15

Johansson, Karl G. and Kleivane, Elise, '*Konungs skuggsjá* and the Interplay between the Universal and the Particular', in *Speculum septentrionale: Konungs skuggsjá and the European Encyclopedia of the Middle Ages*, ed. Karl G. Johansson and Elise Kleivane (Oslo: Novus Forlag, 2018), 9–34

Bibliography

Johnson, Janell, 'Negotiating Masculinities in Dinah's Story: Honor and Outrage in Genesis 34', *Review and Expositor* 115.4 (2018), 529–41

Jónas Kristjánsson, 'Learned Style or Saga Style', in *Speculum Norroenum: Norse Studies in Memory of Gabriel Turville-Petre*, ed. Ursula Dronke et al. (Odense: Odense University Press, 1981), 260–92

Jordan, Mark D., 'Words and Word: Incarnation and Signification in Augustine's *De Doctrina Christiana*', *Augustinian Studies* 11 (1980),177–96

Kalinke, Marianne, *Bridal-Quest Romance in Medieval Iceland* (Ithaca, NY: Cornell University Press, 1990)

——, 'The Cowherd and the Saint: The Grateful Lion in Icelandic Folktale and Legend', *Scandinavian Studies* 66.1 (1994), 1–22

Kamesar, Adam, *Jerome, Greek Scholarship and the Hebrew Bible: A Study of the Quaestiones Hebraicae in Genesim* (Oxford: Clarendon Press, 1993)

——, 'Jerome', in *The New Cambridge History of the Bible*, ed. James Carleton Paget and Joachim Schaper, 4 vols (Cambridge: Cambridge University Press, 2012–15), 1 (2013), 653–75

Kaminsky, Joel S., *Yet I Loved Jacob: Reclaiming the Biblical Concept of Election* (Nashville, TN: Abingdon Press, 2007)

——, 'The Theology of Genesis', in *The Book of Genesis: Composition, Reception and Interpretation*, ed. Craig A. Evans, Joel N. Lohr and David L. Petersen (Leiden: Brill, 2012), 635–56

Karkov, Catherine, 'Hagar and Ishmael: The Uncanny and the Exile', in *Imagining the Jew in Anglo-Saxon Literature and Culture*, ed. Samantha Zacher (Toronto: University of Toronto Press, 2001), 197–218

Karp, Sandra, 'Peter Comestor's *Historia scholastica*: A Study in the Development of Literal Scriptural Exegesis', PhD thesis, Tulane University, 1978

Kawashima, Robert S., *Biblical Narrative and the Death of the Rhapsode* (Bloomington, IN: Indiana University Press, 2004)

——, 'Literary Analysis', in *The Book of Genesis: Composition, Reception and Interpretation*, ed. Craig A. Evans, Joel N. Lohr and David L. Petersen (Leiden: Brill, 2012), 83–104

Kedar, Benjamin, 'The Latin Translations', in *Mikra: Text, Translation, Reading and Interpretation of the Hebrew Bible in Ancient Judaism and Early Christianity*, ed. M. J. Mulder and Henry Sysling (Assen: Van Gorcum, 1988), 299–338

Ker, William Paton, *Epic and Romance: Essays on Medieval Literature* (New York: Dover, 1957)

Kessler, Edward, *Bound by the Bible: Jews, Christians and the Sacrifice of Isaac* (Cambridge: Cambridge University Press, 2004)

Kessler, Stephen, 'Gregory the Great: A Figure of Tradition and Transition', in *Hebrew Bible/Old Testament: The History of its Interpretation. Volume*

Bibliography

I: From the Beginnings to the Middle Ages (Until 1300). Part 2 The Middle Ages, ed. Magne Sæbø (Göttingen: Vandenhoeck & Ruprecht, 1996), 135–47

Kirby, Ian J., *Biblical Quotation in Old Norse-Icelandic Religious Literature*, 2 vols (Reykjavík: Stofnun Árna Magnússonar, 1976–80)

——, *Bible Translation in Old Norse* (Genève: Librarie Droz, 1986)

——, 'Biblical Literature', in *Old Icelandic Literature and Society*, ed. Margaret Clunies Ross (Cambridge: Cambridge University Press, 2000), 287–301

Klein, Lillian R., *From Deborah to Esther: Sexual Politics in the Hebrew Bible* (Minneapolis: Fortress, 2003)

Kleivane, Elise, 'There is More to *Stjórn* than Biblical Translation', in *Speculum septentrionale. Konungs skuggsjá and the European Encyclopedia of the Middle Ages*, ed. Elise Kleivane and Karl G. Johansson (Oslo: Novus, 2018), 115–47

Kochenash, Michael, 'Trojan Horses: The Counter-Intuitive Use of Dinah, Helen and Goliath in Joseph and Asenath', *Journal for the Study of Judaism* 52 (2021), 417–41

Konráð Gíslason, *Um frumparta íslenzkrar túngu í fornöld* (Copenhagen: Trier, 1846)

Kopár, Lilla, *Gods and Settlers: The Iconography of Norse Mythology in Anglo-Scandinavian Sculpture* (Turnhout: Brepols, 2012)

Korpel, Marjo C. A., *The Structure of the Book of Ruth* (Leiden: Brill, 2001)

Kraus, Matthew A., *Jewish, Christian and Classical Exegetical Traditions in Jerome's Translation of the Book of Exodus: Translation Technique and the Vulgate* (Leiden: Brill, 2017)

Kugler, Robert A., *The Testaments of the Twelve Patriarchs* (Sheffield: Sheffield Academic Press, 2001)

LaCocque, André, *The Feminine Unconventional: Four Subversive Figures in Israel's Tradition* (Minneapolis: Fortree, 1990)

——, 'An Ancestral Narrative: The Joseph Story', in André LaCocque and Paul Ricœur, *Thinking Biblically: Exegetical and Hermeneutical Studies*, trans. David Pellauer (Chicago: University of Chicago Press, 1998), 365–97

Lassen, Annette, 'The Old Norse Contextuality of *Bárðar saga Snæfellsáss*: A Synoptic Reading with *Óláfs saga Tryggvasonar*', in *Folklore in Old Norse – Old Norse in Folklore*, ed. Daniel Sävborg and Karen Bek-Pedersen (Tartu: University Press of Tartu, 2014), 102–19

——, 'Indigenous and Latin Literature', in *The Routledge Research Companion to the Medieval Icelandic Sagas*, ed. Ármann Jakobsson and Sverrir Jakobsson (London: Routledge, 2017), 74–87

Lee, Brian S., 'Transforming the Vulgate: Comestor and the Middle English *Genesis and Exodus*', *Mediaevistik* 31 (2018), 133–52

Lethbridge, Emily, Icelandic Saga Map, at http://sagamap.hi.is/is/#

Bibliography

Light, Laura, 'Non-Biblical Texts in Thirteenth-Century Bibles', in *Medieval Manuscripts, their Makers and Users: A Special Issue of Viator in Honor of Richard and Mary Rouse* (Turnhout: Brepols, 2011), 169–83

Linafelt, Tod, 'Private Poetry and Public Eloquence in 2 Samuel 1:17–27: Hearing and Overhearing David's Lament for Jonathan and Saul', *Journal of Religion* 88.4 (2008), 497–526

——, 'The Pentateuch', in *The Oxford Handbook of English Literature and Theology*, ed. Andrew Hass, David Jasper and Elizabeth Jay (Oxford: Oxford University Press, 2009), 214–26

——, 'On Biblical Style', *St John's Review*, 54.1 (2013), 17–42

——, 'Poetry and Biblical Narrative', in *The Oxford Handbook of Biblical Narrative*, ed. Danna Nolen Fewell (Oxford: Oxford University Press, 2016), 84–92

Linafelt, Tod and Beal, T. K., *Ruth and Esther* (Collegeville: Liturgical, 1999)

Lindow, John, *Trolls: An Unnatural History* (London: Reaktion Books, 2014)

Livingston, Michael, 'Introduction', in *The Middle English Metrical Paraphrase of the Old Testament*, ed. Michael Livingston (Kalamazoo, MI: TEAMS, 2011), 1–43

Lobrichon, Guy, 'Un nouveau genre pour un public novice: la paraphrase biblique dans l'espace roman du XIIe siècle', in *The Church and Vernacular Literature in Medieval France*, ed. Dorothea Kullmann (Toronto: Pontifical Institute of Mediaeval Studies, 2009), 87–108

——, 'Le mangeur au festin. L'*Historia scholastica* aux mains de ses lecteurs: Glose, Bible en images, Bibles historiales (fin XIIIe–XIVe siècle)', in *Pierre le mangeur ou Pierre de Troyes, maître du XIIe siècle*, ed. Gilbert Dahan (Turnhout: Brepols, 2013), 289–312

——, 'The Story of a Success: The *Bible historiale* in France (1295–1500)', in *Form and Function in the Late Medieval Bible*, ed. Eyal Poleg and Laura Light (Leiden: Brill, 2013), 307–31

Lönnroth, Lars, 'Rhetorical Persuasion in the Sagas', *Scandinavian Studies* 42.2 (1970), 157–89

——, 'Sverrir's Dreams', *Scripta Islandica* 57 (2006), 97–110

Louth, Andrew and Conti, Marco, *Genesis 1–11* (Downers Grove, IL: Intervarsity Press, 2001)

Lowden, John, 'The *Bible moralisée* in the Fifteenth Century', *Journal of the Warburg and Courtauld Institutes* 68 (2005), 73–136

Luscombe, David, 'Peter Comestor and Biblical Chronology', *Irish Theological Quarterly* 80.2 (2015), 136–48

Marchand, James W., 'The Allegories in the Old Norse *Veraldar Saga*', *Michigan Germanic Studies* 1.1 (1975), 109–18

——, 'An Old Norse Fragment of a Psalm Commentary', *Maal og Minne* (1976), 24–29

278

Bibliography

Marner, Astrid, 'glosur lesnar af undirdiupin omeliarum hins mikla Gregorij, Augustini, Ambrosij ok Jeronimi ok annarra kennifedra: Väterzitate und Politik in der Jóns saga baptista des Grímr Hólmsteinsson', PhD thesis, University of Bonn, 2013

Marsden, Richard, *The Text of the Old Testament in Anglo-Saxon England* (Cambridge: Cambridge University Press, 1995)

——, 'The Bible in English in the Middle Ages', in *The Practice of the Bible in the Middle Ages: Production, Reception and Performance in Western Christianity*, ed. Susan Boyton and Diane Reilly (New York: Columbia University Press, 2011), 272–95

Matis, Hannah W., *The Song of Songs in the Early Middle Ages* (Leiden: Brill, 2019)

McAllister, Patricia, 'The Middle Low German *Historienbibel* Helmstedt 611.1: A Critical Edition of Genesis and Exodus', PhD thesis, Indiana University, 1988

McBrine, Patrick, *Biblical Epics in Late Antiquity and Anglo-Saxon England* (Toronto: University of Toronto Press, 2017)

McDougall, David, 'Pseudo-Augustinian Passages in *Jóns saga baptista II* and *The Fourth Grammatical Treatise*', *Traditio* 44 (1988), 463–83

McDougall, Ian, 'Studies in the Prose Style of the Old Icelandic and Old Norwegian Homily Books', PhD thesis, University of London, 2013

McGraph, Elizabeth, 'Jacob Jordaens and Moses' Ethiopian Wife', *Journal of the Warburg and Courtauld Institutes* 70 (2007), 247–85

Melinkoff, Ruth, 'Sarah and Hagar: Laughter and Tears', in *Illuminating the Book: Makers and Interpreters*, ed. Michelle Brown and Scott McKendrick (Toronto: University of Toronto Press, 1998), 35–51

Miller, William Ian, 'Feeling Another's Pain: Sympathy and Psychology Saga Style', *European Review* 22.1 (2014), 55–63

——, *Hrafnkel or the Ambiguities: Hard Cases, Hard Choices* (Oxford: Oxford University Press, 2017)

Minnis, A. J., *Medieval Theory of Authorship: Scholastic Literary Attitudes in the Later Middle Ages* (Philadelphia: University of Pennsylvania Press, 1988)

Molan, Steven, 'The Identity of Jacob's Opponent: Wrestling with Ambiguity in Genesis 32: 22–32', *Shofar* 11.2 (1993), 16–29

Molland, Einar, 'Les quatres filles de Dieu', in *Épektasis: Mélanges patristiques offerts au cardinal Jean Daniélou*, ed. Jacques Fontaine and Charles Kannengiesser (Paris: Beauchesne, 1972), 155–69

Moore, Rebecca, *Jews and Christians in the Life and Thought of Hugh of St Victor* (Atlanta, GA: Scholars Press, 1998)

Morey, James, 'Peter Comestor, Biblical Paraphrase and the Medieval Popular Bible', *Speculum* 68.1 (1993), 6–35

Bibliography

Mortensen, Lars Bøje, 'Hugh of St Victor on Secular History', *Cahiers de l'institut du Moyen-Age grec et latin* 62 (1992), 3–30

Munk-Olsen, Birger, 'Trois étudiants danois á Paris au XIIe siècle', in *Mélanges d'histoire, de littérature et de mythologie Hugur offerts à Régis Boyer pour son 65e anniversaire*, ed. Claude Lecouteux (Paris: Presses de l'Université de Paris-Sorbonne, 1997), 87–96

Munro, Hector H. and Chadwick, Nora K., *The Growth of Literature*, 3 vols (London: Cambridge University Press, 1932–40)

Najork, Daniel C., *Reading the Old Norse-Icelandic 'Maríu saga' in its Manuscript Contexts* (Kalamazoo, MI: Medieval Institute Publications, 2012)

Neff, Robert W., 'Saga', in *Saga, Legend, Tale, Novella, Fable: Narrative Forms in Old Testament Literature*, ed. George W. Coats (Sheffield: JSOT, 1985), 17–32

Nelson, Richard D., 'The Former Prophets and Historiography', in *The Cambridge Companion to the Hebrew Bible/Old Testament*, ed. Stephen B. Chapman and Marvin A. Sweeney (Cambridge: Cambridge University Press, 2016), 215–32

——, 'Historiography and History-Writing in the Ancient World', in *The Oxford Handbook of the Historical Books of the Bible*, ed. Brad E. Kelle and Brent A. Strawn (Oxford: Oxford University Press, 2020), 6–19

Niditch, Susan, *A Prelude to Biblical Folklore: Underdogs and Tricksters* (San Francisco: Harper & Row, 1987)

——, 'The Role of Orality and Textuality, Folklore and Scribalism in the Historical Books', in *The Oxford Handbook of the Historical Books of the Hebrew Bible*, ed. Brad E. Kelle and Brent E. Strawn (Oxford: Oxford University Press, 2020), 393–405

Nordal, Sigurður, *Hrafnkels saga Freysgoða: A Study* (Cardiff: University of Wales Press, 1958)

Ocker, Christopher, *Biblical Poetics Before Humanism and Reformation* (Cambridge: Cambridge University Press, 2002)

O'Donoghue, Heather, 'What has Lamech to do with Baldr: The Lethal Shot of a Blind Man in Old Norse Myth and Jewish Exegetical Traditions', *Medium Ævum* 72.1 (2003), 82–107

——, *Skaldic Verse and the Poetics of Saga Narrative* (Oxford: Oxford University Press, 2005)

——, *Narrative in the Icelandic Family Saga: Meanings of Time in Old Norse Literature* (London: Bloomsbury, 2021)

Orlov, Andrei A., 'Overshadowed by Enoch's Greatness: "Two Tablets" Traditions from the *Book of Giants* to the *Palaea Historica*', *Journal for the Study of Judaism* 32.1–4 (2001), 137–58

Paasche, Fredrik, 'Esras aabenbaring og Pseudo-Cyprianus i norrön litteratur', in *Festskrift til Finnur Jónsson*, ed. Johns. Brondum-Nielsen et al. (Copenhagen: Levin & Munksgaard, 1928), 199–205

Bibliography

Páll Eggert Ólason, *Menn og menntir siðskiptaaldarinnar á Íslandi*, 4 vols (Reykjavík: Bókaverslun Ársæls Árnarsonar, 1919–26)

Pardes, Ilana, 'Zipporah and the Struggle for Deliverance', in *Countertraditions in the Bible: A Feminist Approach* (Cambridge, MA: Harvard University Press, 1992), 80–97

Paulmier-Foucart, Monique, 'Vincent de Beauvais et l'histoire du *Speculum Maius*', *Journal des savants*, 1–2 (1990), 97–124

Pelle, Stephen, 'A New Source for Part of an Old Icelandic Christmas Homily', *Saga-Book* 36 (2012), 102–116

——, 'Twelfth-Century Sources for Old Norse Homilies: New Evidence from AM 655 XXVII 4to', *Gripla* 24 (2013), 45–75

——, 'An Old Norse Homily and Two Homiletic Fragments from AM 624 4to', *Gripla* 27 (2016), 263–89

Perkins, Richard, 'An Edition of *Flóamanna saga* with a Study of its Sources and Analogues', PhD thesis, Oxford University, 1972

Petersen, David L., 'Genesis and Family Values', *Journal of Biblical Literature* 124.1 (2005), 5–23

Pettit, David, 'When the Lord seeks to kill Moses', *Journal for the Study of the Old Testament* 40.2 (2015), 163–77

Poland, Lynn M., 'Augustine, Allegory and Conversion', *Literature and Theology* 2.1 (1988), 37–48

Potz McGerr, Rosemarie, 'Guyart desmoulins, the Vernacular Master of Histories, and his *Bible historiale*', *Viator* 14 (1983), 211–44

Quain, E. A., 'The Medieval *Accessus ad Auctores*', *Traditio* 3 (1945), 228–42

Quick, Laura, 'Decorated Women: A Sociological Approach to the Function of Cosmetics in the Books of Esther and Ruth', *Biblical Interpretation* 27.3 (2019), 354–71

——, 'The Book of Ruth and the Limits of Female Wisdom', *Journal of Biblical Literature* 139.1 (2020), 47–66

Rajak, Tessa, 'Moses in Ethiopia: Legend and Literature', *Journal of Jewish Studies* 29 (1978), 111–22

Remley, Paul G., *Old English Biblical Verse: Studies in Genesis, Exodus and Daniel* (Cambridge: Cambridge University Press, 1996)

Römer, Thomas, 'The Narrative Books of the Hebrew Bible', in *The Hebrew Bible: A Critical Companion*, ed. John Barton (Princeton, NJ: Princeton University Press, 2016), 109–32

Roughton, Philip, 'Stylistics and Sources of the *Postola sögur* in AM 645 4to and AM 652/630 4to', *Gripla* 16 (2005), 7–50

Runnalls, Donna, 'Moses' Ethiopian Campaign', *Journal for the Study of Judaism* 14.2 (1983), 135–56

Sapir Abulafia, Anna, 'The Bible in Jewish-Christian Dialogue', in *The New Cambridge History of the Bible*, ed. James Carleton Paget and Joachim

Bibliography

Schaper, 4 vols (Cambridge: Cambridge University Press, 2012–15), II (2012), 616–37

Sayers, William, 'The Alien and Alienated as Unquiet Dead in the Sagas of the Icelanders', in *Monster Theory: Reading Culture*, ed. Jeffrey J. Cohen (Minneapolis: University of Minneapolis Press, 1996), 242–63

Sävborg, Daniel, 'Kärleken i *Laxdœla saga* – höviskt och sagatypiskt', *Alvíssmál* 11 (2004), 75–104

——, 'Style', in *The Routledge Research Companion to the Medieval Icelandic Sagas*, ed. Ármann Jakobsson and Sverrir Jakobsson (London and New York: Routledge, 2017), 111–26

Sävborg, Daniel and Bek-Pedersen, Karen, 'Introduction', in *Folklore in Old Norse – Old Norse in Folklore*, ed. Daniel Sävborg and Karen Bek-Pedersen (Tartu: University of Tartu Press, 2014), 7–13

Schier, Kurt, 'Iceland and The Rise of Literature in "terra nova": Some Comparative Reflections', *Gripla* 1 (1975), 168–81

Schipper, Jeremy, *Ruth: A New Translation with Introduction and Commentary* (New Haven, CT: Yale University Press, 2016)

Schoenfeld, Devorah, *Isaac on Jewish and Christian Altars: Polemic and Exegesis in Rashi and the Glossa ordinaria* (New York: Fordham University Press, 2013)

Scholes, Robert and Kellogg, Robert, *The Nature of Narrative* (New York: Oxford University Press, 1966)

Schroeder, Joy A., *The Book of Genesis* (Grand Rapids, MI: William B. Eerdmans, 2015)

Schrunk Ericksen, Janet, *Reading Old English Biblical Poetry: The Book and the Poem in Junius 11* (Toronto: University of Toronto Press, 2020)

Selma Jónsdóttir, *Illumination in a Manuscript of Stjórn* (Reykjavík: Almenna Bókafélagið, 1971)

Shemesh, Yael, 'Rape is rape is rape: The Story of Dinah and Shechem (Genesis 34)', *Zeitschrift für die Alttestamentliche Wissenschaft* 199.1 (2007), 2–21

Shereshevsky, Esra, 'Hebrew Traditions in Peter Comestor's *Historia scholastica*: I. Genesis', *Jewish Quarterly Review* 59.4 (1969), 268–89

Sherwood-Smith, Maria, 'Die "historia scholastica" als Quelle biblischer Stoffe im Mittelalter', in *Die Vermittlung geistlicher Inhalte im deutschen Mittelalter*, ed. Timothy R. Jackson, Nigel F. Palmer and Almut Sauerbaum (Tübingen: Niemeyer, 1996), 153–65

——, 'Old Friends: David and Jonathan', *Oxford German Studies* 36.2 (2007), 163–83

Sicard, Patrice, *Diagrammes médiévaux et exégèse visuelle, Le libellus de formation arche de Hughes de Saint-Victor* (Turnhout: Brepols, 1993)

Sif Rikharðsdóttir, *Emotion in Old Norse Literature: Translations, Voices, Contexts* (Cambridge: Brewer, 2017)

Bibliography

Signer, Michael A., '*Peshat, Sensus Litteralis* and Sequential Narrative: Jewish Exegesis and the School of St Victor in the Twelfth Century', in *The Frank Talmage Memorial*, vol. I, ed. Barry Walfish (Haifa: Haifa University Press, 1993), 203–16

——, 'Restoring the Narrative: Jewish and Christian Exegesis in the Twelfth Century', in *With Reverence for the Word: Medieval Scriptural Exegesis in Judaism, Christianity and Islam,* ed. Jane Dammen McAuliffe, Barry D. Walfish and Joseph W. Goering (New York: Oxford University Press, 2003), 7–82

Ska, Jean-Louis, 'Genesis 22 or the Testing of Abraham: An Essay on the Levels of Reading', in *The Exegesis of the Pentateuch: Exegetical Studies and Basic Questions* (Tübingen: Mohr Siebeck, 2009), 97–110

Smalley, Beryl, *The Study of the Bible in the Middle Ages* (Notre Dame, IN: Notre Dame University Press, 1964)

Smith, Lesley, *The Glossa ordinaria: The Making of a Medieval Bible Commentary* (Leiden: Brill, 2009)

Sneddon, Clive R., 'The Old French Bible', in *A Companion to Medieval Translation*, ed. Jeannette M. A. Beer (Leeds: Arc Humanities Press, 2019), 23–36

Sørensen, Preben Meulengracht, 'Murder in Marital Bed: An Attempt at Understanding a Crucial Scene in *Gísla saga*', trans. Judith Jesch, in *Structure and Meaning in Old Norse Literature: New Approaches to Textual Analysis and Literary Criticism*, ed. John Lindow et al. (Odense: Odense University Press, 1986), 235–63

——, 'Freyr in den Isländersagas', in *Germanische Religionsgeschichte: Quellen und Quellenprobleme*, ed. Heinrich Beck et al. (Berlin: De Gruyter, 1992), 720–35

Southern, R. W., 'Aspects of the European Tradition of Historical Writing: 2. Hugh of St Victor and the Idea of Historical Development', in *Transactions of the Royal Historiographical Society* 5th ser. 21 (1971), 159–79

Sparks, H. F. D., 'Jerome as Biblical Scholar', in *The Cambridge History of the Bible, Volume I: From the Beginnings to Jerome*, ed. P. R. Ackroyd and C. F. Evans (Cambridge: Cambridge University Press, 1970), 510–41

Springer, Otto, 'The Style of the Old Icelandic Family Saga', *Journal of English and Germanic Philology* 38.1 (1939), 107–28

Stefán Einarsson, *A History of Icelandic Literature* (Baltimore, MD: John Hopkins, 1957)

Stefán Karlsson, 'Fróðleiksgreinar frá tólftu öld', in *Afmælisrit Jóns Helgasonar 30. júni 1969*, ed. Jakob Benediktsson et al. (Reykjavík: Heimskringla, 1969), 328–49

Steinberg, Naomi A., 'The Genealogical Framework of the Family Stories in Genesis', *Semeia* 46 (1989), 41–50

Bibliography

——, 'The World of the Family in Genesis', in *The Book of Genesis: Composition, Reception and Interpretation*, ed. Craig A. Evans, Joel N. Lohr and David L. Petersen (Leiden: Brill, 2012), 279–300

Steinhauser, Kenneth B., 'Job in Patristic Commentaries and Theological Works', in *A Companion to Job in the Middle Ages*, ed. Franklin T. Harkins and Aaron Canty (Leiden: Brill, 2017), 34–70

Sternberg, Meir, *The Poetics of Biblical Narrative: Ideological Literature and the Drama of Reading* (Bloomington, IN: Indiana University Press, 1985)

Stone, Timothy, J., 'The Search for Order: The Compilational History of Ruth', in *The Shape of the Writings*, ed. Julius Steinberg and Rachel Marie Stone (Winona Lake, IN: Eisenbrauns, 2015), 175–86

Storm, Gustav, 'De norsk-islandske bibeloversættelser fra 13de og 14de Aarhundrede og Biskop Brandr Jónsson', *Arkiv for nordisk filologi* 3 (1886), 244–56

Svanhildur Óskarsdóttir, 'The Book of Judith: A Medieval Icelandic Translation', *Gripla* 11 (2000), 79–124

——, 'Universal History in Fourteenth-Century Iceland: Studies in AM 764 4to', PhD thesis, University of London, 2000

——, 'Prose of Christian Instruction', in *A Companion to Old Norse Icelandic Literature and Culture*, ed. Rory McTurk (Malden, MA: Blackwell Publishing, 2005), 338–53

——, 'Heroes or Holy People? The Context of Old Norse Bible Translations', in *Übersetzen in skandinavischen Mittelalter*, ed. Vera Johanterwage and Stefanie Würth (Vienna: Fassbaender, 2007), 107–21

——, 'Arctic Garden of Delights: The Purpose of the Book of Reynistaður', in *Romance and Love in Late Medieval and Early Modern Iceland*, ed. Kirsten Wolf, Johanna Denzin and Marianne E. Kalinke (Ithaca, NY: Cornell University Press, 2008), 279–301

——, 'What Icelandic Nuns Read: The Convent of Reynistaður and the Literary Milieu of Fourteenth-Century Iceland', in *Nuns' Literacies in Medieval Europe: The Kansas City Dialogue*, ed. Virginia Blanton, Veronica O'Mara and Patricia Stoop (Turnhout: Brepols, 2015), 229–48

Sverrir Tómasson, *Formálar íslenskra sagnaritara á miðöldum* (Reykjavík: Stofnun Árna Magnússonar, 1998)

Thompson, John, *Writing the Wrongs: Women of the Old Testament among Biblical Commentators from Philo through the Reformation* (Oxford: Oxford University Press, 2001)

Tomassini, Laura, 'Attempts at Biblical Exegesis in Old Norse: Some Examples from *Maríu saga*', *Opuscula* (Bibliotheca Arnamagnæana) 10 (1996), 129–35

Torjesen, Karen Jo, *Hermeneutical Procedure and Theological Method in Origen's Exegesis* (Berlin and Boston: De Gruyter, 2011)

Bibliography

Trible, Phyllis, *Texts of Terror: Literary-Feminist Readings of Biblical Narratives* (Philadelphia: Fortress Press, 1984)

Tulinius, Torfi, *The Enigma of Egill: the Saga, the Viking Poet, and Snorri Sturluson*, trans. Victoria Cribb (Ithaca, NY: Cornell University Press, 2014)

Turville-Petre, Gabriel, *Origins of Icelandic Literature* (Oxford: Clarendon Press, 1967)

Tveitane, Matthias, 'The "four daughters of God" in the Old Norse King's Mirror', *Neuphilologische Mitteilungen* 73.4 (1972), 795–804

——, 'The Four Daughters of God: A Supplement', *Neuphilologische Mitteilungen* 81.4 (1980), 409–15

——, 'Arbor sapientiae', in *Festskrift til Ludvig Holm-Olsen på hans 70-årsdag den 9. Juni 1984* (Øvre Ervik: Alvheim & Eide, 1984), 308–17

Tveito, Olaf, 'Wulfstan av York og norrøne homilier', in *Vår eldste bok: Skrift, miljø og biletbruk i den norske homiliebok*, ed. Odd Einar Haugen and Åslaug Ommundsen (Oslo: Novus, 2000), 187–215

Valdez, Maria Ana Travassos, *Historical Interpretations of the 'fifth empire': The Dynamics of Periodization from Daniel to António Vieira, S.J.* (Leiden: Brill, 2011)

van den Toorn, Karel and van der Horst, Pieter, 'Nimrod before and after the Bible', *Harvard Theological Review* 83.1 (1990), 1–29.

van Deusen, Natalie, 'Sworn Sisterhood?: On the (Near-)Absence of Female Friendship from the *Íslendingasögur*', *Scandinavian Studies* 86.1 (2014), 52–71

van Liere, Frans, 'Andrew of St Victor and his Franciscan Critics', in *The Multiple Meanings of Scripture: The Role of Exegesis in Early-Christian and Medieval Culture*, ed. Ineke van't Spijker (Boston: Brill, 2009), 291–309

——, *An Introduction to the Medieval Bible* (Cambridge: Cambridge University Press, 2014)

——, 'Introduction to Richard of St Victor, *On Emmanuel*', in *Interpretation of Scripture: Practice. A Selection of Works of Hugh, Andrew, and Richard of St Victor, Peter Comestor, Robert of Melun, Maurice of Sully and Leonius of Paris*, ed. Frans van Liere and Franklin T. Harkins (Turnhout: Brepols, 2015), 349–452

van Seters, John, *The Biblical Saga of King David* (Winona Lake, IN: Eisenbrauns, 2009)

van't Spijker, Ineke 'The Literal and the Spiritual: Richard of St Victor and the Multiple Meanings of Scripture', in *The Multiple Meanings of Scripture: The Role of Exegesis in Early-Christian and Medieval Culture*, ed. Ineke van't Spijker (Boston: Brill, 2009), 225–47

van Wolde, Ellen J., *Ruth and Naomi* (London: SCM, 1997)

Bibliography

——, 'Love and Hatred in a Multi-Racial Society: The Dinah and Shechem Story in Genesis 34 in the Context of Genesis 28–35', in *Reading from Right to Left: Essays on the Hebrew Bible in Honour of David J.A. Clines*, ed. Cheryl J. Williamson and Hugh G. M. Williamson (London: Sheffield Academic Press, 2003), 435–49

Venuti, Lawrence, *The Scandals of Translation: Towards an Ethics of Difference* (London: Routledge, 1998)

von Rad, Gerhard, 'The Beginnings of Historical Writing in Ancient Israel', in *The Problem of the Hexateuch and Other Essays* (Edinburgh and London: Oliver & Boyd, 1966), 166–204

——, *Genesis: A Commentary* (Philadelphia: The Westminster Press, 1972)

Wanner, Kevin, 'Purity and Danger: Excrement, Blood, Sacred Space and Society in *Eyrbyggja saga*', *Viking and Medieval Scandinavia* 5 (2009), 213–50

Well, Barry, *The Book of Judges* (Grand Rapids, MI: Eerdmans, 2012)

Wellendorf, Jónas, 'Ecclesiastical Literature and Hagiography', in *The Routledge Research Companion to the Medieval Icelandic Sagas*, ed. Ármann Jakobsson and Sverrir Jakobsson (London: Routledge, 2017), 48–58

Wenham, Gordon, *Genesis 1–15* (Grand Rapids, MI: Zondervan, 2014)

Westergård-Nielsen, Chr., *To bibelske visdomsbøger og deres islandske overlevering* (Copenhagen: Munksgaard, 1957)

Westermann, Claus, *Genesis 1–11: A Commentary* (London: SPCK, 1984)

Westra, H. J., 'Augustine and Poetic Exegesis', in *Poetry and Exegesis in Premodern Latin Christianity: The Encounter between Classical and Christian Strategies of Interpretation*, ed. Willemien Otten and Karla Pollmann (Leiden and Boston: Brill, 2007), 11–28

Whitmarsh, Tim, *Dirty Love: The Genealogy of the Ancient Greek Novel* (New York: Oxford University Press, 2018)

Wilken, Robert L., 'Melito, the Jewish Community at Sardis, and the Sacrifice of Isaac', *Theological Studies* 37.1 (1976), 53–69

Williams, Benjamin, 'Glossa ordinaria and Glossa hebraica midrash in Rashi and the Gloss', *Traditio* 71 (2016), 179–201

Williams, Megan Hale, *The Monk and the Book: Jerome and the Making of Christian Scholarship* (Chicago: University of Chicago Press, 2006)

Wolf, Kirsten, 'Brandr Jónsson and *Stjórn*', *Scandinavian Studies* 62.2 (1990), 163–88

——, 'Peter Comestor's *Historia scholastica* in Old Norse Translation', *Amsterdamer Beiträge zur älteren Germanistik* 33 (1991), 149–61

——, *Legends of the Saints in Old Norse-Icelandic Prose* (Toronto: University of Toronto Press, 2013)

Wollin, Lars, '*Stjórn* och Pentateukparafrasen: Ett sannordiskt dominikan-projekt i högmedeltiden', *Arkiv for nordisk filologi* 116 (2001), 221–99

Bibliography

Würth, Stefanie, 'History and Pseudo-History', in *A Companion to Old Norse-Icelandic Literature and Culture*, ed. Rory McTurk (Maldon, MA: Blackwell Publishing, 2005), 155–72

Yearley, Janthia, 'A Bibliography of *Planctus* in Latin, Provençal, French, German, English, Italian, Catalan and Galician-Portuguese from the Time of Bede to the Early Fifteenth Century', *Journal of the Plainsong and Mediaeval Music Society* 4 (1981), 12–52

Young, Frances, *Biblical Exegesis and the Formation of Christian Culture* (Cambridge: Cambridge University Press, 1997)

Zacher, Samantha, *Rewriting the Old Testament in Anglo-Saxon Verse: Becoming the Chosen People* (London: Bloomsbury, 2013)

Zinn, Grover A., '*Historia fundamenta est*: The Role of History in the Contemplative Life according to Hugh of St Victor', in *Contemporary Reflections on the Medieval Christian Tradition. Essays in Honor of Ray C. Petry*, ed. George H. Shriver (Durham, NC: Duke University Press, 1974), 135–58

——, 'The Influence of Augustine's *De doctrina christiana* upon the writings of Hugh of St Victor', in *Reading and Wisdom: The De doctrina Christiana of Augustine in the Middle Ages*, ed. Edward D. English (Notre Dame, IN: University of Notre Dame Press, 1995), 48–60

——, 'Hugh of St Victor's *De scripturis et scripturibus* as an *accessus* treatise for the study of the Bible', *Traditio* 52 (1997), 111–34

——, 'Exegesis and Spirituality in the Writings of Gregory the Great', in *Gregory the Great: A Symposium*, ed. John C. Cavadini (Notre Dame, IN: University of Notre Dame Press, 2001), 168–80

Þórir Óskarsson, 'Rhetoric and Style', in *A Companion to Old Norse-Icelandic Literature and Culture*, ed. Rory McTurk (Malden: Blackwell, 2005), 354–71

INDEX

Aaron   74, 75, 128, 205
Abel   17, 81–82, 84, 111, 114
  as protomartyr   100–01, 106–07
  in *Stjórn I*, 157–60, 165, 169, 188 n. 54
Abelard   97, 139, 247 n. 7
Abiathar   237
Abigail   98–99
Abimelech   116, 225
Abner   234–35
Abraham/Abram   81, 89, 96, 100, 171,
  192
  'saga' of   17–18, 20
  in the fire of Chaldea   64, 107, 114
  sets out from Haran   3–4, 174, 179
  and Lot   4, 168, 173–74
  defeats Chedorlaomer   174
  drives out Hagar   175–79, 189
  institutes circumcision   106
  visited by three angels   174
  sacrifice of Isaac, *see under* Isaac
Abraham Ibn Ezra   58
Absalom, David's son   20, 108, 131,
  236–38
Absalom, Archbishop of Lund   53
Achish, King of Gath   232
Acts of the Apostles   62, 150
  see also Apostles' Sagas
Adam   49, 64, 81, 82, 111
  creation of   151
  sleep and prophecy   105, 112, 151
  eats the forbidden apple   125–28,
  152–57, 159–69
  see also Fall of Man
Aeneas   206, 248
Ahab/Achab, King of Israel   94, 250
Ahasuerus, King of Persia   125

Alcuin   63, 106 n. 15, 139
Alexanders saga   4, 9, 104
Allogia, Queen   248
Allegoriae in novum Testamentum, see
  Richard of St Victor
Allegory, *see under* Exegesis
Amalekites   78–79, 131
Ambrose, St   47, 92, 139
Andrew of St Victor   53, 58–59, 62, 64,
  144
Angels, *see* Fall of Angels
Anthopomorphism, *see* God
Anti-Semitism   50, 52, 60, 59, 80, 109
Apostles' sagas (*postola sǫgur*)   39, 86,
  99
  see also Acts of the Apostles
Ari Þorgilsson   110
  Íslendingabók   193–94
Árni Magnússon   8
Arnórr *jarlaskáld* ('poet of jarls')   238
Asael, Joab's brother   234–35
Asenath, Joseph's wife   114
  and Joseph   13, 199–201, 206, 208,
  246–47, 249
  and Pharaoh's son   202–03
  see also Oddr Snorrason, Romance,
  Vincent of Beauvais, *Yngvars saga*
  víðfǫrla
Áslákr *fitjarskalli* ('from Fitjar')   227,
  235
Assumption of the Blessed Virgin
  Mary   80, 87
  see also Homilies
Assyrians, *see* Holofernes
Athalia, Queen Consort of Judah   239
Auðr Vésteinsdóttir   252

Index

Auerbach, Erich 27–28
Augustine, St 41–43, 56, 58, 98, 148, 161
 in Iceland 50, 87–88, 92, 94, 101
 Confessionum 47–48
 Contra Faustum 49–52
 De civitate Dei 50, 101, 130
 De doctrina christiana 43, 48–49, 54–55, 74, 103–4
 De genesi ad litteram 126, 139–40, 142, 143–44, 146, 152–57,
 De genesi contra Manichaeorum 139–40, 143, 150–51, 156
 De sermone domini 130
 Enarrationes in Psalmos 137
 Tractatus in Evangelium Iohannis 50, 73 n. 16
 see also Exegesis, Six Ages of the World, Sign Theory
Augustinus saga 9
Æsir 237

Baal 250
Babylon/Babylonian captivity 66, 90–91, 100, 112–13, 210
Bilhah/Bala, Dan's mother 189, 203
Balaam and Balak 14
Baptism 43, 56, 76, 96, 194, 204
Bárðar saga Snæfellsáss 34–35, 245
Barthes, Roland 31–33
Barlaams saga ok Josaphats 5
Barzillai the Gileadite 238–39
Basil the Great 139
Bathsheba 94, 108, 131, 233
Bede 58, 72, 87, 97, 103, 139
Benjamin, Joseph's brother 198–99, 203
Beowulf 15–17
Bergen 4, 8, 72, 121
Bergr Sokkason 6
Bible, see Hebrew Bible/Old Testament
Bibles historiales 9, 11, 43, 65–69
 see also Peter Comestor, Guiart Desmoulins
Bible moralisée 65
Bláland, see Ethiopia
Boaz 221–26, 256
Bolli Bollason 202
Bolli Þorleiksson 29, 253–54

Brandr Jónsson, Abbot of Þykkvibær 5–7, 9, 69, 92
 see also Maccabees
Breta sǫgur 104

Cain 17, 81, 100, 161, 192
 kills Abel 107, 114, 157–60, 165, 169
 cast out 64
 builds city 111–12
Canaan, Ham's son 165
Canaan 196, 201, 210
Cantemus domino ('Song of Moses') 172
Cataflua/Kataflua, Noah's daughter-in-law 114
Christ 4, 10, 69, 100–01, 107, 111
 in biblical exegesis 42, 44, 49, 55, 92, 144
 and Abraham 180
 and Adam 64, 86 n. 46, 105, 151
 and David 108, 212, 233, 239
 and Egill 247
 and Isaac 45, 59, 183
 and Job 83
 and Joseph 109, 200
 and Melchizedek 172
 and Moses 75
 and Óláfr 248–49
 and the paschal lamb 204
 and the Exodus 109
 and Samson 80
 and Wisdom 137, 142
 Temptation of 3, 246
 Wedding of Cana 73
Chronicles 54, 90
Cicero 38, 47
Constantinople/Miklagarðr 168–69
Convergent evolution 11, 39–40
Conversion 21, 41, 47–48, 193–94, 201, 206
Creation 3, 71, 104, 107, 111, 139
 as primeval saga 18
 in Augustine 48, 103
 in Hugh and Richard of St Victor 55–56, 59
 in *The Icelandic Homily Book* 76
 in *Konungs skuggsjá* 126, 136–37
 in *Stjórn I* 142, 148, 150, 159, 164, 168–69

290

Index

see also Hexamera, Six Ages of the World

Cursor mundi 67

Dan, Joseph's brother 203–04, 213
Daniel 62, 66, 103, 113
David 3–4, 89, 221, 234, 244
  saga of 13, 17, 21–22, 23, 226
  youthful exploits 228–30
  defeats Amalekites 78–79
  fights Goliath 230–32
  relationship to Saul 12, 108, 131–34,
    227
  feigns madness 232–33
  lament for Jonathan and Saul 134, 246
  and Abigail 98–99
  adultery with Bathsheba 94, 131, 135,
    233–34
  lament for Absalom 236–37
  old age 238–39, 247
  as psalmist 123–24
  see also Konungs skuggsjá, Stjórn III,
    Veraldar saga
Deuteronomistic history 21, 23, 211
Deuteronomy 5, 91, 210, 156
Dido 205–06, 248
Dinah 13, 191–96, 202–03, 208
Diomedes 169
Dixin 248–49
Dominicans 8–9, 61
  see also Vincent of Beauvais
Durandus, William, *Rationale divinorum*
  officium 9, 140, 159–60

Egils saga Skalla-Grímssonar 222–23,
  230–31, 238, 244, 245–46
Egill Skalla-Grímsson 13, 167, 212, 220,
  239, 246–47
Egypt 21, 40, 76, 176, 196
  Joseph in Egypt 108, 188, 198–202
  Moses in Egypt 204–06, 248–49
Einarr *þambarskelfir*
  ('string-shaker') 227
Eiríkr Ívarsson, Archbishop of
  Niðaróss 53
Eli 3, 4
Eliezer 173, 174,
Elijah 82, 93–94
Elisha 228, 240
Emotion 98, 108–09, 138, 178, 222

economy of 17, 23, 28–30, 83, 117, 177
  and verse 26
  and rhetoric 89, 94, 179, 183–85, 187, 209
  divine emotions 162
Encyclopaedic Literature 40, 62, 102,
  113, 121, 140
  and exegesis 12, 103–04, 138, 169
  see also Konungs skuggsjá, Stjórn
    I, Universal History, Vincent of
    Beauvais
Enoch, Jared's son 82, 84, 89, 107, 112
Enoch, Cain's son 111
Ephraim, Joseph's son 199
Erlingr Skjálgsson 227, 235
Esau 57, 81, 188–90
Eskil, Archbishop of Lund 53
Esther 62, 66, 124–25
Ethai 238
Ethiopa/Bláland 149, 204–05
Etna (Sicily) 168
Eusebius of Caesarea 103
Eve 94, 105, 219
  created from Adam 49, 64, 112, 151
  eats forbidden fruit 107, 127–28,
    154–55
  in *Konungs skuggsjá* 125–28
  in *Stjórn I* 151–57, 159–60
  see also Fall of Man
Exegesis, biblical 10, 12, 42–43,
  66–67,103–04, 139–40
  allegorical 43–52, 70–71, 73–80,
    86–89, 92–95, 105–10
    in *Stjórn I* 150–51, 159–60, 172,
      179–87
    in *Stjórn III* 212, 239
  as poetry 48–49, 88–89, 91–92, 101,
    135–37
  Jewish 46–47, 57–59, 60, 62–64,
    68–69, 121
  literal/historical 69, 79, 96, 101, 138
    in *Stjórn I* 142–43, 155, 169, 172,
      179, 182
  moral/tropological 80–86, 94–95, 97,
    124–35, 160
  Victorine 52–62, 107, 122–24, 126, 138,
    140–44
  see also Christ, *Glossa ordinaria*,
    Hebrew Bible/Old Testament, New
    Testament, Translation

Index

Exodus
  book of 18, 54, 74, 109, 128, 171
  events of 43, 76, 204
  in *Stjórn I* 4–5, 7, 140, 172, 202,
    206–07
Eyjólfr Þórðarson 252
Eyrbyggja saga 229, 245–47
Eysteinn Ásgrímsson 9
Eyvindr *skáldaspillir* ('the plagiarist'),
    Hákonarmál 242
Ezekiel 38, 60, 66

Fáfnir 167
Fall of the Angels 3, 144–48
  see also Lucifer
Fall of Man 3, 18, 139, 252 n. 32
  in *Heimsaldrar* 111, 114
  in *Konungs skuggsjá* 125–28
  in *Stjórn I* 129, 152–60, 161, 165, 169
  in *Veraldar saga* 106–07
  see also Adam, Eve, God
Fenrir 229
First Grammatical Treatise 35
Flateyjarbók 4
Fliva, Noah's daughter-in-law 114
Flood 18, 89, 107–08, 113, 114
  as allegory 56, 76, 89, 100
  in *Stjórn I* 140, 150, 160–66, 168, 169
  see also Noah
Flóamanna saga 245–46
Flores Hugonis de Sancto Victore, see
    Richard of St Victor
Folktale 17, 31–32, 34–35, 228
Fornkonunga saga 201
Four Daughters of God 58, 121, 125–26,
    130
Freyr 33
Færeyinga saga 230

Gad, Joseph's brother 203–04
Gaza 80, 216, 219
Gefjon 169
Geira, Óláfr Tryggvason's wife 248–49
Genealogy 11, 13, 15, 19, 40, 111
  in *Stjórn III* 171, 213, 221, 226
Genesis 16, 27–29, 31–32 , 37–39, 220,
    247
  as allegory 43–45, 48, 52, 59
  as 'family literature' 171–72

as history 54, 57, 61, 63–64, 66, 141
as primeval 'saga' 16–20
commentary on 139–40
in *Heimsaldrar* 111–12
in *Konungs skuggsjá* 71, 125–28, 136–37
in *Stjórn I* 4–5, 12, 140–46, 150–69,
    172–99, 208
in *Veraldar saga* 105–08, 111–12
see also Abraham, Adam, Creation,
    Dinah, Eve, Fall of Man, Flood,
    Hagar, Noah, Jacob, Joseph, Sarah
Genesis and Exodus 67
Genesis Rabbah 64, 121
Gideon 116
Gísla saga Súrssonar 13–14, 197, 232 n.
    90, 244, 247, 250–54
Gísli Jónsson, Bishop of Skálholt 5, 9
Gísli Súrsson 197, 212, 220, 232 n. 90,
    250–54
Gizurr Hallsson 105
Gizurr Ísleifsson, Bishop of
    Skálholt 193
Glámr 17, 33–34
Glossa ordinaria 43, 97, 109, 248 n. 15,
    249
  and the *Bibles historiales* 66–67
  and Comestor 62–63
  and *Konungs skuggsjá* 121–26, 128–29,
    135, 106
  and *Stjórn I* 10, 140, 142, 143, 148
God 49, 52, 55, 78–79, 88–91, 95–96
  anthropomorphism 16, 47, 160–63
  as Creator 56, 105–06, 142, 144–45, 149
  command to Abraham 28–29, 38, 45,
    57, 63, 82–83, 179–83
  command to Adam and Eve 154–55,
    160
  delivers Manasseh 90–91
  dining hall of 61, 140–41
  image of God 54, 148
  incarnation 44, 49, 56, 77, 107, 137
  lamb of 97–98, 241
  meaning of 'God said' 142–43
  rejects Saul 131–35, 227–28
  revealed in history 56, 75–76, 103
  tests Job 84–85
  see also City of God, Creation, Fall
    of Man, Four Daughters of God,
    Flood, Wisdom

292

Index

Goliath 90, 133, 228, 230–32
Gospels 54, 62, 76, 123
  see also under Gregory the Great
Greek 17, 41, 43–44, 96, 143, 199
  biblical translations 36, 41, 42, 46, 57
  see also Origen, Philo, Septuagint (LXX), Translation
Gregory the Great 11, 54, 61–62, 69, 87, 92
  Dialogues 114, 222
  Expositio in Canticum Canticorum 51
  Homiliae XL in Evangelia 12, 70–72, 74–75, 77–82, 86, 101
  Homilies of Ezekiel 9, 52, 144
  Moralia in Job 51–52, 109, 128–29, 143
  see also Exegesis
Grettir Ásmundarson *inn sterki* ('the Strong') 13, 17, 33–34, 97, 212–13, 220
Grettis saga Ásmundarsonar 11, 16, 86 n. 44, 213
Grímr, see Þórr
Grímr Hólmsteinsson, *Jóns saga baptista II* 12, 92–99
Grosseteste, Robert 172
Guðbrandur Þorláksson, *Biblia* 70
Guðrún Gjúkadóttir 120 n. 80, 219, 222, 237
Guðrún Ósvífrsdóttir 21, 29–30, 223, 253–54
Guiart Desmoulins 11, 65–66
  see also Bibles historiales
Gunnarr Hámundarson 20, 21, 202
Gyðinga saga, see Brandr Jónsson
Gæfa ('luck, good fortune') 13, 196–97, 199

Hagar 43, 114, 171, 173
  in *Stjórn I* 174–78, 187, 189, 203, 207, 247
  face of 179–80
Hákon Sigurðarson *jarl* ('earl') 202
Hákon Magnússon, King of Norway 4, 5, 8, 10
Hallfreðar saga 232–33, 244
Hallfreðr Óttarsson *vandræðaskáld* ('the troublesome poet') 232–33
Hallfreðr, Hrafnkell's father 32–33
Hallgerðr Hǫskuldsdóttir 20, 201

Ham (Cham), Noah's son 81, 100, 166–67, 169
Haman 125
Hamor, Shechem's father 192–94
Hannah 4
Haraldr the Fine-Haired, King of Norway 219
Haraldr Sigurðarson, King of Norway 234, 238
Haran, Abraham's brother 64
Haran, Abraham's departure from 3, 173–74, 179, 180–82
Harold Godwineson 234
Heaven 80, 100, 148, 149, 164
  creation of 76, 136–37, 144–45
  joys of 74, 89, 97
  see also Babel, Fall of Angels, Flood
Hebrew 35–36, 57–59, 63–64
  in the Parisian schools 57–59, 63–64
  in *Stjórn I* 143, 163–65, 176–77, 182, 191–96, 206–8
  in *Stjórn III* 216–17, 221, 241, 252, 256
  traditions 90–91, 96, 102, 107, 182–83
  see also Andrew of St Victor, Genesis Rabbah, Exegesis, Peter Comestor, Hebrew Bible/Old Testament, Hugh of St Victor, Jews, Midrash Rabbah, Peshat, Rashi
Hebrew Bible/Old Testament 1–3, 10–14, 42–43, 58, 65–66, 191, 210–11, 227
  and exegesis 43–46, 48–49, 54, 56–60, 75–76
  and sagas 13–14, 15–26, 39–41, 78, 143–44, 245–57
  and style 22–26, 101, 165
  as historical narrative 11, 43, 54–56, 60–64, 66–67
  in Iceland 70–71, 73, 77, 86–87
  see also Exegesis, Genesis, Greek, Hebrew, Exodus, Jerome, Judith, Kings, Sagas, Samuel, Septuagint, *Stjórn*, Style, Translation, Vulgate
Hebrews, Epistle to the 45, 183 n. 41
Heimsaldrar 110–13, 138
  see also Ages of the World, Universal History
Heimskringla, see Snorri Sturluson
Hekla (Iceland) 168
Helga, King 201

293

Index

Helgafell 4, 9–10, 244
Hell 76, 80, 94, 100, 146, 148
Herdís Bolladóttir 223
Herod 93–94
Herodias 93–94
Herodotus 113
Hexamera 139
Hezekiah, King of Judah 130
Historia scholastica, see Peter Comestor
Historiebijbel van 1360 68
Historienbibeln 11, 68
Historye of the Patriarks 67
Hólar 70
Holofernes 116, 118–20
Homer 27, 43
Homilies 2, 12, 69, 70–73, 86, 101–02
  for Ember Days 75
  for Assumption Day 80
  for Christmas Day 81–82
  for All Saints 75, 82–83
  on Wedding of Cana 73–74
  on Moses' Prayer, *see under* Moses
  Resurrectio Domini 76–77
  see also Augustine, Gregory, Icelandic
    Homily Book, Job, Norwegian
    Homily Book, Origen
Honorius Augustodunensis 113, 114, 115
  n. 55
Hrafnkell *Freysgoði* ('Freyr's
  priest') 32, 254–55
Hrafnkels saga 32–33, 167 n. 98,
  245–46, 247, 254–56
Hrefna Ágeirsdóttir 29–30
Hugh of St Cher 65
Hugh of St Victor 11, 43, 53–54, 105,
  107, 245
  Adnotationes in Pentateuchem 56–58,
    144
  Chronicon 55, 104
  De archa Noe 89, 121
  De fructibus carnis et spiritus 121
  De sacramentis 56
  De scripturis 54–55
  Didascalicon 54, 57, 61–62, 93, 122,
    141
  see also Andrew of St Victor, Four
    Daughters of God, Richard of St
    Victor
Hulda-Hrokkinskinna 238

Iceland 2, 10–11, 168, 211, 244
  as provenance of *Stjórn I* 9–10
  Augustine and Gregory in 50–51
  Comestor in 68–69
Icelandic sagas, *see* Sagas
Ingibjǫrg, Princess of Norway 29
Ingjaldr Alfarinsson 34–35
Illuminations, *see under* Manuscripts
Interpretatio norrœna 169
Isidore, *Etymologiae* 12, 103, 114
  in *Stjórn I* 9, 140, 148, 168–69
Isaac 3–4, 18, 44, 81, 112
  birth 173, 175
  plays with Ishmael 176–77
  sacrifice of
    in Hebrew 27–29
    in Vulgate 29, 38
    in Origen 45
    in Hugh of St Victor 57
    in Richard of St Victor 59–60
    in Comestor 63–64
    in the *Icelandic Homily Book* 82–83
    in *Stjórn I* 179–87
  deceived by Jacob 106, 179, 188–89
Isaiah 58, 75, 95, 136–37, 256
  martyrdom of 90–91
Ishmael 168, 171, 173–79, 189, 203, 247
Íslendingabók, see Ari Þorgilsson
Israel/Israelites 98, 129–30, 202, 241–43,
  254–55
  history of 45, 144, 171–72, 206, 210–12
  kings of 132, 226, 239–40
  prose literature in 21, 23, 25
  tribes of 96, 115
Ívens saga 169

Jabal, Lamech's son 112
Jacob 18, 57, 82, 84, 112, 171
  wrestles with an angel 11, 16–17,
    31–35, 50, 52, 206
  trickster figure 187–89
  usurps Esau's blessing 3–4, 81, 106,
    190
  and Laban's daughters 173, 189–91
  twelve sons 191–95, 198–99, 102–03,
    172, 213
Jael 116
Japheth, Noah's son 81, 165
Járn-Skeggi 250

294

Index

Jehu, King of Judah 250
Jeroboam, King of Israel 100
Jeremiah 38, 66
Jericho 3
Jerome 62–64, 87–88, 96–97, 138, 205
  'Hebrew truth' 11, 46–47, 58, 107
  translations 36–38, 41, 42, 44, 103
  Liber interpretationis Hebraicorum
    nominum 74, 78, 112
  Quaestiones Hebraicae in Genesim 46
  Tractatus sive homiliae in psalmos 89
  see also Hebrew, Hebrew Bible/Old
    Testament, Septuagint, Translation,
    Vulgate
Jerusalem 168, 182, 210, 238
Jesse, David's father 3 n. 11, 221, 226,
  228
Jews 50–51, 60, 100, 205, 227, 231
  see also Anti-Semitism, Hebrew,
    Hebrew Bible/Old Testament, Philo
Jewish exegesis, *see under* Exegesis
Jezebel, Ahab's wife 94
Joab, David's nephew 131, 233, 234–37
Joash, King of Judah 228
Job 9, 21, 65, 70, 77, 83–86
  see also Gregory the Great, *Moralia in*
    Job
Jochebed, Moses' mother 114
John, Gospel of 55, 73, 143, 247
John the Baptist 71, 86, 88, 93–97
Jón Halldórsson, Bishop of
  Skálholt 8–9
Jóns saga baptista II, see Grímr
  Hólmsteinsson
Jonah 130
Jonathan 134
Jordan 33 n. 88, 93–94, 96
Joseph 17, 57, 81, 173, 188, 190
  and Asenath 114, 199–204, 246–47
  and Potiphar's wife 124–25
  as dreamer 197–98
  story as romance 13, 108–09, 138, 170,
    196–99
  see also Gæfa
Joseph Bekhor Shor 58
Joseph Kara 58
Josephus, *Antiquitates* 68, 91–92, 111–12,
  125, 161, 205
  influence on Comestor 62–64

in *Stjórn I* 161, 182, 186
and Oddr's *Óláfs saga*
  Tryggvasonar 248–49
Joshua 3, 4, 100
  book of 54, 62, 97, 210, 245
  translation of 5, 7, 68, 114, 211–12
  see also AM 226 fol., *Stjórn III*, *Stjórn*
    IV
Jubal, Lamech's son 112
Judges 54, 210–12, 221, 244, 245, 254
  see also Abimelech, Delilah, Rape
    of the Levite's concubine, Ruth,
    Samson
Judah, kingdom of 210, 239, 240, 250
Judah, son of Jacob 199
Judith 62, 66, 219
  in AM 764 4to 12, 113–14, 116–20, 138
Jǫrmunrekkr 78 n. 26, 237

Kári Sǫlmundarson 238
Keturah, Abraham's wife 114
Kings (LXX Kingdoms) 54–56, 62, 46,
  71, 114, 210–11
  1 Kings 226–27, 239
  2 Kings 90, 228, 240–44
  in *Stjórn III* 5, 7, 69, 211–12
  see also 1 Samuel, 2 Samuel
Kings' sagas (*konungasǫgur*) 13, 23,
  228, 244
Kjartan Óláfsson 29–30, 253–54
Kolbeinn *svarti* ('the black') 238
Konungs skuggsjá 71, 124–35, 138, 144
  and *Stjórn I* 152–54, 237 n. 109
  and *Stjórn III* 5–7
  and wisdom literature 135–37
  Victorine connections 12, 58, 121–24
  see also Aaron, David, Fall of
    Man, Four Daughters of God,
    Encyclopaedic Writing, Esther,
    Joseph, Moses, Saul, Universal
    History, Wisdom
Kormáks saga 247
Kristni saga 193

Laban, Jacob's uncle 173, 187–88,
  190–91
La Bible abrégée 65–66
La Bible du XIIIe siècle 65
Lagarfljót 33

295

Index

Lamech 58, 112

Lavinia 205

Laxdœla saga 11, 13, 21, 29–31, 201–02, 213

and *Stjórn III* 220, 223, 230, 244

Leah, Jacob's wife 114, 189–91, 195, 198

Lectio divina 10, 52, 135

Leo, *Sermones* 9

Leoninus, *Historiae veteris testamenti* 65

Levi, Jacob's son 191, 194–95, 203–04

Li Quatre Livre des Reis 65

Liber exceptionum, see Richard of St Victor

Líknarbraut 241–42

Lincoln 53

Liturgy 10, 12, 35, 140, 159–60, 172

see also Lent, Septugesima

Lot, Abraham's nephew 3, 4, 168, 174, 182

Lucan 104

Lucifer 127, 145

see also Fall of the Angels, Satan

Luther 9, 68

Maccabees 5, 59, 62, 65–66, 69

see also Brandr Jónsson

Magnús Hákonarson, King of Norway 5

Magnús Þórðarson 4

Manesseh, King of Judah 89–91

Manesseh, Joseph's son 199

Manoah, Samson's father 213, 215

Manuscripts 2–10, 68–69, 156, 244

AM 225 fol. 4–5

AM 226 fol. 4–5, 9–10, 144, 150, 172–73, 214

alternate readings 141, 200, 213, 226

AM 227 fol. 3, 6, 8–10, 217, 226

illuminations 3, 128–29, 146–47, 179–82

marginalia 10, 148, 172 n. 9, 204

rubrics 142, 172–73, 196, 202, 213, 224, 226–27

AM 228 fol. 5, 7

AM 335 4to. 5, 7, 213

AM 617 4to. 5, 213

Maríu saga 12, 87–91, 92–93, 102

Mary, Blessed Virgin 71, 86, 87–89

see also *Maríu saga*

Melkorka 31, 223

Mesopotamia 21, 40, 173

Methodius 161

Michael, Archangel 200

Middle English Metrical Paraphrase of the Old Testament 67

Midian 206

Midrash Rabbah 58

Miðgarðsormr ('middle-earth-serpent') 77

Miriam 172, 204–05

Moabites 240–43

Mordecai 125

Moriah 27, 57

Morkinskinna 13

Mörtu saga ok Maríu 10, 68

Moses 43, 89, 107, 129–30, 168

childhood 114–15, 248–49

story as 'heroic saga' 18–19

Moses' prayer 74–75, 172

wives 114, 204–08, 248

author of Pentateuch 57, 144

see also *Cantemus domino*, Exodus, *Konungs skuggsjá*

Naamah, Lamech's son 112

Naomi 221–26, 255–56

Nabal, Abigail's husband 98

Nebuchadnezzar, King of Babylon 117

New Testament 43, 54, 59, 71, 86

in relation to Old Testament 44, 86, 106, 183, 257

Nimrod/Nymrod 111, 113, 167–68

see also Babel

Njáls saga 15, 19–21, 201, 238, 245

Norway 2, 7–8, 35, 120, 204, 227

Norwegian Homily Book 71–72

Numbers 14, 205

Obed, Ruth's son 221, 225–26

Oddr Snorrason, *Oláfs saga Tryggvasonar* 13, 219, 245–46, 247–50

Oddrúnargrátr 237

Óðinn 233, 236–37

Óláfr Haraldsson, King of Norway and Saint 202, 211, 235, 238, 244

Óláfr Hǫskuldsson 30, 220

296

Index

Óláfr Tryggvason, King of Norway 219, 227, 232, 244
see also Oddr Snorrason
Old English Hexateuch 67
Old Icelandic Homily Book 69, 71–73, 106, 190, 245
and allegory 73–74, 75–77, 86
and moral exempla 81–85
see also Exegesis, Homilies
Old Latin/*Vetus Latina* 36, 38, 43, 47, 62, 117
Orality/Oral Tradition 15–19, 22, 40, 58, 63–64
Origen 42, 83, 183–85, 209
and allegory 43–46, 47, 51, 54
Ormr Stórólfsson 17
Orpha, Ruth's sister-in-law 221
Ovid, *Metamorphoses* 169

Páls saga II 68
Paraphrase 11, 69, 146, 156, 192, 207
as exegesis 66–67
see also Translation
Pharphia/Parphia, Noah's
daughter-in-law 114
Parisian schools 11, 53, 58, 61, 64, 69
see also St Victor
Pascharius Radbertus, *Cogitis me* 87
Paul, St 43, 154, 175
Pentateuch 21, 245, 246
Swedish paraphrase of 8
commentary on 56, 60, 62
translations of 5–7, 67, 144, 211
see also Hebrew Bible/Old Testament, *Stjórn I*, *Stjórn II*
Peshat 57
see also Exegesis
Peter Comestor, *Historia scholastica* 43, 60–64, 245
as source of *Jóns saga baptista II* 10, 92, 96, 98
as source of *Konungs skuggsjá* 122, 127–30, 132, 138
as source of *Stjórn I* 9, 146, 161–62, 166–68, 188–91, 206–8
prologue 140–42
on Creation 148–51
on the Fall of Man 152–59
on Noah's drunkenness 166–68

on Sarah and Hagar 174–79
on Abraham and Isaac 183–86
as source of universal histories 12, 104–05, 107–09, 111–12, 114
translations and adaptations 5–6, 11, 64–69
use in Iceland 5–6, 68–69, 71, 90
see also Exegesis, Hugh of St Victor, *Stjórn IV*, Victorines
Peter Riga, *Aurora* 65
Pétrs saga postola I 10, 68, 71
Pharisees 96
Pharaoh 100, 115, 188, 196, 200, 203–06, 248
Philistines 215–16, 218, 219–20, 232, 251–52, 255
Philo 43–44, 47, 175
Plato 43
Poarpa/Phuapara, Noah's wife 114
Potiphar 125, 199, 201
Potiphar's wife 108, 124–25
Prophets 38, 46, 60, 70, 86
'Former Prophets' 210
Prosimetrum 11, 26
Proverbs 65, 66, 122, 136–37
Psalms 70, 86, 89, 124, 137
Pseudo-Jerome, *Quaestiones Hebraicae in Libros Regum et Paralipomenon* 91
Putiphare, priest of Heliopolis, Asenath's father 199, 201
see also Potiphar

Queen of Sheba 4, 168

Rachel, Jacob's wife 60, 114, 173, 189–91, 198
Ralph d'Escures, Archbishop of Canterbury 72, 79
Rangá 33
Rape of the Levite's concubine 115–16
Rashbam (Rabbi Samuel ben Meir) 58
Rashi (Rabbi Samuel ben Isaac) 58, 60, 63
Red Sea 76, 100, 204, 208
Rehoboam, King of Israel 100
Rémundar saga 201
Reuben, Jacob's son 81
Reynistaður 113

297

Index

Richard of St Victor 11, 53, 59–60
  Liber exceptionum 9, 12, 59–60, 105, 109, 212
  see also Stjórn III, Veraldar saga
Rebecca (Rebekah), Isaac's wife 4, 106, 114, 179, 187, 189
Rijmbijbel 11, 68
Romance 7, 29, 66, 99, 169
  Joseph and Asenath 13, 109, 196–97, 198–99, 200–03, 208
  Moses and Tharbis 204, 206
Romans 83, 154 n. 52
Rome 103, 205
Rómverja saga 4, 104
Rudolf von Ems, *Weltchronik* 65, 68
Rufinus of Aquileia 44, 45
Rúnólfr Sigmundarson 9, 92
Ruth 210–11
  in *Stjórn III* 212, 219, 220–26, 244
  and *Hrafnkels saga* 255–57

Sachsenspiegel 65
Sadducees 96
Sagas 19–22, 29–31, 39–41, 138, 208–09, 243–44
  and biblical influence 245–57
  and the Hebrew Bible 1–2, 10–14, 15–19, 171
  in homilies and saints' lives 78, 86, 97, 99–102
  see also David, Kings' Sagas, Joseph, Samson, *Stjórn I, Stjórn III*, Style
Saints' Lives 2, 12, 40, 69, 71, 86, 101
  see also Jóns saga baptista II, Maríu saga, Tveggja postula saga Jóns ok Jakobs
Sallust 104
Sámr Bjarnason 255–56
Samson 7, 13, 212–13, 215–16, 220, 244
  kills lion 214–15
  composes riddle 217–18
  in Gaza 79–81, 216–17
  betrayed by Delilah 3 n. 11, 116, 218–20, 224
  and *Gísla saga* 250–54
Samuel, prophet 3–4, 132, 227–28
Samuel, book of 7, 17, 46, 71, 210–12

1 Samuel 68, 78, 98–99, 226, 228, 230, 232
2 Samuel 20, 233–37
Saracens 175
Sarah 3, 43, 114, 182, 192
  rivalry with Hagar 173–77, 179–80, 189, 203
Satan 85, 145
  see also Fall of Angels, Lucifer
Saul, King of Israel 4, 12–13
  persecutes David 108, 114, 232, 237
  rejected by God 131–35, 227–28
  death 134, 231
Sephora, see Zipporah
Septuagesima 140, 159–60, 162
Septuagint (LXX) 42–43, 46, 57, 117, 210, 241 n. 147
Sermons, *see* Homilies
Seth, Adam's son 100–01, 112, 161, 192
Shechem 191–203
Shem, Noah's son 81, 100, 165
Sign theory 48, 54–55, 79–80, 87–88
  see also Exegesis
Simeon, Jacob's son 191, 194–95, 203–04
Sir Gawain and the Green Knight 32
Sirach 9, 136–37
Sisera 116
Six Ages of the World 56, 73, 89, 103–04, 107, 110
  in *Stjórn I* 148, 150, 159
  see also Universal History
Skaldic verse 13, 26, 238, 239–43
Skálholt 3, 4, 5, 50, 71, 92
  and AM 227 fol. 8–10
  and St Victor 53, 105
Snæfríðr 219
Snorri Sturluson
  Edda 15, 21, 167, 222, 229, 246–47
  Háttatal 243
  Heimskringla 13, 211, 219
Sodom and Gomorrah 168, 174
Solomon, King of Israel 3, 4, 48, 100, 131, 227
  Solomon's temple 63, 239
Song of Songs 49, 87–88, 91
Speculum historiale, see under Vincent of Beauvais

Index

St Victor 11, 35–36, 52–60, 61, 105,
121–23
see also Andrew, Hugh, Richard,
Victorines
Stamford Bridge 234
Stephanus saga 68
Stephen, Protomartyr 106
Stephen Langton 61
Stígandi 220
Stjórn 4–10, 12–14, 54, 68–69
meaning of *stjórn* 8, 244
Stjórn I
levels of interpretation 158–60,
182–87
multi-vocality 155–57
sources 87, 139–40
ways of reading 140–44
and *Konungs skuggsjá* 152–55
and saga literature 165–68, 171–73,
191–96, 197–98, 200–03, 208
Stjórn II 5–8
Stjórn III
and AM 764 4to 113, 115–16
and *Hrafnkels saga* 254–57
and *Konungs skuggsjá* 121
and saga literature 7, 211–14, 219–20,
222–23, 226–36, 243–45
Stjórn IV 5
see also Bibles historiales, Hebrew
Bible/Old Testament, Manuscripts,
Translation, Vulgate
Storytelling 16, 18, 39–41, 245–47, 257
in the Hebrew Bible 16, 18, 25
in biblical translations 86, 101, 118
in *Stjórn I* 13, 69, 172, 208
in *Stjórn III* 211, 244
Sturla Þórðarson, *Hákonarkviða* 242
Style 2, 10–13, 15, 20–29, 32, 35–36, 40
in the homilies 71, 77, 86, 101
in *Jóns saga baptista II* 94–95, 97–99
in Judith 12, 117–18
in *Konungs skuggsjá* 137–38
in *Stjórn I* 13, 140, 145–46, 149,
163–66, 183–84, 208
in *Stjórn III* 7, 13, 211, 219, 240–43,
245
in the Vulgate 36–39, 41, 47, 57
'saga style' 10, 12, 22–26, 32–35, 71,
117–18

variation between styles 12, 91–92,
169–70, 172–73, 179–80, 187, 209
see also Exegesis, Jerome, Translation,
Vulgate
Styrbjǫrn *inn sterki* ('the strong') 213
Svanhildr, daughter of Sigurðr and
Guðrún 237
Sverris saga 245, 246

Talmud 58
Tamar, Judah's daughter-in-law 199
Tamar, David's daughter 236
Tharbis, Moses's wife 204–06, 208, 248
Theodoricus, Bishop of Hamar 53
Theodoricus, Archbishop of Niðaróss 53
Thermutis, Pharaoh's daughter 248–49
Third Grammatical Treatise 36
Tickhill Psalter Group 3
Tobias 62
Translation, biblical 2–5, 12–14, 42–43,
54, 70–71, 257
in medieval England 67
in medieval France 65–67, 69
in Old English 2–3
and style 36–39, 117–19, 163–65,
183–85, 243
and sagas 40, 138, 211, 220, 243–44,
254
see also Bibles historiales, Daniel,
Guðbrandur Þorláksson, Hebrew
Bible/Old Testament, Jerome,
Judith, Luther, Maccabees, Old
Latin, Septuagint, *Stjórn*, Vulgate
Troyes 61, 63, 64
see also Rashi

Trójumanna saga 104
Tubal-Cain, Lamech's son 112
*Tveggja postula saga Jóns ok
Jakobs* 10, 71, 99–102

Universal history 12, 62, 113, 121, 138
and biblical exegesis 103–04
see also AM 226 fol., AM 764 4to,
*Heimsaldrar, Konungs skuggsjá,
Veraldar saga*
Ur 74–75
Uriah, Bathsheba's husband 108, 131,
135, 233–34

299

Index

Valdamarr 248–49

Vanir 237

Vastes (Vashti), Queen of Persia 125

Veraldar saga 12, 68, 71, 104–11, 114–15, 138
  see also Universal History

Vermundr Þorgrímsson 202

Vesuvius (Italy) 168

Victorines 10, 47, 52–62, 69, 144
  in *Konungs skuggsjá* 12, 121–24, 138
  see also Andrew of St Victor, Hugh of
    St Victor, Peter Comestor, Richard
    of St Victor

Víðarr, Óðinn's son 229–30

Víga-Styrr [Þorgrímsson] 167

Viðey, Augustinian abbey 50

Vincent of Beauvais
  Speculum historiale 45, 65, 71, 87,
    104, 172
  in *Stjórn I* 8–10, 140, 148, 161, 165, 169
    on Creation 142, 149
    on the Fall of the Angels 145–46
    on the Fall of Man 156–57
    on the sacrifice of Isaac 183–87
    on Joseph and Asenath 199–203
    on Moses and Tharbis 205–06
  see also Dominicans, Encyclopaedic
    Writing, Universal History

Vitae Patrum 4

Vǫlsunga saga 222

Vǫlundr 169

Vǫluspá 237

Vulgate 16, 35, 42–3, 62, 68, 117
  and biblical style 36–39, 163–65, 184,
    187, 199
  in *Stjórn I* 6, 8, 151, 163–65, 190, 208
    compared with Hebrew and Old
      Norse 175–76, 192–95, 206–07

compared with Old Norse 168–69,
    175–79, 182, 188, 190
  in *Stjórn III* 213, 215–20, 222–25,
    228–38, 240–43
  see also Jerome, Old Latin (*Vetus
    Latina*), Septuagint (LXX), Style,
    Translation

Wedding at Cana, *see under* Homilies

Weltchronik, see Rudolf von Ems

Wisdom 60, 121–22, 135–37, 142

Yngvars saga víðfǫrla 245

Zilpah/Zelpha, Gad's mother 203

Zipporah/Sephora, Moses's wife 114,
    204, 207–08

Þingeyrar (Benedictine monastery) 3,
    8–9, 246–47, 249

Þorbjǫrn at Hóli 256

Þorgeirr Ljósvetningagoði 194

Þorgeirr Þjóstarsson 255–56

Þorgerðr Egilsdóttir 201, 253

Þórhaddr 197

Þorkell Eyjólfsson 167, 202

Þorkell Þjóstarsson 255–56

Þorlákr Þorhallsson, Bishop of Skálholt,
    Saint 53, 69

Þormóðr Kolbrúnarskáld ('Kolbrún's
    poet') 238

Þormóðr Trefilsson, *Hrafnsmál* 243

Þóroddr Þórbrandsson 229

Þórólfr Skalla-Grímsson 230–31, 238

Þórr 35, 77 n. 24, 215, 250

Þorsteins þáttr Síðu-Hallssonar 197

Þykkvibær (Augustinian abbey) 9–10,
    69, 92

300

Studies in Old Norse Literature

1 EMOTION IN OLD NORSE LITERATURE
Translations, Voices, Contexts
Sif Rikhardsdottir

2 THE SAINT AND THE SAGA HERO
Hagiography and Early Icelandic Literature
Siân E. Grønlie

3 DAMNATION AND SALVATION IN OLD NORSE LITERATURE
Haki Antonsson

4 MASCULINITIES IN OLD NORSE LITERATURE
Edited by Gareth Lloyd Evans and Jessica Clare Hancock

5 A CRITICAL COMPANION TO OLD NORSE LITERARY GENRE
Edited by Massimiliano Bampi, Carolyne Larrington and Sif Rikhardsdottir

6 THE *MAPPAE MUNDI* OF MEDIEVAL ICELAND
Dale Kedwards

7 FRENCH ROMANCE, MEDIEVAL SWEDEN AND THE
EUROPEANISATION OF CULTURE
Sofia Loden

8 DISCOURSE IN OLD NORSE LITERATURE
Eric Shane Bryan

9 SAINTS AND THEIR LEGACIES IN MEDIEVAL ICELAND
Edited by Dario Bullitta and Kirsten Wolf

10 KINSHIP IN OLD NORSE MYTH AND LEGEND
Katherine Marie Olley

11 POETRY IN SAGAS OF ICELANDERS
Margaret Clunies Ross